PRACTICAL
MENTAL
MAGIC

PRACTICAL MENTAL MAGIC

Theodore Annemann

Edited by John J. Crimmins, Jr.
Illustrations by Nelson Hahne

DOVER PUBLICATIONS, INC.
NEW YORK

Published in Canada by General Publishing Company, Ltd., 30 Lesmill Road, Don Mills, Toronto, Ontario.

This Dover edition, first published in 1983, is an unabridged republication of the work originally published by Holden's Magic Shops, New York, Boston, Philadelphia, in 1944 under the title *Annemann's Practical Mental Effects*.

Manufactured in the United States of America
Dover Publications, Inc., 180 Varick Street, New York, N.Y. 10014

Library of Congress Cataloging in Publication Data

Annemann, Theodore.
  Practical mental magic.

  Reprint. Originally published: Annemann's Practical mental effects. New York : Holden's Magic Shops, 1944.
  Includes index.
  1. Conjuring. 2. Tricks. I. Title.
GV1547.A57   1983   793.8   82-17745
ISBN 0-486-24426-1

FOREWORD

In offering this book of practical mental effects to the magical fraternity, we are paying tribute to the one man who probably did more to popularize this branch of entertainment than any other. To Ted Annemann, then, we bow in grateful appreciation for the many brilliant creations he left as his legacy to the world of magic. Each of the effects to follow were either performed by him, or were products of his editorship, for he attracted to his Jinx Magazine contributions from all the leading performers in recent years. In him they found a kindred soul, a man whose entire life was devoted to giving the audience what it wanted . . . Entertainment! We quote him: "My ideas and conceptions differ a great deal from those of some with whom I am acquainted. It is my theory that any effect to be successful must first be founded upon a simple method, and then be performed with a direct, to-the-point presentation. It is my contention that the moment one deviates from this straight line, he is not doing what a genuine magician or mind reader would do."

The popularity of his magazine bore out the truth of his convictions. In that bible for mentalists and magicians live effects that will be performed for many years to come. We have taken a fair share of these remarkable effects, edited them, arranged them for ready reference in separate chapters, and offer them to you for your pleasure. You will find considerable overlapping in the various catagories, but that is the nature of mental tricks. Not all the card tricks are in the card section, nor all the slate or envelope tricks in their respective chapters. Likewise, you will find book tests under various headings. We have endeavored, however, to segregate the effects using the dominant feature of the trick as our yardstick. Tricks of every type are included . . . those requiring a serious presentation or a humorous one; some are weird, such as "Voodoo," others spooky, such as "Sefalaljia," but all are solid entertainment and, as the title implies, practical.

MAX HOLDEN
JOHN J. CRIMMINS, JR.

TIME MARCHES ON

"There was a time, about twenty-five years ago, when the art of crystal gazing was dominant in vaudeville. Audiences of that era sat enthralled while the 'master mind' looked into a glass ball and gave answer after answer, ad nauseum, to queries written by the customers who either were actually troubled or highly interested. Redundant as that may sound, it's true. Magic magazines of that period abounded with advertisements clamoring for $100 to $200 as a reasonable return for a trunk full of gadgets plus a twenty odd paged manuscript, the possession of which would assure the buyer's success in the theatrical field.

Time, like trouble in the hearts of men, marches on! The crystal ball, with handbox reader beneath; the nickle-plated sphere (they didn't have chromium then) with a cog wheel controlled spinning band inside; the pedestal prompter with its pulpit appearance; the various electrical devices, either direct contact or induction, from carpet to turban; all of these means to an end have had their day. Contemporary with these were the change baskets, the mirror bowls, and the end-for-end ladles with which to secure the information and make it ready for material passage through the first mentioned devices to the omnipotent man on the stage.

As time marched on, audiences became more acute and sensible. While mediums, fortune tellers and psychics still abound in private consultation shelters, the stage seer has had to find honest work. All of which finally brings us to a point. Question answering, plus the revelation of supposedly unknown thoughts, when kept within reasonable limits of time, can be a very important part of the magician's program today! And, we mean the program of the performer who entertains platform, social and club types of audiences.

Audiences today 'go for' the mental type of trickery more than ever. It is more of a 'grown up' phase of magic and mystery, and there seems to be a greater element of wonder when the performer can reveal unknown knowledge or something personal about the members of his audience.

I'm not in any way slighting magic as a whole when I say this, but I've found it to be true so far as my own work is concerned."

Theo Annemann

Reprinted from Theo. Annemann's magazine, "The Jinx".

CONTENTS

THEODORE ANNEMANN

Whose brilliant contributions to the field of Mental Magic will remain as an everlasting memorial to his genius

BERT REESE SECRETS

ANNEMANN

Down through the ages have come but few noted billet readers, and invariably such men have been able to fool Kings, Premiers, Presidents, and scientists. Dr. Lynn, and Foster, the medium, were two of renown, but in the past 30 years one man stood out as a charlatan par excellence at the business of reading the folded slip. The man was Berthold Riess, born in 1841 in Posen, which was then in Prussia. Later he became known universally as Bert Reese and before his death in 1928 had crossed the ocean over 50 times to humbug such people as Charles M. Schwab, Ignace Jan Paderewski, Premiere Mussolini, Woodrow Wilson, Warren Harding and Thomas Edison.

As I look through my file of articles, clips and stories about the doings of Bert Reese, I marvel at the constantly appearing statements that he never touched the written-on paper. This is a psychological point of importance to all performers who do anything of this nature. Only a trained observer can give an accurate account of every move, even though they may not know the method of trickery. What, to the ordinary spectator, may be the most natural of movements, can be the one detail that would solve the problem in recounting the experience.

Thus Reese's actions, being psychologically different in their entirety from the technique of magic, may seem brazen and bare-faced to a magician not acquainted with this type of deception. These very same actions, blended into a routine by Reese that lead up to a startling revelation, were looked upon by his audiences as phenomena far removed from the realm of sleight-of-hand or trickery. *It is important to remember, therefore, that an audience is in a different frame of mind at the time it watches a billet reading exhibition,* and that all traditional magical gestures of sleeve rolling or of showing the hands empty are ridiculous, not to mention ruinous. Also keep in mind that the really successful humbugs in this line do not demonstrate from the theatrical stage. Rather they confine their activities to the lecture platform and to the semi-privacy of the home and drawing rooms where theatrical atmosphere is not present, and their demonstrations are cloaked with a scientific or almost religious demeanor.

Reese did not care whether his subjects called it telepathy or spiritism, being content to let people credit him with whatever solution of power they deemed most fitting. Here was a good point as he did not antagonize any particular group but left it to their own individual credulity and gullibility.

He ever was ready to demonstrate at any moment or place, another point which emphasized his benign sincerity of purpose in making use of his apparently strange faculty.

Routine with Three Sitters:

Illustrated is one of his routines using three sitters. Reese is sitting at the left. Borrowing a piece of writing paper, he tore it into slips about two by three inches. He would be standing at the time, and did the tearing while the others were sitting down and making ready. Five slips were put on the table, the rest of the sheet being crumpled up and tossed away. However, Reese really would make six slips and retain one, folded once in each direction, as a dummy for his own use. A detail here was that afterwards, the sitters would relate that he had used their own private tinted or watermarked paper rather than any of his own. Now he walked around the room while questions were being written to dead people on the slips and folded once each way. The folded papers were mixed together on the table and Reese would take his seat, the dummy billet being finger-palmed in the right hand.

He then said, "Give one to this lady to hold," pointing to the one farthest away, and the sitter opposite him (a man in this case) would hand her one paper. Reese had not touched it but the pointing was being done to accustom all to the gesture. "Give one to this lady," he'd say next, pointing as before but to the lady next to him. The gesture was once more planted, and moreso when he repeated it again by having another paper given to the first lady. Now he would tell the gentleman to keep the remaining two, but as an after thought would say, "Perhaps we'd better let this lady have another." This time he would casually take the slip being passed over to the lady next to him, complete the six or eight-inch journey, but in that space make the switch for the dummy which she would get to hold. The stolen slip was dropped into his lap and opened with the left hand while, with his right, he'd make marks on a sheet of paper on the table. He apparently got his answer from these, and his scribbling served to attract the attention of the sitters while he glimpsed and then refolded the slip with his left hand under the table.

Now he would extend his left hand, with finger-palmed billet, towards the lady next to him, and say, "Give me that paper," pointing not to the dummy but the other one. Taking this it was apparently opened and spread on the table. In reality the one taken was drawn back into the finger palm by the thumb, while the paper in hand was pushed out by the fingers from where the right fingers took hold and opened it up. Thus the one opened on the table was the one just glimpsed, and the one finger palmed was a fresh one. Again the "business" would be gone through and new marks made and a new answer given. This time a slip from the second lady would be requested and apparently opened. Following this, the man's paper would be taken, then back to the second lady, and lastly the lady next to him again which would bring the dummy back to him in return for the final slip.

Routine for Single Sitters:

For single sitters Reese had a slightly different routine, although practically everything he ever did was based on the one-ahead idea. Four or five slips would be given a man to write questions on and fold. They would be thrown onto the table as written and Reese would mix them a little with his finger, but in doing so would switch the dummy slip he had palmed for one of the papers. As the gentleman was writing his last paper, Reese would walk away, and in his wandering would open and read the stolen paper. The single fold each way of these papers made them very easy to open with one hand. As the person finished the last question, Reese would return to the table and ask him to put one paper in his left coat pocket, another in his right coat pocket, one in his left shoe, one in his right shoe, and the other perhaps inside his watch. Reese only watched to be certain into which spot went the dummy slip of the five. Knowing the contents of the finger palmed slip in his left hand, he would walk back and forth around the room and give the answer. Then he would point to one of the locations on the spectator's person and ask for that paper. Taking it, he would open and read it aloud, actually reading what was on the slip he knew and memorizing what he now saw. Folding this paper he would finger palm it in the right hand, and left hand would toss the other onto the table. Reese invariably smoked a cigar and the action of taking it from his mouth with thumb and finger of either hand served as an admirable mask for the finger palmed paper.

He would proceed by answering the next question and so on until the last, always leaving the dummy in its resting place until that time. It was a regular procedure of his to have the papers placed about the person in odd places, such as the watch case, for instance, and my theory for this is that such places, being unusual in character, were always remembered by the sitter in preference to the more common spots. Afterwards, in telling about the ordeal, the sitter could be depended upon to swear that he had put the paper there and that Reese had answered it without being near the sitter or having touched the slips.

Another angle that Reese brought into play often was in asking people to write the name of their favorite school teacher when a child; the name of the town or city where they were born; their auto license number; their telephone; their mother's maiden name; and any number of odd but personal bits of information to which he could have no access but which would be vividly personal enough to be remembered and talked about by the sitter. Such items are far better than merely having any number or any word written.

Routine for Telephone Test:

In many cases when Reese was going to work for someone he knew, it was a simple matter to check up on the person's telephone number before starting. In such a case, he would sandwich the request for a telephone number in among the other slips as they were being written. A steal was made of one of the others and read as already described. Watching the telephone number slip on the table and also the dummy, he would have them pocket or conceal the slips as usual. However, when they picked up the telephone slip he would have it placed in a pocketbook, between the pages of a notebook or in some other difficult spot. The rest of the slips would be read as usual but the telephone slip apparently forgotten. Then he would recall that there was another slip out, and merely taking the article which contained the slip and holding it to his forehead he would answer the question and hand it back. The sitter had been told so many things no one else could know that the idea of Reese getting his number would never occur to him.

Not alone can the telephone number be used, but there are many little bits of information about a person that are dropped by others, and of these most anything can be used. Much information about doctors, for instance can be secured from a medical directory and it is possible to have the name of their college on one slip and the name of a professor at that college on another. The first you know, and the second request makes it logical to have the other.

Routine for Groups:

Reese, when before a group of people, also had slips written, folded and collected. He would absently pick them up again, hand them to another person and ask him to put the papers under objects around the room. Of course, the switch had been made, Reese would light his cigar and read the slip in his cupped hands. He would then walk around the room to the various spots, pick up the paper concealed at each point and apparently read it, always leaving the dummy until the last. In all of these variations, it is to be noticed that the effect was what counted. The stories that are told about these happenings afterwards are unbelievable. Like the famed Dr. Hooker's Rising Cards, there were so many variations of the same thing that afterwards, one had difficulty to remember exactly the procedure on each test, and not get them confused with each other.

Some Final Remarks:

And now I want to give a bit of information which I doubt has ever seen print. Much has been said about soft paper that will not crackle as it is furtively opened. Invariably it has been left to the reader to search out a soft quality and experiment. Reese used a soft paper but he took it from a most natural spot. At his home, especially, when giving a test for visitors, he would pick up a book, and tear out the blank page at the back. Pulp paper books give you this perfect soft paper, and right in front of people, too, without the necessity of bringing out prepared sheets. This detail alone was one of his most potent secrets.

I haven't exhausted, by far, the many incidents and stories about Reese situations. However, I have given a practical and working knowledge of how he worked, and the fact that this man traveled the world over for years, and in the highest circles, while being looked upon by many as a competent psychic advisor, proves that such work is worth developing and extremely effective on the audience. As far as I know, and I keep a fairly complete file, nothing has been written about the man for magicians, although reams have been printed in the press about his marvels. Of one thing I'm sure. This type of work is more sought after, better liked, and talked about more than any other phase of the mystery game. And last but far from least, the monetary gain of those successful in this line far outdistances that of those successful in other branches of magic. *But watch your presentation, and forget about magical movements that immediately class you as a manipulator.*

BILLET SWITCHING
ANNEMANN

There are two essential switches of folded paper slips that everyone doing mental work should learn. The first or simple method is not new and is merely an exchange of folded slips. The second method, or folding switch, is my own and consists of reading a paper slip which is then switched for a palmed dummy as you refold it. The dummy is then handed to someone to hold, while the one just read is finger-palmed and retained in your hand.

The size of the paper should be 2½" x 3½". Hands differ, however, and the individual should try out sizes in proportion with these dimensions until the right size for his own hand is found. A printer will cut up a bunch of these and pad them, about fifty to a pad, for a small sum.

The folding of the slips is important. Fold them once the long way, and then twice the opposite way, i.e.: after the first fold you then fold the left end in to the middle after which the right end is folded over all. This will result in a folded slip a little narrower than the width of your second finger and long enough to be held easily, yet firmly, between the root and first joint of the finger. Thus, with the second finger slightly curled, the slip can be safely held and will be invisible from the front as long as the hand is not turned directly around. It is also invisible from the sides and

FINGER PALM

C·C·C·

from the back, too, providing the hand is not held too far (more than eight or ten inches) from your body.

The First Method:

With the slip in your left hand between second finger and thumb, practice pulling it back with the thumb into the finger-palm position, and keep at it until you can push the slip out and get it back easily and quickly. Then practice this with your right hand as well.

After you have mastered this simple move, you are ready to try the first method of switching. Finger-palm one slip in your left hand and, with the same hand, pick up a second slip and hold it at the finger tips between your second finger and thumb. Slide this second slip back with your thumb until it overlaps the one that is finger-palmed. The thumb continues to pull this second slip even further back till the thumb tip rests on about the center of the finger-palmed slip; then with the help of the finger this finger-palmed slip is pushed forward into view. This will be found to work easily and smoothly, and it leaves the originally palmed slip in view at your finger tips while the second slip is now in position to be palmed.

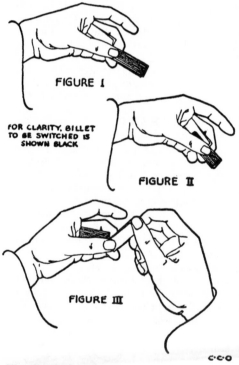

FIGURE I

FOR CLARITY, BILLET TO BE SWITCHED IS SHOWN BLACK

FIGURE II

FIGURE III

The right fingers can now take the switched slip which is in view and hand it to someone. Simultaneously, the left thumb holds the newly palmed paper in place against the second finger of the left hand until the fingers curl a little and secure the slip in the proper finger-palmed position.

I repeat that this must be practiced until the switch can be done without looking at your hand at all. During such a switch, the hand is not held still and you are not doing a trick to switch papers, remember that! Keep the hand in motion, using it to gesture with and the switch will never be seen.

The Second Method:

The second switch is a little harder but quite useful and perfect. Finger-palm a folded billet (paper slip). Now take another folded billet and open it at the finger tips of both hands, just as you would do normally. Read this open slip and refold it. On the last fold let it come right on top of the palmed slip, and your right thumb and forefinger takes the two slips, as one, and holds them in full view for a second. Do not make any obvious move to show your left hand empty. However, you can act freer than before until you reach the party who is to receive the formerly palmed slip instead of the one just read.

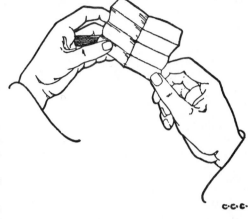

c·c·c·

At this point the two slips are again taken by the left thumb and second finger, with the back of your hand towards the audience. The slip nearest you, on which your thumb now rests, is drawn back into your palm as you offer the visible (switched) slip to the person who is to hold it. He may be the person who had written on the original slip, so it is important that your switch be clean and perfectly executed so as not to raise any suspicion in his mind that the slip he gets is anything but his original one.

Now you have two methods of switching folded paper slips, and a third method will be found on page 216 under the heading of the "Dollar Bill" Switch." The rest is routine work and showmanship of presentation which all comes under the same heading.

You will never get enough practice on this type of work. You have to do it all without looking at your hands, which are always held in front of you naturally at waist level. When you read a slip and start to refold it, don't look down again at it but rather look at the writer while you refold the slip in a natural manner, switch it and return it. All these points are important and there's nothing theoretical about them. I've learned them all from hard work and application, and I've used them just as described for many years so I know what I'm talking about.

A QUESTION AND THE ANSWER
ANNEMANN

It would be easy to call this a super effect. I have used it continuously and from the audience standpoint the effect is direct and easy to follow.

Effect: The performer asks a spectator to write a question on a slip of paper, some question to which he would like an answer. The spectator does so and then folds the slip. It is initialed by another person and is held in full view. The performer, standing at some distance, picks up another slip of paper and proceeds to write something on it. As soon as he finishes, he crumples up the slip and hands it to a third person to hold for a few seconds.

Returning to the person, who is still holding the first slip, the performer opens it and reads the question aloud. The third spectator now stands and reads what the performer had written, and finds that it is a direct answer to the question asked!

Preparation: Effects as simple as this will always appeal to the practical performer. The only materials needed are a few pieces of paper about 2″ x 3″ in size, a pencil and a thumb tip. Fold the papers once the long way and then twice the other way. Such a folded slip will fit into the thumb tip nicely. Have one in the tip and keep it in the right, lower vest or trouser pocket. Open out the remaining slips and have them in the left side coat pocket with the pencil.

Routine: Start by selecting someone to write the query. Take the paper slips from your left coat pocket, give him one and replace the remaining slips in your pocket. While he writes the question, your right hand secures the tip on your thumb, with the slip inside of it under the ball of the thumb. When he has finished writing, you step up to him, hold out your left hand and ask him to refold his slip and lay it on your palm. Now bring your right hand up and place your thumb, with its thumb tip, right on top of the slip. Simultaneously you close the fingers of the left hand over the right thumb. Now pull your right thumb out of the thumb tip and out of the left fist, bringing with it the dummy slip which is clipped between the tips of the right thumb and first finger. The thumb tip and the original slip are still hidden by the closed fingers of the left hand, which casually drops to your left side. Without any hesitation at all, you ask someone to initial the (dummy) slip which you hold in your right hand. After he has done so, you ask him to take the slip and hold it high above his head for a few minutes, so that everyone can keep their eyes on it. This entire switch, when smoothly done, is very natural and should cause no suspicion on the part of anyone.

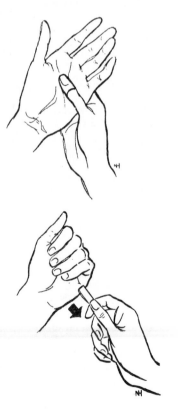

Now as you walk away you casually put your left hand in your left coat pocket, remarking at the same time about what's been done so far. It only takes a second to drop the thumb tip and to open the original slip against those already in your pocket. Bring them out immediately with the written slip facing you. As you draw off the bottom slip with your right hand you read the first person's question and then return the remaining slips to your pocket. This time when your left hand comes out of your pocket you bring out the pencil and explain that you will attempt some automatic writing.

Changing the slip over from your right hand to your left, and the pencil to the right, you write an appropriate answer to the person's question. Crumple up the slip and give it to someone to hold.

Now return to the man who is holding the dummy slip, supposedly the original one, take it from him and apparently read the question. Of course, you merely repeat the question you have just read. When you have finished, direct attention to the person holding your slip as you crumple up the dummy and pocket it. Now ask the person with your slip to read aloud what you wrote in answer to the question. The answer is correct, so make the most of your climax!

THE AL BAKER THREE BILLET TRICK
ANNEMANN'S VERSION

Fifteen or sixteen years ago, Al Baker originated an effect using a deck of cards, three pieces of paper, and a borrowed hat. To the audience the procedure was to have three cards selected and thought of while the pack of cards was in their hands. The names of these selections were written on pieces of paper, folded, and collected in the hat. One by one, the performer would take out the papers, and apparently by divination reveal the selected or thought-of cards. I first obtained the original method in 1924 and later, around 1929, added somewhat to the general effect by using switches so as to be able to return the slips as read. In the meanwhile, Mr. Baker personally had given me three or four variations for the handling of the billets. About the same time I discovered that a stacked deck could actually be shuffled without impairing to any great degree its subsequent use in a trick. Its most common application was in conjunction with a code, and Mrs. Annemann would reveal the chosen card from a distance when to the onlookers there wasn't a chance of my knowing it or finding it. Combining this principle with the three billet trick, I have been doing the trick as given below, ever since.

Effect and Routine: Here is the working of this quite perfect mystery. Three pieces of paper are at hand and a deck of cards arranged in your favorite system. Hand the deck to someone to shuffle overhand. As he starts mixing, you cause him to hurry by asking him to put the deck face down on his left hand. Then as an afterthought, tell him to give the deck a complete cut and square the cards. During this you have turned away. Now request him to look at the top card of the deck, and then insert it any place in the center of the deck and square the cards well. Turning back, you hand him a piece of paper and take the deck. Ask him to write the name of the card he just looked at on the paper slip. Now, as you start towards another person, note the bottom or face card of the deck. By counting one ahead in the system, you know the first man's card which he is writing on his paper slip.

Give the deck a quick riffle leaving the noted bottom card in place, and then an overhand shuffle bringing the bottom card to the top. The second spectator receives the deck, face down, on his left hand; pulls a bunch of cards from the center, notes the face card and drops the packet on top. Squaring the deck, he cuts them once and again you take it and give him a paper for writing. Picking a third person, you ask that he fan through the deck and merely think of any card he sees. For example, you illustrate by fanning through the cards carelessly. However, you watch for the card you first noted, and the one directly behind it is the card the second man chose! The third man then takes the deck, thinks of a card and fans through them to see if his mentally selected card is there. When he locates it, he closes up the deck, lays it down and writes the name of his selection on the third slip of paper.

All you have to remember are the first two cards selected. Now collect the folded papers in a borrowed hat, watching them as they are dropped in so you know which is the first, second, and third. Reach in with the right hand and, finger-palming the first slip with the second finger, bring out the third billet openly at fingertips. Look at the first person and little by little name his card. Just as it is acknowledged, open the visible slip, the third one, nod your head as you refold it and apparently return it to the writer. However, you have now found out the identity of the last, or mentally thought-of card; and after refolding the slip, switch it for the first paper you have finger-palmed and return that. (For those who can't master a finger switch the following method is very simple. Do it as above to the point where the third slip is refolded. Holding it in sight at left fingertips, start towards the writer and put it apparently in your right palm. Actually, however, finger-palm it in left hand and open your right hand revealing the substitute paper.)

Return now to the hat and pick it up with the fingers of the hand, holding the palmed billet, inside and drop the slip into the hat. Remark that there may be some suspicion that the handling of the papers enables you to learn the names of the cards. Pass the hat directly to the second person and ask him to reach in and take out one of the two remaining slips. He is to open it and say whether or not it is his slip. If it is his slip you impressively reveal the name of the card while he holds the paper billet himself. If it is not his slip, ask him to hand it to the third person for a few minutes and then to reach into the hat again and take out the last slip which must be his. Thus you are able to leave the actual thought-of card for the last and get a better effect when you reveal its identity. This routine will leave well informed magicians baffled because you not only twist them up on the card selection but also in the handling of the papers as well.

The first thought of many people will be to figure out a way of discovering the name of the third thought-of card without opening the billets. However, there is no way that will compare with having a spectator just think of a card, and that one point alone makes this trick one effect that will be talked about.*

A DAY OF YOUR LIFE
ANNEMANN

Most billet reading routines depend upon the assistance of several spectators, and there is a need for "reading" tricks wherein only one person is the subject throughout. I recall occasions when it would have been to my advantage had I been in a position to do a good, solid test for a single person, such as Bert Reese used to enhance his reputation. It is very essential that a test of this sort be personalized so that the subject can truthfully swear that he was given information absolutely impossible for the performer, or medium,

*(Editor's Note: There is one excellent method of discovering this "Thought-of-card" that has been suggested since this effect was published in 1936. That is to use the "Mental Masterpiece" impression pack, which gives you a carbon-wax impression of the person's writing. When using this pack you will, of course, have to reverse the process to let the person "just thinking" of a card write his slip first. He uses the card case as a support. The deck can then be dumped out for the other two selections. During this maneuver you note the carbon impression, and continue with the trick as outlined.)

to know. Besides, when you are making someone think of his personal doings, he has to keep his mind on himself which is to your advantage in "working."

Effect: Seat your subject in front of you and tell him that you want to get "impressions" of some of the ordinary happenings in a day of his life. If you are performing in the evening, you may use that day's happenings, otherwise try and make him recall the day before.

Give him a piece of paper and ask him to write on it one single item of food he had for dinner the night before. As he writes this and folds the paper you have secured another. Take the "dinner" slip, giving him a fresh one, and put the folded billet under his right foot. On the second paper he writes one article of food he had for "luncheon." It is folded, exchanged for a third fresh slip, and the "luncheon" billet is placed under the subject's left foot. On the third paper he writes one thing he had for his "breakfast." After being folded, the performer has the subject hold it clenched in his fist. Then, as a last wish, the subject is asked to write down the hour he got up that morning, not exactly, but as close as he can remember. During this last bit of writing, the performer gets an ash tray and matches close at hand.

The folded billet bearing the hour noted is openly burned, and from the smoke the time the subject arose is revealed. The performer next touches the subject's forehead and announces his favorite breakfast food. Then, in turn, he correctly divines the luncheon dish and the dinner course. He may conclude, saying, "And those are only minor details of your day. It probably is just as well that I do not try to get impressions of the important phases of your business."

Preparation: All you need is a pad of paper about $2\frac{1}{4}$ inches by $3\frac{1}{2}$ inches in size. Tear off five or six sheets, folding each once the long way and then twice the opposite way. This makes just the right size billet to finger palm and finger switch with ease. The creased paper billets are opened and with the pad are placed in your side coat pocket. Have the loose papers nearest the body. One paper is left folded, as a dummy, and this is kept in the same pocket.

Routine: Take out the pad and sheaf of papers. Remove the top one and give it to the subject for his "dinner" notation. Put the packet back in your pocket, finger palm the dummy billet, and bring out the next loose paper. When the spectator has refolded his paper, you take it with the hand holding the finger paimed dummy while giving him the fresh paper with your other hand. Then suggest putting the dinner" billet under his right foot, which is done, but the switch has been made and the right foot is placed on the blank dummy. (See "Billet Switching," page 11.)

Now take another paper from your pocket, but keep the first ("dinner") billet finger palmed. Take the "luncheon" paper in exchange for a fresh slip, as before, and, after an exchange, put the "dinner" billet under the subject's left foot, saying that you are placing the "luncheon" paper there. The same routine is followed the third time. The "breakfast" paper is taken (but no fresh slip this time) and finger switched as you ask where this one should be placed. Then you suggest that he hold it cleanched in his fist. This is important, for afterwards he will always remember that he held his own paper and will not recall that you touched it.

Your hand, with the "breakfast" billet palmed, goes into your pocket and, as you say there is one thing more—the arising hour, the paper is opened against the front of the papers and the pad. The pad and papers are now brought out and one paper is taken from underneath the top one. As you take this paper, you instantly read what is written on the top one which gives you the answer to the "breakfast" problem. Replace the pad and the extra papers in your pocket, which leaves you holding the blank page you had withdrawn.

On the center of this blank piece draw a circle, saying that it will represent a clock face. Give it to the subject asking him to draw in the hands of a clock at the time he arose. During this get an ash tray and matches ready. He folds the paper as before, but, as you take it from him at your fingertips, unfold the first fold to make it a paper folded but once each way. Hold with the four loose corners to the lower right. Tear, from top down, through the paper a little to the right of the center crease. Put the right hand portion in front (towards spectator). Turn paper crosswise before you, the bottom circling towards the right, and tear through again, a little to the right of the center. Put the right hand portion in front. Hold at left fingertip and thumb as your right hand moves the ash tray in place and hands the matches to the subject. The left thumb draws back the rear portion and the right fingers take the pieces that remain and puts them on the tray to be burnt. The left hand drops to your pocket and opens out the stolen piece which, because of the folding and tearing, contains the full clock face you so helpfully drew in the center of the paper!

Bring out the pad and paper while the useless bits burn and smoke, and draw out a blank piece of paper, getting a good look at the clock face and the time. Repocket the packet and then proceed to duplicate the clock face and time being thought about in your best psychic manner!

With this acknowledged as correct, you finger-palm from your pocket the refolded "breakfast" slip as you pace back and forth before the subject. Now name the "breakfast" food he had. Deliberately take the paper he had held clenched in one fist and open it. Nod your head, refold the paper, switch and toss it on the table. Now you know the "luncheon" data and have that billet finger-palmed. Ask which "under foot" paper was the "luncheon" one (as if you can't remember). He gives you what he thinks is right, but really it is the "dinner" slip. You divine the "luncheon" paper, open and read the "dinner" billet, refold and switch so that you can toss the correct "luncheon" billet on to the table. Lastly you pick up the dummy billet and, as you say you are coming to the most important meal of the day, merely finger switch for the "dinner" billet which you have palmed. Then give this directly to the subject and ask him to place it against his forehead and imagine tasting his food. Then finish your effect and he has all the papers in his possession as they should be.

The routine shouldn't take over eight or nine minutes. Once you've gotten acquainted with the setup of moves you'll have an impromptu stunt that is psychologically perfect.

THE GERMAIN GEM

Effects of Karl Germain's seldom see print. A master of magic, a great showman of several decades ago, this gentleman believed that a trick should only be given to an intimate friend, or learned through apprenticeship. We feel proud, therefore, to be able to present this authentic presentation of a Germain effect.

Effect: "Do you believe in spirits?" "I am not prepared to do a trick for you, but I am conversant with a method wherein we might be able to call forth the spirits to do something for us.

"Now suppose you name some personage who resides in the world beyond, either north or south as the case may be. Kipling? Fine.

"You say that you do believe in spirits? Oh, you're not sure. May I say that when I first saw you I had a very definite impression that there is a certain bond between us. I believe exactly as you do.

"Will you take one of these little cigarette papers, examine it, and roll it into a ball. Put it on the table. Here is a pencil which I'm going to ask you to hold in a certain manner. I want you to take the little pellet and put it right on top of the pencil—stick it on the end of the point. Now hold the pencil up vertically with your very fingertips.

"The reason for this is simple. There are no material things in the spirit world, and, when we are visited by the spirits, we must provide the materials for them. They need them to show their presence.

"You named a person deceased, yes? Custer. General Custer, the man killed by the Indians—Oh, Kipling, I'm sorry. The man whose 'Kim' and 'Tommy Atkins' are unforgettable. Now it may be that you feel a very slight tremor about the vicinity of the pencil you hold, but please do not let that disturb you—yes—I feel as though Mr. Kipling is trying to get through to us—here, look at the paper and see if he hasn't left visible proof of his presence!"

The action has followed Germain's own patter, and the spectator un-ravels the ball of paper to find thereon the signature of Kipling. Germain has done this unassuming but potent effect for many people to their belief.

Preparation: The most important secret is to be prepared to write the name in your pocket the very moment it is given. Germain has been known to get the little pellet all written out, rolled up and finger palmed with hands on the table in less than half a minute after the name was given. Like so many well done effects, getting set before you start the trick is the thing that makes it a real miracle.

Writing the name on the paper with a large piece of lead, or a very small stub of pencil, is just something learned by practice. A good plan is to have several well known names, such as Lincoln, Washington, etc., already written, (copying their actual autographs) and hidden in pockets easily accessible should one happen to be called.

The best papers are those that come in an orange colored book called "Riz-La." Two books are needed, one to hand to the spectator when you ask him to take out one and examine it. (During this time you write the name on the book in the pocket, tear off the paper, and ball it up.)

The book in the pocket is prepared as follows: Bend one cover all the way back so that it lays against the other cover. Snap the attached rubber band around it this way, and tear one paper (top) almost loose. It makes it very easy to tear off and wad up the paper after writing on it.

Routine: Follow Germain's routine as outlined in the patter. Hand the spectator the duplicate book of cigarette papers, have him select one, examine it, roll it into a ball and lay it on the table. Then hand him a pencil with your left hand, all the while keeping up your flow of patter. In the mean-time, your right hand has been busy writing the chosen name on the cigarette paper in your right coat pocket, crumpling it into a ball and finger palming it. By the time he has laid his paper ball on the table, your right hand is resting on the table edge also. Help him to get the paper ball on the tip of the pencil point and to hold the pencil, as illustrated, between his fingers. You, of course, switch the pellet which the spectator has examined, for the one you have pinched between the tips of the fingers which wadded it up. This should be easy, for you pick up his pellet to show him how to place it on the point of the pencil . . . and at that point the switch is made.

If the moves are fitted to the patter, given here in Germain's words, and presented with evident sincerity, the trick takes on an aura of great significance.

Germain has been known to go into a simulated trance from the time the spectator started to hold the pellet on the pencil point, and otherwise made it evident that his mental faculties were under terrific strain.

In short, the effect is worth cultivating. In Mr. Germain's hands it was a veritable masterpiece.

TERVIL
ORVILLE MEYER

This is "Tervil," a prophetic demon. The effect is one of prophecy, and I shall describe the working along with the effect as presented.

Three paper billets are used. They are about 2½ inches by 3¾ inches in size. Fold them once the long way and then twice the opposite way. This makes a billet just right for finger palming. Two of them are opened and dropped on the table. The third is in one trouser pocket as a dummy.

You announce that you will write a prophecy of what someone is going to think about later. Pick up one of the papers and write a three-word prognostication. It doesn't matter what you write. You will understand that in a moment. The prophecy is folded and tossed on the table. You say, "That is what I am sure is going to happen."

The second, unfolded paper is handed to a spectator who is requested to write down any color, any number from 1 to 99, and the name of any city in the world.

During this interval you finger palm the dummy billet from your trouser pocket. The spectator folds his written billet, being guided by the creases of the original fold, and you take the paper from him. Hand it directly to another person to be initialled, and this person hands it back to the first person (the writer) to hold up over his head so that everyone may keep their eyes on it. However, when you took it from the writer you switched it for the dummy, and it was the dummy that was initialled and handed back to the writer.

As the situation stands now, your "prediction" is on the table. The spectator holds what he believes to be a record of his thoughts, and finger palmed you have the billet actually bearing that person's writings.

Pick up your "prediction," saying, "I said I was going to attempt a feat of prophecy, and try to pass beyond that veil which hides the future. All of you must realize that though but a few minutes have passed, I did put down in black and white what I felt sure was going to be thought of." This patter sets your audience and serves as a necessary stall. At its start you have picked up the blank from the table, switched it, and have casually opened the paper upon which are the spectator's choices. As the patter makes the action natural you gesture with and glance at the open paper, all of which suffices to give you the information thereon. At once you refold and walk towards another person at some little distance. He stands, you saying, "I want you to take charge of my prophecy. It is only right that my audience check on every detail throughout."

May I get away for a moment? This last person is given the billet you just have read. It actually is that written by the first man now holding a blank. But—don't make it apparent that you have opened, looked at, and closed the paper as you talked. The patter takes care of all angles, the audience is watching and listening to you, and it is perfectly natural for you to glance at your own prophecy anyway, just as long as you don't make it decidedly apparent that you have to or must do it. This half minute procedure can make or break things. And don't worry or be self-conscious. It may seem bold or brazen to you, but after becoming accustomed to its working you'll find out that even magicians won't know or remember that the paper has been opened.

The first person still holds a blank (he's holding it high "for everybody to see" and this subtle maneuver prevents him from opening it) thinking it his own. The person last approached is standing with your prophecy clenched in his hand. It's really the paper belonging to the first man and containing his written thoughts. And you now know what those thoughts are. So far the procedure from the view of the audience has been direct and clean. There has been nothing done to confuse them, and at this point the trick is over except for the unbelievable climax.

You take the paper from the first person. The dummy has been ditched after giving the last person your paper. Your hands are empty. You open this paper, look at it for a split second, and then read aloud his written thoughts. This is pretense for you are naming the items just gleaned from the other paper. You point directly at the man and ask if he believes it possible for you to have known beforehand what he was going to think. Make this definite and outstanding. Then have the other person read what you foretold. Approach him as he reads, take the paper, take a bow, pocket both, and go on with the act.

MENTAL HAT PIN
Dr. Jaks

The subtlety involved in this pellet trick offers you a cute method for switching pellets. Any long decorative pin, such as a corsage pin, will do very nicely, and the fact that it may be borrowed on the spot makes everything look very impromptu.

Effect: You pass out several small squares of paper and at the same time borrow a corsage or hat pin from one of the ladies present. Have the person holding the paper pellets select one and write some short question on it. He then crumples the pellet into a small ball which you impale on the pin. With the pellet isolated in this fashion, the pin is given to someone to hold until the completion of the experiment.

You now produce a small pad on which you scribble a note or two in an apparent effort to get an answer to the question through automatic writing. After due deliberation, you interpret the scribbling into a full answer to the question asked by the writer. The pellet is removed from the pin, opened up and the question read to verify that you have given the correct answer.

Preparation: A duplicate pellet is, of course, necessary and this you have crumpled into a small ball and hold it concealed in the crotch of the second and third fingers of your right hand. Have a small pad in your left side coat pocket, as well as several loose pages of the pad. These loose sheets should be torn in half so as to offer but a small writing surface, and also for ease in handling as will be explained later. If you prefer, you can remove several pages from the pad in view of the audience and then tear them in half. However, I like to have them all ready in advance. A pencil should also be handy in a convenient pocket.

Routine: Step forward with the duplicate dummy pellet palmed in your right hand as already described. Announce that you will try an experiment in automatic writing and request the loan of some lady's hat pin. While this is forthcoming, reach into your coat pocket, remove the loose slips and hand them to some gentleman in the audience. Drop your right hand to the side and, as you receive the hat pin with your left hand, the right thumb rolls the dummy pellet from the crotch of the two fingers into a position between the thumb and first finger tip. Instruct the man holding the slips to select one page and write on it some simple question. While you are explaining just what you want him to do, you apparently grasp the point of the hat pin between the thumb and first finger tip of the right hand, which is held palm upwards, and hold the pin horizontally in front of you with its head retained by the thumb and first finger tips of the left hand. What you actually do, however, is to insert the point of the pin into the paper pellet being held between your right thumb and first finger. Now just give the pin a push which will impale the pellet on the pin as its point comes into view on the right side of your right thumb and first finger. Push the pin through the pellet until this dummy is about half way up on the pin, then release your left hand and hold the pin up in view as illustrated. Your right thumb and first finger will effectively hide the dummy. Time your patter, so that this maneuver appears but an unconscious and unimportant handling of the pin. As you finish your instructions, you should be motioning with your right hand and the pin in an unconcerned manner without causing the least suspicion.

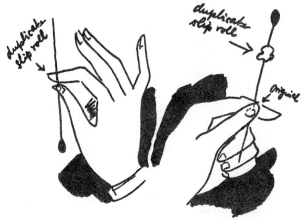

Now tilt your right hand so that the bent fingertips face to your left, which will bring the pin into a vertical position directly in front of you with its point straight up. Ask the person who has written the message to crumple up the paper slip into a small, tight ball and to impale it on the point of the hat pin which you are holding. Either have the person push his pellet down the pin to about half way to where you are holding the pin, or you aid him by pushing it down with your left first finger tip. Now turn your right hand so that the back of the hand is upwards and so that the pin is horizontal with the floor and pointing towards the left. Grasp the pin with your left thumb and forefinger directly over the written pellet; open your right thumb and forefinger slightly so that the dummy is visible and push this dummy along towards the head of the pin. If you do this as one movement, it appears as though you merely shifted the pin to the left hand and moved the pellet up the pin with your right finger tips. Hold it in view for a few seconds and then ask someone to grasp the head of the pin, remove it from your left hand and hold it. As he does this, the original written pellet remains between your left thumb and forefinger, and you immediately drop this hand to your side. So much for the switch, which is a beautiful piece of deception.

Reach into your left coat pocket with the palmed pellet, open it out against the face of the pad and then remove the pad and pretend to mark down the vibrations and impressions you are receiving. Hold the pad with its back to the audience, and with the pellet opened and facing you. Read the question and make some notes on the first sheet of the pad, above and below the opened pellet. Drop the pad back into your pocket just as you finish with your reading. Roll the spectator's pellet into a small ball and bring out your hand with the paper ball pinched between your thumb and forefinger. Step up the spectator holding the pin and grasp it with your right fingers. As your right thumb and forefinger moves down the hat pin they momentarily cover the dummy pellet. Step back towards the original writer as your left hand apparently finishes removing the pellet which you give to him. In reality, however, you give him the original pellet you have palmed in your left hand. Now reach over towards the lady who loaned you the pin, thank her and have her pull it out of your hand. This will leave the dummy pellet in your right hand, which you dispose of shortly.

DEVIL DEVICE
Magnuson

Effect: The sitter is ushered into the "reading" room of the medium. He is seated behind a flat top desk or table. The seeker of enlightenment is seated opposite and invited to write his or her most important queries, not upon a pad or fileboard, but upon a plain blank business card.

From a small box the seer takes a crystal ball. He gazes into the sphere of so many hidden mysteries, shakes his head, and then advises the sitter to drop his card into the now empty box, writing side down. The box is closed and remains in full view before the subject.

Now, and without opening a desk drawer to get at the spirits, and without doing anything that might seem out of the way or uncalled for, the medium proceeds to answer question after question. As the last one is answered the seer opens the box, reaches in and hands the dumbfounded (?) onlooker his question card. Thereupon the believer leaves, thoroughly (we hope) satisfied that here, at last, is a strange man with a strange power—and for weeks to come he shows the card to skeptics, his story growing with each telling—which same happens to the mental marvel's reputation to his benefit, if not to that of his subsequent and eager patrons.

Preparation: This effect is thoroughly practical and it can be duplicated by anyone with no practice or study. The secret, of course, lies in the box. At any 5 and 10 cent store or stationers you can buy what is known as a file cabinet. It is a little hardwood box used for filing cards, recipes, etc.

Fake the box with a fine hacksaw and you have the "slickest" piece of mental apparatus today. Remove the lid from the box by taking out the small nails or screws that hold the hinge on to the box proper. This is not a hinge in the regular sense of the word, but two pieces of metal at each side of the cover. Now, with the fine saw, cut down the back of the box following the side of the box as closely as possible. When you come to the bottom lay the box on its face and continue cutting right through the bottom of the box, too.

Stop when the saw blade touches the front of the box. Then duplicate this cut on the other side of the box.

Next, with a razor blade, or sharp knife, follow the inside of the front of the box, cutting from one cut side until you hit the other cut side. Soon you will have two separate parts to the box. Paint the insides of the entire box with a dead black paint. Do this also with the cover. When dry, you are ready to complete your "crystal box."

Place the two parts of the box together as they were before you cut them apart. Then, using two pins or fine nails, fix the box so the bottom and the back side will pivot. It works just like the old Turnover Production Box, so well known to magicians. First drive one nail into the lowermost back corner of the side of the box, and holding the cut out back portion of the box in place, drive the nail straight through the side into the edge of the cut-out bottom and back portion of the box. Turn the box over and repeat this on the other side.

Now replace the lid onto the box proper. Use the same small nails that were in the hinges originally. One last operation and the box is ready. In the back of the box near the top, but not in the lid, drive a cut off pin. Let it project just a sixteenth of an inch—just enough so you can catch it with your finger-nail.

Routine: A two and a half inch crystal just neatly fits into the box. Having it there is an excuse for the box on the desk. Having the sitter put his card into the box strikes him as being an afterthought—as it's supposed to. The minute the sitter is through writing ask him to turn it writing side down. Take the crystal from the box and gaze into it for a moment. Shake your head and push the box over to his side of the desk, the back of the box toward you. Have him drop his card inside, writing side down. As he does this, drop lid into place and pull box over to the center of the desk—at the same time catching the pin with your finger-nail. With a little flip towards you the back and bottom of the box do a turn-over. The part that was the bottom is now the back, and the original back lies on the desk in back of the box which hides it from the sitter. On this "shelf" is the sitter's card, but the writing is now face up so as to be read easily when the crystal is held close to the box and "gazed into."

The angles are against the sitter so he sees only the front of the box. If the writing happens to be upside down it is overcome by having the sitter hold out his hand. Walk over to his side of the desk, and because you are standing you can look over the box at the questions in the act of "reading his palm."

With all the information gained the box is slid towards the sitter and the back flipped up into place. Everything is now as it was at the start, and the card is in the box face down. If one's movements are natural and he takes his time for acting the part he is playing, no other piece of apparatus will duplicate the effect as neatly as this device.

THE OM BILLET SWITCHING BOX
Otis Manning

Because I am a firm believer in using simple looking items in magical effects, I have spent considerable time in devising an innocent looking box for switching billets. After making several boxes, this fool-proof and very plain-looking idea was finally built. It has proven its worth in several ways.

I use a Schrafft's candy box, $8\frac{1}{2}$ x $4\frac{1}{2}$ inches and in the top, at center, is cut a small slot to take the folded billets. Immediately below this slot is a small secret box, pasted or taped to the top, size 3 x $3\frac{1}{2}$ inches. When billets are dropped into this slotted box they go into the secret box and not into the candy box proper.

After the billets are collected, and the box is shaken up a bit, the lid is lifted and a spectator allowed to select any one inside. Thusly a billet is forced for the simple reason that all inside the box proper are alike.

The drawing shows the secret box when pasted to the lid at points marked X. Billets drop into the box through slot A. On each side of the small box, in box proper, have the faked billets—each containing the informa-

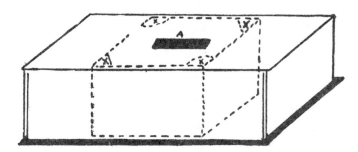

tion which you wish forced. I have a ribbon tied around the box in orthodox fashion, missing the slot, of course, and it can be passed into the audience from person to person, for the insertion of slips. After a good shaking by the last person who brings it to you, the lid is removed, care being taken that the inside of the lid is not shown to reveal the faked box, and a selection is made from those seen in the box proper. The lid then is replaced and the box is tossed aside.

Note by Annemann: Many years ago we tried to work out methods of forcing which would eliminate the change bag and change basket so prevalent at that time but so out of keeping in the surroundings of drawing rooms and intimate clubs. We didn't succeed to the extent of publishing our results, and now Mr. Manning has provided a self-proven, practical device really worth consideration. He concluded his instructions for construction and use by saying: "The rest is up to the performer and the effect he might wish to do."

The point now is that such a fine principle, with its natural dress, should not suffer by a drawn-out passing about only to be used for a single selection, unless, of course, that picking be for a tremendously effective stunt.

In the case of numbers there is little choice. In fact, there is no use for them except when the box is a part of an effect being performed before only from ten to twenty people. No number effect within our ken deserves or warrants the time necessary to have written and collected the individually written billets.

Mr. Manning mentioned, in his copy, that he was using the box for a name selection, but he didn't go any further. It might not be difficult to figure that he could reveal the selected cognomen in some startling way, available to all of us, but still we wonder as to the practicability of spending time for the ultimate choice unless the denouement be worthwhile.

Our last thought upon the matter has to do with questions and their answers. In other words, maybe the box is useful as a force for more than one thing. This may open the minds of some readers to new possibilities. For instance, here's an effect I worked out to utilize the box. Let's call it

THE GHOST OF A CHANCE

The five and dime (Woolworth) emporiums sell small packets of pads in assorted colors. Suppose you were to pass a red pad into one part of your audience, a white pad into another section, a green pad elsewhere, and a yellow pad through what is left. The spectators write a query upon the top sheet, tear it off and fold, passing the pad and pencil on to another sitter. It really doesn't matter if they cross—it's the effect of the beginning that counts.

During this time the performer does a couple of quick mysteries not requiring audience participation. Then the box is started around for the collection of the folded billets. And during this time a couple of more mysteries are presented. In short, the audience members write on various colored papers, fold, and insert them in the passed around box. It all builds up to a watched for climax, but it does not stop the performer's presentation of numbers on his program. Otherwise there would be a long "stall" during the writing time and the collection period. At the beginning of the maneuver the master mind may say that he wishes questions for a later test. And when the box finally is returned to the front or platform he lets someone shake it well.

He recalls the use of the various colored papers, and says that because of time limits he can answer but few queries. Thus, on account of color, he can have picked, by chance, some one spectator from each part of the audience.

The performer unties the box and discards the lid. The person who brought the filled box forward takes it and hands the performer one paper of any color. He holds it upon his open palm and answers the question. The assistant takes it and reads the question aloud.

He then is asked to pick one of another color, and the same result occurs. This happens with the other two colors. With four questions answered the program item is concluded.

It all is accomplished by having the box proper filled with four "forced" questions, each one duplicated upon its own color of paper. The utter duplicity of the affair is psychologically hidden by the fairness of the pad passing and box passing while the performer concerns himself with other deceptives. It is not necessary, as in other question answering cases, to identify the writers. The performer gives his stock answers (according to the colors as picked out) and the assistant then reads the papers. I hope it isn't too late to mention that the spectators are asked to write questions of import but not to write names or initials.

This leaves the performer safe when the assistant reads the paper which the performer has answered, for, until that time, the audience does not know if he is actually giving a reply to the billet selected from amongst the others. Without identifying initials, the writing may be from anyone in that colored-paper sector.

The reader must recognize this. The effect is just an effect among others in the program. It is done simply as a program item. No time is lost in distribution, write-up, or collection. The spectators do it all themselves. The performer "answers" one of each color to make it a fair selection—and the audience knows that. And he may even have the box proper passed to various front row observers for each choice, merely telling them to take any one of a color not yet chosen.

The questions? And answers? Better people than I have written books upon the subject of answering freely given queries, but here you have a set-up. You not alone know the question for each color, but have an answer ready to recite by rote.

CRYSTAL CLEAR
OTIS MANNING

We are indebted to "The Phoenix Magazine" for this ingenious method of delivering information to the mindreader right under the nose of the audience. This is Mr. Manning's own method which he used for years in conjunction with his OM Billet Switching Box, described above. It is probably one of the cleverest ruses you'll ever run across.

Let's assume that your assistant has collected a batch of questions in the OM Box, has returned to the stage and dumped the dummy billets into a bowl in view of the entire audience. She then walks off stage with the box, the lid of which still retains the original questions.

The mindreader now attempts to set fire to the billets in the bowl, runs into a little difficulty, and calls off stage for the assistant to bring him some alcohol. This is immediately forthcoming, and the mindreader sprinkles some of the spirits into the bowl and soon has a merry fire burning. He then proceeds to give his readings to the satisfaction of all concerned.

The means employed to obtain the questions he answers is simplicity itself! It all rests in the bottle, as follows: While the assistant is off stage, she copies off a number of the questions retained in the OM Box, in abbreviated form, on the back of the label. The front of the label has lettered on it in bold letters, ALCOHOL. When she has written down the questions, she pastes the label on a bottle of alcohol and brings it to the mindreader when he calls for it. As he pours the alcohol on the dummy billets in the bowl, he reads the information off of the back of the label through the bottle. The bottle and the alcohol acts as a magnifying glass, thus making it easy to read the information.

Like most of the real, dyed-in-the-wool, actual mindreading secrets this may not strike you forcibly at first reading—but take our word for it, it's perfect for actual performing conditions.

Publicity Effects

MINDREADING PUBLICITY EFFECT
ANNEMANN

Good publicity stunts for newspapermen and offices are not easy to find. This not only fills that need but is also useful for impromptu tests anywhere at any time.

Effect: Tearing a piece from any newspaper that happens to be handy, the performer has his witness look it over and encircle any word thereon with a pencil. The paper is folded and the witness is asked to concentrate upon the word he selected. The performer tears up the piece of paper into little bits, drops them into an ash tray and sets fire to them. As soon as the paper is burned, he reveals the chosen word correctly! There are no duplicate papers nor dummies, and no switching is necessary. I released this subtle secret several years ago in a different form. In using the newspaper, however, it can be done at a moment's notice thus making it that much more effective.

Routine: There is no preparation necessary, although the test will work best if you are sitting at a table. Pick up any newspaper and tear out a piece about two by three inches. Tear it out of solid reading matter rather than an advertisement. Hand it to the subject and ask him to ring one word with a pencil, and then fold the paper once each way with the circled word on the inside.

Take it with your left finger tips, holding the long folded side to the left with the closed corner of the doubly folded paper at upper left. Tear it lengthwise slightly to right of center. (Note illustration.) Place the right hand pieces in front of (audience side) those in the left hand, tip them to left and tear the pieces again slightly to right of center. Place the right hand pieces in front of the left hand pieces again, and the left thumb draws the rear folded section back while the paper is again torn in half. These right hand pieces are put in front of those in the left hand, and the right hand reaches into coat pocket for a box of matches which you hand to the subject.

Your right hand now takes the torn pieces from the left finger tips, with the exception of the torn center which is being held under the ball of the left thumb, and crumples them up and drops them in a nearby ashtray. At the same time, your left hand, with the folded center piece hidden between thumb and finger, drops to your side or in this case into your lap. The subject lights the papers in the ashtray and, as he watches them burn, you open the stolen center piece in your lap, glance down and read the circled word. Then as the papers burn to ashes, reveal the word in your best dramatic fashion.

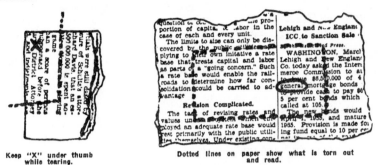

Keep "X" under thumb while tearing.

Dotted lines on paper show what is torn out and read.

The two illustrations will make the maneuvers clear, and five minutes practice will be sufficient for the mechanics. The secret is subtle and one of the cleverest methods of getting information I have ever known. After using it for a short time, you will get used to the handling and it all becomes second nature. The fact that the piece is torn from any paper on a moment's notice is a strong point and it is obvious to all that no duplicates could be employed.

NEWS EVENT PREDICTION
ANNEMANN

For publicity purposes, the following test will be found hard to beat. I have used it myself, just as explained below, with gratifying results.

Effect: During a recent election in a city where an independent candidate was running against two regular party nominees, I stopped into the local newspaper office and offered to predict the winner. The editor took me up on it immediately, so I wrote a prediction on a slip of paper, folded it once and sealed it in an envelope. Then I asked the editor to sign his name across the face. The envelope was then put in the newspaper safe. Later when the results of the election were certain, I returned to the newspaper office, asked for the envelope, opened it without switching or any other underhand business and my prophecy was found to be correct!

Preparation: All that is required for this space-grabbing effect is my "Original Faked Envelope," described on page 137. Two compartments of this envelope already contained the names of two of the candidates, and the third and regular compartment was empty when I arrived at the office. I also carried a plain, unprepared envelope to match the fake envelope.

Routine: After I wrote my prediction which, of course, was the name of the third candidate, I folded the slip and sealed it in the unprepared envelope. Then I asked the editor to sign his name across the face. As I blotted it, I stopped, picked up the envelope and crumpled it up and said that I was sorry but that I had just had a flash that there would be an upset. I dropped the crumpled envelope into my side coat pocket and took out another slip and wrote the same prediction over again. I folded this slip, reached into my inside coat pocket for the faked envelope and sealed my prediction in it. I then had the editor write his signature across the face of this envelope, and had him put it away in his safe with the promise that he wouldn't open it till the election was certain.

As soon as I had the results, I cut open the original crumpled envelope at the same end where I would later cut open the faked one and threw the slip away. Then I crumpled the envelope again and put it back in my pocket and hied over to the newspaper where everything was bedlam in the editorial offices; with election returns coming in and being totaled. When I could make myself heard I got the editor to fetch the signed envelope from his safe. He verified his signature and I cut open the envelope at the proper end and dumped my prediction into his palm. I crumpled up the envelope and dropped it into my pocket, switching it for the first crumpled envelope. While the prediction was being read, I brought out the original signed envelope and, as I was leaving, I dropped it on the editor's desk.

THE UNKNOWN SUBJECT
ANNEMANN

I thought for quite a while before deciding to release this secret because I've used it a lot for press work and the effect is absolutely original.

Preparation: Pick out a friend's name from the telephone book. Count down and remember its position from the top of the column. Make 26 one-inch card squares containing letters of the alphabet. Make 25 more all containing the first letter of the friend's last name. Put the 26 duplicate letter cards in your right coat pocket. Put the 25 different letter cards in the small watch or coin pocket at the top of this same pocket. Select two cards, one red and one black, whose values will add up to the required number to count down to in the book to locate the friend's name. Tip off this friend to the names of the two cards. (I manage to get to his phone and paste the names on the bottom so he won't lose them.) Take the book and dog-ear or otherwise mark the correct page so you can get to it quickly. So far this may not appear as much, but please visualize the following effect on those witnessing this test.

Effect and Routine: Explain that you will demonstrate a test of mind-reading with the telephone book. A name must be selected at random so you have a set of letters. Reach into your pocket and take out the set from the small coin pocket. Show that they are all different and mixed and put them back. Your hand goes on down after leaving them in the coin pocket and stirs up the duplicates. Have some person reach in and take one out. Right after this you take out the top set and throw them on the table. This set, being minus the one forced, makes everything check.

Now explain that an "R" (for example) has been picked, the name shall be among the "R" section. Pick up the telephone book and run through it, stopping at the marked page, saying, "Here is a page of Rs. We will use it." Turn the book down, still open, and pick up the deck of cards. "Now we need a number of two figures," you continue. If, for instance, the forced name is 36th down from the top, you force a three and a six. Use your own choice of methods here, but for your sake as well as mine don't let it be complicated. Use an alternating two-kind deck if you wish, and have two removed from anywhere in a spread. Call the cards 36, and turning the book over, point to the proper column and tell him to count down and mark the name. You walk away. If you'll only go right through this as written without dragging, it is the best method of which I know. Now you dramatically suggest that you would like to make a test of telepathy. Ask the person to go to the phone and call up the selected name in the book. This party called is to be told something about a University or committee that is checking laws of averages and sequences, and would he be kind enough to name two playing cards at random for the record. The person at the other end can hem and haw a little to build it, but does as requested, *and names the two selected cards!*

Imagine the effect created by this double test! I could rave for an hour but the information is all here, and if you'll think for a minute you'll feel like raving too!

PUBLICITY STUNT
ANNEMANN

Here's a publicity stunt from my preferred list that's a stunner. Have a few reporters in to your hotel for an interview and state that you will present a test of thought transference with your partner in a distant city by long distance phone. First they are to select a number up to 10,000, then a mixed up series of five letters. The keys on anyone's key ring are counted and noted down. Someone else names a color. In fact, the tests are unlimited. You now give one of the reporters present the medium's name and telephone number, and the reporter selected puts through the out-of-town call. When the medium answers, the reporter explains that he is conducting an experiment with you and that a series of tests have been agreed upon. The medium replies that he seems to sense the nature of the various tests, and describes each one of them to the satisfaction of everyone!

The best part of this stunt is not that it is simple, but because it doesn't cost a long distance call. A box of candy, a couple of theatre tickets, or a couple of dollars will fix it up with any hotel switchboard operator as a joke. The operator, upon getting the call, merely takes it and says as usual, "I'll call you back." The call is stalled for three or four minutes and then put through to an adjoining room or a downstairs' phone booth. Your partner has listened in on the selection of tests from an adjoining room, or outside the door, and reveals them as coming from a distant city. This is a perfectly practical feat and I wouldn't write it so positively if I had not used it myself.

ON THE WIRE
ANNEMANN

For many years I have used the following effect as a publicity stunt for newspaper editors, and at other times as an impromptu stunt after a performance in private homes. The working is far from difficult, but the effect on the spectators is very striking. There is something about mental stunts on a telephone that create unusual interest. The business of naming cards over a phone has been tossed around so much that it isn't of much value anymore, so my thoughts along these lines have been to make them one man tests, but still use the telephone.

Effect: The performer is near a phone and says he will try a rather interesting feat. Selecting the host, or someone else to assist in the experiment, the performer asks him to think of some friend who can be reached by phone at this time. When the assistant signifies that he has decided upon a number to call, he is given a slip of paper upon which to write the friend's name, and the slip is folded several times and put under the phone. The performer asks for the telephone number and proceeds to call it. Upon the call being answered, the performer *asks to speak to the person thought of, although seemingly he has had no way of knowing the person's name!* When the person asked for comes to the phone, the performer explains that he is at the home or office of Mr. . . . . . ., is conducting a test of mental powers, and that Mr. . . . . . . was thinking of him (the man at the other end of the wire) so you have called him up. He hopes he hasn't bothered the person called and thank him for his cooperation. The performer then hangs up the receiver and takes the paper from under the phone and returns it to the writer. Eight times out of ten, the person called will call back to find out what it is all about, and naturally learns about you being an unusual person, which is an ad in itself.

Routine and Presentation: My method for this is a mere switch. In left coat pocket have a pad of paper about 2¼ inches by 3½ inches. These small pads may be obtained in the Woolworth stores. Tear off two sheets and fold them once the long way and then twice the short way. Open out one of these and lay it on top of the pad, then place the pad and the loose sheet in your right side coat pocket. Put the folded dummy billet in the left pocket, ready to be palmed out.

Generally, try to select a person as the subject, who is sitting a little way from the phone. Take out the pad with the separate top slip and give it to your assistant together with a pencil. Ask him to write the name he has decided upon, and then fold the slip. While he is doing this, you replace the pad in your *left* coat pocket, and, as your hand comes out, finger palm the dummy slip with the second finger. Take back the pencil with your right hand and the folded slip with your left. As you move to the telephone, pull back the written slip with your thumb and push forward the dummy slip to be dropped under the phone. Your left hand goes directly to the pocket as you ask the person for the telephone number. Always ask the person first if he knows the number, and then ask for it. This gives you a few seconds longer to stall, while your left hand opens the slip against the pad.

Take out the pad, pull off the top sheet from under the open slip, and in doing this you get a glimpse of the name. The pad and open slip are replaced in the pocket, and on the blank sheet you write the telephone number. Now sit down with the number before you and make the call. There is a lot of time now to drop your hand to your pocket and refold the slip and finger palm it again. Then at the finish, your right hand moves the phone, as your left picks up the slip and makes the switch again as it is returned to the person who wrote it.

You will find a finger switch here the most practical, and you can master it with but a few hours' practice.

Although this may sound simple, it has a stunning effect upon those watching because it is different and unusual.

WIRED THOUGHT
ANNEMANN

Do you happen to have a set of the old card from the pocket indexes among your souvenirs? If you have, then you have the makings of a stunning press and drawing room stunt.

Fill the indexes, not with the usual cards, but with folded slips of paper on which are written the names of the 53 cards in the deck, like this: "The stranger selected will think of the ...." Fifty-three of these papers are indexed, and the containers are put in your pockets, one in each pants pocket. Now, when you are at someone's home or in a news office, write a prophecy, fold it and apparently drop it into a hat or a bowl, but finger-palm it out. Ask the editor to think of some friend and to call him on the phone. this person, who is unknown to you, is asked to think for a few moments and then name any card that comes to his mind. You immediately request the editor, or the person making the call, to ask the stranger if he had any particular reason for picking that card or if it was just a blind selection. This stall allows you a full twenty or thirty seconds during which time you have pocketed the first slip and have secured and finger-palmed the correct paper from the index in your pocket. Now pick up the hat with that hand, fingers inside, and drop the finger-palmed slip to the bottom of the hat. Request the editor to take the slip out of the hat, open it and read your prediction to the person at the other end of the wire. Imagine that person's feelings!

Having people phone their own friends, all strangers to you, is what makes this perfect.

THE IMPRESSION MODERNE
ANNEMANN

Sealed letter tests have come and gone, but in this case we have one which differs enough in effect to make it appear new in the eyes of the sitter.

Effect: Only one envelope and sheet of note paper is in use at any time, and the effect is presented as a combination of psychometry and automatic writing. The sitter (who doesn't sit in this test) is handed a sheet of note paper and a letter envelope. He writes a question about something concerning himself personally, folds the paper several times, and seals it securely in the envelope. Taking the envelope and pencil in his otherwise empty hands, the medium feels it, stares into space, grunts, foams at the mouth, and otherwise becomes very psychic. He asks the sitter to take it back, hold it to his forehead and mentally think the question over. The medium grabs the envelope almost immediately, and scribbles across it an impression that turns out to be an answer to the question which still remains sealed and untampered with in the envelope.

Preparation and Routine: Nothing is needed except the envelope, paper and pencil. Use the cheap type of envelope obtained at Woolworth's stores. Coat the entire face of the envelope with parafin wax that is cold and hard, by laying the envelope on a hard surface and rubbing the cake over it. Now burnish the surface with the Mount of Venus (the heel of the thumb) on your right or left hand, being careful that said Mount is clean as the parafin picks up all dirt. This gives you a smooth, shiny surface very susceptible to all impressions. Have a sheet of paper that can be folded several times. Contrive to keep the sitter in a standing position for the test. Hand him the paper after you have asked him to think of a question. Now give him a pencil and, at the same time, back up the paper he is holding with the face side of the envelope. He now writes his question and seals it in the envelope.

Now you take the sealed envelope. Pretending to feel it, and turning it over and over in your hands, you read the impression in dulled writing on the face of the envelope! In short, an impression has been made on wax rather than by wax on paper. And most important, in handling, the dulled lines are obliterated by merely rubbing the envelope between the hands!

From here to the climax it is only "the business" as far as working goes. Reading the impression is a matter of tipping the envelope surface slightly so that the light strikes it right. I pretend to start writing on this side which gives you all the opportunity needed for reading. Before writing, however, ask if such-and-such means anything to them, describing something at random. Hand the envelope to them for the forehead action, and taking it back you scribble the answer on the back because writing won't "take" on the waxed surface and this maneuver makes turning the envelope over after reading go unnoticed. This is a nice effect for publicity purposes as one can always go about with a couple of prepared envelopes and paper.

A CUTE PUBLICITY STUNT

The following clipping appeared in the Public Notice Column of the New York Times, and illustrates a cute effect which has been written about a few times but seldom used in actual practice.

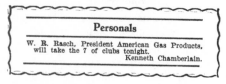

Personals

W. R. Rasch, President American Gas Products, will take the 7 of clubs tonight.
                              Kenneth Chamberlain.

Perhaps the fact that someone else is actually doing it will start magicians off on the same track. It's possible of many, many variations, and as a publicity effect is very strong.

DEATH FLIGHT

Tom Sellers

Excellent for press and publicity work is this very effective and out of the ordinary trick. The preparation is very simple and quickly done with a minimum of material.

Effect: The performer hands a spectator seven blank cards, one of which he is asked to take and write upon it the name of a dead person. He is then told to shuffle the seven cards and they are placed in an envelope, sealed, and the envelope initialed, whereupon the spectator may pocket it. Then seven more blank cards are shown and examined. These are sealed and this envelope likewise is initialed and held. The "Death Flight" takes place when the performer causes the dead name card to travel from one envelope to the other. Upon opening the first only six cards are found, all blank. In the second envelope are found eight cards and the dead name card among them!

Requirements: A packet of blank cards; a packet of small envelopes which will hold the cards neatly; a pencil.

Preparation: Place six blank cards in one of the envelopes, seal it and place it second from the top of the packet of envelopes, they all being flap side down. In the top envelope place a single blank card.

Routine: Count out seven cards and give them to a spectator. He selects any one of them and writes upon it a dead person's name. Then have him mix them with the writing side of the "dead name" card down. You have taken the top envelope from the stack. Take the cards, insert them in the envelope (the single bank card is already in it) and hand the envelope to the spectator for sealing. As he does this, pick up the packet of envelopes and the pencil. Take back the sealed envelope and place it on top of the packet with the flap side down. Ask for his initials, turn the two top envelopes over, as one, and write the initials on the back. Slide this envelope from the packet and hand it to him to put in his pocket. The spectator thinks he has his own envelope, but really he has the one with the six blank cards. (His envelope is now on top of the stack in your hand).

Hand the second spectator seven blank cards which he counts and examines. As he does so, you turn over the stack of envelopes in your hand, and pick off the top one and give it to him, asking him to seal up his cards. Take it back from him and place it face down on top of your stack of envelopes and finish sealing it by pressing down on the flap as you talk. Turn it over, singly and openly, and then, in getting a pencil again for marking, turn the whole stack over again. The envelope now on top is the first person's containing the "dead name" card and seven others. It is also face down, so you proceed to initial it with the second person's initials and hand it to him. (Editor's note: If you don't think you can work this stack turnover imperceptibly, you can follow the same routine as was used with the first envelope. However, the subsequent routine for the second envelope gives you a little variety.)

As far as you are concerned, the trick is over except for the build up and the revelation of the transposition of the "dead name" card. When the first envelope is opened only six blank cards are found. The second envelope is is opened and found to contain eight cards and the "dead name" one is among them.

IMPROMPTU VISION
J. G. THOMPSON, JR.

Effect and Routine: Borrow a business card and ask the owner to write a question, line of verse, or name of a dead person on its back. Take the card from him, written side down, by grasping it at one end with your left thumb on top and the first finger underneath the card. Your right hand now pulls out your pocket handkerchief, holding it by one corner, and covers the card by drawing the corner back along the forearm until the card is covered by the center of the handkerchief. Now, with the right thumb and forefinger (finger on top) grasp the inner end of the card through the

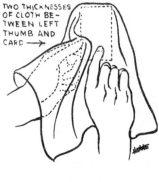

TWO THICKNESSES OF CLOTH BE-TWEEN LEFT THUMB AND CARD →

handkerchief close to where it is being held by the left finger. The left fingers let go but immediately regrasp the card and handkerchief near the top end, this time through a fold of the handkerchief. (The thumb at this point should have two thicknesses of the handkerchief between it and the top of the card.) The right hand now goes forward and picks up the front corner of the handkerchief that is hanging down. This corner is brought directly back along the arm to show that the card is still there with the written side down. Now drop the left hand with a sort of throwing motion, letting the two edges or corners of the handkerchief resting on the arm fall forward and down. The card is now apparently held securely in the center of the handkerchief. (This is the old coin move.)

The right thumb and forefinger (finger on top) grasp the inner end of the card and hold the card and handkerchief bundle vertically, while the left hand reaches down and twists the hanging ends of the handkerchief. At this time, the card will be on the back of the folded handkerchief with the message looking right at you! (Hold the bundle in front of you at about chin level.) This bundle is then tucked into the breast pocket, leaving the corners of the handkerchief sticking out.

Take hold of the writer's hand and answer the question any way you see fit, or reveal the contents of the card. At the finish, reach up with the right hand, grasp a corner of the handkerchief and pull it quickly from your pocket, when the card will drop to the floor.

I have found this a perfect press stunt and it can be done with a drawing or sketch which you can reproduce. Being impromptu, you have quite an effect. By using your own business cards you can leave them with the spectators, thus garnering some nice publicity.

A NEAT PUBLICITY TRICK
NAT SCHERZER

Any trick can be redressed and changed at will to create an entirely new effect. Envelopes are used in this case instead of cards. It sounds simple and is, but where cards might be used and passed off as an old story the use of envelopes makes this effect a novel mystery.

Use letter envelopes that have gone through the mail but have been opened carefully at one end without mutilating them. About seven or eight are enough and all of them are addressed to different people in different cities. It shouldn't be hard to collect quite a lot of these from friends throughout the country.

Carry them around and you are always ready. Pull them out and toss them around to be looked at. Now write something down on a piece of paper, fold it and let someone hold it. Stack the envelopes, fan, and have one selected. They read the address on the front and you have prophecied it correctly! Simple? Certainly, but the effect is neat. Just force the envelop any way you please. The straight fan force is always good and most natural with envelopes, as you will find when you try this stunt. It's really good!

TELEVISION COMPACT
Dr. Jaks

Reading messages in sealed containers make very impressive feats of clairvoyance, and this impromptu method from continental Europe will be found very practical as an interlude in your performance, or as an excellent publicity stunt.

Effect: This is direct, easily followed and beautifully deceptive. Remove your card case from your pocket, take out one of your business cards and tear it in half. Now ask one of the ladies to loan you her compact. Whoever offers one is given half of your card on which to write a single word or name, and is then instructed to insert the card into the case and snap it shut. This case is now handed to you behind your back as you face your audience. Almost immediately you say that the second letter is exceptionally clear and is round like the letter "o" or "e." Then, with proper showmanship, the complete word is revealed, and the compact is returned and the word verified.

Routine: There is no preparation necessary. The compact is just a borrowed one, and your cards are unprepared. However, engraved cards work best because then you can tell by feel which is the front and back of the card.

Commence by removing one of your cards and tear it in half so that it will fit easily into the compact. When you hand it to the young lady ask her to write a word on the back or blank side of the card. She does so and then encloses it in her compact which she hands to you behind your back. State at once that the second letter in the name is round and you'll be correct in the majority of cases, because usually this second letter is a vowel. At the same time, silently open the compact, remove the card and palm it in your right hand with the engraved side of the card against your palm. (If you do not use engraved cards, better nail nick the card so that you can distinguish  on which side the writing is.) Hold the compact at the finger tips of the the compact at the finger tips of the right hand and bring this hand around to the front with its back towards the audience. Transfer the compact to the left hand, which has also been brought around to the front, and read the name on the palmed card which will be facing you. Put your right hand behind your back again as you turn the case over openly in your left hand. Seemingly sense another letter or two and call them out. Suddenly you get the full impression so you rearrange the letters and spell out the word. Just as you give the last two letters in a slow and hesitating manner, your left hand goes behind your back and the case is opened and the card reinserted. As you finish spelling the word, you close the case and then repeat the word, asking for verification as you return the compact. Be sure to replace the card in the compact as it was originally, that is with the same side up as put in by the young lady.

G R A P H O L O G Y
L. Vosburgh Lyons

Handwriting is something which may or may not identify one person from another. It's a moot question and therefore leaves the path open for an astute performer to make the most of things.

Effect: The performer explains that he is a student of graphology and will give a test of his ability to read people's characteristics from their handwriting. He passes out ten to twenty business cards and asks those receiving them to write a certain sentence on the blank sides of the cards, while he is out of the room. These cards are collected by an obliging spectator in a hat and shaken up. When the performer returns to the room, he picks a card at random from the hat, studies it for a moment . . . looks over the faces of the guests, and then hands it to the person who had written it. He proceeds to do the same thing with the rest of the cards, to the amazement of those present, not making a single mistake.

Preparation: The performer uses from 10 to 20 personal cards and naturally, one side bears the performer's name and address, which subtle angle prevents the spectator from using that side for writing.

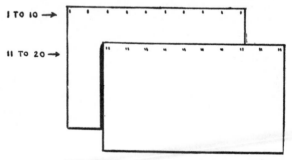

CODE MARKED ON EDGES OF BLANK SIDE OF CARDS

This allows of the cards being "marked" with the edge reader principle, otherwise, should the cards be writeable on both sides, this cute and practically indetectable idea would not be available.

Take a packet of twenty such cards in hand, all facing one way as far as the blank sides are concerned. Divide the long edge into two parts and, with a dot on the edge of each card, mark them from 1 to 5 and then 5 to 10. Ten cards remain. Instead of one dot this time, make two close dots for each number and these markings identify cards from 11 to 20.

Turn the whole packet around, end for end, and the newly presented long edge is marked again from 1 through 20. Now, as long as the printed sides of the cards are faced in one direction, the performer can take the packet, glance at the edges, and pick out any one of the cards from 1 through 20.

This is, insofar as I have been able to test under practical conditions, the best possible method for finding the right cards under the strictest conditions and surveillance.

Routine: At the start the cards are in order from 1 to 20. They are handed out, after a preliminary talk on the way a person's hand-writing reveals his characteristics to one who can read the hidden signs. Although the performer is set for 20 cards, he may hand out only 8 or 12 as the case may be and pocket the rest. This is done from the left to right or in such order that the performer can remember those who have been given cards.

The performer now picks up a book at random and reads a short sentence of five or six words. A book of prose or blank verse will be found the best to use.

It matters not what this sentence or line may be, for all those who have cards write the same thing. The performer retires while the writing and collecting is taking place.

Upon his return the performer takes the hat containing the cards, dips his hand amongst them and take out one. He studies it for a moment and looks the spectators over carefully. Then he approaches one and hands him the card he is holding. It is acknowledged as correct!

Faster and faster the action is continued. The performer obviously "gets hot" as he "swings" into the judging and one by one the cards are handed back to their rightful owners.

(Editor's Note: A similar effect, but using paper billets, is "Alias Divination" by Oscar Weigle, Jr. in that excellent book of mental tricks, "You'd Be Surprised" Ted Annemann considered this to be one of the finest and most unusual effects of modern mentalism.)

Dead or Alive

FROM BEYOND THE GRAVE
ANNEMANN

Here is an effect which is original with me and one that has been reposing in my notebook for several years.

All you need is a packet of at least 35 blank cards which you hand to a spectator and ask him to select any one of them and then return the rest to you. Request the person to think for a moment of a relative or friend who is not living. This name (first and last), he is to write on one side of the card, and hold it writing side down. The card is returned to the packet of blanks and another spectator shuffles them well. The performer now takes them and as he drops them off the top, one at a time, the spectator who wrote is asked to spell the dead person's name letter by letter. As the last letter is reached, the performer holds the card at which he has arrived. The spectator repeats the name and the card is turned over. It is the card with the name of the dead person and everything is left with the audience.

If you do not consider that a different and effective bit of business, I've been sadly fooled by the number of people before whom I've done it. When torn apart it is nothing but a card spelling trick in a weird dress. Some may prefer doing it with blank playing cards because of the ease in manipulation, but I don't agree with this because cards of this type immediately give the impression of a card trick. My safe and sure method has two variations depending upon the performer's desire for cleanness. After the selection of a card I take back the rest and hand the spectator a pencil. Turning my back while he wrote, I'd cross my arms and exchange the packet for one trimmed a little narrower. Don't make them shorter as they are shuffled at the ends. Have the name card returned and mixed by the spectators themselves. Now take them for a further bit of mixing (being careful to have the packet kept right side up throughout). Then cut them several times, bringing the wide card to the top. Cut one more card on top of this making the name card second from the top. Do this carelessly while describing the affinity existing between the card written upon and the deceased person, and how differently it now vibrates from the rest. As you ask the writer to spell aloud, letter for letter, as you deal, gesture with the left hand holding the packet and turn it completely over. No difference can be seen. Now deliberately deal a card each time the spectator gives a letter. I have never had any trouble knowing when the end of the name is coming up. As you deal off the card for the letter third from last and still with two to go, turn the packet over with your left hand as your right hand lays the card down on the table. That is why it is best to put each card down with a deliberate, sweeping motion. Now the dead name card will show up on the last letter, and can be dealt off as described in the opening paragraph, or you may allow the spectator to lift it off the packet himself.

If you don't care to switch packets you can previously trim one a little shorter and force this card on the spectator for the writing of the dead name. I have used this when doing the trick impromptu with a packet of business cards, but still I prefer the switch because of the freedom allowed the spectator at all times. However you do it though, you'll find here is one effect away from the usual run that is certain to excite comment.

TWO PAPERS AND A SPECTATOR
ANNEMANN

Here's a mental stunt that may be done practically impromptu yet has the appearance of genuine mindreading. I would suggest, however, that you follow the routine with the material in hand and you will grasp the principle without difficulty.

Effect: The performer has a spectator write a dead name on one slip of paper, and a date, connected with the name, on another slip. The performer now picks up a blank slip and writes something on it, which later proves to be the same date as written by the spectator. The dead name slip is now held against the performer's forehead and he reveals the dead name, letter for letter.

Preparation: All that is needed is a thumb tip and seven or eight pieces of paper, 2 inches by 3 inches. Fold these once the long way and then twice the opposite way. Open them out, except one, and put them in your left trouser pocket. This folded slip is placed inside the thumb tip which is placed in your right trouser or vest pocket so that it can be secured easily. You are now ready.

Routine: In starting, the packet of papers is removed from the pocket and two are taken, the packet being replaced. One is handed to a spectator with the request that he write the name of some dead friend or relative and then fold it as it was before. The other piece of paper is left on the table and the performer turns back and walks away while the first slip is being written.

At this time he secures the thumb tip, containing the dummy, on the right thumb and when he returns, picks up the paper he left on the table with the right hand. With the left hand he takes the dead name slip from the spectator and, at the same time, hands him the slip in the right hand. The right hand should be held back up with the thumb underneath. On this second slip the spectator writes down some particular year, for instance, some year in which he and the dead party were closely connected, or perhaps his birth year or year of death.

As he gives these instructions, the performer has the dead slip on his left palm and the thumb tip containing the dummy on his right thumb. He lays the right thumb onto the slip on left palm, the left fingers close around it and the right thumb comes out with the paper which is tossed onto the table. Actually, however, the dummy is drawn from the tip instead while the dead slip remains in the left palm under the tip. The left hand drops to the side, and the performer turns and walks away again while the date slip is being written. This switch is smooth and clean. It shouldn't be watched or accentuated, but is done as a matter of course while explaining the procedure with the second slip.

Now, while the second slip is being written, the performer has his back turned and quickly reads the dead slip. He refolds it and holds it in the same position in his left hand under the tip as he returns to the spectator.

Picking up the dummy from the table (apparently the dead name) he asks the spectator into which of his pockets he would like to keep it and, at the same time, apparently puts it into his left hand which opens and holds it on palm. Actually it is put back into the thumb tip and the spectator picks up the real dead slip and pockets it. The performer now has the tip on his right thumb again with the dummy inside.

The left hand picks up the date slip which the spectator had placed on the table, and once more the switch is made as at first. The right hand gives the dummy slip to the spectator, asking him to place it somewhere in view and to cover it with a paper weight or a book.

The date slip in the left hand under the tip is pocketed as the performer asks the spectator to explain whether the date written was a birth, death or important event. During this slight stall, the slip is opened against the packet of papers in your left pocket and the packet brought forth. A glance at the top opened paper gives the performer the date as he takes a blank paper from the bottom of the stack. The packet is returned to the pocket and on the blank slip the performer writes the date that he has just read. This is given to a party seated a little distance away and, as the performer returns, his left hand drops to his pocket and the date paper is folded, pushed into the tip and the left hand comes out with the thumb wearing the tip.

Walking to the table or wherever the date slip has been covered, the right hand picks it up, holds it on the right palm. The left thumb covers it for a second, the right fingers close, and the left thumb draws out carrying the slip from inside the tip and this is handed directly to another party while the tip in the right hand is pocketed for good.

The person to whom the slip was handed is asked to read aloud the date. When he does, the party holding the performer's written slip is asked to read what was written and it is the same.

Now the performer states that with the name slip he will try a quicker way and he asks the spectator to take the dead slip from his pocket and hold it against the performer's forehead. Very slowly the performer spells out the dead name letter by letter.

When you try this you will find that the few stalls come at the right time to cover the moves. The principle of switching by thumb tip is Al Baker's and does away with all necessity for sleight of hand. However, if one wants to practice enough, it is possible to improve the working a good deal through the use of a straight method of pellet switching which requires no apparatus.

MORE LIVING THAN DEAD
ANNEMANN

Effect: You pass out four paper slips on which your subject writes three living names and one of a person who has passed on. He folds the slips once each way with the names inside. You take the slips one at a time, tear them up and drop them into an ashtray. As you do so each time, you burn the pieces by holding a lighted match to each separate pile. Suddenly, as the third one is burning, you say, "This is the dead name slip which is burning now!" Then reveal the dead person's name. The fourth "live" slip is left on the table.

Routine: There is fine misdirection in this routine. Use four pieces of blank paper, size 2 inches by 3 inches. Have a person write living names on three of them, and a dead name on the fourth. Previously you have secretly marked the slip upon which the dead name is to be written. A nail nick is best. Hand your subject three of the papers, one after the other, requesting him to write names of living people on each. On the fourth slip, the one that is nail nicked, you ask him to write the name of some dead person. Have them folded, with names inside, and dropped on the table where they are mixed up a bit. You pick them up one at a time, tear them once each way and drop them in an ashtray where you proceed to burn them. Each time you shake your head and declare it to be a living paper. Select the nicked slip for your third, tear in half both ways, drop into the ashtray, but steal the center section as explained in the "Mindreading Publicity Effect" on page 30. Drop your hand into your lap and read the "dead name" as the pieces burn, then reveal it. The third live slip is left on the table. Give this a trial and you'll find it very effective and an excellent impromptu table trick.

DEAD OR ALIVE
ANNEMANN

This is a clean and simple method for an effective living and dead test. At the finish all material used may be left behind as there is nothing wrong to find.

Effect: Use five or six blank cards and a drug envelope. Four people write the names of living persons and the fifth writes the name of someone who has passed on. The cards are collected by one of the spectators, and mixed. Taking them with the writing sides down, the performer also mixes them a little more and puts the entire packet into the envelope. He now holds the envelope to his head and slowly and correctly reveals the dead name! Opening the envelope, the cards are removed and spread out with the writing side downward. The performer finishes by waving his hand over them and correctly picks out the dead name card and hands it to the writer.

I consider this a very practical method for any close up opportunity, especially press work.

Preparation: The drug envelope used is faked in a far from new manner. Across the face side, a half inch from the flap end, a slit is made large enough to accommodate easily one of the blank cards. The five or six cards used are ordinary except for one which has a nail nick in the upper left and lower right corners. If one takes such a card, holds it between the thumb and the first finger with thumb on top, and presses hard with the thumb nail, a nick is made that becomes an easily felt bump on the other side.

I put these cards, with the nicked one on top, into the envelope and carry it in my vest pocket ready for immediate use.

Routine: Take out the envelope, being careful not to expose the slit on the face side, and remove the cards. Leave the envelope laying on the table face side down. Show the cards and ask someone to think of the dead person. Hand him the top card for writing and hand the rest out for the writing of living names.

Now have them collected by someone else and mixed with the writing sides down. Take them and mix them a little more and in doing so bring the nicked card to the bottom or the face side of the pile. Don't try to shuffle them like playing cards or do anything fancy. Just mix them carelessly with your two hands while they are held horizontal with the floor.

Pick up the envelope with the left hand, flap open and with the right hand insert the packet. The right fingers are underneath the packet and, as you start this, the bottom card is pushed a little ahead of the others and going into the envelope goes through the slit. The rest of the cards on top are slightly tilted down at the end being held and go on into the envelope proper. Try this several times with the material in hand and it will be found an easy move. Now lift the envelope up, moisten the flap with the right forefinger and seal the flap while this side is towards the audience.

At this time, because you are making it apparent that you are sealing the flap, the back or face of the envelope is towards you and the dead name card is looking right at you.

If the name is upside down it doesn't matter, because you still have to bring the envelope to your head and it can then be turned around in your hands while you ask the person to think intently of the name. Slowly reveal the name of the person who has passed away.

Hold the envelope in your left hand at the lower end with the flap side towards the audience and the card facing you. With a small pair of scissors cut the flap end away. However, the left thumb has drawn the card back about an inch to clear the slit, and the envelope is cut across on the slit, which destroys all evidence of trickery in the envelope.

Reach in the opened end with the right first and second fingers which grasp the cards inside. The right thumb goes against the card on the back and, with one move, the cards are removed with the card from the back along with them.

Toss the envelope aside or to the spectators and holding the cards, with the writing downward, mix them a little and spread on the table. Waving your hand over them finally pick up the correct card and return it to the writer.

For clearness I think this a welcome routine. At any rate try it out a few times.

THE SECRET
DUNNINGER

While this effect has been sold under different names and credited to many different people, no one as yet has published the presentation which I first used over 25 years ago. Here is the effect:

On a piece of paper about 3 x 2½ inches in size the performer draws three short lines across the paper as he holds it lengthwise. This is given to the sitter for a short question, or better, for the name of one who has gone into the "happy summer land"; not now living.

The paper is folded once each way and is given to the performer. He tears it up into small pieces and gives them back to the spectator, who drops them into a goblet of water on the table before him. Both watch the floating papers intently. They burst into flame and disappear. The performer picks up the goblet with one hand, gazes into it and reveals the secretly written information, or the "dead name," as the case may be.

Preparation and Routine: This effect makes use of the stolen center ruse. Mark the dividing lines on the paper slips, as explained above, and have someone write a dead person's name in the center panel. Or draw an oval in the center of the paper and have the name inscribed within it.

Now comes the subtle part. In his left trouser pocket the performer has put, just previous to the performance, a packet consisting of folded and torn bits of flash paper. In the center of this packet is a small piece of potassium. He finger palms this flash paper packet in his left hand during the writing and folding of the paper billet by the spectator.

Taking back the written slip, and keeping it plainly in view, the performer tears it into little pieces, using the routine described in Annemann's "Mindreading Publicity Effect," page 30. He is careful, however, to tear this billet by holding it between his right thumb and forefinger so that, at the finish, he will have the torn center piece under his right thumb. Once the slip has been torn, he pretends to leave it in his left hand, actually palming the original pieces in his right hand, and bringing the flash paper pieces into view with the left hand. The performer asks the spectator to pick up the pieces from off his left hand and drop them into the glass of water.

Now both the performer and the spectator watch the paper pieces floating in the glass, the spectator being asked to concentrate on the dead person's name. Under cover of this misdirection, the performer puts his right hand, containing the pieces of the original slip, into his right trouser pocket. He releases all the pieces except the center section, which he has under his thumb and opens it out against the base of his fingers.

The potassium loaded flash paper pieces will float on the surface of the water for about twenty seconds, and then will burst into a grand flame—and they're gone! As the flame flashes up, the performer brings his right hand out of his pocket. He now reaches for the glass and picks it up with his right hand which, you will remember, contains the stolen and opened up center of the original slip. His fingers encircle the bowl of the glass and conceal the palmed slip from the view of both the spectator and the audience. By looking into the water, the performer can read the name written on the slip, for the glass helps to magnify the writing. Thus the master mind reveals the name on which the spectator has been concentrating!

DR. DALEY'S DEATH DIVINATION

Effect: Have the spectator sitting opposite you and, in the following manner, proceed to convince him that a strange power is yours to command. Five or six pieces of rather heavy tissue paper (about two by three inches in size) are put in front of the subject. He is asked to pick up one and write upon it the name of someone living. He folds it once each way, puts it back on the table and takes another slip. This time he is told to write the name of a dead relative or close friend. He folds it as before, you take it from him, at the same time handing him another slip, and this time he writes another living name. The rest are living names also, until all slips are folded and on table. You then idly touch them with a cigarette, one after the other, one suddenly flaring up and vanishing. You ask the sitter to check the remaining slips for the dead name. It is gone! For the climax you impressively reveal the name.

Method: The secret is flash paper, which any magical dealer can supply in large sheets. Take the paper from the spectator each time and place it on the table, but switch at the dead name. Then read it under the table edge while he is writing the others. The rest just works itself. The effect is marvelous.

THE GHOST HAND
HENRY HARDIN

Here is a masterpiece from the fertile brain of that marvelous creator of subtleties of years ago. To be precise, this effect was advertised and sold by Mr. Hardin in 1907, yet today we find it is true magic because it isn't complicated. Its effect is truly amazing and will prove exceptionally worth while.

It is a "Living and Dead" trick dependent upon the now presumedly ancient "rough" and "smooth" edge principle. But it is the presentation, once more, that was Hardin's forte. Following are his original instructions:

Tear off one leaf of a sheet of note paper, and one of the edges (length-ways) will be quite smooth, and the other edge will be rough. This is the secret of the trick. First ask a party to take a sheet of note paper and tear off one half. Now ask him to tear this paper lengthways into five strips (of course one of these strips will have a smooth edge, and can be readily distinguished from the others, which will have two rough edges). Now you take these strips in a careless manner, square them up and hand them back.

However you are careful to leave the smooth edged one at the bottom of the packet of papers. Next request the party to write on the first strip the name of some live friend, fold the strip and lay it on the table. Ask him to do the same with each succeeding slip, but when he arrives at the last or bottom strip ask him to write the name of a dead friend. Next ask him to mix all the papers well together and to bring you two hats, and two handkerchiefs. (At this point, the original instructions should have been written in caps.)

You stand the hats on the table and picking up the strips one by one, you drop them openly into one of the hats. Now when you pick up the strip with the smooth edge you pretend to drop it in the hat with the others, but in reality you thumb palm and retain it in the right hand. Now picking up the two handkerchiefs, you spread them over the two hats. However, in doing this you secretly drop the concealed strip in the empty hat. You then announce that the spirit of the dead person will reach into the hat, pick out the slip with his name on it and put it in the other hat. Invite inspection of the hats, and the strip will be found in the empty one.

This effect cannot be improved upon for directness of action or for ease of working. How many of my readers knew of that hat transfer, with a ghost hand taking part in the proceedings?

DEAD

ORVILLE MEYER

A Living and Dead test should concentrate upon the wallop of the effect rather than upon the method. This is impromptu, and while the presentation idea involved belongs to Eddie Clever, the method of handling and using billets instead of envelopes and cards is mine. In this form the billets can be torn out of borrowed paper without preparation or notice.

Use five or six billets about 2x3 inches. These are folded three times, to an easily manipulated size. One is secretly dotted on the outside, or given an extra bend or kink. The slips are passed out, and the person getting the marked one is asked to write a dead name. The others write living names. The writers refold the billets and drop them into a hat, the collecting being done by a spectator.

The performer picks out a slip, making sure it isn't the "dead one", and announces it as a living name. He opens to verify, nods, refolds and gives to the man who collected the slips. As an afterthought he has this man read the name on the slip aloud so that the writer can claim it. Now reach in and take out the dead name slip, at the same time finger-palming one of the living name slips. Hold this to your forehead and announce it to be another live one. Open it for verification as before, note the dead name, nod, refold it and switch slips in handing it to the assistant. He reads the live name and this second slip is claimed by its owner.

Take out the third slip, dropping the dead name billet back into the hat. Repeat the same procedure with this live name slip. By now you have accustomed the audience to your way of handling the papers, and twice (first and third times) your hands are actually empty. For the fourth time, take out the dead name slip. Build this up. Announce it to be the dead name and ask for the owner. Return the paper to him and ask him to keep it closed. Then reveal the name, letter for letter, for a smashing and baffling climax!

HADES CALLING!

Here's an idea for those using a Living and Dead test. For paper use a heavy tissue. Five pieces are written upon, four living and one dead. They are mixed and someone holds a match. One by one the folded slips are passed through the flame. The first disappears in a flash. This happens to the second, too. The third stays unharmed. As a check you try the fourth and fifth, both of which vanish in smoke and flame. The spectator opens the one unharmed slip and it is the dead name! There's nothing to it because the dead name is on the only piece that isn't flash paper! The effect on an audience is remarkable!

NYCTALOPIA

PAUL CURRY

Rather a nightmarish effect is this, it going slightly beyond the pale of things. It is the only feat of its kind, to our knowledge, in which the materials used never leave the possession of the spectator, and at no time is he approached by the performer.

Effect: A pad, pencil, and envelope are put before a spectator. He thinks of someone who is dead and unknown to the performer. Another spectator now turns off the light and, with the magician in the corner of the room, the first person prints on the pad the name of the thought-of person. He then tears off the written sheet, rolls it into a ball, seals it in an envelope, and holds it to his forehead. After due concentration, the performer, although he has never left the corner of the room, successfully spells out the name in question!

Requirements: A pencil, two small pads about the size of a playing card, a pay envelope, a fountain pen flashlight, and a small piece of carbon paper called "Auto-copy" and obtainable at Woolworth's. "Auto-copy" is a new idea in which the paper itself takes the impression.

Preparation: Cut a piece of "Auto-copy" the width of one pad, but a trifle shorter. Attach a 20-foot length of black silk thread to the upper right corner of the "Auto-copy" by pasting a small sticker over thread onto paper. The "Auto-copy" is placed under the top sheet of the pad. The prepared pad is placed in upper left vest pocket with the thread tucked in loosely beside it, and its free end tied to one of the vest buttons. Wrap a small piece of red cloth around the end of a pen flashlight. Tie tightly, and have the cloth of a quality that only a red glow comes through. Put this in inside coat pocket. The unprepared pad, pencil, and envelope are placed before the spectator on a small table, upper right corner of the pad being towards that part of room where magician is about to retire.

Routine: When the lights have been put out, the magician removes from his pocket the prepared pad with a few feet of thread. He picks up the articles on the table one at a time and replaces them, telling the spectator he had better leave them as is so they won't be knocked off of the table. In so doing, the prepared pad is put down in place of the ordinary one. The magician now goes to his corner of the room, letting out thread so it will lie along the floor.

After the spectator has printed the name he thought of, he is told to tear the sheet from pad and roll it into a ball between his hands. This is an important point as it not only keeps both his hands occupied, but also makes sufficient noise to cover any possible sound produced as the performer, from his corner position, draws the "Auto-copy" towards himself by means of the thread.

During this time, the performer may keep talking and direct the spectator in sealing the paper inside the envelope, and then holding it to his forehead. In the meantime, he has secured the "Auto-copy", turned his back so as to face the corner as closely as possible, removed the pen flashlight, and in a space of about five seconds learns the thought-of name! He now finishes by spelling it out correctly, and stays in his place until the lights are on and everything is checked, he, of course, having done away with his apparatus of charlatanism. In closing, it can only be said, and it's a truly old saying too, that the effect should not be confused with the method. Just give it one or two fair trials!

ENTITY ALONE

LYONS-ELLIOTT

Effect: The following is an unusual version of "The Quick and the Dead." All sitters present are given slips of paper on which to record the name of some living friend. That is, all but one sitter, who is asked to write the name of some close friend or relative not now living—someone in the happy summer-land or another world.

The performer picks up a pitcher of water and fills a goblet standing nearby. One sitter is asked to collect the papers and see that they are well mixed before handing them to the performer. One at a time, he drops them into the goblet, while muttering, just audibly, a verse from Longfellow's translation:

" 'Twas right a goblet the Fate should be
Of the joyous race of Edenhall!
Deep draughts drink we right willingly;
And willingly ring, with merry call
Kling! klang! to the Luck of Edenhall!"

As the last paper drops within, the performer picks up the glass and asks the attendant who collected the papers to reach into the glass and take out, in a bunch, the papers floating there. The glass is held high while the

performer approaches and stands before the person who wrote the dead name.
He says, simply:

> "The drinking-glass of crystal tall;
> They call it the Luck of Edenhall."

And that person is called upon to notice one lone paper at the bottom of
the glass of water. He is asked the name of whom he wrote. The pitcher is
asked for. The water is poured from the goblet. The spectator gets the paper
from the glass and reads it aloud. It is the dead name!

Preparation: Now to undermine the proceedings with factual data.
The dead name paper must sink while the others stay, naturally, on the
surface of the water. The slips of paper are cut from absorbent paper towels
(in U. S. A., Scott Tissue Towels) and when of a size about 1 x 2 inches, any
crinkled property is not noticeable. If you take such pieces of paper and
singly push them into water edgewise they will rise to the surface. It therefore is necessary to indetectably prepare one piece, that given out for the dead
name, so that it will sink to the bottom of the glass, alone.

At any drug store procure a "mouth spray" device. At any paint or
hardware store buy a small can of white shellac. Cut a goodly supply of
papers. Take as many as you wish to prepare. The ratio will be about seven
to one. With the spraying device inserted into the can give the "dead" papers
a coating of the shellac—both sides. Keep these separate from the unprepared papers for it will be impossible to tell them apart. That is all.

The prepared paper will sink—the others will stay on top. As long as you
put the papers into the water edgewise, in order to completely inundate them,
the proper paper will sink to the bottom, even while you don't know by sight
or feel which it is. The floating papers are taken out "en masse" by the col-
lector—the right one is at the bottom. In a few minutes you can prepare
enough papers for a long while. With one added to a bunch of unprepared
papers, a goblet and a pitcher of water, you have all you need to convince
your "guests" that something strange is at work.

Routine: As described under "Effect."

BETWEEN THE LINES
ANNEMANN

Book tests come and go about the same way as do Four Ace Tricks, for it seems as though one is on the search continually for improvement. Of course, favorite methods vary according to the individual. I've seen some people who would swear by a method that to me seemed cumbersome, drawn out, and obviously a fake because of the round about way of getting to the word. However, the advantage of using or knowing several methods for a test makes it possible for one to repeat it at some later time without fear of anyone following the old method of procedure.

In this particular method, I've tried to get away from the adding of cards, etc., all of which tend to make the feat appear mathematical. And more often than not, people don't understand just what you want and do just the opposite.

Another good psychological point is that the selections appear fair because you have a spectator select more cards than are needed and then eliminate the picture cards. And lastly, the fact that the spectator never tells you anything, in fact hardly says a word, really impresses an audience tremendously.

Presentation: Start by giving the deck a false shuffle or several straight cuts. Put the deck on a table with the book and walk away. While your back is turned, you ask someone to give the deck a complete cut. Then say, "Better give it another." Continue, "Now hold the deck in your hand and deal three cards, from the top of the deck onto the table in a face up row from left to right. These cards are going to indicate a page and a word in the book. By the way, are there any picture cards among the three?"

If the spectator says, "Yes," you say, "They're too confusing. Push those three cards aside and deal three more in the same way. Are there any picture cards there now?" Suppose he says, "No."

You go on, "Look at the first two cards. If they are a 6 and a 7, open the book to page 67. If they are a 5 and a 2, open the book to page 52."

"You have it? Now look at the last or third card. I want you to start at the top of the page and count across on the top line to the word at that number. If the card is a 3, count to the third word. If the card is an 8 spot, count to the eighth word."

"Now turn the cards on the table face down, so I can't see them, and keep your finger right on the word you have located. Have you got your finger on it? Fine! Please hold your finger on the word, look intently at it and concentrate on it." At this point you turn around, and proceed to reveal the word.

Method: This effect can be obtained only through the use of the Si Stebbins' card stacking system and no other. There are only four possible combinations of three cards without pictures: A-4-7; 4-7-10; 2-5-8; and 3-6-9.

With these four combinations in mind, you previously have looked up and memorized four words in the book you intend using: the 7th word on page 14; the 10th word on page 47; the 8th word on page 25, and the 9th word on page 36.

Furthermore, two of these page numbers are even and two are odd.

When you turn around to face the spectator holding the book, as already explained, you note whether his finger is resting on a right or left hand page. This is your clue, because all even numbered pages of all books are on the left, and all odd numbered pages are on the right when a book is opened for reading. (As you stand facing the person holding the open book, just remember this rule in reverse.) Therefore you know immediately whether the word is one of the two words on the odd pages, or one of the two words on the even pages. Thus you automatically eliminate two words, and have but two words to "work on." Start by giving the first letter of one of the two words. If right, continue. If wrong, say "Well, the last letter is . . . ." And you name the last letter of the other word, and spell out the word backwards.

Whenever a spectator deals three times onto the table and has a picture card each time in his group of cards, you know automatically that the next or fourth deal, always will be the A-4-7 combination. In such a case, you don't even have to turn around but can name the word immediately. When you get used to working this trick with a certain book, you can also judge which of the two words it is, for the odd numbers are 22 pages apart and the even numbers are 22 pages apart also.

THE YOGI BOOK TEST
ANNEMANN

This method of presentation has been a great favorite of mine for homes and spots where it can be presented in an apparently impromptu fashion. Many times when out for an evening, the opportunity will arise to pick up one of your host's books and secretly prepare this test. It only takes a few minutes' time to get ready.

Effect: The performer picks up three books and asks to borrow a deck of cards. A subject is selected to assist and he makes an obviously free choice of one of the books. He then shuffles the deck of cards, cuts them, and retires to a corner of the room with half the deck and the book. He now looks at the top three cards of his half deck, opens the book at a page corresponding to the values of any two of the three cards, and counts along the top line on that page to the word that occupies the number corresponding to the value of the third card. Ask him to hold his finger on that particular word and concentrate on it. Then you reveal the word correctly!

Preparation and Routine: In effect, it differs a lot from the usual routine. I know that my original way of having the page and number looked up from cards is extremely effective and a throw-off in every respect.

At an opportune moment you pick up two books, apparently at random, from a table or bookcase. Deciding that you need three, and being at a loss as to which you will take, you call upon one of the spectators to make a selection and hand you a third one. This is just a little wrinkle but will be remembered later.

Place the three books on a chair or on the floor and ask someone to pick up two of them. This is going to be an out and out force so I may as well explain it as I go along. If the person assisting leaves the right one behind, merely tell him to lay aside the books he has picked up as they won't be needed again. If he includes the right one among the two, ask him to hand you one. If you are handed the wrong one, thank him, pick up the book on the floor and lay them aside. If he hands you the right one, thank him, read the title of the book and mention that you are using for the test a book taken from the case and selected at random. Just take this part easy and don't stall or hesitate, and you have the prettiest force that you'll ever need.

Now for the cards. Any borrowed deck is used and you fan through the cards to get a Four, a Five and an Eight spot on top in any order. Take the book in your right hand and, in covering the deck for a second, add the three top cards from the deck to the bottom of the book. Hold them against the book with your right fingers. Now have the deck shuffled, and take it back on your outstretched left palm. Ask someone to cut off a good quantity of cards and discard them. As they do this, you drop the book from your right hand onto the lower half of the deck on your left palm. Immediately hand the book with the cards beneath it to the person who is to assist you in the test. Ask him to take them both to a corner of the room and to turn his back. If he likes, he may leave the room entirely, just as long as he stays within hearing distance of you.

Now you instruct him to look at the three top cards of the packet he holds. Tell him to take any two of them and, combining their values to represent a two digit number, open the book he has to that page. At this point you have a neat point. After telling him the above, continue and say "Just take any two of the three cards and open at that page. If you have a six and a nine you can call it either sixty-nine or ninety-six, it really doesn't matter as long as the book is opened at a page selected in some manner by the cards as I want everything left to chance." Now tell him to use the remaining card as a number and count along the top line to that word. When he locates the word, he is asked to remember it. You then, with only a word or two, reveal the word correctly!

The real kick I get out of this test is the handling of the page and word numbers from the three cards. And I am sure that that point is as fair as any could be in the eyes of the audience. However, fair as it may seem to the audience and complicated as it may seem to you, *there are only six possible pages and words that can be arrived at!*

Take three cards as follows and check with this table:

Page 45 Word 8
Page 54 Word 8
Page 48 Word 5
Page 84 Word 5
Page 58 Word 4
Page 85 Word 4

That's the secret in a nutshell. Beforehand you memorize the six words as per the table. I say memorize because I know it to be the best way in the long run. The order in which you memorize them doesn't matter a bit. I generally change them around and form a sort of mental sentence made of the six words in their easiest remembered order.

First pick out the books and have the right one selected. If you have been using the cards before this, you can have the three proper cards already on top. You have nothing else to do after the person cuts the deck and leaves the room, or stands in the corner, except to tell him what to do. When he returns, or turns to face the audience, you know he is thinking of one of the six words, and it is up to you to find out which one. Nine times out of ten you can pump it out of him with a question or two or by stabbing at letters.

Ask him does the word begin with a "T," etc. If wrong, try a last letter of another word. When I say, "Ask him," I mean, "Tell him," but in a more or less questioning manner. You'll always get a reaction and know whether or not you are on the right track. As there are only six words you shouldn't have much trouble. More often than you would think, you'll hit upon the right word the very first time. Remember that in the mind of the audience you have the most difficult task in the world—that of finding out what word is being thought of. And to the audience it might be any word in the English language.

As a variation, I someitmes hand the person a pencil and a pad and ask him to print the word on the top page of the pad and then place the pad in his pocket. Standing across the room, I can invariably spot a letter or two by the action of the top of the pencil and can also judge the length of the word. In this way you can hit the right word the first time, in practically every case.

THE PERFECT BOOK TEST
ANNEMANN

This "Perfect Book Test" is an effect put on the market some years ago at $2.50.

Effect: In working, three books are handed to a spectator in the audience and he selects one. The medium is blindfolded and is sitting at the front with her back towards the audience. The spectator opens the book at any page, runs his finger along the first line and stops on any word. He shows it to several around him, closes the book, puts it between the other two, and someone else carries them to the medium. She tosses one to the left, one to the right, and keeping one, riffles the pages and correctly announces the chosen word.

Routine: The performer stands to the left of the spectator. He takes the two unused books back with his left hand and, as he tells the spectator what to do with the chosen book, puts his right hand in his trouser pocket where a waxed business card and pencil stub repose. The moment the book is opened and a page selected, the performer jots it down on the blank card in his pocket. He tells the spectator to run his finger along the top line and to stop at a word he likes. This done, the performer jots down the position of the word in the chosen line while the spectator shows it to those close by. As he tells the spectator to close the book, the performer palms the card from his pocket and transfers the two books to his right hand, pressing the card against the under side of the bottom book. He takes off the top book with his left hand, has the spectator put his book on top, and on this drops the book from his right hand, the card being stuck beneath. The three books are given to someone else to deliver to the medium who removes the card, tosses the outside books away and finds the word.

WHIM OF TITUBA
(Tituba—The Original Witch of Salem)
ANNEMANN

The effect is the thing, and this effect is different. Three books or magazines are shown and one is selected. The performer has three piles of envelopes, each of a different size so they can be nested one within the other From the smallest pile he gives a spectator one into which he puts a blank piece of paper and then seals it. The envelope is placed into one of the next larger size and the spectator writes his name across the flap. This set of two envelopes is now sealed in the third and largest envelope.

With the envelope in hand, the performer addresses a number of people, obtaining a figure from each. With these jotted down in a column, a line is drawn beneath and the envelope is given to the man who signed the second envelope. He adds the column and calls aloud the total. We will assume it to be 54.

The performer asks the person with the magazine to open it to page 54—but page 54 is found to be torn out, and in its place drops out the blank piece of paper.

The performer acts annoyed to no slight degree, explaining, "Tituba likes to have fun in her witchy way. She was the West Indian slave who started the witchraft scare back in 1692 with her voodoo stories. I generally have a word selected on the chosen page of the book and Tituba, believe it or not, scrawls the word on the piece of paper inside the envelope. She never knows what the word means because she was burned at the stake just when the children of Samuel Parris were trying to teach her to read and write. She duplicates the printing as best she can and I've noted quite a bit of improvement over a period of five years since I learned of her presence, but when she gets impatient, mad, or just wants to play a joke, she'll rip the entire page out. Books never meant much more to her than something with which to start a fire. I'm sorry things have gone wrong. I can finish now only the way she'll let me."

The spectator with the envelope opens the first and identifies his signature on the flap of the second envelope. When this second envelope is turned over, right across its face is scrawled in large crayon figures the page number 54. Underneath the figure is the name Tituba in a childish scrawl. "You see," says the performer, "one never knows for sure what will happen. Maybe she thinks she knows enough about the alphabet and wants me to teach her arithmetic."

The envelope is opened and the inside one removed. When this is opened there is found inside the missing torn out page, and the performer finished wryly, with "Well, if a word could have been selected on the page, Tituba certainly made sure that it would be found in the envelope."

Preparation: Have three magazines or books of a decidedly different appearance. From one tear very roughly and jaggedly a page in the 50's or 60's. Leave at least an inch-wide strip near the binding. At that spot insert a blank piece of paper, one of the sheets from the pad you will later use in the effect. Now pile up the three books with the prepared one in the center.

Have three stacks of envelopes. Call the smallest size 1, then 2 and 3. The 1 and 3 piles are ordinary and unprepared. The top envelope of pile 2 (flaps up) has its flap entirely cut away. Then the flap of the next envelope under it overlaps the top envelope and everything appears right. Fold the torn out page, not nicely, but at angles, until it fits into the smallest envelope. Seal it and place this inside the second envelope of pile 2 whose flap overlaps the top flapless one. Then, on the face side of this second envelope which now contains the sealed page, scrawl the page's number and Tituba's name. A duplicate piece of blank paper and a pencil completes the set-up.

Routine: Lay the three books in a row with the faked one in the center. A spectator steps up and you ask him to give you two of them. Seldom will he give you the two end ones but when it does happen, toss them aside and tell him to hold the other. When the faked book is among the two given you, immediately say, "Now take one back." If he takes the faked one, say, "Hold it for a few minutes." If he takes the other, you hold up the faked one, saying, "One book out of three. Put the others aside and watch this one carefully." The whole thing must be done quickly and without hesitation or stalling.

The No. 1 stack of envelopes is picked up in the left hand with flaps upwards and to the right. The top one is taken off and given to a person to blow in. Then he is given the piece of paper to seal. During this you lay down the first pile and pick up the No. 2 pile in the same manner. Take back the sealed envelope with your right hand and apparently put it into the top envelope. The audience sees the flap lift up but it's really the second envelope's flap, and the sealed envelope goes into the top flapless envelope. Grasping the opened flap, the right hand pulls the envelope away from the pile. You swing to the right as this is done and your left hand lays its pile on the table. The face side of this envelope is kept down and with a moistened finger you seal the flap and hold it for the spectator to sign across the flap side.

Pick up the No. 3 pile and slide the envelope into the top one of the pile. Hand it to the spectator for sealing. Then take it back for the addition part. Each of six or seven people whisper figures from 1 through 9 to you as you approach them. You write the figures on the face side of the envelope. However, you add them as you go along keeping the total in your mind after each figure. When the total reaches less than 9 from the page number you want to force, stop. Say that you will have them added up and, at the same time, make a flourish of drawing the line beneath the column of figures. However, you have just added another figure before that, a figure that brings the total to the page number desired. Simple as it is, the subtlety hasn't found its equal for simplicity in years.

The trick is done but for the histrionics. I recommend that it be presented without any fussing around, or any attempt to justify your actions other than a simple detailing of what you are doing. The time for the audience to think is when you find the page gone, give them the patter and rake Tituba over the coals, and then wind things up with the discovered page plus the plaint that you're sorry. Just impress them that you are embarrassed by failure and go into your next item as if you are sure this will work and make up for the one which just went wrong. You'll find out that they'll remember Tituba longer, sometimes longer than they'll remember you.

DICE AND A BOOK
ANNEMANN

Most readers will have a set of the five dice used in Heath's Deciphering Dice Trick. After using it for a time, I discovered that the dice were peculiarly adapted for a subtle book test.

Effect: Produce the five dice and mention that they are used for some money game (without going into that part further) as an excuse for their being numbered with three digits to a side. Let someone shake and roll them. You line them up in a row, and turning your back ask the person assisting to add up the figures and get the total. Then ask him how many figures are in the total. He replies that there are four, and you tell him to look at the first two and the last two. Now toss him a book, and have him open it at the page represented by the higher of the two numbers. Then, taking the other number, he counts to that word on the page and remembers it. You take out a pocket notebook, jot something down on a page, tear it out, crumple it and hand it to another person. The word is now disclosed, and your written divination is found to be correct.

Preparation and Routine: I have found that the use of the dice make the test appear very fair. There is never a thought that in the moment of putting the dice in line, or in instructing the spectator what to do, you have learned the total by the short cut process possible with this trick. The opinion they have is that there can be hundreds of variations.

As a matter of fact, there are only 27 different grand totals possible. Going still further, if one separates the four figure totals in half, using them as large and small two-figure numbers for page and word, there are only 15 possible words that can be selected. Thus, on the inside cover of your notebook, you have the list of the 15 words—from the book you intend using—followed by the 15 smallest figures in all possible totals. It's an easy matter, then, to steal a glance at the prepared list as you open your note book to jot down your written word.

The combinations are as follows:

PAGE	WORD	PAGE	WORD	PAGE	WORD
39	11	34	16	29	21
38	12	33	17	28	22
37	13	32	18	27	23
36	14	31	19	26	24
35	15	30	20	25	25

(Variation by F. F. Clark: Use the above test with a telephone directory. Vary by having two of the figures represent the page, the third figure the column, and the last figure the name in that column. It is easy for the spectator to find the name and telephone number as he never has to count down more than nine, i.e.: 3119 would be page 31, first column, ninth name. When there happens to be a nought in the last one such as 3020, the page would be 30, second column, and then, as long as there is a nought, you can tell them to look at the first name.)

A monstrous variation of this test is possible for those who are at home with a set of books or encyclopediae, whose pages run consecutively through the volumes as high as 3,911. In such a case, you tell the person assisting to look through the set and find the page represented by the entire total. Then they are to add together the figures of the total reached and count to that word. You successfully reveal the word in this case, also, because there are only 27 pages that can be selected. When you add the four figures of any total you get 14 in every case except two, when it is 5. Your notebook, of course, carries the 27 totals with the correct word after each.

THE WORD ON THE PAGE
ANNEMANN

I've used the novel principle employed in this trick many times for an impromptu book or magazine test. With but a minute's access to a book and a few minutes to set your cards, you have as clean a test as you'll find anywhere.

Effect: You ask two spectators to step forward. To one of them you hand a book, while the other one selects four cards from the deck which you have ribbon spread across the table top. He gives two of these cards to the man with the book and retains the other two for himself. One man totals the values of his cards and the book is opened at that page. The other man totals his cards and counts down to the word on the page at that number. You have moved away from the table while the selection of a page and a word has been going on, but once they decide on the word you are able to reveal it.

Preparation: The deck for this trick is stacked and utilizes the 14-15 stack now generally known to magicians. It's a case of arranging the values (disregarding the suits) so that any two adjoining cards in the set-up will total, when added together, either 14 or 15. For instance: 7-8-6-9-5-10-4-J-3-Q-2-K-A-K-2-Q-3-J-4-10-5-9-6-8-7-7, etc., until all the cards in the deck are used except two Aces, which can be left in the case or in your pocket. This deck can be cut indefinitely and any two cards removed together will total either 14 or 15.

My simple, but extremely useful discovery was this. If you spread the deck across the table and remove two together, the card above and the card below this pair always have a definite and unvaried relation. If the inside pair total 14, the outside pair will total 15 or 16. If the inside pair total 15, the outside pair will total 13 or 14. Therefore, it is only necessary to remember the 13th and 14th word on page 15, and the 15th and 16th word on page 14.

Routine: When ready to present the effect, false shuffle the cards and have someone cut them on the table. Now ribbon spread the deck face down across the table, and walk away a short distance. Hand the book to a spectator, ask him to select someone else to assist and the two of them step up to the table. Now have one of them remove four cards together from anywhere in the spread. Then say that you want the cards divided and ask the first person which two he would like to have, the middle two or the outside two. Whichever he wants, tell him to take them and ask the other person to take the remaining two cards.

You now know that the person getting the center pair has a total, when the two cards are added, of 14 or 15. Ask him to add the values of his two cards together and then open the book to that page. Then ask the second person to add the values of his two cards and to count along the top line on the selected page to the word at that number. Both men are asked to remember the word. When this second man counts to the selected word on the selected page, you know the page immediately because 14 will always be on his left, and 15 will always be on his right as the book is open before him.

Now you know the word must be one of the two you have remembered. Ask your two assistants to concentrate on the selected word, and then you say, "The first letter looks like . . . ." If right, continue and finish. If wrong, say, "Well, perhaps I should try it backwards. The last letter looks like a . . . . . .," and you proceed to spell it out backwards. You merely spell the other of the two words at this time. Always start with the 13th word on page 15, and the 16th word on page 14 and you will be right nine times out of ten—for there are only six instances in the stacked set-up when the others will pop up.

MONKS MYSTERY
JACK VOSBURGH

Effect: Say, in starting that you wish a word selected, one in the English language. To prevent your mind and speech from influencing the subject, you continue, it shall be made by chance, with cards and a book. And, you finish, to make impossible the reading of the subject's mind by yourself, of course, you shall write down first what thought has come into vision of your foresight.

Introduce two slates. Pick up the top slate and proceed to write on it. Pick up the other slate and drop it over what you have written and lay the slates, as they are, in a visible spot.

A volunteer assistant now is given a book and a deck of cards. You turn your back. He is told to cut the deck once or twice and then cut it into two piles. Next he is asked to take the top and bottom cards of each pile. You remark that the picking is made as mixed up as possible.

With these four cards in hand, the spectator is to add their values together for a total which represents the page in the book to which he is to turn. When he announces that he has it, you ask that he put the cards back among the others and forget them. Turning, you request that he locate a word on the page by first adding together the figures of the page number at which he is looking, and then counting across the printed lines until he reaches the word at that spot.

Whereupon, the word being disclosed for all to know, the performer picks up his slates to reveal that he has foretold successfully the choice of that particular one of many thousand words.

Preparation: Remove two aces from a deck and arrange the remaining 50 cards by values so that each adjoining pair, when added together, total either 14 or 15. (7-8-6-9-5-10-4-J-3-Q-2-K-A-K-2-Q-3-J-4-10-5-9-6-8-7-7-8, etc.) The deck may be cut indefinitely without harm. In the book you will use, note, and remember, but three words—the tenth word on page 28, the eleventh word on page 29, and the third word on page 30.

Take two slates and a flap to fit. On one slate write one of the words. On the flap write another of the words. Cover the slate writing with the flap, its own writing inside. Lay this, with the flap side up, on your table. Put the untouched slate on top.

Routine: Follow the presentation as described in the beginning, by handing a spectator the book and the deck of cards.

It will be seen that with the arranged deck and the adding together of the top and bottom cards of two cut piles, the total can be only 28, 29, or 30. And, the tenth, eleventh, and third words, respectively, are all that can be noted by the spectator.

Two of these are written on the slate and flap as described. The third you write on the other slate during the effect, and onto this unshown writing drop the other "casually shown blank" slate with flap side down.

Knowing the positions of these written words inside the slates, it is no skillful problem at all to finally take them apart to reveal the proper word of the three. Should it be the one just written, only the top slate need be lifted and shown. For either of the other two the slates must be turned over, allowing the flap to drop from one to the other of the inside surfaces. The "lift-off, in this case, must be more careful, for only one of the written-on surfaces is disclosed while the other slate is tossed back onto the table. The action is not reprehensible, in a way, because the audience has seen, at one time or another, both clean surfaces of both slates. And, having seen you write something on one, they accept what is shown as that writing.*

THE DOUBLE AD TEST
ANNEMANN

In most tests with newspaper ads, there is but one way of getting the information as to the contents of the ad as far as the audience is concerned. In this instance, I've tried to change the effect for each and at the same time make it very easy for the performer.

Effect: A want ad, or renting ad page is removed from a local paper. A column is cut from the page and six or seven people clip out ads from the column strip. The most practical way of presentation is for you to clip the strip of ads apart on a saucer, and then let several people each select

---
* (Note by Annemann: I thought that I exhausted the 14-15 deck stack principle long ago but Mr. Vosburgh has a decidedly new angle for its use in a book test. Besides this "break-down" of chances to a three-word possibility there is included a revelation via slates which, for the first time to our knowledge allows of the word being foretold by the performer without the use of a definite force.)

one ad. Each person is handed an envelope in which to seal his ad. Each is asked to pick out an ad and put it in the envelope without looking at it, as you are trying a test of clairvoyance and do not want to get any telepathy mixed in. The envelopes are sealed, collected, and given to you in a bunch. The lights are then turned out. One of the spectators takes the envelopes in the dark, mixes them, keeps one and tosses the rest onto the table. The lights are turned on again, and you stress the point that you had the selection of an envelope made in this way to prevent anyone from saying, or thinking, that you could keep track of any ad or any envelope.

You now concentrate, hedge around a little, and finally give the import of the ad that the spectator is holding. I do not advise giving the ad word for word. The envelope is opened, the ad removed and checked. Now repeat the test, but this time with the lights turned on. Ask another person to mix the envelopes that are on the table and then select one of them. You stand before him and slowly reveal the contents of his ad. The envelope is opened, the ad checked and you are found to be correct again!

Preparation: No other ad test has allowed of these conditions, i.e., each choice a free one. The basic method, however, is far from new. It's only the combination that counts. Only six or seven ads are necessary. Pick up seven papers, for instance, if you are going to use six, and cut from six of them two different ads. Try to pick out ads that are about different subjects. This gives you six duplicates of each ad.

Now obtain twelve No. 2 drug envelopes that open at one end. Trim the closed ends and sides of six of the envelopes and you'll have six envelope fronts with flaps attached. Insert these fronts into the other six envelopes so that the flaps come together. In the back compartment of each envelope, put the six duplicates of ad No. 1. Wet the flap of the whole envelope and stick it to the flap on the fake insert. The envelope now appears to be an ordinary one. Put into the front compartment of each of these envelopes the six duplicates of ad No. 2. Now seal the envelopes in the regular manner. You now have six envelopes, each with two compartments, and with six duplicate ads in the front section of each, and with six different duplicate ads in the rear section of each envelope.

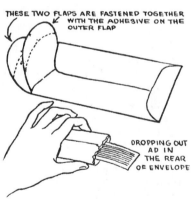

THESE TWO FLAPS ARE FASTENED TOGETHER WITH THE ADHESIVE ON THE OUTER FLAP

DROPPING OUT AD IN THE REAR OF ENVELOPE

Put this packet of six prepared envelopes in your left side coat pocket where you can reach it quickly. Have your seventh newspaper handy, together with a pair of scissors and six more envelopes.

Routine: When ready, open the newspaper and take out the ad page. Cut out a column of fifteen or twenty ads and snip them apart into a saucer or cup. Pass the saucer around and have six people select ads and seal them in the unprepared envelopes you hand them. Take the envelopes back with your right hand, and the moment the lights go out drop them into your right coat pocket. Simultaneously bring the prepared packet of envelopes out of your left coat pocket with your left hand. Give this prepared packet to someone to mix and to make a selection of one envelope. You walk over to the light switch and put on the lights yourself. Everything looks fair because the spectator has his own envelope and is just laying the rest on the table. You step up to him, and disclose the contents of the first ad in the back compartment of the envelope. Take the envelope from him, tear off the flap end, pinch the envelope open, shake it and the ad from the rear compartment falls out. If the envelope has been made correctly, you can flip the center section—dividing the envelope—to either side as you pinch the envelope open. In this case, you manage to open the rear compartment only thus letting out the ad in the rear. In doing this, the center section is squeezed flush up against the front of the envelope thus securing the other ad. No matter how much you shake the open envelope, this second ad cannot become dislodged.

Now have someone else take the remaining five envelopes and make a choice of one of them. Stand before him and disclose the contents of the other ad, the one in the front compartment. Open the envelope, but this time squeeze the center section against the back of the envelope which allows only the ad in the front compartment to fall out. Have the ad verified and checked with your revelation. Pick up the remaining four envelopes and drop them into your right coat pocket, but to the inside of those already there. Later you can take out four of the unprepared envelopes and drop them on a nearby table—just in case someone wants to look them over.

SYMMYST

ORVILLE MEYER

This is a magazine test wherein the performer reveals words selected by two different people. The repetition raises the effect above its first climax, for interest has been whetted and the second revelation is more confusing than the first.

Effect: The performer exhibits three different magazines and has one selected by one spectator and a second one selected by another person. The performer then announces that he wishes to have a page selected for the test he is about to attempt and, so that there will be no question but that the page is chosen fairly, he takes a small pad down into the audience and has several people whisper a series of numbers in his ear. These numbers are written on the pad, which is then handed to one of the assistants holding a magazine. This person totals the column of figures and opens his magazine at that page. He then, of his own accord, selects a word on that particular page. The performer picks up a slate and starts to write down a series of letters, finally combines them into a single word which surprisingly enough turns out to be the chosen word.

Now the other assistant opens his magazine to a page suggested by anyone in the audience, and counts down to a word at a number suggested by someone else. He concentrates on this word and the performer successfully reveals it.

Preparation: The magazines are prepared, but once they are fixed up they are good for quite a few performances. Use Collier's or Liberty Magazines, the latter being more practical because of its smaller size. Buy two copies of the same issue. Now buy one copy each of two different issues. From one of the latter remove the cover, which comes off easily because it it is only stapled on. Exchange this cover with the cover on one of the duplicate issues. Throw away the odd copy and the cover. You will now have three magazines, all with decidedly different covers, but two of which are alike in contents.

You will also need a small note pad and pencil, and a slate and a piece of chalk.

Routine: The three magazines are brought forward and a spectator is asked to select two of them. Usually he will take two that are different, which is exactly as it should be. If he takes the two like magazines, then immediately hand the one left to another spectator and ask the first man to hand back either one of his two. In this way you will always end up with two people holding different magazines, and with you holding the duplicate of one of them.

For the moment you lay your magazine aside, but close at hand, and concentrate upon the person holding the odd magazine. From your pocket take a small pad and pencil. Say that you desire everything left to chance. Pass to four or five people, each of whom whispers a single figure in your ear, and in every case you write down the figure before that person's eyes. Then you hand the pad and pencil to the man with the magazine. He totals the column and opens the book at that page. It's forced quite simply and cleanly. Let's say you previously picked page 42, one having reading matter. You put down the figures as given, but silently add them to yourself. When the total hits 33 (9 less than 42) or more, start back towards the man and his magazine. You know the exact figure needed to make your desired total. You stand before the spectator. Say, "Here's a column of figures taken at random. You total them, and no matter what the result is, open the magazine at that page." As you talk you openly draw a line under the column, but a bit below the last figure, and as you indicate that he is to add and total what's there, merely add in that needed figure.

He takes the pad and you return to the front and pick up a slate and chalk. He totals and gets the page. Now ask him to think of a figure himself; 1 to 9. He is told to count along the first line of reading matter on the page, noting the word at that number. You pretend to write letters of the alphabet on the slate, where, quite visible, is a lead pencil list of the nine words of the first line on that page. You have judged his counting across his page. Start from where you think he is and pump. "It's a long word." "It's a word you can picture. A name of something." "The word you have in mind denotes action. It's something a person does." "It's a very simple word that's common." Such pumping does not hurt a bit. You are reading a mind. You get a first letter. If wrong tell him to think of the next letter, you naming the second letter of another word. It will never take as long as it reads in print. Once you are sure write it on the slate and have him call it out. Then show the slate.

The foregoing is far from original but it has points which fit in this test and build for the second. Regardless of how hard it is, say, "You're a difficult subject. It's hard to get impressions. You should make a good poker player." And turn to the other person. Put the slate aside. Point to someone and ask for a number not over 50. Then point to someone else and ask for a number from 1 to 9.

Have the second man stand. Be serious. Tell him to open his magazine at the page called. At the same time pick up your magazine saying, "Hold it up so no one but yourself can see the page." Illustrate, and open your magazine to the correct spot. Keep your finger there. He does his part. Then tell him to count along the line to the second number decided upon. Again illustrate, stressing that no one must get a glimpse. Only a glance gets you the word in your duplicate magazine. Lay it aside. Now turn on your best showmanship and build this second revelation to a smashing climax!

BEHIND THAT DOOR!
CLAYTON RAWSON

Effect: You begin this effect by having the medium leave the room. Have her hide in an adjoining room with the door closed, and play this fact up. As soon as she has left, bring out a deck of cards, shuffle them, and then have a spectator cut the cards and replace the cut. Then with the deck face down before him, a spectator cuts off any number of cards up to half the deck. Without looking at it, he places the bottom card of his cut-off portion in his pocket, keeping the rest of the packet himself. The performer, with the half deck remaining, goes to spectator number two who also cuts off a portion. This person, however, looks at the bottom card of his heap and then shuffles it into the packet he holds, along with those the performer has left.

Leaving him to his shuffling, the performer has a word chosen in a dictionary, a spectator riffling through and stopping anywhere at all. Next someone names a color. Then any spectator takes the shuffled half deck of cards to the medium and passes it to her through the slightly opened door.

Within a short while the medium comes back. She carries the card that was shuffled into the deck and on its face is written the name of the chosen color, the word in the dictionary, and the name of the card the spectator has in his pocket which, as yet, no one has looked at!

Routine: Card Code: A Si Stebbin's set-up takes care of the cards. Your first shuffle is false, naturally. After the first spectator has cut off some cards and put the bottom one in his pocket, you nick the top card of the remaining half deck along the side edge with your finger nail.

When the second spectator cuts to a card, you repeat the process by nicking the next card down, except that this time you nick it on the end.

When the medium gets the cards, she looks for the card with the nick in the end, adds three and takes the next suit which gives her the name of the chosen card. She looks through the deck and removes this card. Then she locates the card with the side nick, adds three, takes the next suit and thus knows the name of the card reposing in the spectator's pocket. She writes the name of this card on the card she has removed from the deck.

Color Code: The color is cued according to a simple code. Think of Governor Bryan but in abbreviated form, like this: GOV. BRY. Each letter in these abbreviated initials stands for a different color, i.e., G means Green, O means Orange, etc. Further, if a man brings the deck to the medium, the color is in the GOV group; if a woman, in the BRY group.

IF A MAN BRINGS DECK	IF A WOMAN BRINGS DECK
Color is:	Color is:
G ....Green	B ....Blue
O ....Orange	R ....Red
V ....Violet	Y ....Yellow

To identify the color, a fountain pen is used. Have the person bringing the deck to medium take your pen with him. If the pen is still capped, that indicates the first color on the list; if the cap is on the opposite end from the point, it indicates the second color; if the pen arrives without a cap, it indicates the third color. (Example: A man brings the cards and a capless pen. The color is violet.) The medium writes the correct color on the card.

Word Force: The word, of course, is forced. The medium knows it beforehand and writes it on the card before returning. Use Holden's "DeLuxe Dictionary Trick" or Baker's version here, and you're all set. If you do not have either of these, then the following force is excellent:

Pass out two or three pocket dictionaries. Then bring out a match box, open it and dump four small dice on the table. A spectator picks them up, examines them and drops them into the half opened match box which you are holding. Explain, as you close the box and shake it, that the first two dice, reading from left to right, will designate the page number and the last two, the word on that page. Push the drawer of the box out and the spectators, who have the dictionaries, take a look. They open their dictionaries and find the "forced" word, because the dice always land the right way up. This is due to the fact that the four dice they see have been glued in place at the end of the drawer which you open. The original four dice, which they heard rattle, are at the other end of the drawer. Drop the box into your pocket and go on with the trick, but later take out an unprepared box with four loose dice and leave it on the table. Somebody will be sure to look at it!

The small dictionaries have two columns of words per page. I've found it best to avoid forcing a column. As the spectators are noting the dice merely tell them to count down in the first column and, if the number is too large, to continue the count in the second column. You always keep that number low to avoid mistakes in counting, but they don't know that, and your statement sounds as if you don't know what the dice show.

An alternate method of forcing the page and number is to use the torn newspaper corners as explained in "The Twentieth Century Newspaper Test" on page 68. Furthermore, you can eliminate the use of the thumb-tip by having several torn corners, all bearing the same page number, in your pocket to start, the ones you tear from the newspaper in sight of everyone going into your change pocket. When a person reaches down into your pocket for one of the corners, he naturally gets one of the duplicates. Since there are two numbers on the corner of each piece, you have them multiplied to get the page, and added to get the word.

THE 20th CENTURY NEWSPAPER TEST
Stuart Robson

This is the best and cleanest way of presenting a newspaper test yet conceived. The method for securing the numbers, which in turn are used to indicate a column and ad, is most disarming and highly original. In book tests and effects of this nature I have always objected to the introduction of outside and otherwise foreign objects such as cards, dice, counters, numbered papers and whatnot that immediately gave the effect an air of preparedness and trickery.

In the case at hand there is nothing ever seen by the audience except the newspaper, and it becomes a means unto itself. That is what gives the entire stunt a veritable air of nonchalance and fairness.

The other important point is the ease with which it may be done and the fact that the performer has little to get ready. He can purchase a paper on the way to his engagement and use it with but two minutes of perusal. Or, if desired to perform the feat impromptu, he may use a paper at hand with no more than two minutes of preparation. Professionals will appreciate this point.

Effect: A copy of the daily newspaper is shown, and the performer states that he will try a feat of telepathy with the classified advertising section. The paper is opened and one page of the classified ads is torn out and given to a member of the audience to hold.

Now the performer says he will have one of the ads selected in an open and obviously fair manner. So saying, he holds the newspaper in front of him and, with one motion, tears off the upper right corner of the entire paper. This includes all the pages and also all the numbered corners of the paper to which he calls attention.

Laying the paper aside, the packet of corners is tossed into a borrowed hat or bowl and mixed well by anyone. The performer asks this person to reach in without looking, to select just one of the corners, crumple it up small and drop it on his (performer's) hand. The performer in turn hands it directly to the person holding the torn-out page, and then walks to a far corner of the room. This person is told to look at the selected corner. On both sides of this corner will be a number. He is to select either number and use that to count across the page to a column. Then he is to use the other number and count down that column to an individual ad. He now concentrates upon the wording and subject matter of this ad, and calls out when he is ready. The performer returns and effectively reveals what the ad is all about even if not able to give the wording in its exact form.

Preparation: The effect always wins applause because of its directness. Previously the performer has torn out a corner, it being, for instance, the corner bearing the page numbers 5 and 6. Turning to the page that he will remove later and which contains nothing but classified ads, he reads the sixth ad in column five and the fifth ad in column six. The main thing is merely to know what it is about and not bother to learn it word for word.

In his pocket he carries the well known and respected thumb tip. Into this he puts this stolen corner after crumpling it up into a pellet.

Routine: Now the effect proceeds as described. The corner selected is crumpled up small by the spectator and placed on the performer's outstretched left palm. While this is being done, the performer secures the thumb tip on his right thumb. In going to the person holding the page of the newspaper, the right thumb is placed over the pellet on the left palm, the left fingers close and the right thumb comes out with the stolen pellet from inside the tip. This is handed to the spectator while the left hand pockets the tip and the other pellet as the performer walks away. He watches the spectator from a distance while the counting is done and therefore knows which of the two ads has been selected. Newspapers have columns on both sides of the page and both sides line up with each other. It only remains for you to give as impressive a description of the ad as you are capable of delivering. Properly presented this test is most convincing.

THE JAIPUR JINNEE

EDDIE CLEVER

Natural looking methods for the selection of a book page and word are seldom seen. With the following method, the principle of a recent illusion, and an older die and frame trick, has been brought into play, and provides a perfect way of getting to the proper page.

Effect: The mentalist makes either a prediction on a slate, or cleans two slates for a spirit message. The slate or slates are laid aside, and a book or dictionary shown. A length of ribbon is picked up and handed to a spectator. The performer holds the book and the spectator holds an end of the ribbon in each hand. He brings it over the pages of the book which the performer is holding by the ends, and is told to pull the ribbon down between the pages somewhere near the center. The slate is picked up and the book is handed to someone. This person opens the book at the ribbon, adds the page numbers together on the left hand side, and counts down to that word. *It is the word prophecied by the mentalist; or written by the spirits on the inside of one of the two slates!*

Preparation: There is a bit of preparation and practice necessary for this feat, but those who try it will have a stunt that can be done anywhere with a moment's study of any book.

Get a spool of spring steel piano wire No. 3 at any large music store for ten cents. Cut off a piece of wire several inches longer than the book. At one end of the wire twist a loop, and through it stick the other end of the wire. This will make a noose which can be pulled fairly tight. On the other end of the wire fasten a small ring of thin stiff wire of such a size as to fit over the end of your finger. Paint the wire and loop either flesh color or black. You will also require a piece of ribbon about two or three inches longer than the book, and about half an inch wide.

Lay the wire between two pages of the book, off center towards the back. The running loop is out at one end, and the ring at the lower end. The wire should be long enough, so that when you have a loop about three-quarters of an inch in diameter at the top, the ring at the other end is against the pages at the bottom of the book.

Note the page number figures on the left hand page, add them together and count down to the word on the page represented by the total of the page number. Either write this word on a slate and cover it with a flap, or make a straight prediction.

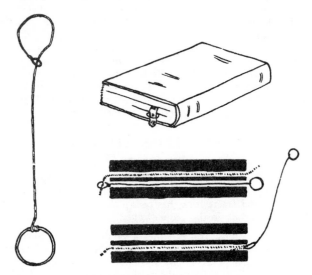

Routine: If working a prediction, pick up the slate, write the name of the forced word and lay the slate on the table or chair, writing side down. If working this as a spirit test, show the two slates to be blank, place them together so that the flap will fall onto the lower slate and lay them on the table. Thus, by picking up the top slate later, you can show the word written by the spirits.

Bring forward the book, holding it with your right hand at the outer edge (edge nearest audience: loop end) and riffling the pages as you do so. Riffle through before a spectator, stopping however before coming to the pages with the wire between them. Have the ribbon in your left coat pocket. Hand it to someone. Hold the book between your hands, each hand covering one end of the wire. Ask the person with the ribbon to insert it anywhere between the pages. As he does so, pull the book slightly towards you so that the ribbon goes in ahead of the wire.

Now step back and explain what has been done. As you do so, stand with your left side somewhat towards the audience and with both hands holding the book. The end of the book from which the loop projects is away from the audience, and your fingers slip the end of the ribbon through the loop! When you say, "And on the slates on my table," you swing sharply to the left (table should be on your left) and, at the same time, your left hand with the book moves away from your right. The right hand with the loop remains stationary. This action pulls the ribbon around and in between the pages where the wire lies. The sharp pull also drags the ribbon through and out the other end, and the wire slips off the ribbon! As you swing left and the wire comes loose, pick up the slates with your right hand and drop the wire on the table. Bring the slates forward, and hand the book to someone. And that's all there is to it!

Sometimes the pull does not bring the end of the ribbon free at the top of the book. It remains between the pages. If this happens, pull it out with a flip of the finger as you look for someone to take the book. Be sure the table is close by so that it requires only a turn of your body to pick up the slates. And remember that the right hand remains still, only the left hand moving away.

This has been tested. The ribbon is never seen in its flight, the swing of the body and hands concealing everything. It is strictly a method which requires practice, rhythm and confidence. No one will suspect that the ribbon in the book is changed to an entirely different spot! And when the spectator takes it to look up the word, the book and the ribbon are unprepared!

40,000 WORDS
SID LORRAINE

Effect: The performer introduces a pocket dictionary. The spectator looks through it, has a free choice of any one of the thousands of words, then writes his selection on a card. This card is inserted momentarily in the dictionary. After a moment of concentration, the spectator removes the card

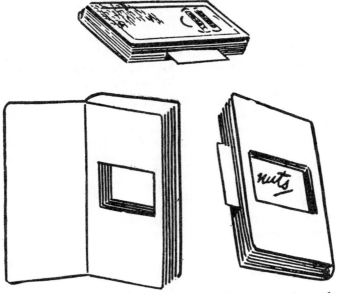

and places it in his pocket. He then hands the dictionary to the performer who opens it and immediately announces the chosen word and reads its definition.

Preparation: The working is simple, and there is ample misdirection to cover the few necessary moves. The secret lies in the use of a second dictionary, unknown to the audience. The type used by me is about 3 inches by 6 inches, with the cover title "Webster Dictionary—40,000 words." The duplicate is mutilated by cutting out a section from every inside page *and* the back cover—in other words, your dictionary has a complete cover but the balance of the book has a window through its middle. The illustration will make it clear.

Several visiting cards are also required. They should be of such a size that when one is inserted in the sides of the book, as per the illustration, about one-quarter of an inch protrudes. The size of the window in the book really is governed by the card's size. The idea, of course, is that when a card is inserted, a glance through the window will reveal whatever is written on the card. Have a pencil at hand, and of course, the legitimate dictionary.

Here's the set-up: In the right coat pocket is the gimicked dictionary— in your left coat pocket have the cards. I don't care where you keep the pencil. The presentation should be casual throughout.

Routine: Start by saying that the average person, when asked on the spur of the moment to think of a word, finds it difficult to think of a real hard one. He may suggest "house" or "rabbit," but offhand will never think of "muscovado" or anything like "ethnographic." So that your audience may have an opportunity of choosing a really difficult word, one that even may be a headache for you, you will use one of Webster's pocket dictionaries. Explain that the spectator who is to assist is to take the dictionary, run through it till he finds a word that suits him, and then read its definition so as to impress the word firmly on his mind. Next he is to write it upon a card, which you hand him.

Ask him to turn the card with the writing down, and at the same time you retrieve the dictionary. Don't mention this action—don't mention the dictionary at all—keep talking about the word he has written. During the talk casually place the dictionary in your coat pocket and instantly come out with the gimmicked one. You are looking at and talking to the spectator. If anyone notices your hand and the book he should get the impression that you tried to insert the book into your pocket, and, finding it difficult, have placed it aside—which you do.

Still talking to the spectator you walk away from where you have placed the gimmicked book, and try to get an impression of the chosen word. You fail, after a couple of attempts. Picking up the book you ask the spectator to insert the card, writing side down, somewhere between the pages. Be careful not to expose the back of the book during this time.

Turn the book on its edge and quickly steal a glance at the written word, which you can read easily through the book's window. As you turn the dictionary around, still apparently looking at the edge, you say, "I see you've inserted the card at about where the letter R starts (or mention whatever other letter the word may begin with). Immediately return the card to the spectator and say, "That's a bit of unconscious help you've given me— I know the word begins with that letter, and as there are only 8,000 words beginning with R it narrows my field considerably."

At this point you open the dictionary, still being careful not to flash the back or cut pages, and look up the word you now know. If it isn't there, due to the cut-out pages, you know it so can name it just the same. If it should be there, then the best presentation is to give the name and read the definition. At the conclusion put dictionary in your pocket, or switch back and leave it around.

As you pocket the dictionary, or to cover the exchange, you can say, "I'm glad you picked that word, sir. Last evening a fellow picked the word "nothing" and when I asked him to concentrate he had "nothing" on his mind. It made it extremely difficult for me."

ANOTHER DICTIONARY EFFECT
OTIC MANNING

I have found this effect to be a perfect follow-up to Sid Lorraine's "40,000 Words" just described. No extra book is needed, and the immediate repetition of the word test with someone else will upset no little those who try to check up on your actions.

Effect: A ten-cent store pocket dictionary is given a person for a free selection of a single word from any place within its covers. The performer takes back the book and gives the spectator a slip of paper, 2 inches by 2 inches in size. The word is written down, for, as the performer says, "I don't want you to think of one of the remaining 39,999 words in there." The spectator then is to fold the paper once each way, making it one-quarter of its original size.

In the meantime you have put the dictionary into your upper left vest pocket out of the way, and your hands are empty. Next appear to concentrate and pace around a bit. Mention the letter "e". "It's in the word?" The chance is good. Try another, asking the person to visualize the word, and, if possible, its meaning. If it hits try another. The moment you fail, take out the dictionary and glance through it, telling the subject to remember exactly what he did. Suddenly you stop and read a definition. It fits his word. You reveal the word.

Preparation: The secret of this seemingly impossible feat lies in your breast pocket. For it is in this pocket during the effect that you tuck the spectators folded paper. The drawing shows that about one inch below the top edge of the pocket is a slit which has been cut through the coat, and

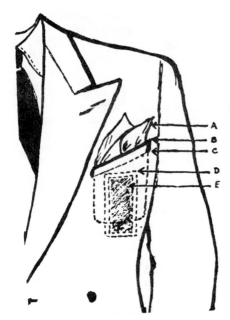

the edges sewn with a button-hole stitch. Thus any paper pushed down into the pocket goes through the slit and also into the dictionary which is in your vest pocket. The dictionary protrudes just enough from the upper left vest pocket to receive the paper perfectly.

The details of the pocket are shown in the drawing, and are as follows:

A—Pocket handkerchief in pocket proper, and behind which, also in pocket proper, is a dummy folded slip of paper.

B—Top edge of breast pocket on coat.

C—Slit through inside of coat one inch below top edge of pocket. Finish edges with buttonhole stitching.

D—Outline of vest pocket, upper left side.

E—Dictionary in vest pocket ready to receive slip through slit. (This isn't exactly shown as the book generally will protrude above the pocket and offer more ease in the placing of the paper.)

Routine: Proceed with the trick as already described and have the the spectator write a word on the paper square and fold it. Take back the dictionary and place it in your upper left vest pocket. Now take the folded paper, glance around a bit, as though at a loss where to put it, and then push it down into your breast pocket behind the handkerchief. The paper, of course, goes right through the slit in your pocket and into the dictionary as already described.

When you remove the book for further aid, it is only necessary to open at the spot where the paper is and you'll be surprised to find how simple it is to open the folds with your thumbs. Only a glance is needed and you continue to run through the book until you find that word. Just leave the paper where it was.

With the book in your hand, after the revelation, take out a dummy slip from your breast pocket and apparently verify the word. Fold the dummy and put it into the dictionary which you place in your pocket. In case the slip is requested you need only open the book and give back the original slip.

It may be well merely to read from the book without mentioning the word, and say, "Does the definition fit what you are thinking about?" Then reach into your pocket, open the dummy slip, and apparently read the word.

As you put it in the book and replace it in your pocket, say, "Well, that's the word to which I was attracted by your concentration."

This effect is perfectly practical for performance by itself by those who don't care to use the faked extra book of Lorraine's version. However, it is six of one and a half-dozen of the other, considering the faked pocket. That's why a combination of the two, with his method as the lead-off, makes for what is most desired in mental magic: i.e., the repetition of an effect using an entirely different means of accomplishment. Unlike visual magic, mental magic almost always can stand being done over again when the effect use only one person in the audience.

In the first effect a plain card is used for the writing. In the second method a piece of paper is used. Why? Probably because the performer doesn't have another card, so uses the next best thing, a slip of paper folded.

DAVID P. ABBOTT'S BOOK TEST

This effect was a favorite with David P. Abbott, and in his hands was a veritable miracle. He used eight books and allowed anyone a free choice of any book. Next he had a card selected, the numerical value of which was to indicate the line on any page of the book the person cared to open. Once the line was found and acknowledged, the performer gave the correct reading of it even though he was standing some distance away. Like other Abbott effects, it was built on simplicity and created a tremendous impression.

The following description is Mr. Abbott's own just as he wrote it in a letter to Ted Annemann on January 10, 1927:

"You will need a force book of a certain type. The best I have run across—with short lines and very few part lines at paragraph ends, and with every page full of printing with no pictures—is 'Hidden Years at Nazareth' by G. Campbell Morgan, published by Fleming H. Revell Co., N. Y., price 35 cents. It has 48 pages and light board backs. Or get some kid's story book, the kind with large type and few pages.

"On strips of adding machine paper write, very small, the number of each page followed by the line which is to be forced later. You can get about ten or twelve of these to a strip, which you paste on the face side of some extra cards to match your deck. Use two decks, one ordinary, the other prepared as described later.

"Now you have eight books, seven of any nature and your force book. Lay them in two rows of four each, with the force book third from the left in the row nearest you. You have four small cards with the numbers 1 and 2 printed on them and these you put under the top covers of the end books as illustrated:

$$(2) \quad * \quad * \quad * \quad (1)$$
$$(1) \quad * \quad * \quad x \quad * \quad (2)$$

"When ready for the book selection, ask someone to choose row 1 or row 2, saying that the rows are numbered. If he says "1," open the covers of the books on the left end of the rows to show which row he has selected. If he says, 'Row 2,' open the covers of the books on the right end. Lay the other row aside. Now he hands you two of the books left. If he does not give you the force book, tell him to pick up one of those left. Ask him to keep it or lay it aside, as the case may be. If he gives you the force book in the first two, ask him to take one back. He uses the book he takes or puts it with the others, and the one left with you is used.

"Now you pick up the deck of cards and slowly overhand shuffle it with the faces of the cards towards the spectator. The prepared cards, bearing the lists, are at the back of the deck, and these are held back with seven or eight others and are dropped as a bunch on the back of the pack as you finish the shuffle. As you make this shuffle, you explain several times that you want the spectator to have an absolutely free selection of a card. That you are going to riffle the cards very slowly and he is to insert his finger in the deck anywhere and take any card he pleases.

"Hold the deck up vertically and pass the cards from left to right hand, showing that they have been well mixed. Then square up the deck and illustrate the riffle, doing it slowly. When the spectator understands what he is to do, riffle the deck once more and have him insert his finger in the end of the deck. Stop riffling at this point and ask him if he would care to change his mind, or if he is satisfied with the card he has his finger on. If he wants to change his mind riffle once more and finally have him withdraw a card. All this convinces the audience that your subject has had a free choice in the fairest way possible.

"The card he gets, however, is a force card because you are using one of Donald Holmes' forcing decks. This consists of a deck made up of triplets. Each triplet consists of two cards hinged together at one end, the face card of the pair being shorter than the rear card, and in between is a single loose short card. There are seventeen of these triplets. The loose card, in between, are all duplicates, and it is one of these duplicates which you force in the manner outlined above. My force card is a Five Spot. Riffling such a deck, face down, allows the cards to slip by your finger in threes, and the spectator's finger can only go in and pull out one of the force cards. Such a deck may be freely fanned, faces out, and also overhand shuffled, face out, to show all the cards different.

"When the card is selected you step over to a far corner of the room and ask spectator to name the page number of the first page in the book where the reading starts, as well as the number on the last page of the book he has selected. Then he is asked to decide upon any number between the first and last page numbers and call it out for all to hear. During all this instruction, you have been standing in the corner with your back turned to the audience. As soon as he names a page, fan the deck of cards which you still hold and locate the list card for the page he has just named. Tell him to open to the page he has selected and, using the card he holds as a bookmark, to count down to the line on that page that corresponds to the value of his card. When he has located the line, he is to read it to himself. Long before he has done all this, you have discovered the line for yourself on the slip card.

"Put the hand holding the force deck in your pocket and, as you turn to face the audience, switch the force deck for the ordinary deck. Bring this latter deck out of your pocket and absentmindedly lay it on a nearby table for the future inspection as anyone who cares to examine it. Now slowly reveal certain words in the selected line, in a mixed up order, and finally give the whole line complete with as much showmanship as you are able to muster."

thought foretold

THE STORY OF THE POCKET INDEX

POCKET PROPHECIES

ANNEMANN

"Before you begin concentrating," says the performer, "I'll write something for you, something that may occur in the near future, an event, or happening over which I have no possible control."

Such is the general opening remark to the type of trick which has been ever popular with mystery workers and audiences. The prophecy of occurrence—whether it is a number to be thought of, a word to be pictured, or a playing card to be chosen.

In studying prognostication effects, two basic principles have been found to be useful. First, carbon paper for impressions via pencilled reference notes, or its counterpart, the thumb nail or thumb tip stylus secretly used for the same purpose, and the graphite thumb nail writer for writing secret notations upon the unsealed surface of a card, billet, etc. Haden's Swami Holdout, either in the stylus or pencil lead style, will be found excellent for introducing the nail writer for use without fumbling. Haden's DeLuxe Swami nail writer, which writes with a bolder stroke is a more recent improvement. These may be obtained from any of the leading magic dealers.

The second principle, and the one with which this chapter will deal, is the Pocket Index File. Such Indexes, when loaded and placed in your trouser pockets, provide a quickly accessible set of indexed billets covering all possible selections for the effect being presented. All that is necessary is to finger palm the proper billet and substitute it for the dummy prophecy which you apparently write before the event or the selection has taken place. To do this, the dummy is dropped into a hat or a bowl and then palmed out. Later the correct paper, obtained from one of the indexes, is introduced into the container as the latter is picked up and handed to a spectator. Magicians have differed as to the construction of indexes, and most have been impractical. For proof, the reader has only to wonder why he hasn't used the principle, and whether or not he knows someone who did use it. From here on, I'll attempt to make very clear, and very attractive, what I've done with pocket indexes, and why.

Over 15 years ago Al Baker conceived the idea of substituting a set of 52 paper billets, each bearing the name of a different card, for a full deck of playing cards in the then popular pocket indexes. Herbert Brooks was in the United States featuring the effect of producing any card called for from his pocket, after shuffling a deck, cutting it in two halves and placing a half in each trouser pocket. The idea was a happy one, but no one ever seemed to make anything of it. The card indexes were themselves too big for paper billets, and while the initial use of indexes did not hide the fact that one was getting something from his pocket, the use of such gadgets for secretly obtaining paper billets entailed too much fumbling for the misdirection possible in a mental effect. That's my answer as to why "pocket prophecy" tricks have not been among the popularly used subterfuges.

A year or so later, I received a letter from the late Bob Gysel suggesting the idea of a special billet index. I immediately made up a set of indexes to hold and deliver quickly 52 separate paper billets. I used what was handy and followed, as closely as I knew, the principle of the Brook's indexes. This original set of indexes served me well, for it was almost six years later in New York that I finally had to make a new set. There were but two minor changes that I made after using the originals constantly, and I might say here that frankly I can't remember an engagement when I haven't used an index of some sort.

Thus, after 14 years of constant use, I honestly think that what I have to say here about pocket indexes is the last word to date. In that time I would say that the two sets that I made have seen use in over 700 shows. Up until February, 1940, only three people have looked at my indexes. I thought too much of them. And those three people were members of my immediate family, for even Mr. Baker never saw them. Of late, there has been a very definite increase of interest in indexes and pocket "pick-outs." So I'll explain herewith how to prepare the indexes that have served me so well, and also a few of the very best effects I could evolve during recent years.

CONSTRUCTION OF THE ANNEMANN BILLET INDEX

Let's take up the mechanics of the indexes first. With that out of the way, effects and possibilities can be covered later.

You will need a pack of cards of regulation size, not bridge size. They do not have to be new, but on the other hand they should not be too old either. It is preferable to use cards of good linen quality, too, rather than the cheap paper type, for once made up you will want your indexes to last for as long a time as possible.

Other tools and accessories are a ticket punch, scissors, ruler, three paper fasteners of the type about three-quarters of an inch long with shanks that spread out, and a box of paper fasteners of the V-type that fold over the end of papers and then are pinched together. A paste pot and a hammer complete the workshop tools.

The indexes are the size of a playing card and we'll take up the making of one. Both are exactly alike.

First cut up enough cards to make 13 pieces each measuring ¾ inch by 2½ inches. One card will make four such pieces, the playing cards in a regular size pack being 3½ inches by 2½ inches. At ⅜ of an inch from one of the long sides, and equally spaced, punch three holes for insertion of the shank clips later on. These ¾ of an inch strips are to be used as "in betweens" for holding papers later, and are important.

Now there are 14 index parts to cut, each one different from the other. Keep cards in front of you during this description, check it all with the illustration, and we'll call the nearest (to you) end of the cards the bottom—the far end, the top.

Take the first card and cut it cleanly across just two inches up from the bottom.

Take the second card—cut it across from left to right—two inches from the bottom, but leave a tab on its right edge—just three-quarters of an inch long and one-quarter of an inch high.

Take the third card, cut it across from left to right—two inches from the bottom, but leave a tab on its right edge three-quarters of an inch long. This tab is twice as high as the first—one-half inch.

The fourth card—its tab is the same width, but it is one-quarter of an inch higher than the tab on the third card.

The fifth card—its tab is one-quarter inch higher than that on the fourth.

The sixth card—its tab is one-quarter inch higher than that on the fifth.

The seventh card—its tab is the length of the card.

Please keep in mind when looking at the illustration that the numbers shown there are indicators of playing card values and that we are one ahead of those in detailing the cutting of the index cards.

The eighth card (seven on the sketch) has its three-quarter-inch long and one-quarter-inch high tab in the center.

Beginning with the ninth card (eight on the sketch) the tabs are found on the left side of each card. Each is one-quarter inch higher than the last, and and this continues through the 13th (Q on sketch) card. The last, or 14th (K on sketch) card is left intact and it acts as a back-

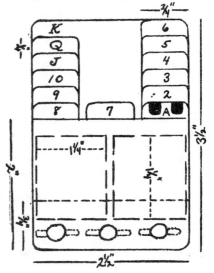

ing to protect the rest of the index cards and tabs.

Next, at the bottom of these 14 cards, and at the same positions as was done with the small "in between" strips, punch three holes.

Then comes the assembly. Put the three shank clips through the first square cut (no tab) card and lay it on the table so the shanks are sticking upward. Onto these three shanks you put the remaining 26 punched pieces. First—a narrow strip—then the second card (Ace tab)—next a narrow strip—then the third (2 tab) card—a narrow strip—fourth (3 tab) card—and so on until finally the whole (K) card completes the pile.

The shanks are now bent apart and pounded flat with the hammer. You can hurt only the table and your thumb so don't be afraid to make it all very secure.

The last operation is to use the V shape clips on the edges of the tabs as shown on the Ace tab in the sketch. Each tab gets two. These were a later improvement to protect the edges and make them much easier to count in the pocket.

Now for the loading. Upon 52 pieces of paper, 2½ inches by 2½ inches square, are written the names of the cards in a deck. Keep the suits separate. Fold the paper slips once each way. Each index is made up to contain all black or all red. Two of these slips, each representing an Ace, go into the first section of the index *in front* of the Ace tabbed card, and *are pushed in in between that card and the narrow binder strip at the bottom.* Without that strip the indexes are not worth a cent as holders. Keep all the Hearts on one side and all of the Diamonds on the other. Then fix the other index in the same manner using the black cards. Don't mind if the newly filled index flares out like a stuffed fan. It takes a week or so pressed tightly before they close down as much as they will.

Two such indexes placed together with tab sides inward and in a reversed position to each other are just about the thickness of a pack of cards. Keep them in a heavy telescopic type of card case. That holds them flat and protects them.

In your trousers pockets, the tab sides are *towards* the body, and the thumbs do the finding. Any paper can be found with a maximum of *three* counts—from top down, or bottom up in either tab row. The thumb is pushed into the opening and it forces out whichever paper is wanted.

And that's the most practical paper holder I've yet to see or try out. It lays flat in the pocket and holds the largest size paper slip of any. Blocks of wood with holes in them may be all right for up to 10 papers, but not more than that, and they are not any too good then. The index for Zingone's Dual Prophecy trick was worthy of ten years in the bastile. The papers were tiny and you had to be an accomplished piano accordionist to find your place. Besides you always were knocking others out of place.

THE ORIGINAL EFFECT

The indexes are filled with papers bearing names of cards. The performer asks a spectator to shuffle an ordinary deck, and while this is taking place the performer writes something on a slip of paper, folds it, and drops it into a hat, or cup. However, he finger-palms the slip, on which he has written "Joker." The spectator is asked to think of a card, then to remove it from the deck and place it on the table, face up. A few seconds are taken up with queries as to whether the spectator was "made" to take any particular card. The proper paper has meanwhile been secured, and that hand picks up the hat or cup with fingers inside (dropping the paper) and offers it to someone. This person removes, opens, and reads the prophecy.

This effect also can be worked as pure mindreading by having the person think of the card before the performer writes.

LADY AND GENTLEMAN

This was my own combination of the indexes with the "Two Souls" trick of Al Baker's. It eliminated the necessity of counting. The indexes are loaded with papers reading, "The gentleman will get the—(name of card) —." A deck is stacked with your favorite system of arrangement. Approach a lady, false shuffling the cards. Put them on her hand and ask her to keep her mind a blank while you write something for her. Scribble anything on a piece of paper, fold, and pretend to put it in a hat or bowl. Finger-palm it out.

Now tell her to give the deck a cut. Then she is to look at the top card and push it anywhere into the deck and square them up. Take the deck from her and hand it to a nearby gentleman. He is to shuffle the cards while you write something for him. However, you have glimpsed the bottom card and therefore know at what card the lady has looked. On another piece of paper you now write, "The lady will choose the—(writing the name of the card she did take)—." Fold and openly drop into the hat. Now have the gentleman choose a card in the same manner.

Ask him the name of his card, at the same time reminding him that you have written something for each of them before they acted. When he names his card, turn and ask the lady the name of her card. This gives you the necessary ten-second stall, during which time you secure the paper billet bearing the name of the gentleman's card from the index. Then pick up the hat, drop the paper inside with the other billet and have someone else reach in, pick them out and read them.

A variation here is to let each person keep his card. Then they not only name them but show them as well, and are allowed to keep both cards and paper prophecies as souvenirs.

THE OMEGA CARD PROPHECY

This is really my reason for writing this chapter. I couldn't explain the trick correctly without describing the index, so I figured I might just as well cover as much as possible.

Years ago Walter Gibson thought up a clever trick wherein you handed a deck of cards to a person to be shuffled, or he could use his own deck if he preferred. Following the shuffle, the spectator turned the deck face up and separated the cards, one at a time, into two heaps, one heap consisting of all the red cards, the other of all the black cards. These heaps were then turned face down, and he picked up one heap. He turned up the two top cards of the heap he held, added together the values of both cards, and then counted down to the card resting at that number in the other heap on the table. While this was going on, the performer wrote a prediction and laid it on the table, under a book, vase, etc. When the spectator reached the card he was counting to, he withdrew it and showed it to all. Then the performer's prediction was opened and read and was found to be correct! Remember, this was done impromptu without the performer touching the deck and, as we mentioned at the start, it could be the spectator's own deck.

The secret lay in the fact that the cards were dealt single into face up piles. The performer stood watching and noted the first two cards dealt into either heaps. Quickly totaling the values of both of these cards, the performer then counted the cards falling on the other heap until he spotted the card in that heap which hit the preferred position! During the rest of the dealing, he busied himself writing the name of this card on a slip, which he then folded and laid on the table. After the spectator had finished separating the cards and had turned the two piles face down, he was asked to pick one up. If he picked up the pile whose two top cards you had used for your tally, he was asked to take the two top cards and add their values together. If he picked up the other pile, he was asked to put it in his pocket for the moment so that it couldn't be tampered with. Then he was told to turn the two cards on top of the other pile on the table. Finally he counted down in the proper pile to the number he had and looked at your force card. This, of course, corresponded with your prediction.

Now imagine this improvement due to your use of the indexes. The spectator shuffles his own deck while you write a prophecy (dummy) and drop it in a cup on the table. Of course, you palm it out. Then the dealing is done as explained above. The moment you learn what card is set in the deck, you have plenty of time to secure the correct billet from your indexes. drop this billet into the cup as you pick it up and move it closer to the dealer, or hand it to someone else to hold.

Thus everything is done before the spectator is through dealing. You have apparently written your prophecy before any dealing was done, and another spectator is holding the correct billet before anyone sees the card that is chosen, apparently by chance. No one could ask for anything cleaner than that!

ORVILLE MEYER'S TWIN PREDICTION

Two predictions are written, each on a slip of different color. They are dropped into a hat. Two spectators count down to a number mutually agreed upon and note the cards arrived at. The predictions, both of which were written and dropped into the hat before the pack was handed out, prove to be correct.

The Meyer method excludes indexes and makes use of but ten pieces of paper, each bearing the name of one of the ten Hearts. They are in order and held together with a paper clip so that the Ace side of the packet can be told in the pocket. The ten Heart cards of the deck are arranged from Ace to Ten from back to face of the deck and an indifferent card placed between each. An indifferent card is placed on top also which leaves the ten Heart cards at even numbered positions. The deck has a short card at the bottom, and the performer notes and remembers the indifferent card on top.

After a false shuffle and cut the deck is handed to one of two spectators. Pick up a white slip of paper (the set in the right trouser pocket is white also), look at the man with the deck and write something (anything) on the slip. Fold it and drop it in full view near the hat. Look at the second person and pick up the colored slip. On this you write the name of the indifferent card now on top of the pack. Fold this paper and drop into the hat. Then pick up the white slip and pretend to put that in also, but finger-palm it instead.

The person holding the pack is asked to name aloud any number from 1 to 20. No matter what is called the performer will cause one of the Hearts to be selected. For instance, in the case of 11, the performer would ask the helper to count off 11 cards, one at a time (reversing them), then look at the next card, and place it also on the counted-off pile. Had 12 been named, 12 cards would have been counted off, and then the last or twelfth card looked at and replaced. In either event, a Heart card at one of the even numbers is forced, and by halving the number the performer knows the identity of the card looked at.

The helper now drops the remainder of the pack onto the dealt-off pile and gives the deck a couple of cuts. The performer takes the deck, gives it another cut and brings the short card to the bottom again. Then it is given to the second assistant to count off the same number of cards as the first man did (11), look at the next, etc. The second man always is told to do exactly what the first man was told to do, and this automatically forces the original top card of the pack.

During this last procedure the performer's right hand, holding the palmed slip, has gone to the pocket, dropped it, and removed the clip from the packet of papers so that the Ace side is against the thumb. From here on it is a simple matter to thumb off papers to the proper one, and this is finger-palmed.

With the second card noted, the performer reaches into the hat, pushes the palmed slip to the fingertips, picks up the colored slip already there, brings out the hand with the two slips showing, and hands the correct one to each person. Of course, everything turns out to be perfect, and everything stands examination.

For those who can make a pellet switch by hand (see Billet Switching, page 11) the two original papers (dummy white one and correct colored one) can be left in full view on the table throughout. At the last moment, with the correct slip finger-palmed, make a straight switch for the white one in handing it to the assistant.

We know that numbers 7, 13 or 17 will be named more often than others. In the above effect these would represent the 8th, 14th, or 18th cards, or the 4, 7 or 9 of Hearts. By writing the name of one of these cards on the first slip, if one is using the sleight of hand switch, quite often it will not be necessary to make any switch at all!

THE IMPROVED BUCKLEY METHOD

Mr. Meyer's system of stacking the cards was contained in the Buckley effect of about 20 years ago. However, his handling of the papers is much simpler and as practical as was the block of wood with holes in it. Also, Mr. Meyer dispensed with the idea of having a number on one paper to tell the subsequent location of the selected card, changing this part to make possible the prediction of two cards rather than one.

Now we can take the Buckley idea and use it in conjunction with a full set of 52 billets via our pocket indexes, predicting a card to be selected by one person and also predicting the position it will be in the deck afterwards.

The deck is stacked a la Si Stebbins, or in the "Eight King" fashion. The suits rotate over and over in your favorite order. Now you have to practice a little behind the back subtlety. Give each of your right four fingers the name of a suit, using the order in which your cards are stacked. Now touch each finger in turn with the thumb of the same hand, over and over, saying to yourself only the values of the cards as stacked—A, 4, 7, 10, K, 3, 6, 9, Q, 2, 5, 8, J, A, 4, etc., or 8, K, 3, 10, 2, 7, 9, 5, Q, 4, A, 6, J, 8, K, 3, etc., depending upon which system you use. Whenever you stop, you note which finger your thumb is then touching and that tells you the suit. Thus you are able to run through a stacked deck in your mind as fast as your thumb can count.

False shuffle and cut the deck a couple of times. Note the bottom card as you place the deck before a spectator. That tells you the top card's identity, the place from where he will start counting off. Now write upon the colored slip, "and the card will be found 14th from the top of the shuffled deck." Scribble anything on the white piece of paper. Fold both and drop into the container, finger-palming out the white one.

Now ask the spectator to think of any number from 1 to 52. Then he is to start dealing the cards off, one at a time, onto the table so as to make no error, and when he reaches his card he is to look at it. You are standing with hands behind back during this and, knowing the first card, you easily keep pace with the dealing and when he stops you know his card immediately. He then is told to show it to one or two people nearby, and finally to shuffle it back into the deck.

This provides ample time for you to secure and palm the proper paper slip, drop it into the container as you hand it to someone to hold, and then you pick up the deck. Say, "I want you to be certain I haven't done something of a tricky nature and taken your card away. You must be sure that it remains in the pack, and that no one but you and a couple of friends are aware of its identity." As you talk you fan the deck through, standing beside him, watching the cards go by. As you reach his card you start counting and when you pass the 14th card, including his, hold a break in the pack, and continue on. He says that his card is still there. You cut the deck at the break and give it to someone to hold.

The white paper is read first. It correctly names the card. Then the second paper is read. The climax comes when a spectator counts down to that number and finds the chosen pasteboard. And the helper will always swear he shuffled the deck very thoroughly afterwards and no one even touched it!

ANNEMANN'S BALLOT BOX DIVINATION

This effect is proof of the date when my indexes were in constant use. In the Sphinx for May, 1926, was published a note from me asking priority claim to the effect. No method was given. A miniature revolving ballot box of the standard type (screening around the drum to leave contents visible) contained wooden counters of the Lotto type numbered from 1 to 50. It could be turned by a small crank. It was entirely unprepared. The performer would attempt to forecast a drawing of a number, and would ask a committee which draw (first, second, third, etc.) would be for the highest prize.

On a slip of paper the magician would then write something, seal it in a letter envelope, and stand it somewhere in full view. The drawings would then be made in all fairness, and the prediction would be found to be correct!

Needless to say, the pocket indexes were loaded with paper slips reading, "High prize will be won by number . . . ." Twenty-five different slips would be in each index. As you may have surmised, the action of picking numbers in this case is short and to the point. Consequently, a bit of additional action is necessary to balance this, so you add to the pretense of making and revealing the prophecy. In most tricks this is not necessary, but here it is of vital importance, and fortunately you are able to cope with it in a very simple way.

Merely have a letter size envelope in your inside coat pocket. Write the prophecy and fold it once each way. Hold it in your right hand while the left hand removes the envelope from your pocket. The paper slip apparently is placed inside the envelope, but actually it is only pushed under the left thumb which rests on the outside of the envelope on the side facing you. The flap is mostened and sealed. The right hand now pulls the envelope away and stands it up in view, while the left hand drops to your side or pocket with the dummy slip.

After the drawing, and when you have palmed the correct paper slip from your indexes, pick up the envelope with the hand that has the slip finger palmed. The other hand tears off the end of the envelope, and immediately takes hold of the envelope by the long sides as you would do naturally, when raising it up to blow into it. The moment it opens, the fingers of the hand holding the palmed slip grasp the open end of the envelope. The fingers go inside, dropping the slip to the bottom of the envelope, while the thumb remains on the outside. Having thus grasped the envelope, this hand takes it and reaches out towards a committeeman, as you say, "Hold your hand out, please." You turn the envelope open end downwards and shake out the slip onto the person's palm. Say, "Will you read aloud the prophecy I made while the numbers were being mixed?" Crumple up and toss aside the envelope, as you finish with, "And that, ladies and gentlemen, is why I never take chances or bet on events of any kind. I always have to lose, to prove that I'm honest."

FINAL NOTES

That just about winds up my ideas regarding the pocket index principle. I know my indexes are practical for they have aided me to make a living for a long time. I know, too, that each reader will immediately try to improve them, and I wish them luck because I can't. I honestly doubt if it ever will be feasible to have all the paper slips in one pocket index instead of two. There are certain restrictions that are not worth overcoming for other faults will then appear to annoy you.

Outside of the realm of cards, one might play around with the idea of using slips containing first names. 26 male names and 26 female names of the most common type might be indexed, and used in conjunction with some other type of definite prophecy, such as a forced answer to a problem, etc. The system of two papers as used in the Lady and Gentleman effect could be used, and the effect presented as a combination of prophecy and mind-reading. The lady would be asked to think of her mother's or father's first name, a paper written (?), and a prophecy could then be made for the gentleman. He would be forced into the result desired, and the correct name for the lady secured from the index. With the common names the percentage of success would be high, and if the performer didn't have it in his pockets he would merely bring out the one closest to it depending upon the sound. Then he'd have the prophecy correct, and be very close on the mindreading, with the excuse that the lady didn't concentrate well enough but just thought of the name hazily.

I suggest that all who do put this principle to work try and develop the ability to change the papers by pure sleight of hand rather than using a receptacle unless absolutely necessary.

TOMORROW'S CARD

CLAYTON RAWSON

Effect: While a spectator shuffles his own deck, the performer writes a message on a slip of paper, folds it, and puts it some place in full view. A second spectator takes the deck, cuts it, and deals out six cards from any places in the pack. The performer picks up these face down cards, fans them, and allows a third person to select any one of them. The prediction slip is opened by the fourth spectator and read aloud. "One minute after this is written a card will be selected. It will be the ———— of ————." The chosen card is shown. The card of tomorrow has been named!

Feats of this nature usually are accomplished by pocket indexes or the use of a force. Both have their strong and weak points. With indexes the performer must know the name of the card before he can locate the proper billet. Should he desire the prediction read before the card is looked at, a force must take place, and he cannot allow much freedom in the deck's handling or the card's selection. This method combines both principles in such a way that the strong points are retained and weak points pared to a minimum.

The deck is borrowed and shuffled freely by anyone. The spectator has a free choice of, first, six out of fifty-two, and then one out of six. The performer never touches the cards except for a brief moment when he fans

them for the final selection. The prediction is read before anyone sees the chosen card. Psychologically this is very strong for it drives home the belief that the prediction was written before the card was chosen. Only five billets in a simple ready-made index are necessary, instead of 52 billets in bulky indexes. And, finally, once out of every three or four times no switch is necessary at all, the spectators opening and reading the prediction the performer actually wrote.

Preparation: The left trousers pocket contains five slips predicting five different cards, folded and arranged in a paper match folder as shown in the accompanying sketch. The right trouser pocket contains six cards which you have "stolen" from the deck during other tricks. Five of them match the index predictions and the sixth may be any other card. They are in a predetermined order, are bridged at one end, and go into the pocket with the bridge up. Also have a small scratch pad of paper and a pencil.

Routine: During the shuffle write your prediction using the name of the sixth card. Fold and place aside. As you tell the second person to cut and deal out six face down cards at random, put your right hand in your pocket and palm out the six cards there. He finishes and your right hand comes up to

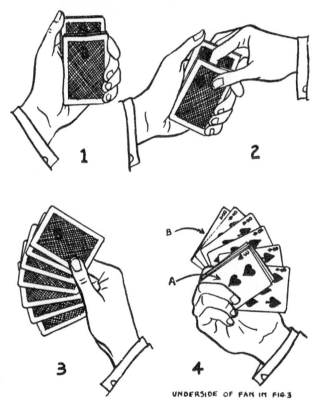

UNDERSIDE OF FAN IN FIG.3

gather the cards, dropping the palmed ones on top. Square the cards in your left hand, cut at the bridge and move the top packet (new) of six downward a half inch, as in Figure No. 1. Insert the right forefinger between the two packets of six, at the top, Figure No. 2, and fan the six added cards between the thumb and forefinger, as in Figure No. 3. The dealt-off six will remain squared and hidden beneath this fan, as shown in Figure No. 4.

If followed with cards in hand these simple directions will make everything clear.

Your left hand goes to your pocket and makes ready to obtain the proper billet. Ask the spectator to touch any card in the fan. This done, accent the freedom of choice he is getting, and ask him if he wants to change his mind. This allows ample time for you to obtain the proper billet with the free hand in pocket, knowing the order, as you do, of the fanned face down cards.

If he chooses the card whose name you actually have written on the exposed billet, forget the index. The trick is done, and the spectator can read it for himself. If that card has been placed third from the left in the fan of six the chances of its being chosen are nearly one in three since the end cards are almost never selected and, of the remaining four, the one just to the spectator's right of center is the most common choice.

If the switch is necessary, have the spectator remove his chosen card and hold it face down. As he does this bring out the left hand with the billet finger palmed, square up the fanned cards, and drop them with the concealed packet on top of the deck.

Pick up the exposed billet and switch it in any manner you prefer before you hand it to the spectator. The prediction is read. The man who holds the chosen card turns it up for all to see. That's the climax, because you never fail.

SEFALALJIA

STEWART JAMES

Introduction by Annemann: I honestly believe that this one man miniature spirit cabinet routine is far beyond, in merit and effectiveness, anything yet conceived. Certainly the manifestations are out of the ordinary and Mr. James has managed to use several magical principles in a way not originally intended. The absence of complicated preparation will be found quite refreshing. The routine that follows will undoubtedly find wide use in the club programs of many performers. The act opens with a very strong effect, follows with a quick surprise item, then runs through three more effects and ends with a weird and startling climax.

Introductory patter theme: "It is the firm belief of many people that walls of a room retain the impressions of violent or unusual incidents that have taken place within that room. People who last were seen in the best of spirits and apparently with everything for which to live, have, after spending a portion of a night in such a room where, unknown to them, some distraught person once committed suicide, in turn re-enacted the tragedy in a manner identical with the first suicide. It is suggested that such individuals were psychic to a high degree and were influenced by the impressions retained in the walls of that particular room."

Effect: The performer offers to demonstrate a few experiments that he has been conducting along that line. He introduces a box which, he claims, was made from material taken from the room of a house said to have been occupied for a number of years by a poltergeist.* The front of the cabinet has been replaced by a curtain that may be drawn back and forth on a rod to reveal or conceal the interior. The inside of the box is painted black. The top of the box is a hinged cover. On top of the box rests a skull and the whole is in full view on a slender and thin topped table.

A bright red rubber ball is carelessly tossed to one end of the box and a drinking glass placed at the other end. The curtain is drawn for a few seconds. When the interior of the box is shown again, the red ball has been

---

*Hereward Carrington describes this word as meaning literally, "Noisy Spirit." A house is said to be haunted by a poltergeist when bells are rung, furniture upset, crockery broken, etc., by no apparent, normal means.

placed in the glass, apparently by a playful spirit. Any spectator may step forward, remove the glass and the ball, and examine both as well as the box!

The inside of the box is concealed again by drawing the curtain. The top is raised and a handkerchief is tossed inside. The spectator, who has stood by, opens the curtains, removes the handkerchief and finds that a knot has been tied in the center of it.

In each end of the box is a hole. In the center of the hinged lid is a screw-hook on the under side. A length of white cotton tape is folded in half and another spectator places a safety-pin through the tape about an inch from the doubled end. The tape is now threaded through the box with the ends protruding out of the holes. Someone in the audience lends his or her finger ring and it is hung onto the hook inside the box. The box is now turned with its curtain side away from the audience. The playful poltergeist's presence is invoked. A volunteer comes forward, grasps one end of the tape and draws it from the box. The borrowed ring actually is threaded on the middle of the tape and is held securely in place by the pin! The ring, still on the tape, is returned to the owner and the volunteer allowed to examine the cabinet.

The cabinet is turned with the curtain side towards audience. A cellophane wrapper is removed from a cigar and the cigar is placed into the glass tumbler. When the tumbler is now put into the open cabinet the spook is found to be a tobacco addict, for the cigar is seen to smoke furiously.

Lastly the lid of the cabinet is raised to accommodate a quart bottle of milk, which remains in full view of the audience. A straw is inserted in the bottle and the thirsty spook immediately imbibes a quantity of the fluid. The performer states, rather apologetically, that his poltergeistic friend always drinks a lot of milk at bed-time, and that now it will be necessary to cease manifestations. "Even spirits have to observe union hours," quips the performer as he takes his bow.

Preparation: The box I use is a radio cabinet. It's size is 7 x 7 x 17 inches. After using it for a long time I find the size just about right. The length may seem long to some, but the greater the distance between the glass tumbler and the rubber ball (first effect), which are placed in opposite corners of the cabinet, makes a very good looking stunt for the opener.

The holes at each end are 1¼ inches in diameter. The size allows of the cord with ring being easily pulled through. The screw-hook is of a No. 5 size. This is in the exact center of the lid, on the inside, being in line with the holes in the cabinet's ends. The final bit of cabinet detail (the only bit of fakery) is a needle size hole in the lid about 2½ inches from one end and at the center of the lid's width (or depth). The small hole will never be noticed.

Routine of Effects in Order of Appearance

THE BALL IN THE GLASS: The red rubber ball is 1½ inches in diameter and made of sponge rubber. At the start of this routine there is a skull sitting upon the top of the cabinet. A thread, about 2 feet long is fastened to the skull and it runs down through the minute hole in the cabinet lid. The other end has been threaded through the ball. The ball has been placed into the glass and when the routine begins the glass and ball are sitting in the center.

After the patter about poltergeists and the building of the cabinet, the glass is picked up and the ball rolled from the glass into the far corner of the box. The glass is placed at the other end (directly under the minute hole in the lid) and the curtain closed.

At this time the performer seems to remember the presence of the skull which is on top of the cabinet. He picks it up with one hand as he relates the fact that it was found beneath the house occupied by the poltergeist. In stepping a bit forward, he causes the thread to be pulled which in turn causes red ball to be drawn against the lid of the cabinet. Pulling the thread just a bit more draws it through and out of the ball with the result that the ball falls directly downward into the glass! The skull is set aside and the performer invites a member of the audience to investigate the cabinet. Of course, he discovers nothing.

THE KNOTTED HANDKERCHIEF: The familiar one-hand knot is made for this effect, when the handkerchief is thrown into the cabinet through the opened lid. The sleight, simple as it is, will be found described in many magic books, the latest description of it appearing in Hugard's "Silken Sorcery." At this point in the routine, psychology plays an important part. The audience is wondering about the ball's passage into the glass; the assisting spectator is worrying both about that puzzle as well as his unexpected prominence on the platform, therefore, so far as he is concerned, a bit of stage fright enters into the situation.

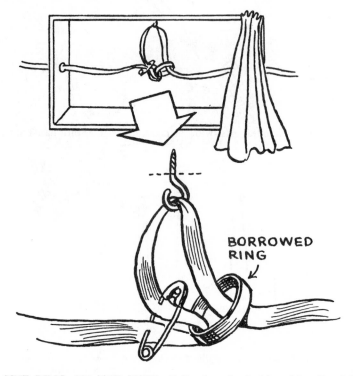

THE RING ON THE TAPE: Following the incidental handkerchief bit, which helps subconsciously to create a feeling that strange powers are at work within the cabinet, we come to one of my original effects.

The tape used is ½ inch wide and, if your box is of the same dimensions as mine, 40 inches long. After the tape is threaded through the box, the borrowed ring upon the hook, and the cabinet turned curtain-side away from the audience, the performer invokes the invisible prankster by rubbing his hands, as he says, inside the confines of the wooden walls. This patter allows of a few quick and very practical moves.

1. Remove the safety-pin and lay it on the bottom of the box.
2. Take the ring off of the screw-hook.
3. Loop the center of the tape and tuck it through the ring.
4. Place the pin through the left side of the loop, thus formed, and the half of the tape that runs out through the left (to performer) hole of the box.
5. Enlarge the loop and place it over the screw-hook as shown in illustration. Now when the left end (to performer) is pulled from the box, the ring is automatically threaded upon the tape and found to be pinned in the center.

THE SMOKED CIGAR: The cigar is of wood and is sold as a novelty pencil. Hollow out one end and insert a piece of felt which, prior to the performance, is soaked in very strong liquid ammonia. When the cigar is properly loaded, wrap it in cellophane. The glass also has to be prepared. Before the performance, put six or eight drops of muriatic acid in the glass (the same one used for the opening) and swish it around a bit.

To present, take the cigar from your pocket, unwrap it and drop it into the glass, open end downward. Place the glass immediately into the open cabinet where everyone can see it. In a few seconds, smoke begins to ascend from the glass in clouds. (A touch of novelty can be added here by tossing a box of matches into the glass with the cigar, in case the spirit hasn't any at the moment. Or you can treat the match box with ammonia and use a borrowed cigar.)

DRINKING THE MILK: The reader should have recognized the DeMuth Milk Bottle trick, used here in an entirely new dress. The placing of the straw serves to release the vent disc and makes the "drinking of the milk" action automatic.

However, for those who do not have the DeMuth bottle, an able and inexpensive substitute may be made. Herb Rungie just inserts a small white-rubber ballon into a milk bottle and partly inflates it. Now push the balloon down to the bottom, and fill the bottle with milk. Take an ordinary drinking straw and load it with a thin wooden stick. Insert the point of a darning needle, about half an inch long, into one end of the plugged straw. When ready for the effect, just insert the straw in the bottle of milk, puncture the balloon, withdraw the point of the needle from the balloon, and leave the straw in the bottle. The effect, as you can visualize, is identical with the DeMuth trick.

TELETHOT

JORDAN-ANNEMANN

The mental transmission of pictures from the performer to the medium has been a bugaboo of telepathists. Everything else has fallen but pictures. So, if one cannot successfully code them, one must falsify the whole proceedings. The following routine will enable you to do this with but 15 minutes practice.

Effect: The performer has a piece of paper perforated for tearing into eight strips. He asks his audience to think of some simple diagrams and then steps among them. The various spectators approached each draw some simple design or figure upon the paper. Stepping back to the platform, the performer tears the paper into eight strips and drops them, one by one, into a

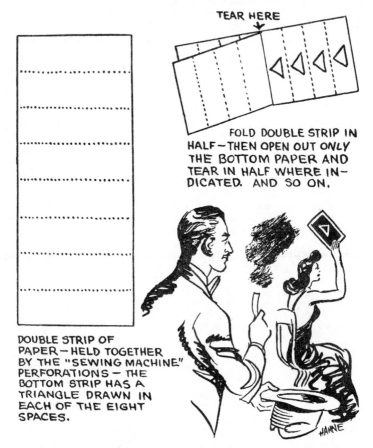

TEAR HERE

FOLD DOUBLE STRIP IN HALF—THEN OPEN OUT ONLY THE BOTTOM PAPER AND TEAR IN HALF WHERE IN—DICATED. AND SO ON.

DOUBLE STRIP OF PAPER—HELD TOGETHER BY THE "SEWING MACHINE" PERFORATIONS — THE BOTTOM STRIP HAS A TRIANGLE DRAWN IN EACH OF THE EIGHT SPACES.

bowl or hat. The medium now enters and is seated with her back to the audience, and is given a slate and a piece of chalk.

Any person from the audience now freely selects from the bowl one slip which he puts in his pocket. He is then given a slate and a piece of chalk and retires with them to a far corner of the room or auditorium, where he waits while the effect goes on.

The performer now reaches into the hat and removes one paper which he looks at in silence. At once, the medium is heard to be writing on her slate. She holds it up to show the picture she has drawn. The performer asks whose drawing the medium has reproduced. The design is acknowledged as correct, and the performer takes another paper. The effect is repeated quickly and, one after another, the spectators acknowledge their drawings, as each is duplicated by the medium. Throughout, the performer remains silent, and does nothing more than pick out slips and look at them.

When the seventh slip has been duplicated, the performer asks the spectator across the room, who is holding the eighth slip and a slate, to draw a picture of the figure on his slip. He does so and then returns to the front where he shows his sketch to everyone in the audience. The medium, who has finished her work and is standing before the audience, turns her slate around and shows it also. Both drawings are the same!

Preparation: Charles Jordan's Yogi Force does the trick. It is still my idea of a perfect force. The paper used by the performer is about 2½ inches wide by 6 inches long. It is of an opaque quality, and there are really two sheets used. Mark off the front sheet in ¾-inch sections. On the back piece draw the design of a triangle eight times so as to conform with the spaces on the front piece. Place the two together, the triangles on the inside facing the upper piece, and run a dressmaker's tracing wheel across the marked-off lines on the top piece, perforating the paper. Putting the two sheets through a sewing machine without thread will accomplish the same thing.

The perforations, dividing the paper into eight sections for tearing apart, hold the sheets together securely until pulled apart. Such a prepared paper can be shown blank on both sides and can be handled quite freely.

Routine: After his opening, the performer steps into the audience. He passes from one to another and each is allowed to make a drawing in one of the perforated sections. Simple design has been stressed as well as the word geometrical. In eight chances, there won't be one in a thousand or more trials when a triangle will not be made. Audiences never think clearly when attacked, and the simplest of patterns are about all of which they can think. However, if a triangle hasn't shown up at the seventh place, merely look at someone a bit away, say, "A triangle for you?" write it in yourself and walk away. And you do not have to yell it so everyone in the place can hear, either.

Hold up the paper so everyone can see that it is all you have in your hands. As you talk about what has been done, tear it up into eight slips as follows:

First, fold the strip in half with the drawings inside. Now open out a single thickness of the triangle sheet and tear it off. Do this deliberately and bring your hands apart showing that you actually have one-half of the paper in each hand. Place this torn-off triangle section in front of the packet, that is on the side of the packet facing the audience. (The triangle drawings are, of course, always kept facing you.) Fold the strip in half again, exactly as before, and open out TWO single thicknesses of the triangle slip, tear them off and again place them in front of the packet. Fold the packet in half again for the last time and open out FOUR single thicknesses of the triangle slip, tear them off and place them in front of the packet. Thus you have separated the forcing (triangle) slip, dissected it and now have eight separate triangle slips in front of your packet. Nothing could be fairer! In the rear of the packet, and under your thumb, you have the original front piece of the paper strip folded up into one bundle; and the original audience sketches are still all in one strip.

At this point, and while the packet is held at your finger tips, you may fan the eight segments, being careful to keep the original bundle behind the fan. Now square up the packet, turn it over in your hand and count the eight separate triangle slips into the bowl. The folded packet remains finger palmed in your hand, and this hand immediately grasps the bowl and shakes up the slips.

The medium is called for and comes on. The performer takes her by the hand and sees that she is seated in a chair with her back to the audience. And in doing so the untorn and palmed packet is left secretly in her hand. When she has been comfortably seated, she is given a slate and a piece of chalk.

Now a spectator steps forward and is offered a free choice from among the slips in the bowl. Naturally, he is not allowed to look into the bowl, this being held above his eye level. He gets one of the triangle slips, of course, and is told to put it in his pocket. He is now given a slate and a piece of chalk and asked to retire to a far corner of the room.

The performer now dips his hand into the bowl and removes one slip, which he looks at without saying anything. The medium immediately draws something on her slate. What? One of the drawings on the strip she has on her lap, skipping, of course, the triangle. She then holds her drawing up for all to see. The performer glances back at his paper (one of the seven triangles left in the bowl), nods, then looks into the audience and asks, "Who drew the ....," naming whatever the medium has drawn. It is acknowledged. Quickly, and as fast as they can be run through, the medium duplicates the other six sketches. In each instance it is apparent that the performer merely looks at the sketch first and, by some mental force, sends the picture to the medium. Anyone who knows about code work will go crazy trying to catch cues and signals.

When the seventh drawing is completed, the person in the corner is asked to make his sketch on the slate he holds and to bring it forward. The medium stands and keeps her slate back outwards. The spectator shows his drawing, and, for the climax, the medium turns her slate around and shows that she has drawn a duplicate of the spectator's sketch.

THE ASTRAL SHIRT
ANNEMANN-DUNCANSON

Here is an extremely effective version of the shirt removal trick that makes a stage item of this otherwise neglected stunt.

Effect: The performer, wearing a white shirt, enters a small cabinet and has his wrists securely tied in the center of a long rope. Throughout the trick two members of the audience hold the ends of the rope, after they have been passed through holes in the sides of the cabinet. A red shirt is now handed into the cabinet and, almost immediately, the performer's white shirt is flung out. Following the white shirt comes the performer, who steps out of the cabinet wearing the red shirt! Everything can be examined as the rope tie is genuine, the red shirt is really on the performer and the white shirt is unprepared.

Preparation and Routine: Two red shirts and one white one are needed, and silk ones will be found the best to use as they take up less bulk.

A bow tie with an elastic neckband should also be worn, such as an evening dress tie that can be removed merely by unhooking the neckband.

The red shirt is put on first with its tail pinned down so it does not pull out later. The white shirt goes on next in skeleton fashion being arranged as per the instructions for the "Shirt Test" on page 99. Snap the tie in place and you're set to work the shirt changing stunt anytime during your program.

When ready to present, have your wrists tied securely in the center of a long rope. Step into your cabinet and have the ends of the rope passed through holes in both sides of the cabinet. Two spectators stand, one on either side of the cabinet, and hold on to the ropes. The curtains are drawn across the front of the cabinet, and a red shirt is handed into the cabinet to you.

As soon as the curtains are drawn, you remove your tie, unbutton your collar button and the two top buttons of the white shirt you are wearing. Unbutton your coat and your vest. Next unbutton the cuffs of the white shirt with your teeth, as you have only to get hold of the cuff at the right spot and pull it off the button. Now reach over your head to back and, bending over, pull the shirt right over your head. You can't do this in one pull, but a series of short pulls will bring the shirt out in a few seconds. When you have the shirt free, stick it between your knees to hold it. Now put your tie on again, and, if you have worked fast enough, you'll be ready when the extra red shirt is handed into the cabinet.

This extra red shirt is either stuffed into your pocket, or into a pocket of one of the curtains forming the side of the cabinet. As soon as it is hidden, toss out the white shirt and step out of the cabinet.

(**Editor's Note:** Although neither Mr. Annemann or Mr. Duncanson mention it, I presume that the two assistants will have to be told to allow you some slack in the rope they are holding.

IMPROMPTU FRAME-UPS
ANNEMANN

Plants and confederates are not always practical, but it is possible with the help of a plant to introduce an impromptu miracle in your program once in a while with striking effect. The frame-up tests to follow all require a little nerve plus the judicious selection of a good-natured spectator to act as your confederate. Don't select one who appears grouchy or of the smart aleck type, but pick out a good-natured person, one who will enter into the spirit of the occasion and get as big a kick out of fooling his friends as you will.

1. ENVELOPE TEST. In your pocket  carry three letter envelopes, nail nicked at the upper right hand corners on the flap side so they can be recognized as one, two and three. Also have a card with the names of five cards written on it, together with a message to your assistant to name the five cards as required, in the order listed, and to stall on the last one. In the opposite coat pocket are the five cards to be forced, and they are set in the proper order.

Start out by having the person, acting as the medium, sit in a chair with his or her back to the audience. Now cover the medium with a sheet and, in the process of doing so, drop the card list into his lap. While this is going on, you have had someone else busily engaged in shuffling a deck of cards. As you explain that you intend to have some cards selected which will be named by the medium, you drop your hand into your pocket and palm the force cards. Taking back the deck, add the palmed cards to the top of the pack.

Step up to your first victim and force the top card, either by the standard fan force after cutting to the middle, or by the riffle and slip cut to the point in the deck where you are stopped. You now hold your finger to your lips for silence and the medium slowly and correctly names the card the first spectator is holding.

This is repeated with another person, the second card being forced and subsequently named. Then follows a variation. State that the first two experimental tests have been by telepathy between the spectator and the medium. This time, however, it will be a case of clairvoyance by the medium as no one will know the names of the cards.

The next three people to take cards, all forced and in order, are each given an envelope into which to seal his card after noting it. The envelopes are pulled from your pocket in each case, and given out in their marked order, one, two and three. Anyone now collects the sealed envelopes, mixes them, and hands them to you. Fan them out carelessly, state that it is impossible for anyone to know which cards are where, and hold up one envelope (holding up the first, of course). The medium names a card, whereupon you tear open the envelope and show it to be correct. This is repeated with the second envelope. With but one left, you hand it to the person not yet accounted for, and the medium finishes off the well-rounded effect by not seeing it clearly. He asks the spectator to open his envelope and stare at the card directly so that he can get a telepathic wave. Then he names it!

As you can see, this test can be built up into quite a sensational effect. Likewise it makes a stunning program item for your regular act, for under these conditions you can have your partner memorize the force cards and be ready at all times. Furthermore, dispense with the sheet and just blindfold her.

2. WATCH TEST. This is another fine test. Take an open face watch and attach to its face a square piece of paper. A dab of wax will hold it in place. Write the following message on the paper: "We can have a laugh and fool the others if you'll help me by setting the watch at ten minutes after eight." Put the watch, so prepared, into your vest pocket and you're set.

When ready to work the stunt, remove the watch and look at it as though checking on the time. Select a spectator and ask him to leave the room with the watch, or go to a far corner and set the watch at any time he may please. He is then to return and give it to you behind your back.

The spectator does as requested. When he hands you the watch behind your back you should be facing the audience. Just hold it in your hand a few seconds and slowly name the hour and then the minutes. You will also find it effective to use a slate in this stunt. After holding the watch for a few seconds, hand it back to your assistant and pick up a slate and write the time —or draw a watch face—on the surface towards yourself. The spectator now shows the watch and calls out the time, and you turn the slate and show that you got the mental impression correct!

3. SLATE TEST. This slate stunt is another variation. Have two slates and on one write, not with chalk but with a slate pencil, "Help me fool the rest of the audience and we'll have a private laugh between ourselves. Rub this writing out with your finger and draw a large square with a triangle inside of it. Thank you."

Pick out your victim and direct him to a corner, going a little ways with him. Hand him the slate and, in doing so, indicate the written message with your finger. Step back to the front and pick up the unprepared slate. Ask the person in the corner to draw some simple geometrical figures on his slate and you'll do the same. When he has finished, he shows his slate and you show yours—and you've both drawn the same figures! Telepathy?

4. ANOTHER SLATE TEST. A variation of the above test has been used successfully by one performer. A slate was handed to someone in the audience and he was requested to stand at a far side of the room and to think of a number of three digits. When he had decided upon it, he was to write it on the slate in large figures and to concentrate on it, being careful to keep the figure out of sight of everyone present.

Now the performer would select a lady to assist in the test. He took hold of her wrist and slowly began counting from One to Zero in a loud voice. The lady was then asked to tell which of the figures called impressed her most and the routine was repeated three times. Thus a three-figured number was arrived at. The assistant with the slate was then asked to reveal his number and it was the same!

Like the first slate stunt, the slate your assistant took with him bore a message asking him to write a particular number. The lady, of course, arrived at the forced number by the simple means of having her wrist pinched by the performed each time he named the proper digit.

This test is not half as difficult as many might think, and though it takes a little affrontery it is as effective as any test of its kind.

5. SHIRT TEST. This stunt will add quite a bit of comedy to any act. In effect, the performer asks for some young man to come up on the platform and, during the course of some trick, proceeds to remove the fellow's shirt without removing his coat.

Of course a plant is necessary, but the time required to arrange the shirt takes but a few minutes. Take off his coat, vest and shirt. Now throw the shirt over his shoulders like a cloak and button the collar around his neck. Also button the first couple of buttons. Now arrange the sleeves around his arm and button the cuffs around his wrist. Put on his tie, vest and coat, being careful to tuck in the shirt tails. He now appears correctly dressed.

To pull the shirt off, unbutton the cuffs. Next remove the tie and unbutton the top three buttons including the collar button. Now by catching the back of the shirt collar, you can pull the shirt right up over the stooge's head.

That's the method and the way it's usually presented. For a spirit act you wouldn't use it so openly or boldly. However, it does offer a bit of comedy to use with your Spirit Cabinet, and if your stooge can learn to remove his shirt in record time and then bounce out of the cabinet it is very effective. The shirt, of course, being thrown out of the top of the cabinet at the same moment your stooge makes his appearance with his hair ruffled.

THE PHANTOM ARTIST
ANNEMANN-NALDRETT

Percy Naldrett first published the effect of this quite perfect program trick under the name "The Celebrity Trick." However, the most important part of the stunt, the cut-out sketches, were not given, and it was left to the individual performer to have them specially made.

Herewith are three of the set which I use. All are pictures of prominent figures, and of such a variety as to cover most every type of performance, whether before mixed audiences, political or children, and of a size to make a really practical club number.

Effect: In appearance this is straightforward and quite startling, as well as being different. The magician announces that he has found it possible to call upon spirits in another plane, and have them control him in such a way that their influence or presence is apparent. Someone from the audience is asked forward. The performer asks for a number of names of famous people or presidents who have passed beyond. The names are written on slips of paper which are then mixed up a bit. One is chosen by the spectator who retains it, unseen, in his closed fist.

At this point the performer picks up a blank sheet of paper and a pair of shears. From now on, he states, everything will be left to another power. He starts folding the paper and clipping away at it with the shears. He continues cutting, clipping, snipping and folding, until the paper is only a couple of inches square and in a bunch. Laying aside the shears, the performer asks the spectator to open the paper he holds and reveal the name. Deliberately and precisely, the performer opens out the cut-up paper, and places it against a black background. *It is a perfect black and white portrait of the person secretly selected!*

Secret and Routine: Probably the success of the experiment lies as much in the credit given to the performer as a clever artist as in the·mystery of the chosen name, but withal, the effect has been well received always and won't fail to get a hand. It seems that no one ever thinks there is any fake in the cutting. They look upon the name selection as the mystery or tricky part, and the cutting as pure skill. However, the simple secret is but a force of a name and a switch of the paper, plus natural ability on the part of the performer to make a good presentation of the cutting and folding.

Reproduced here are three pictures. Let it be understood now that a cut out model from one of these will last for four or five actual performances, and you can make three or four models at one cutting. Lay a sheet of ordinary typewriter paper over a picture. With a pencil outline all of the black sections. Now reproduce this diagram to scale in any larger size you prefer. We suggest 10 inches by 14 inches. Put this enlarged tracing on top of two or three more sheets, thumb tack the corners, and cut out all black sections with a razor blade.

LINCOLN

BRYAN

WASHINGTON

Now take one cut out before you. Fold it in half very sloppily, being careful that small points and parts are folded too and not torn or crumpled. Repeat this each way to reduce the paper to about two inches square in size. As you make each fold *drop in a loose sliver or bit of paper*, so that when you unfold it, these chopped up bits will drop out.

Do the folding so that the upper left corner of the sheet will always be outside. When finished, put the packet under pressure until needed. Then, with a dab of paste, fasten it by this corner to an upper corner of a plain sheet. Fold the paper through the middle the long way, and with the folded packet inside. Place it on your table with shears on top. With a 11x14″ sheet you won't have any trouble finding a background on which to display it. Almost anything with a dark color will do. And if you work with a suitcase show, you can have a black painted sheet of three-ply with two victrola needles along top edge on which to impale the opened out sketch.

Before the paper is shown or cutting is even mentioned, have the name selected. I hesitate to give a method of forcing here because anyone who puts this stunt to work will have favorite methods of his own. Some are sold on the Change Bag, while others will merely have names called and write the same thing on all slips. It doesn't matter much what you do as long as the name selected is the one you want.

Now pick up the paper and shears, letting the sheet drop open, but keeping the attached, prepared packet to the rear and top, that corner being held with the fingers in front and thumb behind. Now fold paper up as it was at start, with packet inside, and start trimming. Each time you fold and cut, cut away all paper in back that covers the packet. Pretend you are cutting a design by your actions. Don't just hack at it. Act as if there is something precise to be cut or trimmed. *But keep folding and cutting until all of the blank sheet is cut away!* And make the pieces small instead of large.

Lay the shears aside and have the name looked at and called aloud. Then open up the paper you have and put it against the background. The small pieces you folded in will drop out, and make it all look very real. And you'll have a stunt which you'll be proud to feature.

TRAVEL THOUGHT
HENRY FETSCH

Effect: From a set of road maps any one is selected, opened to full size and placed on a table. Any three persons then scan the map and each mentally selects a city or town that strikes his fancy. The medium is placed in a far end of the room facing a corner. The performer then instructs each person to write down his mentally selected cities on a small piece of paper so as to have an accurate check at the conclusion of the test.

The last person to write upon the slip of paper is told to fold it and keep in his inside pocket for the time being. Then he is to take the unfolded map to the medium. The three persons now form a circle with the performer by holding hands and the lights are snapped off to aid in the collective concentration. The performer lays stress upon the fact that from now on, until the medium either fails or succeeds in naming the mentally selected places, he will remain speechless. All instructions are carried out and the lights extinguished. Slowly the medium names the three selected places. The lights are turned on and the three places as named by medium are checked by the person who holds the slip. All are correct!

Requirements: (1) A small pocket flashlight with the lens covered with red tissue paper. This is to be concealed anywhere on the medium. (2) A small slip of paper and pencil in the performer's inside coat pocket.

(3) A set of six road maps, more or less, all different. These may be obtained from local gas stations, or by writing directly to any of the large oil companies.

Preparation: These maps have a complete section of the country on one side, while on the other side it is blocked off in a number of smaller sections of cities. On the section nearest the center paste a piece of carbon paper, that fits inside of the section with a clearance of about 1/4-inch all around, with the impression side of carbon facing you.

On top of this lay a thin piece of white paper the same size as the carbon. From a duplicate map cut out this same section and paste it over the carbon on three of its edges. Thus you have formed a pocket over the carbon and piece of paper, the latter being removable from the open side. Fold the map to its original form and prepare as many as you may care to use.

Routine: It should all be very clear by now. Remove the maps from your pocket and have any one selected. The chosen one is spread open with the unprepared side facing the audience and the three cities or towns are selected. Remove the slip of paper from your pocket and lay it on the map directly over the prepared section. When the three people write their selections, carbon impressions are left on the white paper in the pocket of the map under the carbon. The map is taken to the medium who removes the piece of paper from the pocket in the map when the lights are turned off. By means of the dimmed flashlight, which so prepared will not throw a glow, the medium finds out the selections and slowly names them. The rest is presentation and showmanship.

The whole effect is so radically different and so simple and direct in working that a tryout is highly recommended.

TAPS

L. VOSBURGH LYONS

This is probably one of the greatest "little" effects in the mental field. Guard its secret carefully, practice it till you have it down perfectly, and you'll have as stunning a trick as you'll ever find. Its simplicity will intrigue you as it did Ted Annemann, who had planned to include it in the program of his last show.

Effect: The performer explains that he will attempt to produce some spirit raps through the medium of a steel ball and two soup plates, which he exhibits. He drops the ball on one of the plates several times to accustom the audience to the sound. Then he puts the steel ball in one of the soup plates, inverts the other plate on top of it, and holds the two plates between his finger tips. Distinct raps are heard shortly although the performer is careful to hold the plates steady, without any movement of any kind. The performer sets the plates down for a moment, or preferably hands them to someone to hold, while he has a card selected from a deck. He then picks up the plates again, and asks the person with the card to look at each spot on the card in turn, then concentrate on one spot at a time and imagine it is a rap. He is asked to hold the card in his left hand and form his right into a fist. Then as he gazes at each spot, he is to make a knocking motion in the air as one does when knocking on a door. As the spectator does this, the raps follow, one for each spot, a fraction of a second after each knocking motion.

Method: The simplicity of this secret is a perfect example of the inventive genius of Dr. Lyons. All that is needed to produce the raps is a metal finger tip. Wear it on your left or right ring finger, and rap out your answers on the under side of the bottom plate. Be careful to watch your angles, and do not bare your forearms, as the muscles will show tell-tale ripples. The number of spots on the card you know, of course, for it is forced. If you cannot force a card in a natural manner then use a force deck, for the selection must be a free one.

FINGER, FINGER
GRAVATT AND ELLIOTT

This is one of the most thought-provoking little secrets to be evolved in many a moon.

Effect: In action and conception the procedure resembles the popular "finger" game. The performer acts as a medium or thought reader and turns his back upon two spectators who will act as transmitters. Both of these spectators now hold out from 1 to 5 fingers, and the total of the two hands is called aloud. Immediately the performer tells correctly the number of fingers each spectator is showing. Or the two spectators may stand back to back, as Dr. V. Lyons does it, with their sides to the audience. Thus neither can see how many fingers the other holds out. Any third party either calls out the total of the fingers showing, or steps up to the performer and whispers it. Still the performer announces the correct number of fingers each spectator is showing!

Now check that effect against these "perfect" conditions and control features. The medium may be honestly blindfolded or in another room within hearing distance, if desired. Either of the two spectators, or a third, may call out the total. Either of the two spectators may hold out his chosen number of fingers first. This avoids any thought that one spectator may be adding to the other's choice in order to reach a prearranged total. The stunt may be repeated indefinitely.

In short, the conditions under which the stunt is done absolutely allay any suspicion that a confederate is used.

Secret: One of the two spectators is a confederate, however.

The first time it is worked, the confederate always put out 2 fingers. Thus, from the total called, the performer can name how many fingers each person is showing. From then on, however, the confederate always holds out the same number of fingers as did the victim on the previous trial. Knowing the total, the performer merely subtracts and again and again is correct. After any cessation of the stunt, the slate is clean and a new start means that the assistant uses 2 as his starting number.

A variation of the computation can make it really indetectable. Whatever the victim holds out is divided by two and the resultant number of fingers used by the confederate the next time. Where an odd number of fingers are held out, 1 is added to make an even number and then divided in half. Try this out, you'll like it!

LOCK AND KEY
HENRY FETSCH

When in 1931, the Annemann version of "Seven Keys to Baldpate" made its appearance in his marvelous "Book Without a Name," there were quite a number of club magicians who immediately put this novelty in their programs.

Effect: The following is my streamlined version, which is very effective. Several keys and a lock are handed to a spectator for examination. Only one key will open the lock. The performer locks the opened lock into the lapel buttonhole of the spectator, and the keys are mixed in a borrowed hat by anyone. This person takes a bunch of small drug envelopes and drops a key into each and seals them. They are placed in the hat and again shaken up. The performer may be blindfolded if desired, and reaching into the hat picks out one envelope at a time, tossing each aside until he comes to one he "feels" contains the right key. Tearing open the envelope he dumps out the key, and it successfully opens the lock. There is nothing wrong to be found with the keys or lock.

Preparation: You will require two locks, a key to open each, and 8 or 9 other keys that will not open either of the locks. Also have a stack of envelopes with a small bead in the corner of the top envelope, thanks to Mr. Frank Chapman.

Routine: Pass out the keys and have a spectator find the only one that will open the lock. The other lock (spectators only know about one) is in your inside coat pocket along with the envelopes. The key that fits this lock is up your right coat sleeve.

At this point have the spectator mix the keys in a borrowed hat. You have taken the lock from him with your left hand while he does this, and as he shakes you reach into your pocket and get the envelopes. You switch the lock for the other, and your left hand comes out with the envelopes. Don't hurry this move, or try to be clever about it. All eyes are on the mixing of the keys, and you only have to do it naturally. No one ever dreams of an exchanged lock, all action being with the keys and envelopes. Hand the envelopes to the spectator, and then step back and fasten the lock in a second person's buttonhole. At this point let the key in your right sleeve drop into your hand.

Tell the spectator who is holding the envelopes that you want him to seal up the keys one at a time. What you really do, suiting your actions to your directions, is reach into the hat and produce the palmed key. Place this key into the top envelope which contains the bead, and seal it. Thus you have performed the trick right under their very eyes. All that need be done now is have the spectator mix the envelopes after sealing the remainder himself. You then find the envelope with the bead and the rest is showmanship. The trick's greatest feature is that you apparently never handle the key or envelopes, everything being left to the spectator.

TELEPATHY ON THE CUFF!

R. H. PARRISH

In many instances a performer wants to present a two person effect of mentalism, but is prevented from doing so because of intricate codes and methods of communication requiring rehearsal. In this instance we learn of a truly simple way by which the medium (or party of the second part) is able to receive the desired information right in front of those witnessing the test. No practice is necessary on the part of the medium, and so it becomes an ideal "stunt" for those whose wives decline with vehemence to "learn all that stuff."

For illustration of the communication principle we shall use a more or less commonly known problem of mathematics. That is, to magicians. The performer with a pad passes to three spectators in turn and has them whisper numbers of three figures each into his ear. Each time the performer writes on the pad, and, after the third person has given a number, he is asked to add the three rows of figures and think intently of the number. The 9 principle is made use of here. The first row is written as given. The second row is written on the way to the third person and is not the number given to the performer. Instead, the performer puts down numerals which, when added to the figure above, will total nine. The last row is written as given and the pad is handed to the third spectator to add. The performer remembers only the last row. From the last figure he subtracts 1 and puts it in front making a four figured number. Thus if the last number were 248—he would know the total to be 1247. If 320—the total would be 1319.

So far we have brought out nothing new. The performer turns his back while the spectator adds. During this short time he writes on the inside of his left shirt cuff, with the stub of a pencil, the total of the problem as he knows it will be. When the spectator has finished, he is asked to think of the total. At the same time, the performer picks up a slate and chalk which he hands to the medium. She writes, spectator calls out total, and she turns the slate. It just has to be the same because she reads it from the performer's cuff!

NUMBER THOT

DR. E. G. ERVIN

Effect: The performer has members of his audience give him "any single number" until six are named. Should one of these be repeated another is requested. They are marked down upon the paper slip as given and the paper handed another member of the audience. This person is also given a single die which he rolls several times to prove fair. Then he rolls it once more and multiplies the row of figures on the paper by the topmost number on the die just thrown.

The performer explains the impossible nature of the test. It is one of genuine telepathy wherein he is enabled to "read" a group of figures multiplied by a number arrived at by chance, and positively unknown to him, etc. And without further ado the performer apparently fulfills his claims to greatness.

Requirements: A pencil, a slip of paper, and a single die complete the list of necessary apparatus.

Routine: The basic principle of this impromptu mystery is a mathematical oddity which seems to be little known, and, in this particular instance, quite easily overlooked by the very few who might have heard of the idea. It is excusable on their part for misdirection at the beginning makes the feat appear far from being mechanical.

A subterfuge enters into the effect at the very start when the performer secretly writes down his own row of six figures instead of the ones given. The mystic figures are 1-4-2-8-5-7. Asking a person to give another figure, "for that has been named" is a cute bit of "throwing off" for no one of the six people knows what the other gives.

The paper and die are given someone else and the multiplying done. This selection of a figure with which to multiply is so obviously fair that no one will think it possible for the performer to have any idea of the total reached.

However, the oddity of the six figure number used, and as written by the performer, is that it may be multiplied by 1, 2, 3, 4, 5 or 6, and the result will consist of the same six figures in different orders. And further, the six totals possible of being reached, will rotate from left to right in the same relative positions to one another as in the original number multiplied, although each total starts with a different one of the six figures, as follows:

142857 x 1	142857		142857 x 4	571428
142857 x 2	285714		142857 x 5	714285
142857 x 3	428571		142857 x 6	857142

The fact that the resultant number is divisible by 9 allows of an additional effect. Once the total has been computed the performer explains the impossibility of his knowing anything about it. The spectator is asked to concentrate upon one of the six figures and draw a circle about it. Then he is to add together the remaining five figures and name the total thus reached. The performer reveals the circled figure merely by remembering that the six figures total 27 and the circled figure will be the difference between that number and the total called out, i.e., the total of the remaining five.

This over, the performer, knowing the other five component figures, is able to reveal each of them, one by one, in any order that he may choose. Or, he may ask the spectator the position of the first named figure, adding, "And now, which other figure do you just want to concentrate upon, the 1st, 2nd, 3rd, etc., leaving out the one revealed. Knowing its position gives the performer the exact line up of the other five!

THE NEW HALF AND HALF
L. VOSBURGH LYONS

Here is my version of Stewart James' ingenious trick, "Half and Half" on page 184, which I developed after using his method and realizing how impossible the effect seemed to the onlookers and participants.

Effect: The performer selects a subject and throws a typed card (Fig. 1) in front of him on the table. No particular reference is made to it, but it can be seen that it contains a column of figures and a list of word endings. The performer next lays down on the table another strip of cardboard, slightly to one side of the first card, but with its blank side up.

Three dice are given to the assistant to test by rolling them a few times. Then he is asked to hold them tightly in his left hand. The performer tears a piece of paper into halves. On one piece he writes what he calls a prediction. This is put in a conspicuous position and is not touched again. Then the assistant throws the three dice for a final total number.

Whatever it may be, from 3 to 18 inclusive, he looks at the card first put down, and then writes upon the other half of the torn paper the final letters of the word which appears opposite his number. This writing preferably should be in printed capital letters so that "no trouble will be encountered in deciphering handwriting."

The performer picks up and hands the narrow slip of card to the subject. He is told to match the two lists in order to determine what the whole word is. And he also is asked to read some of the other completed words to convince himself and others that all are quite different, any of which might have been chosen by chance.

Finally the spectator is asked to match the pieces of torn paper together and read aloud. It is the same word! And remember, the performer hasn't touched his written paper, which matches the other torn half, since he put it down before the dice were thrown for a free selection of 16 different words!

ICENT ---	1
IFOLD ---	2
ISH -----	3
CUSSION -	4
JURY ----	5
SPIRATION	6
IMETER --	7
CH ------	8
ISPHERE -	9
SIST ---	10
COLATE -	11
SON ----	12
FECT ---	13
FORM ---	14
TAIN ---	15
IL -----	16
PLEX ---	17
CEPTION	18

Fig. I

Preparation: First type a list on index stock as shown in Fig. 1. This is the card you give to the spectator at the start of the effect.

Then type the list shown in Fig. 2, using index stock. Then cut the list into strips remembering that their number values run from 3 through 18. These values are shown at the top of Fig. 2 for your guidance, but should not appear on the lists when in use. The numbers 1 and 2 cannot be thrown when using three dice.

Make two pocket indexes for eight strips apiece, so that you can quickly get any strip you want from either trouser pocket.

Routine: In action, you proceed as has been described with the first list (Fig. 1) thrown down, but for the second, narrow list, you take from your pocket the number 11 strip, putting it writing side down on the table. Be sure to place it quite some distance away from the first list.

The assistant really does toss the dice around with freedom and fairness. Then you tear a piece of paper into two halves and write on one piece the letters "PER." Fold and be sure to put this paper in a spot where afterwards everyone will remember that you didn't touch it a second time.

Now comes the important throw of the dice. You can have both hands in your pockets as it is made. You know the total as quickly as the assistant, and you will have ample time to secure the proper strip from the index in one of your pockets as your assistant looks up the word ending and writes it on the other half of the torn sheet of paper.

3	4	5	6	7	8	9	10	11	12	13	14	15	16	17	18
RET	RET	RET	RET	RET	RET	RET	RET	RET	RET	RET	RET	RET	RET	RET	RET
MAN	MAN	MAN	MAN	MAN	MAN	MAN	MAN	MAN	MAN	MAN	MAN	MAN	MAN	MAN	MAN
PER	SW	SW	SW	SW	SW	SW	SW	SW	SW	SW	SW	SW	SW	SW	SW
DIS	PER	DIS	DIS	DIS	DIS	DIS	DIS	DIS	DIS	DIS	DIS	DIS	DIS	DIS	DIS
CON	CON	PER	CON	CON	CON	CON	CON	CON	CON	CON	CON	CON	CON	CON	CON
IN	IN	IN	PER	IN	IN	IN	IN	IN	IN	IN	IN	IN	IN	IN	IN
TAX	TAX	TAX	TAX	PER	TAX	TAX	TAX	TAX	TAX	TAX	TAX	TAX	TAX	TAX	TAX
COU	COU	COU	COU	COU	PER	COU	COU	COU	COU	COU	COU	COU	COU	COU	COU
HEM	HEM	HEM	HEM	HEM	HEM	PER	HEM	HEM	HEM	HEM	HEM	HEM	HEM	HEM	HEM
SUB	SUB	SUB	SUB	SUB	SUB	SUB	PER	SUB	SUB	SUB	SUB	SUB	SUB	SUB	SUB
CHO	CHO	CHO	CHO	CHO	CHO	CHO	CHO	PER	CHO	CHO	CHO	CHO	CHO	CHO	CHO
REA	REA	REA	REA	REA	REA	REA	REA	REA	PER	REA	REA	REA	REA	REA	REA
EF	EF	EF	EF	EF	EF	EF	EF	EF	EF	PER	EF	EF	EF	EF	EF
UNI	UNI	UNI	UNI	UNI	UNI	UNI	UNI	UNI	UNI	UNI	PER	UNI	UNI	UNI	UNI
OB	OB	OB	OB	OB	OE	OB	OB	OB	OB	OB	OB	PER	OB	OB	OB
DEV	DEV	DEV	DEV	DEV	DEV	DEV	DEV	DEV	DEV	DEV	DEV	DEV	PER	DEV	DEV
COM	COM	COM	COM	COM	COM	COM	COM	COM	COM	COM	COM	COM	COM	PER	COM
DE	DE	DE	DE	DE	DE	DE	DE	DE	DE	DE	DE	DE	DE	DE	PER

Fig. 2

Finger palm the strip along the second finger and bring your hand out of your pocket. Pick up the No. 11 slip on the table with your other hand, as your assistant starts to write his word ending. Have him put the paper down and then hand him the strip. Apparently you hand him the strip you just picked up, but actually you switch the slips, and hand him the one you have just obtained from the index.

He now compares the strip and the card in alignment and discovers the word he won. Then you ask that your prophecy be compared with what the spectator wrote. He lays them side by side, and the word written across the two halves of the paper is the same as the word he won.

I suggest that you use slip No. 11 because 10 and 11 are tops on percentage with three dice. If the dice thrown actually total 11, then, of course, you have a super miracle, because no switch of strips is then necessary.

HORRORS!
STUART ROBSON

Effect: The performer shows five differently colored cards, each of which bears two columns of words. He hands these to someone to shuffle and asks him to lay them on the table. The performer walks to a far corner of the room and asks the spectator to think of any "horror" word, then to look the cards over and pick up those cards that bear that particular word. He puts the cards in his pocket and concentrates upon the word. The performer immediately reveals the word, or describes thoughts, feelings and situations until he finally hits on the word. This latter presentation is by far the best, and should be worked up as impressively as possible.

Preparation: You will need a set of cards like those illustrated. Each card should be of a different color, so that you can identify it at a distance. These can be made easily by typing the lists shown on various colored card boards. The five cards numbered 1, 2, 4, 8 and Extra are the only ones seen by the audience, the other and largest card is your master card, which

Murder	Vampire
Morgue	Frankenstein
Torture	Scream
Undertaker	Skeleton
Suicide	Banshee
Fiend	Strangle
Horror	Poison *1*

Corpse	Black cat
Morgue	Frankenstein
Witch	Trance
Undertaker	Skeleton
Haunted House	Hearse
Fiend	Strangle
Voodoo	Coffin *2*

Corpse	Black cat
Murder	Vampire
Ghost	Dracula
Undertaker	Skeleton
Haunted House	Hearse
Suicide	Banshee
Devil	Insanity *4*

Corpse	Black cat
Murder	Vampire
Ghost	Dracula
Morgue	Frankenstein
Witch	Trance
Torture	Scream
Monster	Grave yard *8*

Corpse	Undertaker
Murder	Haunted House
Ghost	Suicide
Morgue	Devil
Witch	Fiend
Torture	Voodoo
Monster	Horror *Extra*

1	Horror	Poison
2	Voodoo	Coffin
3	Fiend	Strangle
4	Devil	Insanity
5	Suicide	Banshee
6	Haunted House	Hearse
7	Undertaker	Skeleton
8	Monster	Grave yard
9	Torture	Scream
10	Witch	Trance
11	Morgue	Frankenstein
12	Ghost	Dracula
13	Murder	Vampire
14	Corpse	Black cat

you keep in your pocket and consult as needed. Do not, however, number the cards as shown, but remember these numbers as being associated with the various cards. It might be well to number one set, on the back, and keep it for your master set so as to refresh your memory from time to time, particularly just before a performance.

Routine: Have the master list card in your pocket. Show the other five cards, have them shuffled and laid in a row on the table as you step to a far corner of the room. Palm the master list card in transit. Ask the person assisting to select a "horror" word and then pick up all the cards bearing that word. You watch and make a mental note of the value of each of the cards picked up. This will be easy as each one is a different color, and you know the key number associated with each colored card. Mentally add up these numbers, and then look up that (total) number on your key list. If the Extra card is selected also, it simply means that the word is in the first column on you master list card; if the Extra card is not picked up, the word will be at the same number but in the second column. For instance, the person thinks of the word "Vampire." He would pick up cards number 1, 4 and 8, without the Extra card. These cards total 13, so "Vampire" will be found in the 13th place in the second column on your master card. Likewise, if he thought of the word "Morgue," he would pick up cards 1, 2 and 8, and also the Extra card. These cards total 11, so with the Extra card indicating the first column you will find the word "Morgue" in 11th position.

For close up work, you can use plain white cards but dot them on the backs, so that you can identify the numerical value of each. In this case, have the person making the selection turn all the cards face down that he doesn't pick up. Automatically you know what cards he holds.

BLACK PIN IDEA
STEWART JAMES

In this little effect, the performer uses a small black headed pin and a case that formerly contained pen-points. The spectator puts the pin in the case, then closes it and hands it to the performer who has been standing with his back turned. Turning to face the audience, the performer raises the box, without looking at it, to his forehead and divines which way the pin is pointing.

The secret of this impromptu divination is very subtle. You can tell by touch which is the top of the case, for there's a ridge around the cover. Now as you raise the box to your forehead, you do it quickly, and tilt it just as it touches your head. You will hear the pin roll back and forth repeatedly if the point of the pin is at the top of the box. On the other hand, if the head of the pin is at the top of the box this rolling sound is practically non-existant. Don't shake the box, just raise it quickly and be sure to tilt it.

As a patter suggestion, you might use this quip about the philosopher who said, "It's very hard to tell about a pin as it is headed in one direction and pointed in the other."

VOODOO
ARTHUR MONROE

Very seldom does an effect come to light and cover the weird phases as does this. It is strictly a "spook tale" and the reader will see at once that the whole thing is a gigantic "build-up" and must be done seriously to surround it with the right atmosphere. The effect is at its best in a home where you are a guest, or when you are performing at a small party. The room where you are working must be darkened for about four minutes during the "voodoo" portion of the trick.

Effect: A spectator scratches an identification mark on a Chinese coin which he hands back to you. Running a short length of string through the hole in the coin, you allow each of several spectators to tie one or more knots in the string, making it impossible to remove the coin without cutting or untying the cord.

The coin on the string is placed in a small metal box, and with it is put a blank piece of paper or calling card. Rubber bands are snapped around the box and it is handed to the host or hostess. You ask her to hide it in the most remote corner of the house, in an old trunk, under the mattress upstairs, or in the attic. She can go alone or take someone with her, but no one who stays in the room knows where the box has been hidden. When the lady returns, she is asked to select a card from the deck and to keep it in her possession.

The lights are now turned out, and after a moment or two of silence, a small green light glows at the table where you are standing and you are seen to be holding the box! You give it a gentle shake and the rubber bands which are of the heavy type and snapped tightly on, are seen to fall off. The box is opened and string with coin is removed. Another gentle shake and the coin drops off the cord onto the table, leaving only the knotted cord in your hand. The string is replaced in the box and you pick up the piece of paper or card. Writing something on the paper you put it back in the box on top of the string, close the box and snap the bands back on. Now the green light is extinguished, and after a few moments the lights are turned on.

The spectator who marked the coin is asked to pick it up from where it fell on the table, and it bears his identification mark! Then you ask the hostess to go and get the box from its hiding place. Upon returning she opens it herself and finds only the knotted string and the card upon which is written in bright green ink. "The card you selected was the Ace of Hearts."

Read over the above routine again and see for yourself the tremendous possibilities this offers as a super spook stunt.

Requirements: Two P & L card boxes, two duplicate Chinese coins, four wide elastic bands, two black cloth bands to match, three pieces of string, three duplicate paper slips or cards, a pack of cards and a green light. Make the green light with a small flash light set in a lota bowl or similar container that is easily carried. Several pieces of green celophane paper wrapped over the light bulb will give you the proper effect. Set this light in the bowl so that it shoots a beam of light straight up, glowing with weird effect in a darkened room.

Preparation: In one card box place a loop of cord in which you have tied several knots; also one of the slips of paper. Place this card box in your lota bowl together with the flashlight, first, however, slipping over the box the two loose cloth bands. Set the bowl on the table and behind it place two of the rubber bands. Also have the pack of cards, one of the Chinese coins, the other pair of rubber bands, one slip of paper and the duplicate card box in sight on the table. This second card box is prepared as follows: In the bottom compartment place another loop of string which has been knotted, and the third slip of paper. On this slip is written, in green ink, "The Card you selected was the Ace of Hearts." In writing this, make a mistake and then cross it out. Later when you are seen writing under the green light, you apparently make a mistake and have to cross it out. This is a subtle detail, but it will make a big impression! To get back to preparation again, place the third piece of string in your right coat pocket; palm the duplicate Chinese coin in your left hand and your set to start.

Routine: Follow the routine as described, giving it as much showmanship as possible. Have the Chinese coin on the table picked up and marked by someone. You take it and apparently place it in your left hand, really palming it in your right as you bring the duplicate coin into view with the the left hand. Reach into your right coat pocket for the piece of string and deposit the marked coin as you bring out the string. Go immediately to another person some distance from the one who marked the coin, and give this second person the coin and string and ask him to string it and then tie several knots in the string so that the coin cannot be removed. Have him pass it to several of his neighbors who in turn each tie a knot. Pick up the visible card box from the table and the slip of paper. Show them both. Open the top section of the card box (this should be readied in advance), take the coin and string and drop it in the box together with the paper slip. Close the box and snap two of the rubber bands around it. Have your hostess take the box, leave the room and hide it somewhere. When she returns you have her select a card, and force the Ace of Hearts on her. She keeps the Ace in her possession and takes her seat.

Now have the lights turned off as you stand behind the table. Reach into your coat pocket and palm the coin. Then reach into the bowl, light the flashlight and bring out the duplicate card box. Hold it up so that it is visible in the ray of green light and shake off the two cloth bands, which audience think are the rubber ones. Open the box and remove the string with your right hand, at the same time letting the palmed coin slip to your finger tips and hold it against the string so that it is visible to everyone. Shake the string and let the coin drop onto the table. Put the string back into the box and remove the paper slip. Pretend to write on the paper as already described and return the paper to the box; close the box, pick up the elastic bands from behind the bowl and snap them in place around the box. Reach into the bowl with the same hand that is holding the box and snap off the light. As soon as the green light is out, withdraw the cardbox and slip it into your pocket. Your other hand in the meantime has picked up the two cloth bands and slipped them into the pocket on other side of your coat. Now call for the house lights. Ask someone to pick up the coin and have it identified. Then ask the hostess to fetch the box she hid and bring it in. When she does so, she opens it and finds only the knotted string and the slip bearing the name of the card she selected. She produces the card and acknowledges it.

ENCORE VOODOO

EDDIE CLEVER

The following effect is an impromptu variation of the above trick, and one that will certainly appeal to many of you.

To start, the performer announces an experiment in witchcraft. A bit of Voodoo ceremony used to impress ignorant souls that the incantating and muchly overdressed native Witch Doctor is really possessed of powers beyond the reach of ordinary mortals. A power that permits him to send his astral body into far off places during the curious and forbidding rituals of the Voodoo ceremonies.

Effect: A card is selected. An envelope is shown and also a length of ribbon, an inch wide and four feet long. With a knife a hole is made through the envelope and the ribbon is then pushed through so that it runs freely back and forth in the envelope. The card is shown again and a corner is torn from it. The corner is given to a person to hold. The card is pushed into the envelope and sealed. This is handed to your hostess with the request that she wrap the ribbon around the envelope and then carry it out of the room and hide it carefully in some distant part of the house. When she returns the lights are turned out.

Suddenly a green glow appears to surround the performer. Just as mysteriously the envelope appears in his hands. The flap slowly raises as the magician waves his hand over it. The card is removed, also the ribbon. A knife is picked up from the table and a slit is made through the card. The ribbon is threaded through this slit and the ends of the ribbon are passed through the holes. The performer now pulls on the ends of the ribbon and draws the card into the envelope. As a final touch the ribbon is wound around the envelope. Then the green glow goes out. When the house lights are snapped on, there stands the performer empty handed.

Your hostess fetches the hidden envelope. It is opened in the presence of everyone. When the card is removed it is found threaded on the ribbon. The card is now checked with the corner that was being held by one of the guests, and it matches perfectly. Truly a ghostly interlude!

Preparation: The method should require but little explanation. Use the familiar double envelope. A card, with corner torn off, is placed in the rear part of the envelope. Place the corner in your vest pocket. You also require a duplicate ordinary envelope with a ribbon running through it. Inside this ordinary envelope is a duplicate of the force card with its corner torn off. Discard this corner. Place this ordinary envelope in one of your pockets wrapped with a black silk handkerchief. Also have a green light set in a lota bowl as in the preceding effect.

Routine: Follow the routine as given. Have a card selected (forced) and a corner torn off. Switch this corner for the one you have pocketed, and give to someone to hold. Pick up the double envelope (with the duplicate card in the rear section) and

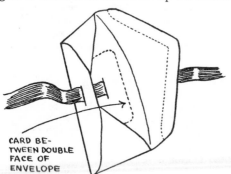

CARD BE-
TWEEN DOUBLE
FACE OF
ENVELOPE

punch a hole through it with a knife. Now thread your ribbon through the hole, insert the forced card in the front section of the envelope and seal it. Wrap the ends of the ribbon around the envelope and have it hidden.

Now have the lights turned off. Reach into the lota bowl and snap on the green light, but stand back from its glow a bit. Bring out the envelope wrapped in the black handkerchief and hold it in your hand. If you stand in the right position it can't be seen until you jerk away the handkerchief. Now hold the envelope slightly tilted towards you and, as you make passes over it with your right hand, push up the flap with your left thumb. From here on follow the routine as already described, pocketing the envelope just after you snap off the green light and before the house lights are turned on. Thus you are empty handed when the room is lighted. When your hostess returns, take the envelope from her, slit open the front compartment and remove the ribbon-threaded card. One suggestion: I strongly recommend that you use a forcing pack because the presentation should be direct.

THE KRAZY KODE

Bert Adams

Effect: The performer takes from his pocket a telegram which obviously bears a coded message, as illustrated:

EASTERN UNION TELEGRAM

THEO ANNEMANN c/o HOLDENS
220 WEST 42 ST NY

I IMPERSONATED PRESIDENT STEIN PEDESTRIAN
SPRINTED INJURED INSTEP STIPEND IS INSUFFICIENT
SITE CHOSEN IS DESPERATION ITS EASY SIT TIGHT
I WILL SEND DETAILS ENSTRIPED TIES ARE TO
FANTASTIC WITH INSET DIAMONDS FORKS HAVE
ONLY FOUR TINES

                              BERTRAM ADAMS

A pair of dice is handed to a spectator along with the telegram, and the performer turns his back. The dice are thrown and the two top numbers are multiplied together. The spectator is asked to count to that word in the telegram and concentrate steadily upon it and its meaning. Nothing has been told the performer and, although he has no idea of the numbers arrived at with the dice, he correctly calls out the letters which make up the selected word.

Preparation: All you need is a telegram as per the illustration, plus two dice. To be really effective, the telegram should be authentic, and all you have to do is send one to yourself. This is much better than typing or writing the message on a telegram blank.

Routine: The spectator actually selects the word as described, and you start to concentrate. After mussing your hair a bit, say, "My dear sir, you evidently have never had your mind read before. The word is coming to me in a jumble of letters. However, I'll call out the letters as I get them, and you cross them off as I call them. When you have crossed out the last remaining one, say 'Right' in a loud voice. Are you set?"

The words in the telegram are so chosen and so arranged that no matter what numbers show on the dice, their product will lead to a word which you will arrive at by repeating the following letters slowly, and in the order given:

I S T E N P D R E A O M

Just try this out. It's easy to do, very effective and makes a fine impromptu stunt.

OPERATOR CALLING

HARRIS SOLOMON

When one can do a trick with the assistance of a telephone operator, he is quite a person, and that is just what seems to happen in the case of this excellent home, office or press stunt. It is short, simple and sweet, depending upon dial telephones and a bit of timing. Most cities of any size have dial phones now, so the inclusion of this feat is warranted.

Effect: Ask for the use of a phone and dial the operator. When she answers, say, "Ring back in a few minutes, operator, as soon as you get my friend's thought impression, and tell him the card by the number of rings. Use the usual suit order . . . I'll call you back." Then hang up.

Now explain that the operator is concentrating, and that you would like to have someone select a card. The puzzled spectator takes a card which you do not see. Tell him that the suits are in a certain order, as Hearts, Clubs, Diamonds, Spades, and are thought of as 1, 2, 3 and 4. Thus a suit can be told by the number of rings on the phone. The spectator concentrates, and in a minute or so the phone rings once, twice, three or four times and then stops. You say, "That's . . . rings. The card must be a . . . . Is that correct? Thank you. Now think of the value please, and listen." The phone starts ringing again and stops when it has rung the correct number of times!

Routine: The stunt has an amazing effect upon a person. The calling of the operator is, of course, just build-up, and the poor operator doesn't know what it is all about. However, operators get so many crackpots on the wire every day with foolish questions that they are used to suffering. Note, however, that you make the above remarks quite fast, pause for the operator to say, "What?" and then say, "I'll call you back." That quiets her down and makes her think you're a bit mixed up.

It is only necessary now for the correct card to be forced and then all stand by for the phone to ring. Your confederate is outside, and calls the number at the agreed time. With all dial phones, one can dial the number and listen to the automatic ringing at the other end. When the correct number of rings are heard for the suit of the card, he hangs up and breaks the connection which stops the ringing. He immediately dials the number again, and this time listens until the correct number of rings have been made for the value of the card before he hangs up. The very slight delay in re-dialing the number is taken up by you asking the spectator if the suit is correct, and telling him to start thinking of the card's value.

As simple as it is, you'll find the ringing of a phone bell most effective. It makes a very spooky bit of business, for although everyone is used to answering a phone, just letting one ring and counting the rings is a strange bit of business.

A DIVINATION WITH MATCHES

FREDERICK DeMUTH

An extremely cute match divination can be presented impromptu with a book of paper matches. It's ideal for close-up work, and although it's based on an old mathematical principle this new dress and presentation makes it completely mystifying.

Effect: Hand a book of paper matches to a spectator and ask him to turn his back and remove several matches. Ask him not to let anyone see how many he's taken and then put them in his pocket. Next he is to count the number of matches remaining and then tear out enough of them to represent that number. For instance, should there be 15 matches left, he is to tear out one and lay it on the table, and then tear out five more and lay them alongside of the first match. He is to put these matches in his pocket along with the first ones. He is then asked to tear out any number of the remaining matches he likes and hold them in his hand.

At this point, you turn around and reveal the number of matches he is holding, although it is obvious that you cannot know how many matches have been torn out.

Secret: It is only necessary to use a new or nearly full pack of matches. In a new pack there are always 20 matches. By following the above directions you will find that there will always be nine matches left after the first two actions. When you turn around, pick up the pack of matches, light your cigar or cigarette and note the number of matches left. Subtract this number from nine, and you know the number of matches being held. As indicated above, this will work just as well if you use a pack that is nearly full.

CALENDAR CONJURING
TOM SELLERS

Calendars may be used effectively in mental routines, and for that reason, the following ideas may be of interest to those who are looking for something just a bit different. It makes a nice close-up stunt as well as a fine program item for large audiences when larger size calendars are used.

Effect: The performer proposes to tell any four dates that are marked off by a spectator. Tear a sheet from a calendar pad and give it to him with a pencil. He is to mark a square around any four dates, as illustrated in the first of the three calendar sheets reproduced below. When the spectator announced the total of the four dates he has circled, you immediately announce the four separate figures making up the total.

Secret and Routine: For this example, the four dates in the first calendar have been encircled. The total named is 80. You mentally divide by 4 which equals 20 and subtract 4 to give yourself 16. This is the lowest

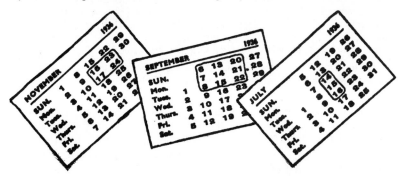

date in the square. It is easy now to calculate the remaining dates as 16 + 7 equals 23, and 17 + 7 is 24. Thus the dates are 16, 17, 23 and 24.

Continue by tearing off another sheet and having another person mark off any nine of the dates in a square. The second calendar sheet illustrates this. Saying that you won't give him so much adding to do, ask him only to give you the total of the highest and lowest dates, in this instance, 6 and 22. This time you mentally divide by 2, and it gives you the center number of the square, or 14. The number to the left of this always is 7 less, or 7 in this instance. The number above is 1 less or 6. Thus you instantly visualize the nine figures as 6, 7, 8, 13, 14, 15, 20, 21, 22.

Again you tear off a sheet and this time a spectator marks off any three figures in a row vertically. We shall use 14, 15 and 16. You are given the total, which in this case is 45. You mentally divide by 3 which gives you the middle figure. By going back 1 and ahead 1 you get the numbers 14, 15 and 16.

Now hand out the rest of the calendar pad and say that you will endeavor to name the days on which any month started and ended. You are given a month and you ask upon what day the 17th landed. If he says Tuesday, you answer by saying that the month started on Sunday and ended on Monday. This is based on the fact that the 15th of the month always arrives on the day the month began, and if there are thirty days in the month it will end one day after the day is started. If there are 31 days in the month it will end two days later than it began. So, when you are told that the 17th was on Tuesday, the 15th must have been Sunday and, if a 30-day month, it must have ended one day later on Monday.

In February, if there are 29 days, the month always ends on the day it starts. If it has 28 days, it always ends one day earlier or before the day on which it starts. There hardly is anyone but knows the jingle by which the number of days in each month is told instantly.

In the example given above, I have used an English type calendar. For the more common type, that is one on which the run of figures goes across in rows rather than in vertical columns, the procedure is the same for the spectator and very little changed for yourself. Where it has been said, in the second effect, that you subtract 7 from the middle figure to get the one at the left, with the more common type calendar you subtract the 7 to get the figure above. In this case, the figure to the left of the one you do know is one less always; and one more, if to the right. If you will just look at any calendar page while going over these instructions, you won't have any trouble understanding the principle.

Dr. Daley has worked out the following formulae, which can be substituted to advantage in the computation of the dates selected.

When the sum of a four-figure square is given, subtract 16 and divide by 4. This gives the smallest figure in the upper left corner. Add 1 to get the figure to right; and 7 for the figure directly underneath, and add 1 to that figure to obtain the figure to right of lower first figure.

For four figures in a vertical row subtract 42 from the sum and divide by 4 for the smallest or top figure. For 5 figures in a vertical row subtract 70 from the sum and divide by 5. You do not have to be told whether 4 or 5 figures are being used as only one of these formulae will come out even.

For any seven figures in a horizontal row subtract 21 from the sum and divide by 7. For a rectangle of six figures, two wide and three deep, subtract 45 from the sum and divide by 6 for smallest number in upper left corner. For a rectangle of six, three wide and two deep, subtract 27 from the sum and divide by 6 for the smallest number in the upper left corner.

DATE SENSE

WALTER GIBSON

Effect: The assistant tears a monthly sheet off the calendar pad. You turn your back on him. He is told to mark off one day in each week. You now ask, "How many Sundays are checked?" "How many Mondays?" "How many Tuesdays?" etc. Immediately after this questioning you name a number. The man with the calendar sheet adds up the dates he's marked and finds that you have called the total correctly!

Routine: Our secret is well hidden. A calendar page is illustrated. Try to use pages wherein 5 lines of dates appear, and the Wednesdays are represented by five date figures. However, those who use this will accustom themselves to the variations. It is only necessary to know the total of the five Wednesday dates, in this case—80.

The subject crosses one day in each of the five lines. More than one date can be checked off on the same day, as long as it's in a different week. You carry seven mental values:

Sunday is minus 3; Monday is minus 2; Tuesday is minus 1; Wednesday is 0; Thursday is plus 1; Friday is plus 2; Saturday is plus 3.

Dates are crossed out in the illustration for example. When asked how many Sundays are checked, the reply is 1. You mentally say minus 3. There is no Monday checked so you repeat minus 3. One Tuesday. You say to yourself, minus 1, and combine it with minus 3 to make minus 4. No Wednesday. Two Thursdays, so plus 1 plus plus 1 are combined with minus 4 which gives minus 2. No Fridays. One Saturday, so plus 3 is combined with minus 2 which gives a final total of plus 1. In your mind you add this to the key number of 80, and 81 is the total of the five dates crossed out.

Remember the key total of the five Wednesdays. This day is neutral. It doesn't matter how many such days are marked. Your mental figures do not change. The day values are 3-2-1-0-1-2-3. Always remember that Sundays, Mondays and Tuesdays are minus; Thursdays, Fridays and Saturdays are plus. In other words, minus to Wednesday; Wednesday neutral or 0; after Wednesday, plus.

SHADES OF SHERLOCK HOLMES !

J. S. THOMPSON, JR.

Here is another "Murder Game" stunt, along the lines of "Who Killed Mr. X," on page 144, but has the added virtue of being impromptu and also uses the assistance of a medium.

Effect: Accompanied by a committee of one, the medium is escorted to another room. As soon as she is gone, the performer explains that a game of murder is to be played. The assembled group is allowed to select from its members the "victim" and the "murderer," and finally the manner in which the crime is to be committed. This being done, the two chosen individuals enact the murder and then resume their seats. To make this playlet a trifle more realistic, the performer explains that at the time of the murder the "victim" is seated in his or her home, playing solitaire and is about to lay a card on the table when the foul deed is done. To determine the name of the card held in the "victim's" hand, the performer borrows a deck of cards and has one selected, noted and returned to the pack by the "corpus delicti," its name being held secret by that person. As a badge of his profession, the performer presents to the "murderer" the Ace of Spades, recognized universally as "the death card," with the request that it be placed in that individual's pocket out of sight. The remainder of the cards are given to a spectator to secrete on his person, and the performer is then escorted from the room under the watchful eye of a committee.

The medium is recalled immediately. She walks about the room finally stopping before the "corpse," and speaks as follows:

"Alas! Poor Yorick. I knew him well! Remarkable life-like in appearance, but I see rigor mortis has already set in. Hm-m-m. Stabbed (or whatever the method employed was) while playing solitaire. I think I'll take a look at these cards (she pretends to pick up an imaginary pack of cards from an imaginary table and looks through them). Just as I thought!"

At this point, the medium moves directly to the "murderer" and accuses him of being the guilty party, saying, "When you killed (give person's name) you thought you had committed the perfect crime. When you stabbed him, he was about to play the Jack of Spades (name the card chosen by the victim). Unable to accuse you in the flesh, his ghost carried that very card into your pocket. Look for yourself. See! It points a silent finger of guilt."

From the above description, it should be clear that the medium finds first the "corpse," discovers the method of the killing, and then locates the "killer" who finds that his badge, the Ace of Spades, has disappeared. In its place is the card selected by the "victim" as the card to be held in his hand at the time of his murder.

Preparation: How does the medium learn all these things? First of all, he or she discovers the "victim" and the "murderer" because the performer has dropped a short length of thread, less than three-quarters of an inch long, on each of their shoulders, when he escorts them to the center of the room to enact the "killing." The thread appearing on the "killer's" shoulder will always be white in color, while the other length may be any one of several colors for it denotes, not only the "victim" but also the type of violent death suffered.

To conform with the story of the "victim" playing solitaire at the time of death, there are only four methods of murdering that could be employed, namely shooting, stabbing, choking and beating. The performer, therefore, will need four different colored threads easily accessible. He can prepare by taking a long length of each thread in turn, placing a needle on it, piercing the outside of one of the vest pockets, tying several knots (overlapping) in the end remaining outside and, with the knotted end pulled tight against the pocket, clipping off the thread inside pocket to the desired length. Arranged thus, any one of the four threads can be quickly procured by grasping the knotted end between the forefinger and thumb and pulling slightly. The white thread, which will always be needed, may be arranged in a similar fashion on the other pocket, if desired. Or the threads may be sewn into the inside edge of each coat sleeve.

Routine: The actual presentation is simple. After explaining what is to be done, the spectators select the manner in which the "victim" shall meet his or her death. This gives the performer ample time to secure the correct thread for conveying the information, the thread being held between thumb and forefinger of right hand. As soon as the "victim" is chosen, the performer asks him or her to come to the center of the room, grasping the person's shoulder in a friendly fashion and dropping the thread thereon with a sort of a slight rubbing motion which makes it adhere to the cloth. The same procedure follows with the "murderer." After enactment of the crime, the performer forces a card, the name of which was previously agreed upon by the performer and the medium. Now the performer goes to the "murderer," locates the Ace of Spades and brings it to the face of the pack just above the chosen card. Two means of switching the cards are available. The performer can either do a two-card lift, turning both pack and double card and laying the latter momentarily on the face down pack, after which it is placed in the "murderer's" pocket or he can execute the "glide" which seems to be the cleaner of the two methods.

After that, it is largely up to the showmanship of the medium. When she returns, she circles the room with much peering into faces, feeling of pulses, etc., which gives plenty of opportunity to locate the two necessary persons and determine the cause of death. The names of the cards she already knows.

TRIUMPH OF THE TRIUMVIRATE
HARRY BLACKSTONE

Here's an effect of strange occurances that all performers who feature a stage show will find effective.

Effect: On your platform are two chairs, back to back and about two feet apart. Resting across the backs of the two chairs is a sheet of glass and on it is a dummy rapping hand.

A side table holds a plate of ten padlocks, another plate of ten keys, and a pack of ordinary playing cards.

To his audience the magician says something like this by way of introduction: "My life of magic has been a much more interesting one because of an intimate acquaintance with orthodox magicians, we magicians do classify ourselves, you know, but after many years of travel and continuous effort to entertain, I've only lately established contact with those contemporary friends who have passed beyond.

"Houdini? A lifetime spent in an effort to subjugate locks and restraining devices to his will. Thurston? One who made the art of stage card manipulation something to be attained by his followers. Carter? An illusionist who sought the bridge between here and the hereafter. Tonight I want to show you how I have made up my own little bridge between where I am and where they are."

The wonder worker asks a spectator to step forward. The plate of padlocks is dumped loudly onto another container. The performer picks up one, hands it to the spectator, and says, "You can open it? No! Not without a key." He takes it back, tosses it into the pile, and picks out another which he hands the volunteer. "Try that one. Can you open it, without a key, any faster than you could the first?"

The magician accepts the negative reply in stride and turns to the audience, requesting and getting a second assistant. For the while he apparently forgets about the lock being held by the first man. "Here is a pack of playing cards. Thurston made a long-to-be-remembered reputation with his smart handling of them. I want you to shuffle them as much as you please."

The performer turns back to his first helper. He picks up the plate of keys. They are dumped into the cupped hands of this man and he is told to lay them out in a row upon the floor in front of himself. "You are holding one of the ten locks. Now you lay out ten keys in any order you please. Only one of those keys fits the lock you hold. I'll show you that the other masters of magic control this experiment and await my joining them."

The magician turns to the second spectator holding the shuffled deck. He takes it, lays it on the floor, has the spectator cut it at any spot, and the cut is held by placing one half crosswise upon the other.

The performer now steps back and shows the dummy hand which has been resting upon the glass plate between the chairs. "Before Charles Carter passed away," he says, "this very close friend of mine studied the possibilities of life after death. He was a famous trickster and knew all about the chicaneries of magical performers. Carter was my mentor."

The performer picks up the hand and gestures with it. "Charles Carter led me to believe that there was something far beyond trickery, and I want to show you now that he may be helping me to make contact with that world in which he is living with his closest friends, Thurston and Houdini."

The hand is placed on the glass inter-chair plate. It raps out a number. The "lock-key" spectator counts to that key—it opens the lock which he holds. Then the hand taps out the name of the card cut at by the second person. And then either of the two helpers may pick up the hand and look it over, as well as the plate of glass and two chairs. There is nothing to find, materially, for the shade of Carter has gone. With him has gone Thurston and Houdini. Only Blackstone remains.

Routine: This trick has been a matter of routining. Ted Annemann wouldn't have wanted it but for the story and presentation.

The deep bowl of locks contains only one you must watch. With them is the card to be forced from the deck later on. First you stir the locks a bit, palming the card, and then dump the locks out. Pick up any one of them (except the right one) and hand it to the spectator. Take it back with the left hand as the right picks out the correct one and gives it in return.

The immediate switch of attention to the card selection is perfect misdirection regarding the free choice of a lock. The key later is chosen by hand raps, and people remember that the spectator had more than one lock in his hand. Taking the deck from the second person, you add the palmed card to the top and at once put the deck face down upon the floor. The spectator cuts it at any place, and you complete the cut by placing the lower half crosswise of the top half leaving it there for the present.

Now pick up the plate of keys and tip them into the cupped hands of the man with the lock. Tell him to shake them up and then lay them out in a row before himself. You watch and help with this, noting the position of the correct key. Mark it any way you choose. Mine is file notched on each side so that it can be caught quickly whichever side is up. Remember that the audience cannot see these keys closely, and the helper is too excited to look for small file marks.

You step to the back and pick up the dummy hand. Use the patter scheme at this point. Then say, "We'll put the hand on the glass and see what Houdini can tell us about your lock. I'm not going to ask you to name a number like two, five, ten, fourteen, etc. I'm going to leave it up to the master in the great beyond." You have thus cued to your assistant the position of the key in the row as laid out by the spectator. The last number you have named is twice the position number. In this case, the assistant knows that the position is seventh (half of fourteen).

You now walk around the chairs once, hold out your hand, and the dummy hand visibly taps out (in this case) the number seven. Ask the first man to count to that key, and try it in the lock. The lock clicks open!

Approaching the second person, you ask him to remove the top crosswise half of the deck and pick up the top card of the lower cut. This is a tried and true force for conditions such as this where the effect is the thing and there is no time for making the selection complicated. The audience always remembers only that the spectator shuffled the cards and then cut them at any spot.

Walk around the hand once more and this time pass your hands directly across from above and underneath. Say, "I'm going to name the four suits, Howard. Make a sign through the hand when I name the one you like best." The hand raps at one suit named. The performer continues, "Now tell us all what value you like best from Ace to King." The hand raps a number of times. The second man shows his card. Thurston has revealed it!

Immediately, ask your two helpers to pick up the hand, the glass, and move the chairs. "You don't see Houdini, Thurston, or Carter?" you say. "Well, they're there, and when the time comes for me to see them I'll tell them all about the times they've helped me entertain my audiences the way they used to do."

The working of the hand is all that remains to be disclosed. It is perfect for stage and platforms where it allows of the performer passing completely around it, and the passing of his hands above and below. One end edge of the glass has a tiny smoothe cut slit which holds a large knotted thread. The diagram illustrates how the thread then runs to a high point at the

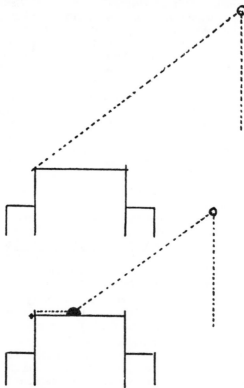

side of the stage, and then to the assistant who operates it. The hand is free at all times and is placed on the thread forcing it down onto the glass where a slight pull tips it to rap as desired. With the thread running as shown, you can walk completely around the set-up and pass your hands directly above and below the glass. At the finish, pick up the hand, and pass your hand across under the thread, which disengages the knotted end from the glass leaving everything free for inspection.

PROPHETIC TISSUE
STEWART JAMES

Effect: The performer shows a piece of white tissue paper to be blank on both sides. It is held at the fingertips, with the hands otherwise empty, and rolled into a ball. This is tossed into a glass on the table. A spectator is now invited to choose a card from a well shuffled pack. When the performer opens the paper ball, the name of the card is revealed in large black letters across the paper.

Preparation: The card, of course, is forced in your favorite manner. The appearance of the name of the card on the paper is managed as follows:

Use two pieces of white tissue about three by six inches. Across one, write in soft crayon the name of your force card. Place the two tissues back to back, with the message on top and facing you. At a spot 1½ inches from one end, at the center of the width, put a daub of library paste about the size of a tack head between the two papers. Press them together and let them dry. Next crumple the message paper, from the four corners in towards the center, making a tight and compact ball resting at its pasted point. You are now ready.

Routine: Pick up the prepared tissue with the left hand. Hold it with the second finger in front and the thumb behind and directly on top of and pressing down on the crumpled ball. The other fingers are kept open and, in this way, the single sheet of tissue can be shown freely on both sides and against a light. Exhibit it, then crumple it up so that the two pieces may be shown as one ball, and even toss it up into the air, if you like. Now throw it into the glass very openly, pick up a deck of cards and force your card. Pick up the glass, roll out the paper ball and open the message side to show that the spirits have written the name of the card for you.

THE BALL OF FORTUNE
STEWART JAMES

Effect: The performer picks up a fair size ball of wool with a pair of knitting needles through it, saying, "This was the property of an old Gypsie who used to be renowned in our village because of her ability to tell fortunes. With your permission, I would like to show you a most peculiar effect using this ball of wool and this glass bowl."

The performer has replaced the ball of wool on his table, and from his pocket has taken a blank card and a lead pencil. He selects two persons as subjects. One is asked to name a number from 1 to 1,000,000. The other is asked to name any color. The performer writes both the number and color on the card, leaving it with the spectators as a check.

Returning to the table he picks up the ball of wool, withdraws the needles, and hands it to a third spectator together with a glass bowl or dish. The spectator puts the ball into the bowl and unreels the wool. In the center of the ball is discovered a cardboard key tag. On one side is written the chosen number, and on the other side is found the selected color!

Preparation: Of course, the reader has beaten me to the denouement, at least part of it. The coin slide comes back into a somewhat new use, but instead of a coin, Dennison or stationery store circular key tags about quarter

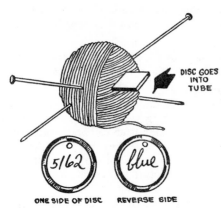

DISC GOES INTO TUBE

ONE SIDE OF DISC   REVERSE SIDE

or shilling size (with metal edge) are used. The knitting needle part is an effective cover for the chicanery. The ball of wool is first wound around the tube in the regular way, leaving a good inch of the tube sticking out. The needles are now pushed through the ball just against the flat side of the tube and about a half inch apart. Such a prepared ball may be picked up and shown for a minute, the fingers on one hand hiding the tube which would hardly be seen anyway, for the yarn is dark red or blue, the needles white, and the tube black. The cardboard disc is also white.

Routine: The wool is returned to the table and the card and pencil taken from your pocket. As they are taken out with the left hand, the disc is finger palmed also. The card may carelessly be shown both sides with the disc concealed, but it isn't necessary. When a number is named you hold the card in front of you and write down the number. The disc is held against the card and the number is written on that, too. You stall a bit by asking to have the number repeated. Then the disc is turned over while asking a color of the second person. This, too, is written on both the disc and the card.

The card is taken in the right hand and given to someone, the disc remaining finger palmed in the right hand. The performer steps up to the table, lets his left fingers touch the top of the ball (which holds it steady) and the right fingers then pick up the ball from the rear, which action allows the finger palmed disc to slide through the tube. With the ball picked up, the performer swings to the left to face the audience. The right fingers curl around the protruding tube and the needles. With one move, the needles and the tube are withdrawn from the ball and put aside.

From here on, the mechanics of the effect are over. It depends entirely upon the individual performer's showmanship and sincerity to make the watchers believe in his prowess.

(**Editor's Note:** The original patter theme of this Stewart James originality was not in keeping with the effects contained in this book, but we felt that the routine was well worth including. As a suggestion, we believe that some logical reason should be given for finding the metal tag in the ball of wool. You may like this. Show a metal tag and a drug envelope at the start of the trick. Apparently drop the tag into the envelope, which you seal and set in the bowl. Just before the climax, pick up the envelope, tear it open and touch a lighted cigarette to it. There is a sudden flash of flames! Then show the envelope empty, and produce the tag from the ball of wool as explained in the routine. The flash can easily be accomplished by having a small slip of flash paper already in the envelope. This unexpected touch should, we believe, add considerably to the effect.) Note 2: The knitting needles shown in the above illustration pierce the ball of wool incorrectly. They should be inserted parallel to and in alignment with the tube.

MY OWN SWAMI TEST

ANNEMANN

Prophecy, in the form known as "The Swami Test," first popularized by Claude Alexander around 1920, has been a much experimented with effect. I have filed exactly sixteen variations and methods that have been marketed at prices ranging from $1 to $10. The following is my own method developed in 1925. Since then I've certainly had ample opportunity to test it out under every conceivable condition confronting the club and close-up worker.

Effect: You use one small card, one small envelope, one pencil and nothing else. Both the card and envelope are examined and initialled. You write a prophecy on the card, seal it in the envelope, and then hold it in full view of everyone throughout the test. A number of three figures is called out, and someone else names any color. The mark on the envelope is identified first, then the envelope is opened and the card withdrawn. On the marked card is found written the exact number suggested as well as the correct color, and everything may be left with the audience at the finish!

Routine: Don't work too close to the audience, but stand back about eight to ten feet. Have the card and envelope examined and marked with a pencil, which is about two and a half inches long. You take back the pencil and card and pretend to write something on the card, but actually you write nothing. Now put the pencil in your right trouser pocket.

Hold the envelope in your left hand, flap up, and with the address side towards audience. Now, from the spectator's point of view, you put the card into the envelope—but it really goes down behind the envelope, where it is held by the left thumb as the envelope is lifted up to your mouth to moisten the flap with your tongue. As the flap is bent down with the right hand, the forefinger of your left hand is inserted between the end of the card and the envelope which allows the flap to bypass the card. Your right thumb and forefinger are now drawn back and forth across the envelope, one on each side, to seal the flap.

The envelope is held between your two hands, forefingers at front and thumbs of each hand at back holding the card against the envelope. Release the side held by the right fingers, and the left hand comes over towards the right wrist and deposits both the envelope and card in the palm of your right hand, with the envelope still hiding the card. The right hand is now held out so that the envelope can be seen plainly for a second while you are talking. The left fingers and thumb now come back and pick up the envelope at the same end as before, bringing it out to the same position as at first, between the thumbs and forefingers of both hands. Under cover of this move, the card is retained in the right hand and palmed. As the backs of both hands holding the envelope are toward the audience, the palmed card is never seen.

Try this and it will be seen at once how easily the card stays in your palm because of its stiffness. The left hand now holds the envelope up in full view. Simultaneously the right hand with the palmed card drops down and is inserted in your right trouser pocket. When well in the pocket, you deposit the card and pick up the pencil. Do not remove your right hand, keep it in your pocket.

HAND WRITING IN POCKET

Now close in on the audience, getting as near as possible. Pick out one person to name a number, which you immediately scribble on the card in your pocket as you look around for someone else who is asked to name a color. The moment the color is mentioned start to write it on the card under the number. In order to create a few second's stall, ask the spectator why he chose that particular color, if it is his favorite, etc. Being close to the spectators makes it difficult for them to watch anything but your face and the envelope which you are holding in your left hand and waving around a bit. When the writing is completed, step back to the front and bring out the right hand with the card palmed, and with the back of right hand towards audience. Rest this hand on your belt, or hold it at about your waist line for a minute, as you recall that you wrote a prediction on the sealed card before anyone had even mentioned or thought of a number or color.

As you say this, bring the envelope down for a second and grasp it between your two hands as before; then place the envelope in your right hand just as you did formerly. This repetition of moves brings the envelope back on top of the palmed card in your right hand. At this point recall that the envelope was initialled for identification. The left hand again picks up the envelope from the right palm together with the card behind it, and holds it so that the card is not visible from the front. Now grasp the envelope at the top with the right thumb and fingers while the left hand tears off the left end of the envelope. Pinch this end with the thumb and forefinger of the left hand, and take this new grip with the right hand: Place the thumb at the bottom of the envelope, the second and third fingers at the top, and with the first finger curled up at back holding the card against the envelope. Now the left forefinger goes into the envelope while the thumb goes behind it, and the card is apparently withdrawn and given to the nearest spectator for verification of your prediction.

Just remember to keep talking when first putting the card into the envelope, and speak about "sealing the envelope" rather than about putting the card inside. They'll take that as natural. All moves are done casually and they work smoothly once you have the routine firmly established in your mind. Try it before the mirror and, once you have gained confidence in the routine, you'll just go ahead and do it without a thought.

TRIPLE COERCION

ANNEMANN

For a nice club or drawing room item, this will be found excellent and it's extremely simple to work.

Effect: The performer writes something on a card and seals it in a small envelope which is displayed in full view on the table. A spectator selects a color, another a card, and finally one is asked to think of a number from 1 to 100. These selections are known to everyone, and opening the envelope a spectator removes and reads the card. It says, for instance, "Three persons will name the color blue, the four of diamonds and the number 73." And all is left with the audience.

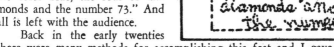

Back in the early twenties there were many methods for accomplishing this feat and I gave my own in "The Book Without a Name." However, the one weak point, to me, was the necessity of jotting down the items as selected when any simpleminded person would find no trouble in remembering them. I honestly think this effect is almost as simple as it can be done.

Use a number two size end opening drug envelope, a card cut a little shorter than usual, and one of the now fairly well known thumb writers. Make a slit in the envelope on the face side about three-quarters of an inch from the bottom edge with the thumb nail, so it will be a little jagged as if torn. Write on the card at the start everything as shown except the number, and space your writing also as shown. Put the card into the envelope with the flap side towards the audience and with the writing away from them.

Tilt the card so it comes out through the slit as pictured. Seal the flap and stand the envelope against something, saying, "We'll place this to one side so all can see it constantly."

Now proceed to force the color on someone using your own favorite method (or refer to my "202 Methods of Forcing") and then follow this by forcing the card on another. At this time be sure to tell the selector to keep it pictured well in his mind. Lay the deck aside and secure the thumb writer on the right thumb as you carelessly pick up the sealed envelope with your left hand. Ask a third person to think of and name any number from 1 to 100. He does so. Turning to the first person, you recall the color chosen. Then ask the second person to name the card he is thinking about. Then repeat the number thought of by the third person. This bit impresses on the audience that the articles are being thought of only, or at least, that's what they go away thinking. The slight stall enables you to bring both hands together and put the number on the card protruding thru the slit.

At this time, the left fingers and thumb pinch the sides of the envelope and tip it a little, so that the card drops back inside. Immediately you tear off the end of the envelope at the slit, which destroys this evidence, and hand the envelope to someone to remove the card and reads it aloud. The psychology of having the last person think of the number is perfect and the people will swear afterwards, as I know, that all the items were merely thought of by the audience. Furthermore, they'll also swear that the envelope was on the table away from you when items were named.

MODERNIZED READING
ANNEMANN

Of all the single or group reading methods that have been invented and created, I think none have been as practical and simple as the window frame idea. I've always thought that it was mine but after eleven years I'm not so sure. I made my first note of it on January 12, 1924, and thought of it while reading about an alcohol envelope fake on page 92 of Alexander's Dr. Q book. I handled a lot of correspondence then and passed it around. Later it was advertised in The Sphinx. Howard Albright used it in his Super-Psychic Mental book, and in June, 1934, it was reprinted (with permission) in The Indian Magician, India's crack magical monthly.

I used it originally, not for a single reading (I didn't see its value as such then), but only "to get" the first question in a one-ahead routine with cards and envelopes. Here is the method of handling. It can be used for the above purpose or for a single reading, and is much cleaner and safer than any of the copies I have read.

Routine No. 1: For those who do not know this envelope it is a regular drug size, end opening type (No. 2 is best) and the face side has been cut out except for a quarter inch margin around the edge. The envelope is on a stack of ordinary ones. Now a card, of a size to fit easily into the envelope, is written on by the sitter and is inserted into the envelope, writing side down, and the flap of the envelope is sealed. Picking the single envelope off the stack and holding it with its uncut side towards the sitter it is burned. Meanwhile the performer has read the question through the window side. There are variations and niceties in handling but we won't go into them here.

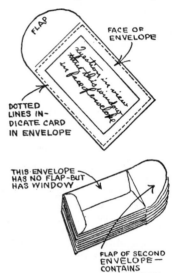

FACE OF ENVELOPE

DOTTED LINES IN- DICATE CARD IN ENVELOPE

THIS ENVELOPE HAS NO FLAP-BUT HAS WINDOW

FLAP OF SECOND ENVELOPE— CONTAINS DUMMY CARD

Routine No. 2: My present method is to have the flap of the window envelope cut off. Six or seven envelopes are in a stack. In one envelope is placed a blank card such as will be used by the sitter for writing a message. This loaded envelope is second from the top of the stack, and on top of this is placed the window envelope with the cut-out side down. The flap belonging to the loaded envelope will now appear to be the flap of the window fake. The stack of envelopes, of course, are being held with the flap sides up.

When the sitter has written on a card, he is told to lay it on the table, writing side down. Approaching with the stack of envelopes in the left hand (hold them from above with the thumb and fingers at the sides, and with flap ends outward) you slide the card to the edge of the table and shove it into the window envelope. Now catch hold of the flap and pull the envelope off the stack. Thus, the loaded envelope is pulled from under the window envelope which contains the written card and which still remains on top of the stack. Sufficient pressure with the left thumb and fingers will retain the window envelope in place, while the back of the left hand hides this "second deal" very nicely.

Now hand the loaded envelope to the sitter and ask him to seal it and write his name across its back and face. As he does so, you turn and lay the stack of envelopes you are holding on a nearby table. With one finger flip over the window envelope on the top of the stack which will bring the message face up. A quick glance at it is all you'll need to read the message. I suggest working at a small table with a drawer on your side. Merely open it and drop the envelopes in, getting the information at the same time. Now take the sitter's envelope and burn it in front of him. This is positively the quickest method of getting sealed information without the sitter having any reason to suspect trickery.

PSEUDO-PSYCHOMETRY
ANNEMANN VERSION

This trick, to my mind, is one of the greatest one-man psychic effects ever conceived. It has all of the elements necessary to make it your most talked about effect, and any performer with but a bit of showmanship can't help but make a hit with it. If you are endowed with a goodly share of showmanship this effect will create a sensation and can be built up to be the feature attraction of your show.

Last, but not least, the effect needs very little preparation, and it can succeed under most exacting conditions. In short, we have before us an idea with unlimited scope. Another of those rare secrets wherein the method is nothing and the effect, from the audience viewpoint, is everything. Your audience will never tumble to the simple detail that makes it possible. The enormity of what the performer attempts completely overshadows the means by which it is accomplished.

Effect: A packet of letter envelopes is all that is needed. About a dozen of these are passed out to different spectators and the performer returns to the front. Requesting those with envelopes to pay strict attention, he instructs them to put into their envelopes some single article and personal belonging that is on their person. It can be a fountain pen, a tie clasp, a ribbon, a coin, a hairpin, a button, a knife, a pencil, a handkerchief, a card, a ring or in fact anything of a similar nature that can be sealed inside the envelope. During this time the performer may be turned around so that he cannot possibly see what is being placed in any of the envelopes. This looks important but actually means nothing insofar as the working of the trick is concerned.

Once the envelopes are ready, the performer has them collected by a member of the audience and brought forward to him. This spectator mixes them and hands them on to the performer. He deliberately tears off the end of the envelope and dumps the contents into his hand. Turning whatever it might be over and over in his hand, he describes a person, giving the sex, type, approximate age (if a man), and a few details of the person's attire. He then holds the article so all can see it and asks the owner to acknowledge it. This person stands, and he or she turns out to be the one just described by the performer!

Another envelope is opened and the article once more seemingly gives a clue regarding the characteristics of the owner. This time, however, the performer walks down into the audience and suddenly returns the article directly to its owner!

As each envelope is handed to him, the performer successfully describes and finds the owner, or describes and merely locates the owner of the property. The patter is about psychometry. Mediums of this type are supposed to have the ability to "see" and locate people by touching some personal belonging. In this case, instead of revealing information about a "dear one," the performer is able, through the same power, to describe and locate the owners of the property he handles.

As I have said before, the audience never realizes that the important detail is right under their noses. They all try to fathom how the performer is able to trace the owner of the trinket each time, it being obvious that he didn't see what any person furnished, or knows in what order the mixed envelopes might be collected and given to him. And thus we have a test that can be made big or small, fast or slow as desired.

Preparation and Routine: The secret lies entirely in the envelope, and it is only necessary to know to whom each envelope belongs!

My method of marking is to open the envelope with the flap towards you, and write a figure lightly on the inside of side which is nearest to you, about an inch from the left end. Have these envelopes in order from 1 to 10.

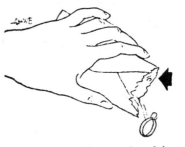

It is far from difficult to remember who gets these envelopes, as they are passed out in numerical order from left to right. By skipping a person between each, or through some other system of layout, the envelopes are spread over the crowd in an order that you can trace. Those who have learned memory principles will be able to pass the envelopes at random and tie up each spectator mentally with the envelope given to him.

In tearing open an envelope, have the flap side towards you. Tear off a half-inch from the right end. Your left thumb and fingers are at the bottom and the top edges with the flap still turned towards you, and the contents are tipped into your right hand. The number is near the edge on the inside looking up at you! Dog ear one envelope instead of marking the inside of it. When you get to it, you know the owner without having to open it. On this one you apparently get a stronger impression, so you describe him, locate him and return the envelope still sealed. It makes a nice variation, and is just different enough from the rest to be remembered by your audience!

An excellent stage version for two people is possible with this test. After passing out the envelopes, the performer introduces a medium and blindfolds her. He then leaves the stage and takes up a position behind the drop from where he can see the audience and communicate with the medium, by any one of several well-known methods. She directs the sealing and the collecting of the envelopes. She sees the key number each time by looking down under her blindfold, cues the performer with a simple finger code, and he gives her a description of the owner's appearance, details about his clothing, etc. This version is a stunner for publicity with Lost and Found Departments!

MODERNIZING THE "ONE AHEAD" PRINCIPLE
This was originally published in the "Jinx" as "Gypsies Won't Tell"
DUNNINGER-ANNEMANN

Probably the oldest and most misused method of answering or revealing written thoughts is that which makes use of the "one-ahead" system. Despite its age we shall try hard to show that the operator is at fault rather than the procedure.

Effect: The performer has questions and notations written upon cards which are sealed inside envelopes provided. They are collected upon a tray by the miracle-man's assistant and placed on a table or in a bowl in full view.

Singly, the master-mind picks up these envelopes and, with each held openly before him, proceeds to answer the question or reveal the thought encompassed within. In every instance the material object is returned to its owner immediately after the revelation.

Preparation: In the past, the performer has had to resort to faking the answer to the first question, and utilized the "one-ahead" method of reading a query as a check up, while actually getting knowledge of the next one. Such a procedure always has entailed the necessity of keeping the messages until the end, when they might be returned in a jumbled bunch.

Obviously, the performer cannot return each question envelope and card as answered. Time is the preventative. But, a helper, an assistant, can, unnoticed, return writing after writing to the owners while the performer, who is the center of attraction, carries on his work without a slackening of interest.

Our main solution is dependent upon that assistant. Audiences watch the man dominating the stage. They pay little or no attention to the assistant. Let us suppose that the performer knows the contents of one envelope among the lot. We'll get to that angle later. While the master-mind may know what is inside one envelope, that which he holds in view contains unknown possibilities. He answers the known question. As he finishes he tears open the envelope and, apparently, reads aloud the query therein. Actually, he remembers what he sees and uses it as the next problem.

In the past, these envelopes and contents have had to be kept on the stage. We want to have each written and sealed question returned to its owner after the answer has been given. If the performer cannot do it, the assistant can. If the performer cannot make a practical exchange of questions, so that the spectator just satisfied gets back his own writing which has just been read by the performer, the assistant can. By that premise we deceive.

So as not to worry about an assistant's sleight-of-hand ability, we build a tray upon which he or she first collects the written thoughts and later returns them to their writers one by one. This tray's peculiar property is that it can change a dropped on envelope for another, and immediately change the next one dropped on for the one secreted before.

Simply constructed of ply wood, the tray is not mechanical. Its value depends upon the assistant's handling of it. It is rectangular in shape and about six by ten inches in size. Around the edge is a narrow siding which gives an inside depth of about five-eighths of an inch. The tray surface is covered with a well-glued on piece of wall paper of striped or squared design. On this is glued a sheet of transparent cellophane and all dried under pressure.

Next secure a piece of tin as wide as the inside tray dimension but only half as long. Punch small holes (use the end of a nail) in the extreme corners of the tin, and, using small finishing nails together with four bits of wood or metal bushings not over three-eighths of an inch high between the tin sheet and tray bottom, secure the metal to the end of the tray. Lastly sandpaper the tin well and cover it with wall paper to match that on the tray proper, followed by a surface of cellophane. Paint the edge of the tray, inside and out, using a color that contrasts with the wall paper.

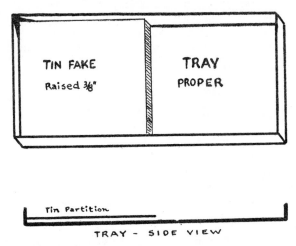

TIN FAKE

Raised ⅜"

TRAY

PROPER

Tin Partition

TRAY - SIDE VIEW

If an envelope is laid on the tray proper and the tray is then tipped, the smooth surface allows the envelope to slide under the tin fake and out of sight. As the tray is never examined, or its surface seen at close range, this preparation has been found the most practical for the purpose.

Routine: Assuming that the performer knows the contents of one message, the procedure is carried out as follows: The assistant collects the envelopes taking the first one received and drops it across the compartment opening, whereupon all others are deposited upon the tray at random. Knowing which spectator's envelope is "the one" he easily keeps it to one end of the tray, the unprepared end, of course. Then, when he returns to the front or stage, and dumps the tray's contents into a bowl or on a table, this one envelope is left behind and is tipped into the slot.

While the performer finishes his introductory talk, the assistant retires or makes himself inconspicuous for the purpose of tearing the end off the stolen envelope. He keeps it at the unprepared end of the tray, where his thumb retains it against the bottom as he holds the tray at his side.

The performer picks up any envelope, holds it to his forehead, and answers that which he already knows. He tears open the envelope as he is concluding, and reads the card inside. The card is replaced and at this moment the assistant presents the tray so that the writing may be returned directly to the person who has acknowledged his whereabouts. The performer drops the envelope on the tray's unprepared end and as the assistant steps away he drops the tray to his side and goes into the audience. The message just read drops into the slot and the original one under the thumb is retained. The spectator removes his envelope from the tray. And on the return trip the assistant need tip the tray but a little to bring out the concealed envelope into the "under-thumb" position in readiness for the next time. The performer, in the meantime, has already picked up another envelope and started his answer which serves to prevent any delay in the continuity as well as to keep attention from the assistant. Assistants are like waiters. They can be all over the place without anyone noticing them.

In this case the performer never answers all of the queries written. There are always too many. He finishes by asking an audience member to pick out a final one from the pile, and he reveals its contents. The remainder of the envelopes are tossed aside or into the crowd.

Readings for Intimate Groups

The foregoing has explained the use of the tray. However, most readers will probably perform for comparatively small groups where a dummy or fake question for the first reading is not to be countenanced. Before large audiences it is a simple matter for the performer to fix up a theoretical query, answer it, and have the assistant deliver it to anyone back in the hall or theatre with the remark, "Kindly check the question, sir," and be sure that no commotion will result. We know of two very good and practical methods for gaining that first question. Rather than ask everybody to "write a question" we prefer to have them jot down "items" such as "events in their lives," "names of relatives," "the place where born," "the name of one's first school teacher," "the maiden name of one's wife," "social security number," etc.

The performer hands out cards and envelopes asking each person to write a specific thing such as those mentioned. Only three or four are asked to write a question. The more varied this array of requests, the more the performer will hold interest during what would otherwise be a dull proceeding. Among these requests, he picks a person for some bit of data *which he knows,* having taken means to find it out. The telephone number generally is easiest. The assistant, naturally, takes care of that particular envelope in his aforementioned way.

The second "out," when no previous information is available, uses that valuable "window envelope." The performer steps into his group of watchers followed by the assistant. He carries a stack of envelopes with cards inside. On the top of the stack is an envelope with most of its face (address) side cut out, opening side down. On top of this is a blank card. The performer asks a person fairly close to the front, "Think of some personal date or event in your life—something which you are certain is unknown to everybody here. Write it on the card so that you won't keep thinking of important happenings, remember something else, and change your mind. Put it in the envelope (he does so, writing side down, you wet the flap and seal, and toss it carelessly upon the tray) and try hard to keep that occurance on your mind. It will aid me a lot."

You hand the rest of the stack to the assistant and tell the audience, "Each of you who take an envelope and card, please do the same. If you do not care to note down (here you recite the various possibilities as already outlined), you may write a question, something about which you would like to be helped. I'll do my very best to give you an answer."

Now, you return to the front and, while your assistant takes care of distributing the writing material and subsequently collects it, you either discourse on the latent power of the mind, or perform some quick mental stunt that will hold the interest of the entire gathering.

The assistant returns, and has the window envelope on top of all with the open side up and turned correctly. He offers you the tray. You mention that you'll take them at random and finger the pile, reading the question before you. Take another one and hold it up. The assistant dumps all but the window envelope onto the table and steps away to a spot where he can open it, remove the card, slide it into a previously sealed and torn open envelope, and retain this on the tray in the thumb position. Everything proceeds quite perfectly.

This exposition of a derided and almost discarded principle has been written to show how it might be rejuvenated by modern day mystics. For once, the performer has relegated the undercover part of the proceedings to his helper. For once, the master-mind can leave the mechanics of his effect to the cleverness of someone constantly before the people yet never noticed. It is simply a case of the ultimate in misdirection when applied this way.

Such a routine might well be used by any couple presenting a telepathic act. For instance, an assistant's help in the opening minutes to set the envelopes, while the performer does one or two psychic tests, accustoms the audience to the assistant's presence. Later the assistant may "come into the open" and be a definitely recognized factor in the experiments to follow.

With personal questions concerning love, business, work, lost articles, etc., taking up only a small portion of the routine thereby holding the interest of the non-participants, this seeming proof of a performer's powers to read sealed messages should be a strong spot in any program. By itself, such a routine ought not to run over 20 minutes in an hour's show. Certainly there are few presentations requiring as little preparation.

AN ORIGINAL FAKED ENVELOPE

ANNEMANN

Faked envelopes all follow the same basic principles, but I think that I have a new variation and also a very practical improvement on the old style. I've never considered such envelopes as sound magic when they are obviously used to change an article. When an audience see the Four of Spades go in an envelope and the Ace of Spades come out, they at once consider the envelope as the medium of exchange and center their interest upon it. However, if a card is freely chosen and sealed in an envelope without being shown, and later it is removed and revealed to be the correct pasteboard, there is no outward evidence of it having been changed. The same applies to something you may write and then subsequently have read. With this thought in mind, I have developed a new faked envelope with three compartments. Two can be loaded at the start. You now write something on a slip of paper and insert it in the envelope and seal it. Upon open-ing the envelope later, a paper is dumped out into the spectator's hand, not pulled out with a lot of fumbling, and this paper slip may be the original one or either one of the other two, as you choose.

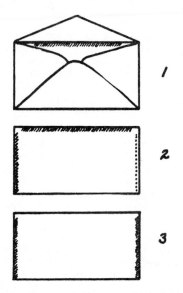

1

2

3

To prepare, have three letter envelopes before you and a small pair of scissors of the one sharp point type.

Envelope No. 1 is left alone. Trim the sides, top and bottom of envelopes 2 and 3 keeping only the address sides. Lay these two inserts in front of you and follow these instructions:

Apply library paste as shown in the illustrations. The shaded sections have paste, while the dotted section on No. 2 indicates paste on the under side. This pasted surface in each case should be only a quar-ter-inch wide, starting a quarter-inch from the upper corners. I find it best to lay down a ruler and then apply the paste to the edge of the envelopes. This will guarantee that the paste strip will be exactly one-quarter inch wide and uniform for its whole length.

Now lay the No. 3 envelope section onto No. 2, and then insert both into the No. 1 envelope. The whole thing goes under a heavy weight and is left to dry. As you look at the sketches, the two loaded papers go into the back and middle compartments. Assemble the sections (Nos. 2 and 3) together with the loaded papers and insert them all into the No. 1 envelope at one time.

Study this for a minute and you'll see what you have made. Now insert a paper or card into the envelope as you would normally do. Seal it. Next open the envelope by trimming an eighth of an inch from the left end. Pinch the envelope at top and bottom, as you would normally do, and blow a little into it to open it. Only the rear compartment can open, and the contents fall out. On the other hand, if you trim the other end, only the center compartment can open. If you want the original paper, stick the point of the scissors under the flap and rip open the top.

Thus, you have complete control of the contents of the envelope and can produce any one of the three you please. No fumbling, or inserting fingers and thumb into the envelope for removal of the slip is necessary. Just tip the envelope, shake it a bit and out comes the very slip you want.

BLUEBEARD'S SEVEN WENCHES

BRUCE ELLIOTT

Those who have read the fairy tale version of Bluebeard and his wives will immediately realize that the *mise en scene* is easily applicable in the case of the seven wenches.

Effect: The performer has seven drug envelopes which he explains represent the seven doors behind which Bluebeard incarcerated his wives.

Seven cards picturing the seven beheaded ladies are shown, and their names are read from the back of each as the performer puts them into the envelopes, that is, behind the doors. For the present, the flaps are not sealed. Smilingly, the performer says, "It is not probable, but it is highly possible that Bluebeard, when on deviltry bent, and desirous of a fresh victim for his chamber of horrors, ambled benignly up and down the corridor selecting the lady by some simple whim or caprice."

The performer offers to let the members of his audience play "cut throat" for a while, and asks that two of them merely think of the name of the lady who might be his next victim. Carelessly mixing the envelopes, the performer places the packet on the outstretched hand of one person and asks him to whisper loudly the name of the fair one destined for a gory fate.

Now the spectator moves an envelope at a time, from the top to the bottom of the packet, spelling a letter of the girl's name with each move. On the last letter he stops and retains the envelope he then holds. From it he removes the beheaded lady. It's the one he had chosen!

The effect is repeated with the second person, and once more an amateur Bluebeard successfully finds the lady he desires!

Then comes the final test. The performer removes the heads from the envelopes. He picks on a third person and asks him to mentally pick the one lady of the seven he'd like to save from an undeserved death. Then he is asked to freely select one of the envelopes. While the performer's back is turned, this third person inserts the card bearing the lady of his choice into the envelope and seals it. He is then told to put the other ladies into the remaining envelopes, sealing them also. Lastly, the seven rooms (envelopes) are well mixed.

The performer, without looking at the envelopes, takes them behind his back and pretends to be Bluebeard. One by one he tosses six of the envelopes aside. The remaining envelope is handed back to the third spectator, who opens it. As he is opening it he is asked to name the lady of his choice, and when he dumps the card out it is that very same lady!

The stunt may get as fantastic as desired, but its dress makes it a somewhat different effect to carry around in your vest pocket.

Preparation: Illustrated herewith are the pictures of the seven wenches. You can scale these up to the size card you want, then copy them in black drawing ink, or have an artist prepare them for you. On the back of each, letter one of the following names: Lois, Julia, Martha, Lucille, Theodora, Jeannette, Evangeline. Each name, you will notice, has one more letter than the one before it.

You will also need seven drug envelopes. Into each, drop one of the smallest size embroidery beads you can get. Keep the packet together with the head cards, and you are set.

Routine: Show the cards and, as you call their names, pick them up in the order given, put them into the envelope and pile them up. Pick up the pile and turn it over. As you talk, carelessly cut three from the bottom to the top, and with the right forefinger and thumb nail nick the top envelope in the right near corner.

With the envelopes arranged thus, any one of the names will automatically spell out when an envelope is moved from top to bottom with each letter. The last letter hits the correct head. After the first spectator replaces his chosen head in its envelope, you put it on the stack and, in passing to the second person, cut the pile a few times to bring the nicked envelope back to the top. The second name now spells out.

Next, remove the heads from the envelopes. It is well to remember that during all of this there is a single bead in each envelope. The spectators do not have much opportunity for handling them, and you, of course, never allow an envelope to be upside down when the flap is open. The third spectator thinks of a lady to save. You spread out the envelopes and have him freely point to any one. Pick it up, pinching its sides and turn your back. Hold your hand with the envelope behind your back towards the spectator, asking him to pick up his chosen lady. Tell him to take the envelope from you and seal her up. Like the old lock puzzle trick, this action has served to turn the envelope upside down without making a visible move of doing so. The bead will fall out, of course, and thus you get rid of it.

With the other heads sealed in the remaining envelopes, it is clear that the chosen head is inside the only envelope without a bead. While the bead principle has been used before it has been necessary to fumble and load in a bead, not the easiest thing in the world to control. In this instance, it is the missing bead that gives the clue.

Behind your back, when holding the mixed packet and facing the audience, it is simply a case of feeling each envelope's corners at the base, tossing aside those containing beads. The empty envelope remains until last and it is given to the third spectator. He first names the lady of his choice, and then opens the envelope to find her safe!

JUST AN ECHO

JAMES T. DEACY

The effect is begun with a few casual remarks about echoes. The audience is surprised and somewhat skeptical when informed that an echo exists not only after a sound has been made, but also before. To substantiate this claim, the performer offers to make a note of a few of the echoes that are now floating around the room, waiting for a sound to give them life. He takes from his pocket a calling card, and has someone initial the printed side of it for later identification. On the blank side of this he then begins to write, pausing impressively at intervals so that he may have a varied collection of the choicest echoes in the room. This card is then sealed in a small coin envelope and two persons asked to initial the sealed ends.

The performer then asks someone to take a bill from his pocket and read aloud the serial number. This is written on a borrowed business card, the sealed envelope being used as a rest for it. Next, someone calls out about ten letters of the alphabet. (I've been getting a laugh lately by asking someone for his Social Security number.)

Four single digits, supplied by four different persons, are now written in a column and added. The envelope is then placed to one side, well out of the reach of any curious person who may wish to examine it. The business card with all the numbers and letters is now handed to one of the audience, and that favored gentleman is formally invited to act as secretary for the remainder of the performance. Someone now shuffles a deck of cards and selects one. Its name is written on the business card by the secretary. The performer then asks the audience for the name of an automobile, and "Ford V-8" is noted on the card.

After a brief recapitulation of the main points thus far, the performer takes up the envelope, produces a scissors, and permits the one who signed his initials first to snip an end off, reach in, and withdraw the card. The original signature is on the card and identified, and the number, letters, etc., are of course identical with those on the card held by the secretary. The envelope is then cut in half, and the persons who signed the ends permitted to retain the halves as souvenirs. Thus, everything used in the mystery is left with the audience, with the exception of the pencil.

Secret and Routine: And now, the inevitable accounting. The envelope used has, across its center, a slit wide enough to permit the card to pass through easily. After the card is initialed, the performer writes at the bottom "Ford V-8" and above that the name of the card which he will force later Before starting, have this card in your pocket. When the deck has been shuffled, palm it onto the top of the pack ready to be forced.

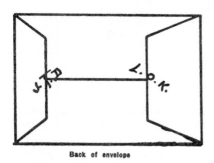

Back of envelope

The performer then stalls a bit, and pretends to write more, frowning something like Rajah Raboid. The card is now slid into the envelope, guided from beneath through the slit, and the flap is sealed. After sealing, it is placed face down on a book, and held there firmly by the performer's thumb while the ends are signed.

Someone is asked to read out the number of a bill, and, as an after thought, the performer borrows a business card so that the number may be noted. While writing, the performer retires to a safe distance so that the slit envelope may not be seen. The borrowed card is placed with its edge half an inch below that of the card in the envelope, and the writing done with a pencil gimmicked in the following manner:

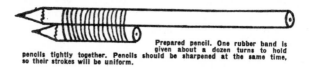

Prepared pencil. One rubber band is given about a dozen turns to hold pencils tightly together. Pencils should be sharpened at the same time, so their strokes will be uniform.

To the sharpened end of a regular sized pencil, the stub of a pencil (about two inches from point to end) is fastened by means of a rubber band. The small pencil is arranged so that its point is about a quarter of an inch behind that of the long pencil. Every performer will, of course, arrange it to suit his own manner of writing. Using this pencil to write the same thing on two cards simultaneously will seem a bit strange in the beginning, but it is much easier than learning to use a thumb writer.

It will be found on experiment that only two sets of double lines may be written across the top of each card by means of this pencil. In order to have sufficient room on the card in the envelope to write the second line without cramping the letters, start the first line at the very top of the outside card with the bottom pencil. This may sound like Einstein talking in his sleep, but the idea will become apparent after a few trials.

After the serial number has been written on both cards by means of the double pencil, move the pencil down a step and you will find no difficulty in writing the double row of letters as they are called out. Before starting this writing though, move the outside card slightly to the right. This will cause the line-up of numbers and letters to be varied slightly on the two ends. It is a small point, but the two cards might be compared later, and this will make them seem different, even though the formation of the letters and figures are individually identical.

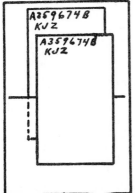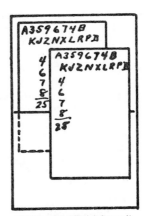

Position of cards for writing first
two lines.

Outside card shifted before writing addition column.

The procedure for the column of figures is slightly different. After the letters have been recorded, slide the outside card to the right, so that its left edge is about half an inch from the left edge of the card in the envelope. As the single numbers are called out, they are written in the following manner. Turn the pencil slightly to the left, so that the upper lead is resting on the card in the envelope, and the lower lead on the outside card. You will find it a simple matter to mark the figures in a column, one under the other. Again, this column is in a different position on each card, a fact that someone may notice. Draw a line and add the column, putting the sum down. The pencil is now returned to pocket, the envelope placed back outward in a conspicuous but safe place, and the borrowed card, together with another pencil, handed to the new secretary.

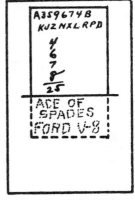

Front of envelope—at finish

Up to this point, the performer has (or should have) acted sublimely indifferent to the numbers and letters given him. This attitude is maintained in the selection of the card, so that no one may have the suspicion of a force. The performer then addresses the audience at large, and asks for the name of an automobile. He should move his gaze from one to another as he makes this request, and undoubtedly at least two will answer. One of these, and probably more than one, will answer "Ford." If anyone at all mentions "Ford," direct the secretary to write down "Ford V-8." In the rare event that no one does, ignore the names suggested, and continue talking. Say that you do not want merely the manufacturer's name, but the motor type also, as for example, "Studebaker Straight Eight." If no one then suggests "Ford V-8," it is because you have put them to sleep and they can't hear you.

I must admit that I can vouch for the certainty of this force only in New York City, as I have never tried it elsewhere. Ford is practically a household word here, and I think it is safe to say that not one woman in a hundred knows how to designate the engine type of any car but a Ford. Anyone who doesn't care to risk this part, may substitute a standard color or book test force.

After the card and auto have been forced, take the envelope, slit side down, and allow one of the signers to clip the end. Be sure he clips the end in which the lower half of the card is enveloped. He is then directed to reach in and remove the card. Take the card and the scissors from him, read the letters and numbers aloud, and after each is called out, ask the secretary to corroborate it. Hand the card to the one who signed it. While he is acknowledging his initials, cut the envelope in half, along the slit, and hand out the halves.

At the start of the performance, have the prepared pencil in the upper left vest pocket, double end up. Next to it is a plain pencil, similar to the long one. This one is used to write on the first card and for signing the envelope. It is replaced in the pocket while the business card is being borrowed. The double pencil is then taken out and the prepared end concealed behind the envelope. With ordinary caution, there is no danger of detection. Do not use a pencil with a rubber tip. For obvious reasons this cannot be used to erase an error. If you think it necessary, carry a small eraser in your pocket. The distance between the pencil points (and consequently between the written lines) can be increased by wrapping a strip of paper around the stubby pencil before fastening it to the longer one.*

WHO KILLED MR. X?

J. G. THOMPSON, JR.

This effect embodies a demonstration of both magic and mindreading, plus a triple mystery and a novel presentation.

Effect: The performer relates the story of a friendless recluse, a Mr. X, who appealed to the police for protection because he feared for his life. To represent Mr. X, the performer shows a small white card labelled Mr. X, which he inserts in a drug envelope and seals. Explaining that the police provided a guard for him, the performer folds the envelope in half and stands it tentwise on the table in front of one of the guests.

Unknown to the police the recluse had one friend in whom he confided the name of the person he feared would harm him. This friend wrote down the person's name. To simulate this friend, the performer has one of the spectators take a plain white card and secretly write on it the first name of one of the assembled guests as the potential murderer. This card is then sealed in a second envelope which is also folded over and stood tentwise on the table beside the first envelope.

*(Note by Annemann: In trying this problem, I found it to be more subtle if you write only the one column of figures on the outside card. Then draw the line, and when you add and mark down the total, write it on both cards. Previously, when you wrote something on the card to be sealed, you also wrote across the center of the card, "The total of the figures called will be." Then you left a little space, and then put down the name of the forced card and auto name. You have already prophesied the figures as found on a bill, so there is no point in prophesying a column. The second time you forecast the total of four figures to be called, and this changes, quite a bit, the appearance of the two cards when and if they are compared.)

Then it happened! One day the old man failed to make an appearance and the police broke in and found him dead, stabbed through the heart. At this point, the person guarding the Mr. X envelope tears it open and finds the "X card" splattered with blood stains and a pin driven through the heart of it.

The police were stumped until the friend of the recluse offered to help them by turning in the name of the man who might have committed the murder. However, when the second envelope is torn open—the card is found to be blank! At this point the police called in a representative of the Depart-

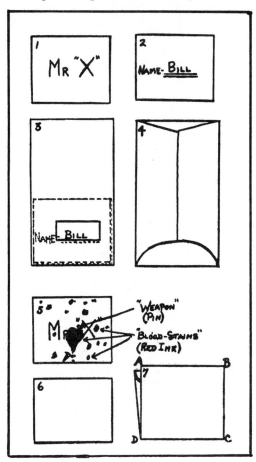

ment of Justice (the performer) who solved the crime by locating the murderer. Acting out the part of the sleuth, the performer walks up to the person who had been secretly designated as the culprit and tapping him on the shoulder, says, "Bill (or whatever the secretly written name was) you are under arrest for the murder of Mr. X."

Acted out, this stunt becomes an interesting story and finishes with a complete surprise to everyone present. It is perfect for clubs, and house parties where the audience is acquainted with one another.

Requirements: You will need several small white cards of a width to fit easily into the drug envelopes. One of these cards has inscribed on it, "Mr. X"; another identical with the "Mr. X" card, but also bearing several splotches of red ink (blood) and with an ordinary straight pin piercing it; a third card on which you have printed the word "Name————————," slightly below the center, so that the underscore line will come exactly even with the window in the cut-out envelope to be described later; and a fourth card, which is just a plain white card.

Also needed is a package of drug envelopes, of the end opening variety. One of these has its flap cut off; another has a small window cut in its face at the end opposite the flap, as illustrated; and a third envelope which is folded in half with the flap side in. The remaining envelopes are unprepared. Have a wide rubber band handy.

Preparation: Place the ink stained "Mr. X" card in one of the unprepared envelopes, tap it to the bottom, and leave the envelope unsealed. Slide the flapless envelope up under the flap of this first envelope, so that they appear to be but one envelope. Place the plain white card into the folded envelope, push it to the bottom, seal the flap and refold the envelope.

To assemble the packet, first lay the folded envelope on the table and on top of it lay several of the unprepared envelopes, flap side up. On these lay the two envelopes with but the one flap, the lower one of which contains the ink stained "Mr. X" card. These are also placed flap side up. On top of these place the "Mr. X" card, writing side up; then the window envelope, flap side up; and on top of all, the "Name————————" card. See illustration. Now encircle the center of the entire packet with the rubber band, bringing the band up high enough so as to hide the folded center edge of the folded envelope. When complete, the package appears innocent of any preparation.

Presentation and Routine: Come forward with the package of envelopes on your left palm, flap side up. Remove the "Name————————" card and lay it to one side. Draw out the window envelope from the package and, holding it flap side up, lay it beside the "name" card on the table. Now exhibit the "Mr. X" card, tell your story and insert it in the flapless envelope, still in place on top of the packet. Grip the flap of the second loaded envelope and, turning the packet slightly towards yourself, pull this second envelope off the stack. This switch is perfectly covered and no one should have any suspicion that you are holding anything but the envelope into which they saw you put the card. Tap this duplicate envelope on the table, ostensibly to drive the card to the bottom. While tapping, turn the packet of envelopes over in your left hand and then replace the tapped envelope on it as you fold it and seal it. Now place it tentlike on the table in front of one who promises to guard "Mr. X."

Pick up the "Name————————" card and hand it to someone who is asked to fill-in the first name of some person present, but not to let anyone see what he writes. As he is writing, carelessly pick up the window envelope with the right forefinger covering the window. Going to the person who wrote the name, you hold out the envelope flap side up and, as your left fingers pull back the flap, you have him insert the card writing side down. Ask him to push the card well in. As an afterthought, bring your hand down on the table to tap the card well down and, under cover of this move, turn the envelope around so that the window is facing you. When the written name is visible in the window, raise the envelope with the flap towards the writer and ask him to moisten the flap. While he does this you read the name. Now lay the envelope, flap side up, on the packet in your left hand, seal it and fold it in half. The folded envelope should be exactly centered over the rubber band on the packet as you finish creasing it.

As you continue with your story this folded envelope, bearing the secretly written name, is also apparently placed on the table in front of the writer. However, you actually make a switch of folded envelopes at this point, for as your right hand approaches the package to remove the envelope you just folded, the left hand turns slightly towards your body and the right hand actually removes the previously prepared and folded envelope instead. Thus, the folded envelope containing the plain white card has been pulled out from under the edge of the rubber band, and it is this one that is stood in front of the writer. The window envelope is still clipped behind or underneath the package of envelopes as they are dropped into your left hand coat pocket. Your story of the eventual murder and the disappearance of the murderer's name continues uninterrupted, and the effect is brought to a startling climax when you enter the case and locate the murderer by tapping him on the shoulder.

THE ASTRAL AD
ED WOLFF

If you could actually do mind reading you would proceed exactly as you do in this astonishing test with a newspaper ad. That is what arouses the amazement of everyone, the entire absence of any apparent method. Every move is done by the spectators themselves. If you notice that one particular spectator has an evening newspaper with him, you can use that or one of your own. It really makes no difference. In short, you are able to go through the test of reading a freely selected ad, word for word, without confederates or assistants.

Effect: Any spectator freely and secretly clips any ten want ads from any page of a daily paper. These ten ads he seals in ten separate envelopes. Another spectator selects one of the envelopes and puts it in his pocket. A third spectator then freely chooses any number up to 12 or 15. The person holding the selected envelope opens it, counts to the word occupied by the number chosen, and concentrates on that word. The performer, after a trial or two, writes a word on a pad or a slate. When the selected word is announced, the performer shows that he has successfully written the very same word. If you like, the performer may give the contents or meaning of the entire ad.

Preparation: A newspaper, or several of them to allow of a choice will be needed, together with a scissors, fifteen or twenty coin envelopes of any convenient size, and a paper pad or slate.

The envelopes are laid on the table in a stack, flap side down and with the flap ends of the envelope towards you. Counting from the top of the stack, the tenth envelope has its flap over the end of the eleventh, so that later you may withdraw this tenth envelope and bring the eleventh one along with it, the two envelopes appearing as one. The eleventh envelope is already sealed and has within it a want ad, of which you have made a copy (lightly) on your pad or slate. Place a pencil dot on the upper left and lower right corners of this eleventh envelope on the flap side, so that you can spot it quickly when you fan the envelopes later.

Routine and Presentation: "There are some people, principally those who are not scientists, who still believe that telepathy is impossible. This is because they have never had satisfactory evidence that mind-reading actually can be done. But we must remember that even scientists can be mistaken. Before the days of aviation a Harvard professor proved mathematically that airplanes could never fly, and when railroads were first introduced some doctors predicted that at any speed above 20 miles per hour the passengers would die of suffocation. Today, they tell us that a bumble bee can't fly, because its weight is too heavy for its wing spread. Fortunately, the bumble bee doesn't realize this unfortunate condition, and flies blithely along and even makes a little honey on the side. However, I am not here to quarrel with the scientists, but to give you a demonstration which you may explain to your own satisfaction.

"Has anyone a newspaper? Any newspaper. Or we can use the one I have here. It makes no difference. May we use your newspaper, sir? Thank you. In order that no one may suspect that you and I know each other, please pass the paper to somebody near you—anybody. Now, madam, you please pass it to somebody else. And you, young man, you too pass it to anyone at all. Excellent. Now, you, young lady, please turn to the want ad section of the paper and select any page—any page at all. (To nearby spectator) : Will you please pass these scissors to the young lady. Now, miss, please clip out 10 of those want ads—any 10 that you choose—only clip each one fairly close to its edges, so there can be no mistake later. While you are doing that, I shall count off 10 envelopes in which we'll seal the ads."

Pick up the stack, flap sides down, and deal off ten envelopes, one at a time, onto the table, counting aloud, "One-two-three-etc." Hold your hands about six or eight inches above the table to start and bring the hand with the envelope down to the table as you count "one"; then raise the hand to the packet and pick off another envelope and lay that on the table, counting "two," and so on. This will help the audience keep count with you, and will also cover the fact that the tenth envelope is in reality two envelopes. Count off the envelopes just about as fast as you would count off cards . . . no hurry, but without losing time.

Lay aside the remaining envelopes and pick up the ten just counted off with your left hand. The tenth envelope is now on top with the eleventh (sealed) one just below it. The envelopes are held flap side down and with the flap ends toward the audience. While explaining that you will have the clipped want ads sealed in these envelopes, draw off the top envelope singly, display it and then return it to the stack, but this time replace it at the bottom of the stack. This leaves the extra sealed envelope on top of the stack.

Approach the spectator who has clipped the ads and ask him to insert one in an envelope and seal it. As you explain this, you turn the stack over in your hand so that the flaps are facing up. Draw off the top envelope and hand it to him. Suggest that he examine it and then seal one of the ads in it. (Your extra sealed envelope is now the bottom envelope of the stack.) When he has sealed the envelope, take it back from him, add it to the bottom of the stack and then hand him another envelope from off of the top. Take back the sealed envelope No. 2, add it to the bottom of the stack, hand him another from the top and continue doing so until all his ten ads have been sealed. As you add the 10th envelope to the bottom of the stack, you will find that your extra envelope will be the top one of the stack. Cut the stack, bringing the extra envelope to the center, and force it on one of the spectators through the medium of the regular fan force used with cards. The pencil dots on this extra envelope makes it easy for you to locate it.

If you have any trouble forcing the envelope, try this method: Fan the envelopes and say, "Will you please stick out your finger and just touch one of the envelopes? Just stick out one finger." Wait until he puts out a finger, then touch the fake envelope to his finger and hold it there. Then say, "Very well, please draw out the envelope you touched. That's right. Just put it in your pocket for the time being. Thank you."

Go back to your table, lay aside the rest of the envelopes and pick up the slate and chalk, or the pad, whichever you are using, and say, "Will someone call out a number up to 12 or 15—anybody at all. What number, Sir? Nine? Thank you. The gentleman selected No. 9 (or whatever the number selected happens to be). Is that satisfactory to everybody present, or shall we choose another number? Very well, then, we'll use No. 9. Will the gentleman who is holding the sealed envelope please open it and remove the ad. Now please count down to the ninth word and concentrate upon it. Don't name it—just concentrate."

To yourself say, in a sort of an audible halftone, "No. 9—No. 9—word No. 9." As you do so, bring up the chalk and pretend to write on the slate, slowly and hesitatingly. As you do so, count off and note the ninth word in the copy you have on your slate. Once you have it, stop writing, hesitate, then rub out the word you started to write together with the copy of the ad. Then start again and write the correct word. Stand the slate on your table against a book, or place it on a nearby chair resting against the chair's back, with the writing away from the audience. Walk away and say to the person with the ad, "Who kept the chosen envelope? Who has it? You, sir? Please stand so we can all see you. Now that I have written a word, will you please read out loud the entire advertisement, word for word. (Wait) I didn't hear you, speak louder please. (Wait) Good! Now count to the ninth word and read just that. A little louder. (Wait) Oh, 'Experience.' Is that right? Yes, 'Experience.' Very well."

"You remember, before the envelope was opened I wrote a word on this slate." Pick up the slate, "and the word that I wrote was 'experience,' as you can see." Turn the slate around for all to see what you wrote.

Additional Hints: Always get the person who holds the envelope to read the whole ad and to repeat the selected word a couple of times in a loud voice. This fixes the word unmistakably in the minds of the audience and creates dramatic suspense.

In cutting your own ad (the one to be forced) from a newspaper prior to the performance, be sure to choose one that has no other ad copy on its reverse side. Otherwise the spectator may read the wrong side. Since the spectator who reads the ad is not the one who cut the ads out, any difference in type, etc., will go unnoticed.

In copying your ad on the slate, put 5 words to the line. This makes it easy to count to the desired number quickly. If you use a paper pad instead, tear off the top sheet, crumple it up and put it in your pocket after the first mistake.

Any envelope will do, but the end opening coin envelopes are the best for most audiences will realize that these Kraft envelopes are not transparent. Also, when asking for a number, be sure that there are that many words in your force ad.

REINCARNATION

Fetsch-Harrison

Effect: In Robert-Houdin's autobiography there appeared an effect wherein the performer has a person write a question on a slip of paper which is then burned. Before the flames have flickered out, the person is handed a sealed envelope, which when torn open reveals a second envelope, then a third, a fourth, a fifth and finally a sixth envelope. When this last is opened there is found the original slip, bearing the message that everyone has seen burned.

A most intriguing effect, you will agree, but Monsieur Robert-Houdin failed to give us the secret. I have, however, worked the following routine with success. The only change being that I use but three envelopes where he used six.

Requirements: A small memo pad, the type that is bound by a spiral wire. Plain paper inside. Size of the pad is about 2 x 3½ inches. A small ash tray and a box of matches, a piece of red or green carbon paper and a pencil with colored lead to match your carbon paper. Most any stationery store can supply this equipment.

Preparation: The first page of the pad is left as is. The second page has a piece of red carbon paper pasted to the underside of it. The lower right hand corner of this page is cut off at a 45-degree angle. The third page is torn away from the binding and then replaced. Another page is torn from the pad and folded in half, to quarters, then eighths. This is placed in your left outside coat pocket along with the ash tray and the matches.

For the envelope part of the effect we will use Mr. Harrison's method. Make a nest of three envelopes as illustrated. Have the flaps open and coat the mucilage sections of the envelopes, and the sections where the flaps hit the envelope, with rubber cement. Let the cement dry. Rubber cement will stick to itself with very little pressure and makes a tight joint. Now sew a pair of paper clips to the lining of your coat just below the edge of the inside coat pocket, so that the clips can engage the ends of the envelopes. The envelopes, with flaps open, are put into place in the clips with the flaps pointing towards the edge of your coat.

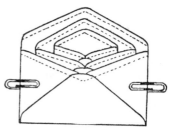

DOTTED LINES INDICATE EDGES OF RUBBER CEMENT

Routine: Open the pad to the first page and lay it on the table with the red pencil. Have a spectator write the name of any person, living or dead, his telephone or social security number, etc., on the first page of the pad. After this is finished, openly tear off this page and lay it, writing side up, on the table beside the pad. Remove the ash tray and the matches from your coat pocket with your left hand, at the same time palm the dummy folded page, and put the tray and matches on the table.

Pick up the pad and apparently tear off the top page which is blank. Fold it so that it matches the dummy slip which you have palmed in your left hand, telling the spectator to do the same with his page which is laying on the table. Explain that this action guarantees that you will not in any way touch or handle the spectator's page.

What really has happened, however, is that instead of removing the top page, you have pulled out the next page instead. When apparently removing the top page your thumb catches the corner of the page underneath, due to the fact that the same corner of the top sheet has been cut away. This underneath page will easily come away, having previously been loosened and reinserted, and will sound like it is being torn away. As soon as this page is clear of the pad, put the pad back on the table and start folding the page to match the one you have palmed in your left hand. Have the spectator follow your actions with his page.

Be careful during the folding of your page that the writing (carbon impression) is not revealed. By the time he starts the folding of his page, your page is completed. While he is finishing the folding of his page, still under your verbal directions, switch the page you have just folded for your palmed dummy, and drop it on the ash tray. Ask the spectator to drop his folded page on the ash tray alongside of yours. Hand him the matches. As soon as he strikes a match, reach inside your coat with your left hand—which has the carbon impression page palmed—apparently to get something from your inside coat pocket. Load the palmed billet into the nest of envelopes, fold the flaps over, giving them a firm rub, bring them out and lay them on the table in full view.

After the paper is burning, begin your buildup. When the spectator's folded page is completely destroyed, have him open the envelopes. Inside the last envelope he finds the very same page he has just burned. Stunning isn't the word for the effect this creates!

The strong points of this routine are (1) The performer never touches the spectator's page; (2) The spectator folds and burns his own paper; (3) if someone knows about colored carbon paper, the fact that the only other page that was handled was burned, erases any thought that he might have along these lines; (4) The nest of envelopes are on the table while the burning page is still in the ash tray; (5) The discovery of the page in the envelopes.

Second Method: In this method the only difference is that the carbon copy is burned by the spectator, while the original page is found in the envelopes.

After the spectator has written on page one, pick up the pad and look at what he has written, saying, "I see you have written so and so. It is strange, but this was written by another person about four weeks ago during another performance." Ask him if he knows this person, giving a name. During this bit of byplay you shove back the corner of the second page and get a grip on the corner of the third page. Pull it out with the tearing sound, making it very realistic, and lay it on the table with the writing side up during the conversation. This gives the spectator the carbon copy. The performer then tears off the top page, the one originally written upon, and then follows the routine as explained. This puts the original page in the nest of envelopes.

NOTE: You could also have the last three pages of the pad set up with a green carbon sheet. Thus a choice of a red or green pencil could be given and the pad opened from either side.

PREDICTION

Sid Lorraine

The following effect, an outgrowth of Annemann's 68¢ Patent" idea, makes a remarkable prediction stunt with numerous publicity angles.

Imagine being able to predict the day's news headlines, by offering your committee a notarized statement in a sealed and stamped envelope that was postmarked days, weeks or even months before! Proof positive that you are blessed with an unfailing power of prediction.

Preparation: Fold a sheet of paper in half and trim its edges down to such a size as to just fit into the envelope you will use. Now apply rubber cement to the three edges of the folded sheet and stick them together. Take this pasted-up sheet to a notary public, have him date and sign the sheet, contents unknown, and then emboss it with his seal which will make an impression through both thicknesses of the folded sheet. Then go to the County Clerk's office and ask for a prothonotary certificate, which is a guarantee of your notary's authority to attest papers as of that date. Now enclose your prothonotary certificate with your notarized sheet and enclose both in an envelope.

Apply rubber cement over the gummed flap of the envelope and also on the surface of the envelope where that portion of the flap will contact. Let stand a while till dry, then seal the envelope. Coat the gum on a postage stamp with rubber cement and stick it over the flap. Rub off any excess dry cement from the edges of the flap and around the stamp, and then write your signature across the flap. Now address the envelope to yourself, stamp it with the proper postage and mail it. Keep this envelope until the proper time comes to work your prediction.

When you want to present the stunt some time later, just select the most outstanding headline of the day. Before going on your date, carefully remove the stamp from the flap, open the envelope and the sealed sheet and write the day's news event as your prediction on one of the inside folds of the paper sheet. If you have any trouble separating the cemented edges, just apply some benzol which will dissolve the rubber cement without leaving any telltale stains on the envelope, stamp or paper sheet. Now glue the edges of the sheet together and reinsert it in the envelope. Remove any excess rubber cement from the envelope and stamp by rubbing it off with your finger. Then only a "lick" is necessary on both the flap and the stamp to seal them down with their original glue, and you're set to confound the most astute audience or committee.

For those who will use this effect time and again, I would suggest that you fix up six or a dozen envelopes at a time and keep them handy.

DARK SORCERY

ALBERT SIDNEY

But little preparation is necessary in order to present this mystery in comparison with the effect obtained. It is one of those stunts which many will like to have ready and prepared in their home for immediate use at a time when the company is in a receptive mood.

Effect: The performer shows a bunch of manilla pay envelopes numbered consecutively from one to fourteen. These are all sealed, although empty, and may be examined at will. A spectator is requested to cut a pack of cards while performer's back is turned, and then to initial the face card of the cut. He is to replace this cut off pile, and then cut the deck again, deeper in this case, remembering the face card of this cut as a numeral only. Thus the assistant has selected and marked a card, and also has selected a number. The packet of numbered and sealed envelopes is on the table with the deck, and now all the lights are extinguished.

In the dark the performer explains that vibrations from those concentrating on the selected card will reveal it while he is passing his hands above the deck on the table. A few minutes elapse, lights are turned on, and the magician states that half of the test has succeeded and that the light has been turned on to break the train of thought. It is again turned out, this time all concerned concenarte on the numeral only.

When the light is on again, the performer announces that he has not only discovered the thought of card and the number, but also, through a legacy of Cagliostro, has caused a strange transposition to have occurred. The spectator picks up the pile of envelopes and looks for the one bearing the chosen numeral. This is opened and inside of it is found the noted and marked card!

Preparation: To obtain this unusual effect, each playing card is treated on the face side with a dot of luminous paint at about the center of both ends. You will also need a duplicate of 14 sealed envelopes numbered like the 14 seen by the audience. Seven are put in one pocket and seven in another, and they are in rotation so that any numbered envelope may be secured quickly.

Routine: To present, lay the sealed set of envelopes and the pack of cards on a table near a lamp, if possible, and put out all the other lights. When the cards are cut, the light strikes the paint and livens it up. The topmost cut is the autographed card, the lower one is the numeral. In the dark fan the deck faces toward you. Transfer the first luminous card (numeral) to the face of the deck; the next one (marked) to the back or top of the deck. When the lights are snapped on to break the train of thought apparently, you pick up and square the deck and the envelopes as you explain this, noting the numeral card. With the lights out again, remove the properly numbered envelope from your pocket and in it seal the top (marked) card from the deck. Count down in the envelope pile and remove the correct envelope (they are in order), putting yours in its place. The light is turned on again, and the effect is brought to a climax.

You will find it best to save most of your patter for the periods when the lights are out. It makes the interval, short as it is, seem much shorter.

(**Editor's Note:** This excellent effect can be all accomplished the first time the lights go out, if the cards used are "pricked" in accordance with the Charlier System as explained by Prof. Hoffman on page 66 of "More Magic". Although the Charlier pack was a Piquet pack of 32 cards this would not be any drawback. However, there is another system of "pricking" the cards so that they may be read by touch, and which employs a full pack of 52 cards. This is the "C-N-H System" which is Wilf. Huggins' application of the Charlier idea to the Nikola set-up.)

slate routines

NELSON
HAHNE

THE PERFECT CLUB SLATE ROUTINE
ANNEMANN

This is an original Annemann effect to which he added a subtlety with colored chalk by Norman Ashworth, a little known medium dodge by Al Baker, and the familiar window envelope to create as perfect a routine as you will find anywhere.

Effect: A prominent spectator is asked to think of some friend of his who has passed on, and to write that person's name on a card which is sealed in an envelope. When this has been done, the performer shows two slates on the four sides of which he writes a jumbled series of letters, which he explains he is passing on into the spirit world so that they may be used for a return message. The slates are now cleaned and another spectator is allowed a free choice of any one of a number of different pieces of colored chalk. He selects one and initials the two slates, which he holds stacked. The performer then picks up the sealed envelope saying, "Now, for the first time we shall learn the identity of the person of whom our friend has been thinking." The envelope is torn open and the name is read aloud. When the slates are opened, one bears the name of the first spectator's departed friend . . . and the name is written in the same color chalk as selected by the second person!

Requisites: Two slates and one silicate flap. On one side of the flap write three rows of mixed letters in white chalk, making the letters large enough to cover the entire surface of the flap. Also needed is a small drug envelope and a blank card to fit it. The envelope is faked by cutting a window in its face side.

Preparation: The flap, writing side downward, is laid on the table overlapping a side edge by about an inch. The two slates lie on top of flap. Also on the table are several pieces of colored chalk, all different, and to one side is a piece of white chalk.

Routine: A prominent spectator is asked to think of some departed friend and, just for the purposes of the test, to write this person's name on a card which you hand him. Have him insert the card, face down, in the (faked) envelope which you hold flap side up on your left palm. Your fingers cover the cut out front, which is against your palm, while your right fingers turn down the flap and hold the envelope open to make it easy for the spectator to insert the card. You assist him by giving the card the final shove, and then you seal the envelope. Finally you write the spectator's initials across the flap, and then stand the envelope against something in full view with the

WINDOW ENVELOPE   SLIT ENVELOPE
BOTH CUT ON THE FACE OR FLAP SIDE OF ENVELOPES

initialled side facing the audience. In doing this, you have ample opportunity to read the name showing through the window, which will be facing you, as you stand the envelope on the table.

You now pick up the two slates (without the flap), show them to be clean and lay them on the table again. Then show the colored chalks and allow some spectator to make a free choice of one color. These colored pieces of chalk should be about two and one-half inches long. When one is selected you pick it up and pass it to the spectator, but just as you pick it up you break off a piece and retain this piece in your hand. It is all done with one hand. Keep this colored piece palmed, as you pick up the white chalk from the table with your fingertips.

Now pick up one slate and proceed to cover both sides of it with mixed letters. To make the slate maneuvers clear, let's call them No. 1 and No. 2, and I suggest that you follow the routine with slates and chalks in hand. Cover the side of slate No. 1 with three rows of mixed letters in white chalk. Turn the slate over, so the lettering faces the audience, and apparently continue, but on this side the dead name is put down in colored chalk. The white piece being held at your finger tips is dropped to your palm, and the colored piece merely worked up to the finger tips. As this switch is made behind the slate, you should experience no difficulty. After writing, switch the two chalks again.

Without showing this side, lay this slate on the table—over the flap—with the name side down. At the same time pick up slate No. 2, and drop the palmed piece of colored chalk out of view among the other pieces of chalk on the table. Now fill both sides of slate No. 2 with mixed white chalk letters. You are holding this slate in your left hand, so you reach to the table with your right hand and pick up slate No. 1 together with the flap. With a slate in each hand, and the flap in place on slate No. 1, you are able to show both sides of each slate freely.

Put slate No. 2 under your right arm and, with a pocket handkerchief, clean slate No. 1 on both sides. Lay it on the table with the flap side down. Now clean slate No. 2. Pick up slate No. 1 again, leaving the flap on the table, and lay it on top of slate No. 2 which you are still holding. Have the spectator, with the colored chalk, initial the two outside surfaces, and then let him hold them. On the inside of the top slate is the dead name in the chosen color.

The envelope is now opened and the dead name is read aloud. The faked envelope, which has been displayed and held with its flap side to the audience throughout, is crumpled up and put in your pocket. Everyone now turns to the person with the slates and watches as he opens them and finds the chosen name in color!

As a variation you can use a slit envelope, instead of the window. This should be an end opener No. 2 Drug envelope. On the face side make a slit across the envelope ¾" from the top when the flap is closed. In using this, lay it diagonally across your left hand with the flap side up and open, and pointing outwards. You aid in shoving the card in, and manage to lead the card through the slit so that it lies between the face of the envelope and your palm. The writing faces your palm, so in setting the envelope aside clip the card against the face of the envelope with your right thumb as you pick up the envelope off your left palm; hold the card side of the envelope facing you and glimpse the name. Now set the envelope on its edge against a book or some other object on your table. When you are ready to open the envelope later, pick it up with your right hand, with thumb at the back holding the card, and push the envelope into your left hand between the left thumb and first finger with the flap of the envelope to the right. The back of the left hand is held towards the audience, and the left thumb draws the card down into the palm and out of the slit. The card will only have to be moved about a half inch to clear the slit. The right hand now grasps the top of the envelope (flap end) and tears the envelope straight across right along the slit. The card is now apparently withdrawn from inside the envelope, really from back of it, and everything may be examined as there is no telltale evidence left.

EXTRA-SENSORY PERCEPTION

ANNEMANN

One of the greatest effects in thought transmission is the coding of pictures freely drawn by the audience. It goes without saying that it is at the same time the most intricate of methods. Julius Zancig was most adept at this feat and developed it over a period of years through undisputed ability, plus a thorough grounding in transmission secrets.

What I am presenting here is quite marvelous to an audience and, at the same time, satisfying to the most exact performer in regards to cleanliness of working.

One needs only a set of 32 five-inch square cards and a large slate with chalk. These cards are best made of white drawing board. This can be obtained from stationery stores in sheets about 22 by 28 inches in size. On one side of each card is drawn a simple sketch with black drawing ink. The sketches are made very heavy and as large as possible. On the illustrated slate I have drawn the ideas I am using myself, although any others can be put to use.

Effect: The set of illustrated cards is freely shown to consist of 32 different and simple ideas. The performer says that he will try a test of

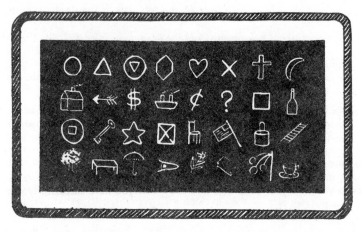

thought transference with members of the audience. Pictures will be used rather than letters or figures because they are better visualized in the mind. The cards, as the performer speaks, are mixed in a fair manner (but not shuffled like playing cards) and then placed in a stack with drawing sides down on the slate. Approaching a subject to be, the performer asks him or her to pick off a number of the cards in a bunch, and hold this stack with face of same close to the body for the time being. Without touching the cards left on the slate, the performer passes to another spectator and has him repeat the procedure. The few cards left are put aside and the performer stands a few yards in front of one spectator with nothing but the slate and chalk in hand. For the first time the assistant is asked to look steadily at his drawing (*i.e.*: The bottom card of his stack) and concentrate upon it. It may be mentioned that at no time can the performer see either the face or back of the drawing being looked at, and that the selection has been left entirely to chance. However, the rest of the audience will know that and it is best not to emphasize the points.

Drawing something on his slate, the performer asks the spectator to show everyone the drawing on the card he selected. Turning his slate, the performer shows his sketch to be the same! Passing to the second spectator the test is repeated, with the performer duplicating on the other side of his slate the picture selected by this man! And everything may be left with the audience, if you so desire.

Preparation: The pictures are stacked but not in any memorized order. Draw these pictures, in the same order, with a pencil across the center of the slate. Your sketches will, of course, be very small.

Routine: Hold the pack of cards face down in your left hand. Take a bunch from the top with the right hand and apparently mix the two bunches together. Really though, a few from the top of the right hand are left on the bottom of the left pile, and then a few from the bottom of the right pile are left on top of the left stack. Repeat this maneuver until all of the cards in the right hand are exhausted, and then repeat the mixing, if desired. Do not attempt to shuffle the cards, but just mix them loosely and apparently at random, and you will have the best false mixing possible. When you have gone through a mixing or two, the cards are in the same order and have only been cut, which does not matter.

Approaching your assistants, they each cut off a bunch of cards and hold them against their bodies. Now lay aside the few remaining cards on your table and, as you drop them face up, your fingers spread them a little so that you get a glimpse of the top card. This is your key to the second person's card, which will be the card just to the left of the key card on your slate list.

As you pick up your slate, you spot the second person's drawing as just explained, and you ask him to look at his card and concentrate on the drawing it contains. Now turn your slate over and reproduce his drawing on the clean side of your slate. Make the sketch large enough for everyone to see it, but do not show it as yet. Ask him to show his card to the audience, and as he does so you turn your slate over and show that you have successfully drawn the same picture.

Take the bunch of cards from this second spectator and lay them aside exactly as you did with the first bunch, spotting the top card of the packet. From this second key card you learn the first person's drawing as already explained. Ask him to concentrate on his drawing while you reproduce it on the opposite (list) side of the slate. Arrange your sketch with heavy lines so that it blocks out the list. Then have this first man show his drawing and you show your duplicate sketch for a smashing climax!

I doubt if a cleaner method of duplicating pictures can be devised for one person. From the viewpoint of the audience, it is very convincing and fair in every way.

NOTARIA

ANNEMANN-BAKER-DALEY

In effect, the performer asks two spectators to come forward and stand on each side of him. He hands a pack of cards to the first spectator and asks him to cut somewhere and remember the card at the cut. The second person is asked to decide upon any simple picture or diagram he may like. Both are given slips on which they jot down their mental ideas. Close at hand is an ash tray. The slips are torn and burned while the performer picks up a slate. Standing between the two people, but a little to the rear, the performer writes and draws on the slate. Now the first person names his card, and the second person shows his thought of picture. The slate is turned, and upon it the performer has duplicated the picture or diagram, and in the center of the sketch has written the name of the card. This makes a telepathic effect suitable for large or small audiences.

There are certain variations that can be used by those who adopt this trick, but as it stands now, it has a double climax which does away with the usual one at a time revelations.

Requirements: As I have been doing it, a one kind forcing deck is used for cleanness. Some may think this a funny idea of "cleanness" but I mean from the audience standpoint. The minute you start messing around, the spectators get lost in following you, so the presentation, as far as they are concerned, must be direct and open.

Have the deck in your right coat pocket with the usual different card at the bottom. You will also need a few pieces of opaque white paper, about two by three inches in sizes, which you have in readiness in your vest pocket, a couple of pencils, an ashtray, matches and a slate. A piece of chalk in your left coat pocket completes the set-up.

Routine: Have the spectators standing on each side of you about three yards apart. Take out the deck and overhand shuffle it, the fingers of the hand holding the deck retaining the bottom odd card in place. Explain to the first spectator that you want him to look at a card by chance while he has the deck in his possession. He is to hold it flat on his left hand, and with his right merely cut off a bunch of cards, look at the card thus cut, and replace those removed. As you say this, illustrate by cutting off a bunch and looking at the face card, but don't let it be seen. Now deliberately put the deck on his left hand and step back. The moment he replaces the cut, step up and take the deck. As you take the deck from him, turn and ask the second person to think of a geometrical design or any simple picture that he likes, and which means something to him. Do not hesitate or stall between taking the deck and giving these instructions. The card selection has been so direct that no one gives it a thought, especially with the immediate request for a picture and because it is a bizarre idea in comparison to a card.

As the spectator says he has a picture in mind, drop the deck in your left coat pocket and at the same time take the two papers from your vest pocket and give one to him. Suggest that he draw the sketch so he'll have a definite and clear cut picture in his mind. Then give the other paper to the first spectator with the remark that he also write down his thought-of card in order to firmly fix it on his mind. (I've tried various routines for this part, and the described actions worked out best.) Now ask them to fold the papers tightly, once each way.

Explain that in ancient times, the soothsayers gazed into the smoke of burning incense, or at some personally owned article to divine secrets pertaining to that person. You will attempt the same thing, but in a smaller way. Look at the first person and remark that you want him to tear and burn his paper. Continue, "Look, tear it and then burn it like this." As you say this, you reach out and take the paper the second man is holding. Still addressing the first person, tear up and steal the center piece as already described in "The Mind-reading Publicity Effect," page 30. The right fingers finally take all the torn pieces, except the center piece which you have clipped between your left thumb and first finger, as you step over to an ash tray where you drop them. As you finish this action, repeat: "Just be sure the pieces are small and will burn easily."

Now watch the first person, the one who selected the card, tear his slip and put it with the pieces you dropped in the tray. Then tell the second person to light them. Up until now you have ignored him since taking his paper. Afterwards both will swear, as do the audience, that they have torn and burned their own papers. The described maneuvering is perfect misdirection for what takes place.

As the second person lights the paper, you pick up the slate and step back. Your left hand reaches into your pocket for the chalk as you direct the burning of the papers, and you flip open the folded center piece you have finger-palmed in your hand. The piece is small enough to be palmed but you only open it half way. Bring it out and put it under the tip of your right thumb which is holding the slate, opening out the paper at the same time.

Now ask both parties to think intently of the card and the picture. Start to make a few rough lines on the slate with the chalk held in your left hand. Just a glance at the paper under the right thumb and you have the picture. Look at the second person and suggest that he concentrate a little harder on the picture, visualizing it as a whole and not as individual lines. Catch hold of the slate with your left hand as your right hand, with the slip, reaches into your pocket for a handkerchief with which to wipe off the slate. Naturally the paper slip is left behind, and you are now free to finish the picture, and write the name of the card in the center of it.

A TORN LETTER

ANNEMANN

Effect: The performer picks up a packet of four-inch square papers. "I have here," he says, "the 26 letters of the alphabet cut from a type of paper not available to the public. You, sir," addressing some member of the audience, "will please think of someone who was a close relative or friend —someone not now living—what is the initial of his first name?"

Let us suppose the letter mentioned to be M. The performer hands the packet to the person with the request that he look through—they all are in order—and remove that particular one.

During this interval the mysticist shows two slates. "These *are* available to the public," he says, "and we shall use them in a way to prove beyond reasonable doubt that something strange is at work here tonight."

He openly shows the slates to be clean of anything foreign and at the same time marks the sides 1, 2, 3 and 4. Put together, the slates are handed to the spectator as the performer takes back the letter, in this case M.

"When people or things on this earth are destroyed," he continues, "the meaning, the spirit, or the soul flies into another level of being." The performer, during this, is tearing the lettered paper into strips and the strips into parts. He makes them into a flat bundle and approaches the man with the slates.

Opening the slates just a little he definitely drops the paper within. And he takes back the remainder of the alphabet papers when he steps away.

"Now let's see if conditions are right for a successful contact with your thought in what spiritualists see fit to call "the happy summerland."

The performer paces back and forth several times, covering a short distance. No talk is necessary. The audience always waits. Then the spectator is asked to get up and come forward. He opens the slates.

"Take the paper," says the performer, who then takes the slates. He shows the inside surfaces. Upon one slate appears a message somewhat like this, "Dear Harry: Conditions are good here. It's not the same as before but I'm as happy as I deserve to be. I've put my initial back together again in case Annemann (or your name) wants to make contact for someone else."

The performer looks at his subject, "You are Harry?" And when the person admits it, he further asks, "Open up the pieces of paper."

The torn pieces are in restored fashion and the letter M goes back to the packet. And there isn't anything to be found wrong with the visible and available objects used before the audience.

Preparation: You need two sets of alphabet papers. The sheets are cut four inches square and large black letters inked on. Only two papers need be replaced at each performance. The paper should be of good linen quality on the heavy side.

One set of papers is folded up in a hap-hazard way to about 1½ inches by 1½ inches in size. These 26 billets are deposited in a regulation "Cards from the Pockets" index as sold by all dealers. Only one of the two indexes supplied is used. It will hold 26 of these papers in place of the half deck it was made to contain. You know them as 1 to 26 and the index is placed in your left trousers' pocket.

The slates? On one side of one slate the message is written. Beforehand, pick some one person in your audience, one not seated in a spot difficult to reach, and learn his or her first name. That's what you fill in after "Dear ———."

Routine: The performer picks up the slates and numbers them. The numbering of the slates is done as follows: In one corner of the message side put the figure 1. This side is at the bottom outward of the stack of two, figure towards the audience as you hold them at first, keeping the message side down. Openly mark the top side with a figure 1 to match. Your right hand takes hold of the slate at the right outer corner, turns it outward like an end-hinged notebook and brings it back underneath the other. The new surface next is numbered 2 on its outer left corner. The same hinge move and come-back underneath is made, but during the action the slates are brought up a bit to face the performer. He writes a 3 on the new surface *and then* lowers the slates to show the numeral. He then lifts them again towards himself and apparently makes the same move for the third time but actually, the hinged out slate, instead of going underneath the other, is brought down on top of the slate in left hand.

Without a pause, he is seen to write the number 4. However, facing him now is the number 1 side and his action is simply that of changing the 1 to a 4. Then the slates are lowered and the audience sees it in all fairness. The slates are given to the spectator with his right hand, and, while he explains that as little light as possible should get between them, the performer's left hand has dropped to his pocket and secured the letter needed. He takes back the selected letter with his right hand, it is shown all and torn. After the pieces are folded to about the correct size a finger switch is made and the performer approaches the spectator quickly, his left hand diving deliberately to his left trousers' pocket again to get rid of the pieces, and comes out with a large rubber band.

"Open the slates just a little," the performer requests, "the pieces of the initial should help to get a direct line open to the hereafter." The restored paper is pushed inside and the rubber band snapped around all. "That should help to keep light out."

The effect is done except for presentation of the finish as described before.

I made this up and have used it recently. The torn and restored initial definitely has possibilities. With other restored paper effects there was little or nothing to differentiate between that destroyed and that restored, except in the simple cases of Chinese laundry slip markings and magazine pages.

In this case we have a restored letter freely picked by a member of the audience, plus a message via slates, and a clean finish that will stand investigation.

HEADLINE HUNTER

ANNEMANN

Effect: From out of the past I have taken a slate writing principle, long off the market, and utilized it in this problem. Bruce Hurling's method for getting rid of a "flap" while standing before an audience in view of all may be used for countless effects. It should not be forgotten.

To his watchers the performer shows a slate blank on both sides and identifies these sides by writing initials on each as called out to him. The slate is stood in full view of everyone for the time being. Next are shown three current newspapers having blatant headlines. A spectator aids in the choice of one, whereupon the performer quickly cuts the headline words apart and puts them onto a table or the floor in crumpled up balls.

Another spectator does his part in the choice of one word, and he reads it aloud for all to hear. He, himself, then approaches the slate and shows both sides. And on the slate, which may be passed around for avid inspection, is shakily chalked the very word picked!

Method and Presentation: In concocting this method I discarded the use of cards, dice, counters, etc., for the choosing of a word because, in the case at hand, they were objects "foreign" to the subject. It is necessary only to have the slate with special flap, two newspapers, chalk, and shears.

Let's cover the "selection" of the word before describing the genius-like qualities of the slate itself. Newspaper headlines are short and to the point with nothing unnecessarily said. Except in terrific times, when one and two words carry great import, there are an average of from three to six words displayed. That the paper may be a few days old doesn't matter. The other paper, of a different name, must have a headline also, but it doesn't matter as to the exact number of words.

Let us say, for example, that we wish to have "selected" the second word of one paper which reads "House Votes Strike Ban." The two papers are thrown down before the first spectator, and to him you say, "Just pick up either one, please." If he picks up the one you want you take it from him, saying, "Thank you," and walk to another person for the next move. If he picks up the wrong one, you say, "It's yours. And when you read it, later tonight, and find out what is happening throughout the world, remember that something strange happened here." Naturally, the "wrong" newspaper always is of current date. And, as you say your piece, pick up the other paper and carry it to the second person.

"There is power in headlines," you continue. "Every word has a meaning of its own." With the shears you slash away at the four word banner, cutting the words apart and dropping them in crumpled balls onto the floor or table. Let them fall as they will, but be careful to note *which one* is the word you want to have "selected."

"Pick up two of them, one with each hand," you say. If the wanted one is among these you continue without pause, "Give me one." If you receive the desired word you open the paper, read it aloud and hand to someone else nearby. If the wrong one is given you say, "Over my left shoulder as appeasement to the spirits beyond (tossing it so), and now will you please open the paper you have and read aloud the word it contains?"

But, if the two papers picked up by the spectator *do not* include the wanted one, say, "Toss them over your shoulders at the same time, for that is a manner of appeasing the spirits beyond. Now give me one of the papers remaining." If given the correct one you open it and proceed. If given the wrong one, toss it over *your own* left shoulder, saying, "After all, I must do a bit of appeasing myself." Then have the spectator open and read the last paper.

Aside from the general explanation I want to insist that you have here one of the very best methods of "forcing" without the use of extraneous apparatus which only too often tends to distract attention from the effect by being "out of place." The method and principle takes practice and assurance, but it will last you throughout a lifetime of magic.

That takes care of the word being the one which appears on the slate. Important no end, in itself, the "message from beyond" is essential, too, and the way it happens goes like this:—

Procure or make a silicate slate with frame, the inside (slate surface proper) dimensions of which are 5 x 7 inches or smaller—no larger. The flap to accompany this slate is made of thinner silicate, or, as in my case, of black art board, obtainable from art stores in 17 x 22 in. sheets, and very pliable. The inside of slate is quartered, and the finished flap takes up three of these, the diagrams making this clear, I hope.

As you can see depicted, the flap is foldable twice which brings it down to quarter size, and that size is palmable, it being no larger than a playing card. Scotch tissue tape, now very prevalent, was used for the hinges. That one which is on the audience side of the slate was sanded with fine sandpaper to take away the gloss, but it isn't necessary because the slate is more or less perfunctorily shown.

At the first showing, the performer draws a chalk line cutting off one-quarter of the slate's surface, and this is done on the flap side at start. The line is drawn along the edge of the flap, or edges of the flaps if you care to make them plural. The initials called are put upon the slate proper, there being a coinciding chalk line on the slate itself just under the flap(s) edge. The word to be forced has been written underneath the flap(s).

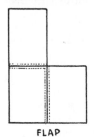

FLAP

DOTTED LINES
INDICATE SCOTCH
TAPE HINGES

The first "quartered-off" section is on the unprepared side, and it is duly initialed. When the second set of initials is given, they are put on the flap(s) side and that person asked to step forward. He is used for the first choice of the papers, and this slight interval allows you to let the top half of flap drop down and engineer the quarter-flap to the right, whereupon the folded flap can be palmed to the pocket when chalk is put away.

That does it. The word is picked freely, and it appears upon a slate mysteriously. What more can be asked of a trick?

PSYCHIC SLATE TEST

ANNEMANN

This is the simplest of slate effects in method, but a moment's thought followed by an actual tryout will convince you of its effectiveness.

Effect: After you have done a card effect or two, state that you will prove beyond doubt that a card's identity can be transmitted by thought waves alone. Spread the deck face down on the table or floor. A spectator freely takes any card he wishes and allows no one to see it. He is told that if his selection be a picture or face card to return it and take another, as it is too difficult to transmit personalities, and so far you have only had definite success with the spot cards.

Hand the spectator a slate and a piece of chalk and ask him to step to one corner of the room. You pick up another slate and step to an opposite corner. Ask him to draw, as well as he can, a picture outline of the card he selected and that you will try to get a thought wave of it and draw it too. He does as he is requested and you draw a picture at the same time. When you both turn your slates around it is seen that you have successfully accomplished your purpose by duplicating the very picture drawn by the subject.

Requirements: Use a stacked deck, Si Stebbins, Nikola, or otherwise, plus two slates and chalk.

Routine: Follow the above presentation to the point where you hand the subject the slate. He has already made his selection of a card, so you pick up the deck and lay it aside. However, you started picking up the deck *from the spot where the selected card was removed,* and then pick up the remaining cards and place these on top of the first group. As you lay the deck aside, glimpse the bottom card (the one that was originally above the selected card) and you know immediately what card was chosen!

No one need tell me that this is simple. I know it, but I use it, too. The followup with the drawings will throw the audience right off the scent, and they will remember this number long after they have forgotten more intricate tricks.

THE GYSEL SLATE

ANNEMANN

Undoubtedly, this is one of the neatest and most subtle of the flap slate methods for home seance work yet devised. I first saw it done by Bob Gysel several years ago, and its operation had me completely puzzled until the whole routine of action was revealed.

Two slates and a flap are used, the flap being prepared at one end with a sharp spring steel hook. A flat piece of spring, about a quarter of an inch wide and one inch long is bent into a V shape. One prong is now filed to a sharp point. The V shaped piece is now put over the center of one end of the flap and the untouched prong is securely fastened to one side by glue and a small piece of black tape. The pointed prong sticks out over the other side as illustrated.

Use a small table, such as a card table, and have on it a loose cloth cover. Write the message on one side of one slate and cover it with the flap, hook sticking outward as per illustration No. 1 Put the unprepared slate underneath and place the two slates to one side until ready to work.

Pick up the two slates together as per illustration No. 2. Turn them over once so that both outside surfaces are shown to be clean. This leaves the flap on the underside and the hook is at the right. Separate them, holding the top slate at the left end with the left thumb on top and fingers underneath; and the bottom slate is held at the right end in the same manner with the right hand. The flap is held in place on the under side of the right hand slate.

Both sides of both slates are shown by turning the hands. Now place the slates back together with the right hand slate going on top. The wooden edge is placed on the wooden edge of the left hand slate and, at this moment, the right fingers let up a bit with their pressure and the weight of the flap allows it to drop about an inch as per illustration No. 3. Then the right hand slate is slid along on top and the flap is thus transferred to the underside of the bottom slate. The situation is now as pictured in illustration No. 4.

The left hand now slides off the top slate, on the underside of which is the message, and drops it on the table. The right hand grasps the remaining slate by the side nearest the body with the thumb on top and fingers underneath, keeping the flap in place. At this point, you apparently think of the table covering, and your left hand pushes the slate on the table to one side a bit, and pulls off the cloth by grasping it at the center of the side nearest you. As this is pulled up, the action covers the right hand and slate for a second, and you'll find the hook in a position to be caught in the cloth. The left hand continues taking the cloth away, and the sides of it will fall down to hang around and effectively hide the flap. Turn a bit to your right and toss or drop the cloth out of the way.

Start to put the right hand slate on top of the other, but turn it around as you do so to show the other side. This is the move that will fool any wise person who may know about flaps. Drop it on top of the other slate and explain that with the slates on a solid surface, a spirit message should appear on the inner surface if at all. As you say this, lift off the top slate to show the inside and, in replacing it, slide it underneath the other slate. Pick up both slates together, tap the edges on the table, and then drop them down turned over. All is now ready for the finish.

Mr. Gysel used this continually as the opening to a series of mediumistic effects to obtain the message, "Good evening, friends." Or one can go further by having the message signed by the "control" supposed to be guiding the seance.

The whole operation takes but a minute, and is done easily and almost carelessly. The writer has seen Gysel do this without the cloth get-away for the flap, but it is not so easy unless one has established the appearance of being erratic in the way of moving around. Using small slates, the handling was exactly the same to the point where the top slate with the message underneath was tossed to the table. At this time, the other slate was held in the right hand which dropped to the side for a second where the flap was hooked onto the clothes a little behind the right hip. When the message was revealed, he turned a bit more towards the right, and the right hand merely grasped the flap by its sides, lifted it loose, and dropped it into the right side coat pocket when he reached in for a handkerchief to be used as a blindfold for his next test. The action, although bold, was done so easily that detection was almost impossible.

BEFORE YOUR EYES

NORMAN ASHWORTH

This effect is one of the most popular slate tricks of recent years because it combines originality, action and a real surprise finish that makes it ideal as a club program item.

Effect: The performer picks up a single slate and with a piece of chalk writes in large letters, "THE NAME OF THE CARD IS . . ." This message fills the slate, which is freely shown to the audience before being laid aside. Now the performer has a card selected, as he explains that the spirits will complete the sentence he has written on the slate by filling in the name of the chosen card. He picks up the slate to prove his statement only to find that nothing has happened, and that the slate still bears the message exactly as he had written it.

The performer looks surprised, remarking that this is the first time the message hasn't been completed correctly by the spirits. Then, as an afterthought, he realizes that there isn't enough room on the slate for more writing, so he decides to erase the message and rewrite it in smaller letters. As he erases his message a strange thing happens, for some of the letters refuse to be wiped off—and those letters remaining in view spell out the name of the selected card: TEN OF HEARTS! The spectator holding the chosen card acknowledges this as being correct.

This startling finish, turning an obvious failure into a complete victory for the performer, has tremendous audience appeal making it an effect worthy of any program.

Preparation: All that you need for this surprising trick is one slate with flap and a deck of cards.

First, write with chalk on the slate the words, "THE NAME OF THE CARD IS," as in the illustration. Then erase the various letters so the slate looks like the second one in the illustration. Erase enough of the letter "D"

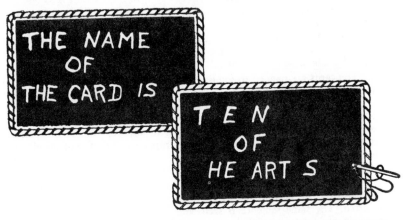

so it is changed to a "T". Now go over the letters, "TEN OF HEARTS" with white paint and set the slate aside to dry. When ready, chalk in the missing letters of the original sentence, being careful to convert the "T" back to a "D" again, so that the slate appears exactly like the first illustration.

Cover this message with the flap and lay the slate on the table together with a deck of cards and a piece of chalk. On top of the deck have the Ten of Hearts ready to force. Also have a cloth handy for erasing the writing.

Presentation: Pick up the slate and show both sides, being careful to hold the flap in place with your thumb or your fingers. Pick up the chalk and print the message on the flap exactly as in the first illustration. Then lay the slate on the table, writing side down, and pick up the deck of cards. Go into your patter theme while you force the Ten of Hearts. Use the method you can do best. (If you can't force a card naturally, better buy a copy of Annemann's "202 Methods of Forcing.") The person selecting the card puts it in his pocket. You now reach for the slate and pick it up, but leave the flap on the table. The message you now show is the prepared one, but to the audience it is the one you have just written! Look surprised for a moment, then disappointed, then brighten up and point out that it was your fault for not leaving enough space on the slate for the spirits to answer. Pick up the cloth and start erasing the message. All the chalked letters disappear, and the painted letters remain forming the name of the chosen card.

Howard Brooks, the night club magician, does the trick without using a flap. He starts off with the prepared message already on the slate. Without showing this side of the slate to the audience, he pretends to write a message, then turns the slate around and shows what he has apparently written. He then hands the slate to someone to hold over his head until time for the finale.

WALTER GIBSON'S METHOD

This method has several nice points that may appeal to some readers in that you can eliminate the force and get away with the flap at the same time.

Follow this closely. The slate is prepared in the same manner as originally described. The Ten of Hearts from the deck is then placed face down upon the written message and the flap is then put on top of both. A second slate, unprepared, is on top of the prepared one, and a deck of cards and a piece of chalk is set on top of all.

The cards are handed to someone for shuffling. The top slate is removed and placed under the arm. Next the sentence is openly chalked upon the flap of the second slate. The spectator who has mixed the deck is asked to stand, fan the cards face down before himself, draw any one he wishes and put it, without looking at it or showing it to anyone, face down upon the written message. The other slate is then dropped on top to cut off all light and give the happy spirit a chance to see the card and write its name for all to see.

During this short interval the slates are turned over together, which lets the flap drop to the unprepared slate. Then the prepared slate, now on top, is lifted. The same sentence is seen, and face up on the other slate is seen the Ten of Hearts, apparently the card which was selected by the spectator. He is asked to take the card and show it around. The slate with flap (and the other card underneath it) is again put under the arm where it is held tightly in place by pressure of the elbow. The slate bearing the message is shown, talked about, and finally wiped off to reveal the correct name of the chosen card.

Thus the stunt is done without forcing, and away from tables in the middle of the floor with people on all sides. A word of precaution is necessary, however. If you find that you cannot prevent the card from slipping out from under the flap when you have the slate under your arm, better lay the slate on the floor and play safe.

PHANTOM HAND

OSCAR WEIGLE, JR.

Effect: A number of white pasteboard cards are shown to be all different and to contain a number on one side, all numbers varying in the hundreds and thousands. The cards are shuffled, and after cutting, a spectator removes five, holding them number side down. On a slate the performer now chalks, "THE TOTAL OF THE NUMBERS SELECTED WILL BE," explaining that a helpful spirit will write in chalk the total of the addition to be arrived at presently. Another slate is given to a spectator, who copies the numbers selected on the slate and then adds them up. While this is being done, the first slate is given to another person to hold.

The copying and adding being finished, the spectator holds his slate for all to see and note the total. The second spectator shows his slate but no spirit writing is yet to be seen. The performer takes it back, saying something must have detained the spirit control, and starts to erase the words. They are seen to change to numbers and, upon comparison with the first slate, every one of the numbers coincide exactly! And not only is the correct total revealed, but all figures of the addition check, so that both slates look alike!

Preparation: The basic principle is the same as that used in "Before Your Eyes," page 168. This presentation is good either for a repeat show, or a place where playing cards are not suitable. The cards used are of white drawing board, playing card size. About 30 or 40 can be used. With bold strokes of black India ink letter the cards, numbering them from 100 to 1999. Make more of the "thousand" cards than the "hundreds," it being in keeping with the effect.

The five cards responsible for the effect are forced. In order from the top down they read: 742, 1072, 1712, 1315 and 1272. When added together they total 6113. The five cards are on top of the deck to start, and are kept there during the shuffle.

The pack is shown with the numbers towards the audience. In squaring the cards, the top 6 or 7 are held by the left hand while the right turns the rest "face down" on them. Advance to a spectator with the pack in your left hand, and have him lift off some of the cards. As you ask if he cut at any point he wished, the misdirection allows you to turn over the packet in your hand and then the top five are taken. That's the force.

For the slate preparation print the words as shown in the first illustration. covering the entire surface of the slate with the message. Make the downstrokes of all "E's" slightly curved—also the "L" of the word "total." The "S" in the word "numbers" is made to resemble a "5" and is unnoticed with the rest of the letters. The "W" in the last line is curved and looped so that the first part of it looks like a "6".

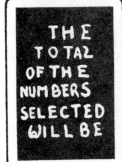  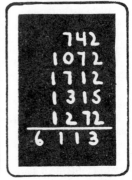

Letters and parts of letters are now erased to leave the figures as shown in the second illustration. These numbers are gone over with white paint. Before presenting, fill in the letters and parts of letters of the original message and cover all with a flap.

This slate, together with an unprepared one, the deck of cards, chalk and a soft erasing cloth are on your table to start.

Effect: After the card selection, pick up the flap slate and write the message on the flap, forming and spacing the letters as you know them to be underneath. You may have them on the flap in pencil. Put the slate on the table, flap side down, and hand the ordinary slate to a spectator. He turns the cards over one at a time and writes the numbers down and adds them. Thus they are put down in the correct order. Before he starts to add, mention that someone else should hold the message slate. Pick up the slate from the table, leaving the flap behind, and as the writing looks the same, all is well and you can be as open and free with this prepared slate as you like. Give it to the second spectator to hold, writing side down in his hands.

The first man adds the figures on the unprepared slate and gets a total of 6113. Ask the second spectator if the total has appeared as yet on his slate. It hasn't! Take the prepared slate from him and start to erase it, holding it so everyone can see what you are doing. The figures appear in full view, and it is but the work of a moment to draw a line just above the total. Everything now checks!

THE ULTRA SLATE MESSAGE
DR. JACOB DALEY

Note by Ted Annemann: Good methods for the appearance of messages on slates are many, but the routine explained here was shown to me by one of America's cleverest amateurs and I have been using it ever since.

Presentation: The psychic shows four pieces of silicate of the flap type. With a handkerchief or dry cloth he casually wipes the upper surface of the top piece, turns it over, cleans the under side and puts the cleaned slate on the table. This is done with all four pieces of silicate in the most open and easy manner and then all four are spread in a row. The spectator is asked to indicate any two of them, and two are laid aside. The chosen two are picked up, put together and the spectator holds them. Upon sliding them apart, nothing is found. A few moments later they are separated again and still nothing is found. Finally, on the third attempt, a real chalk message is found completely covering the entire side of one slate, and all four pieces may be left with the sitters.

Routine: One simple move makes this whole routine possible as well as perfect. When the four pieces of silicate are held in the left hand, the message is on the upper side of the third flap from the top. Dot the top flap so you can always tell which is the top of the stack. Dr. Daley uses pieces of silicate five inches by seven inches as the most practical size. The left little finger holds a break between the third and bottom piece at the start. Hold them flatwise in your left hand. The top piece is cleaned and then turned over with the right finger and thumb at the lower right inner corner. When this side has been cleaned it is slid off and dropped on the table. The top surface of the next slate is now wiped off and the same maneuver is made but this time two pieces are turned over together as one! In short, you merely make a two-card turnover with silicate flaps! The newly presented surface is cleaned and this second piece, bearing a message on its under side, is slid off onto the table. The remaining two pieces are cleaned in the same manner as the others, and are laid on the table so that you have four pieces in a row, of which all have been cleaned and shown on each side in an unquestionably fair manner. The message slate is No. 2 in the row and performer keeps his eye on it.

The spectator now indicates any two. No matter which ones he takes, he must or must not include the message slate in his selection. The performer either keeps the two indicated or uses the remaining two pieces depending upon which set contains the message slate. This message slate is dropped on top of the other and the two slates are held by the spectator. To look at them the first time, the top one is slid off with right hand but nothing has been written on the upper side of lower slate, so the piece slid off is replaced, but goes below the left hand piece this time. Again they are held (message is now on bottom of the lower slate) and this time the top piece is opened out like a book but still nothing has appeared. This top piece again is put underneath the other and, in handing them again to the spectator, the two are turned over. This time when slid apart, the message looks directly up at them.

Once used, I think this method will be found highly effective and practical. I certainly like it and have found it to be one of the cleanest methods of which I know.

THE ANSWER
DR. JACOB DALEY

Every once in a while a principle makes its appearance which may be used in many different ways. The following effect combines Dr. Daley's silicate flap routine with the torn billet and stolen center idea to create one of the most impressive mental tests in years. It makes the magician's dream a reality in that it provides an impromptu method of producing a spirit answer that is a direct reply to any question written by a spectator!

Effect: The performer has someone write a question on a small two inch by three inch piece of paper which is then torn up and burned in a convenient ashtray. While the paper pieces are burning, the performer introduces four silicate flaps, about four inches by five inches, which he shows to be blank. To convince everyone that they do not already bear any messages, he cleans each one individually with his handkerchief and lays them, one at a time, on the table. Two of them are selected. Using these as a writing tablet, the performer proceeds to "get an impression" of the question and writes it on the flap. His first and second attempts are failures, but he cleans the two flaps once more with his handkerchief, places them together, and asks the spectator to put them in his pocket temporarily. When they are removed a few minutes later, they are found to contain a direct answer to the question asked.

Preparation: The few props necessary for this effect may be carried with you at all times. Have the four silicate flaps in your right coat pocket, together with a few slips of papers. The chalk and the box of matches are in your left coat pocket. Also have a pencil or pen handy.

Routine: As already mentioned, this is a combination of two routines. The torn and stolen center stunt will be found on page 30 in Annemann's

"Mindreading Publicity Effect." Follow the procedure outlined there, but use one of your plain white paper slips, with a penciled oval drawn in its center, instead of the newspaper square described in the Annemann trick. After tearing the slip into small pieces and stealing the center section bearing the question, deposit it in your left coat pocket as you reach for the box of matches. At the same time, drop the torn pieces into a nearby ashtray with your right hand. Hand the box of matches to the spectator and ask him to burn the paper pieces which you have crumpled up in the ashtray.

Now reach into your right coat pocket and remove the four silicate flaps. The third flap from the top already bears this message: "It will occur sometime next year," and the flaps should be held so that this message faces up. Work Dr. Daley's "Ultar Slate Message" routine with the flaps up to the point where the two flaps are selected from among four. One of the two selected ones must bear the written message. Put these two flaps together so that the message is on the inside, and then turn them over to bring the message face up beween the flaps.

Hold the two flaps in your right hand, while you talk to the spectator asking him to think of his question. Reach into your left coat pocket with your left hand for the chalk, and secure the stolen paper at the same time. Finger-palm the stolen center piece as you bring out the chalk. Bring your left hand up behind the flaps being held in your right hand, and transfer the flaps from your right hand to your left, as your right hand takes the chalk. Clip the stolen center against the rear of the flaps with your left thumb. The stolen center is folded but twice and is easily opened behind the flap with the aid of the right fingers. The flaps, of course, are held so that the paper is not visible to your audience. Now you apparently get an impression and begin to write on the surface of the flap facing you. Actually you have read the question written on the torn out center of the paper, and you deliberately write a direct answer to it on the flap. When finished, place both flaps under your left arm, drop the piece of chalk into your right coat pocket together with the torn center piece, as you repeat aloud the text of your dummy answer. This dummy answer is on the flap nearest your left arm, so as you finish quoting it, grasp this flap with your right hand and show the dummy message to the spectator. (The flap bearing the correct answer is still under your arm.) Ask the spectator if the answer means anything to him.

The spectator says that the message does not mean a thing. As you discuss it with him, you transfer the flap to your left hand, reach up with your right hand and obtain the flap still under your left arm, and add it to the bottom of the flap in your left hand. Do not let the spectator catch a glimpse of the writing of this second flap. Now carelessly tilt the flaps again so that the dummy message is again visible, reach for your pocket handkerchief and clean off the dummy message. Replace your handkerchief and obtain the chalk again from your right coat pocket.

Make a second attempt to "get an impression," but this time tilt the flaps so that the spectator sees you scribbling a few disjointed words. These mean nothing either, so you remark that perhaps it would be better to let the message come through by itself.

Clean off the last words you wrote and hand the two flaps, still together, to the spectator and ask him to put them in his pocket. Ask him to repeat aloud the question he wrote for everyone to hear. Then suggest that he take the flaps out and look at them. He finds a direct answer written on one of the flaps which he may show to everyone as both flaps will, of course, bear minute examination.

Seriously worked, this makes a fine impression because of the direct answer angle, a feature which heretofore has depended upon assistants or plants. The under arm subtlety is one of Dr. Daley's recent improvements in the handling of the flaps, and the final touch in the perfection of this masterpiece. We are indebted to the Doctor for his permission to include this clever method of switching the flaps in this book.

NEVER FAIL

DR. JACOB DALEY

This effect may be termed a "double-header" for both a rope restoration and a slate writing mystery are accomplished in combination.

Effect: The performer talks of his discovery of a long hidden secret for restoring broken articles to their original condition. He offers to illustrate with a rope. It is looped between the hands and a spectator cuts the loop at the center. The cut ends are tied, passes are made, and the performer sounds off with invocations. The knot is untied and the rope is found in two pieces!

Only a little discouraged, the performer tosses these into the audience and takes another rope. It, too, is cut and the ends tied together. However, the performer admits that he is not too sure of the correct procedure and might rather ask for aid than fail again. He picks up two slates, showing them on both sides to be blank, and writes on one "Dear Houdini: Please help me out with my 'Neverfail' rope trick. (Signed) Dr. Jacob Daley."

The cut rope is hung over this slate with the knot resting on the upper, written surface. The other slate is placed on top. The hanging ends of the rope are crossed underneath the slate, brought up and tied tightly over the top by a spectator.

After a short interval with soft music the slates are untied. Between the slates now lies a loose knot and the rope is seen to be restored. The original slate still bears the Houdini message, but on the other slate is written: "Dear Jack: I had to do it the hard way. You can have the knot. (Signed) Houdini." Everything may now be handed out for examination.

Requisites: Needed are two slates with the usual single flap, two lengths of soft rope, scissors and chalk. The only preparation required is to write the answer on one of the slates and cover it with the flap. Lay this slate on top of the other one with the flap side up, and set to one side on your table.

The general effect being everything, the actual method of doing the rope trick can be left to the individual performer. Any version making use of the small extra or cut off piece, which is openly tied around the rope proper, is all right. I prefer the standard turban trick moves which allow you to do the trick without preparation. This effect has been explained time and time again, but there is one new twist to it which makes this effect possible.

In all versions, the short piece is tied around the center of the long piece, either to be trimmed entirely away, as in the turban trick, or slid off while coiling the rope around the hand. However, when performing this trick, the performer ties the small piece, not around the rope by itself, but around the bight of the rope. The illustration will make it clear, and it has been exaggerated to avoid misunderstanding. When completed, a tight and well tied knot appears to be in the center of the long length of rope. However, a pull on both ends of the long rope will cause the knot to snap free of the rope!

Routine: In order to facilitate the mastering of the subtleties employed, it would be well for the reader to follow the instructions with the articles mentioned at hand.

In the first example, when the rope fails to be restored, the performer uses exactly the same moves he later uses in the second attempt at restoring the rope. However, the necessary turban method move is left out which results in the first rope being actually cut. On the second try, the fake cut provides the short piece and the knot is made as described. The rope is now put around your neck while the slates are brought into play.

Both slates are shown blank. The "Answer" slate is laid on the table, flap side down, while the message to Houdini is being written across one side of the other slate. Holding the writing side of the slate upwards, the rope is now hung across it, from side to side, with the ends hanging down. The knot lays on the top (written) surface. The other slate is picked up from the table, leaving the flap behind, and this slate is laid over the knot, being careful, of course, to hold the "Answer" slate so that no one gets a flash of the writing it contains. Thus the knot is sandwiched in between the two slates.

You are now holding the slates at one end with the left hand in front of your body. The rope ends hang down, one on the side nearest you and the other on the side towards the audience. The right hand takes the end nearest the body and brings it around under the slates and then up over the audience side, across the top, and lets it hang down over the body side again. Then take the end of the rope hanging down on the audience side, bring it underneath towards your body, up and over the slates and let it hang down again on the audience side. But—just as the hand grasps this end, it gives the rope a tug which snaps the knot loose from the rope between the slates!

The right hand now grasps the two hanging ends beneath the slates, the left hand turns the two slates over, which action brings the two ends to the top with the slates hanging underneath, and anyone is asked to tie these ends tightly together. Then that person is allowed to hold the slates.

The trick is finished at this point except for the denouement.

ULTRA ADDITION
Dr. Jacob Daley

Here is Dr. Daley's subtle and convincing method of forecasting the total of an unknown column of figures. There are no loopholes in the routine, and it is as fair as genuine mindreading would be.

Effect: Four people are asked to stand and to think of a three-figured number. The performer looks at each in turn and writes something on a slate he is holding. He then draws a line, is seen to be adding the column of figures and writing the total, and finally he erases the top half of the slate. Laying the slate down without showing it, he announces that he has read the mind of each of the subjects, added the numbers, and now has the correct total written on the slate.

First, though, he suggests a checkup. He approaches the four subjects in turn asking them to jot down their thought-of numbers on a blank card, one number under the other. The problem is then given to a fifth person to add. This person calls the total aloud! Then, as an afterthought, the performer has the original subjects recheck their figures and also call aloud the final total. In short, the total is actually called out five times, during which period the original written numbers are rechecked!

Returning to the front, the performer says, "When I looked at each of you, I read your thoughts, wrote them down, added them up, and now, in absolute proof of the assertion I made originally, I'll show you that my total is exactly the same!" And he does!

Routine: Impossible as this may sound, the convincing details are accomplished by a clever subtlety.

Snap a rubber band around the end of a packet of five or six blank cards. On the bottom card write your fake addition problem, simulating a different handwriting for each row. Draw a line but do not put down the total. Instead, write the total in lead pencil on the frame of your slate. To perform, you need only this packet of cards, a slate, a pencil and a thumb writer gimmick clipped to your thumb nail. (Haden's Swami Holdout is ideal for this effect, and may be purchased from your favorite magic dealer.)

Follow the effect as given. When the slate has been placed on the table after writing, adding and erasing everything but the total, which is that of your fake addition noted on the frame of the slate, you take the packet of cards from your pocket. Approach the volunteers who are or should be standing. Give each one in turn the pencil and ask him to write his thought-of number on the top blank card of the packet, which you hold while he writes. When the fourth person has finished writing his number in the column, drop your hand to your side and turn over the packet of cards as you approach a fifth person. This person is presented with the previously written faked column, the original bottom card of the packet, and asked to total it. He does so while you hold the cards, and then calls the total aloud.

At this time you step to the front, reversing the packet of cards again, and remark that each person has written his own number, another has added the column, and the total obtained is . . . . As you give this slight resume, you glance at the packet and apparently read off the total. Actually, however, you write with your thumb writer the total of your fake addition under the spectator's original figures. You will have ample time for this as you will find out on your first trial.

Now, as an afterthought, go back to the spectators and have each of them check off his own row, and each one calls the total, as well. They have no time to add, and, after all, they are mainly interested in their own individual row of figures. The climax is then up to you. Give it a big buildup. It deserves it!

Dr. Daley's Variation with Mechanical Slate: The general effect is almost identical with the foregoing, and your actions throughout are actually what a real thought reader would do.

Four people each think of a three-digit number and the performer looks at each in turn and writes something on his slate, without letting any-one see it. He now draws a line, totals up his addition problem and is seen to be filling in the answer. He now rubs out the various "thought figures" he has collected, turns the slate around to show the total he has gotten and sets the slate up against a supporting book, etc., so that his total will be in evidence throughout the effect. He now takes another slate around to each of the assistants and has them write their mentally thought-of figures in a row, one under the other. Immediately, he hands the slate to a fifth person who totals the sum. This person stands and announces the total which is seen to correspond with what the mentalist has showing on his slate.

Like the first effect, you write any figures in the column you run up on your unprepared slate, but when you come to the total you fill in the actual total you are going to force with the other slate. This total may be noted in pencil on the frame of the slate, so that you will not forget it.

The mechanical slate may be either Baker's or Thayer's Addition Slate, or Dobrin's Double Locking Flap Slate. Lay the half flap over to one side, draw five horizontal lines across the entire slate surface and fill in the upper four spaces with numbers of three digits each, one under the other. Leave the "total space" empty. The numbers you insert, should vary in the writing but should, of course, add up to the total you are going to force. Now lay the half flap back to the opposite side and lock it. This will hide your figures and leave the slate apparently unmarked. Draw five horizontal lines across the face of the slate with chalk. The working is, of course, obvious. The four assistants write their own numbers on the mechanical slate and, as you hand it to a fifth person to add, you flip the flap over their writing which brings your previously prepared problem into view. As the flap locks, you can hand the slate to this fifth person to add and naturally he gets the same answer that is written on your unprepared slate.

SACRED SCRIPT
GORDON R. McKENNEY

The following is our old friend, the slate trick, all dressed up in new finery and should appeal to those who are looking for something off the beaten path.

Effect: The performer shows four pieces of silicate to be clean on all sides, and two of them are selected by a member of the audience and placed by him in his own pocket, banded together.

Ten cards, each bearing a single figure, and ranging from one to zero, are freely shown, all of them then being mixed by someone. Placing them in his pocket, the performer has four people remove one card each in turn; the selected cards indicating a four-figured number. Let us say that the number selected is 2750. The performer recounts a bit, recalling that two pieces of blank board are being held by the audience, and that a four-figured number has been freely chosen by chance. He throws out the remaining six cards and asks that the boards be separated.

Almost everyone will expect to find the number written on one of the pieces of silicate. But, no! Written in large chalk letters of ancient script is found "NUMBERS IV—36." This is an occasion for conjecture as to what has happened, but suddenly (if no one else has beaten you to it) a bible is mentioned, and the gracious host or hostess provides one. The fourth chapter of the Book of Numbers, verse 36, reads, "And those that were numbered of them by their families were two thousand seven hundred and fifty." And that's the selected number! Everything can now be examined.

Preparation: You will need four silicate slate flaps about 5 inches by seven inches in size. Write "NUMBERS IV—36" on one flap and place it, message up, third from the top of the stack.

The cards are regular numbered cards, and you will need two sets bearing the numbers from zero to nine. If you do not have a set of these cards, you can easily letter the few that you need. Take the numbers 2-7-5-0 from one of the sets and put them in your inside coat pocket in correct order from back to face, and with the faces towards your body. Put the remaining six cards of this set in your upper right vest pocket with the faces towards your body. Lay the other set of ten cards on your table with the silicate flaps and you're ready.

Routine: For the cleaning of the flaps and the showing of them to be free of writing, use Dr. Daley's routine already explained in his "Ultra Slate Message," page 172. At the end of this routine, you have forced two of the flaps, one of which bears your written message. Place these face to face, snap a rubber band around them and give them to someone to place in his pocket.

Next pick up the set of ten cards from the table, shuffle them and show them for what they are. Pass them out if you like and finally take them back in your left hand and put them in the inside coat pocket, on the body side of those already there. Holding the coat open with your right hand, pass to four people in turn and have each reach into your pocket and pull out a card. Work this part without hesitation or stalling, and the force cards will be taken out in the correct order. Have the number on each card announced as it is withdrawn.

This four-figured number is then repeated a time or two, and while doing so you apparently reach into your pocket and take out the remaining cards. However, you really take out the six cards from your vest pocket instead, and toss them on the table. Thus everything will check for the skeptics later.

The climax is now in order. Most people think of the Bible immediately. The effect builds from the point where they expect to see the numbers on the boards and are surprised when they find something else. The trick is really an ideal pocket item and, merely as a suggestion to those with inventive minds, the Book of Numbers has many verses with all kinds of combinations.

TRIBAL TRY

LEN SEWELL

(Editor's Note: The following effect is most unusual. The brilliant originality in the handling of the flap in connection with two boards is far and away superior to the usual slate method, and when properly presented will baffle anyone familiar with slates. We urge you to give it a trial, for it is really very easy once the principle is understood.)

Effect: The performer shows two blackboards which measure about 6 x 9 inches. One board is encircled with two rubber bands, under which the performer inserts a blank piece of white paper. The second board is now placed on top of the paper, and both boards are encircled with two more rubber bands. The slates are now stood against the back of a chair, resting on the seat.

Now a name, number, or object is chosen by the audience. The large bands are removed and the boards are separated. Still attached to one board, by the elastic bands, is the piece of paper. That paper now bears either a picture of he who was named, an inscription of the number mentioned, or a sketch of the object chosen.

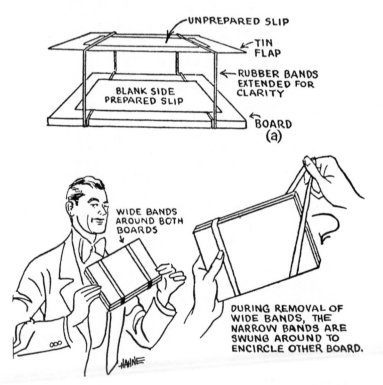

UNPREPARED SLIP

TIN FLAP

RUBBER BANDS EXTENDED FOR CLARITY

BLANK SIDE PREPARED SLIP

BOARD
(a)

WIDE BANDS AROUND BOTH BOARDS

DURING REMOVAL OF WIDE BANDS, THE NARROW BANDS ARE SWUNG AROUND TO ENCIRCLE OTHER BOARD.

Method: It all happens between the boards. The apparatus, if it can be called such, is very simply constructed. The sketches and description to follow will make clear the entire operation. It is a sort of tricky difference between "little" and "big" rubber bands. The small ones hold the paper onto the boards whereas the large ones hold the boards themselves together. Between the two, much happens.

Used are two blackboards, one tin flap to match, four thin elastic bands, two broad elastic bands and two pieces of white paper about 5 inches x 7 inches. On one of the papers write your prediction, name, number or object.

Following is an outline of the principle employed, and if you will follow the moves with three silicate flaps in hand and the necessary elastic bands, the idea will clarify itself very readily. The theory behind the manipulations is simply this: The small elastic bands are utilized to transfer the flap and the papers from one board to the other, under the perfectly natural actions of removing the large bands.

One board (a) is encircled by two small (thin) elastic bands, about six inches apart. Your prepared message is now laid on this board, and across the elastic bands, written side to the board. On top of this paper is laid the tin flap. This is now secured to the board by two more thin elastic bands, also placed six inches apart so that they overlay and coincide with the first two bands encircling the board. Thus the prepared message paper is sandwiched between the board and the flap, and they may be turned around and shown on both sides, appearing as a single board with but two elastic bands encircling it about an inch and a half from each end.

The unprepared slip is shown on both sides to be blank, and is secured to board (a) by slipping it under the elastic bands on the flap side. The second board (b) is now laid on top of the paper slip, and the two boards are secured together by encircling them with two broad elastic bands, which overlap and cover the elastic bands around board (a).

Our problem now is to transfer the flap and both papers from board (a) to board (b), and that is done as follows: Turn the boards over so that board (a) is on top. Hold the boards with your left hand, with the narrow end facing the audience and tilted slightly downwards. Slip your right finger tips under *all* the elastic bands at the far end of the board, lift the elastic bands up and, still holding them clipped by the first joints of the fingers, bring your hand towards the left edge of the boards, then down and around under towards the right edge. As your hand passes the front end of the boards, the thin elastic bands are allowed to slip off the finger tips and immediately are transferred to the lower board. The right hand continues down and away, bringing with it the large elastic band which is now free of the boards. To the audience, of course, this appears as though you just removed the large band from the boards, which is exactly what you want them to think. They know nothing of the thin bands which you transferred under cover of the removal of the large band.

Turn the boards around, end for end, and repeat the same movements with the other elastic bands, taking away the large band. Now remove the top board (a), and things look exactly as they did at first, with the slip secured to the lower board (b) by two elastics. But, the slip now bears your spirit message which can be seen by everyone, because the slip they are looking at is your prepared one, while the blank one is now sandwiched between the flap and the board, and, of course, cannot be seen.

The Force: The request for names, which can be revealed by letters or depicted by sketches, is tricked by the performer writing down names, not as called, but all alike. An excellent alternative is to write names as called, using 2 inch x 3 inch slips of paper. Let a member of the audience watch the proceedings and jot down each name. As each is written, crumple it up and drop it onto a hat, but do not let him see you tuck the first one, the force paper, under the hatband. This one later is retrieved after the hat has been shaken up a bit. All the other papers were honestly written. You pick out two papers, one at a time, and toss them away, then come out with your force paper from under the hatband. Thus you have complete control of your force paper throughout and everything seems perfectly fair.

DUO TELEPATHY

Robert H. Parrish

Many methods of transmitting information are available, but for simplicity of effect and directness of procedure, this slate routine will be found hard to beat.

Effect: The assisting spectator thinks of any card, removes it from the deck, and holds it up for all to see. The medium, notwithstanding the fact that she is seated with her back to the audience, takes the slate and chalk and immediately inscribes on the slate the name of the chosen card. The performer now hands another slate to the spectator and asks him to draw, in view of all, any simple geometric design that occurs to him. It is no sooner completed than the medium cries, "I have an impression!" and immediately reproduces on the slate the very same drawing, although obviously she could not see what the spectator had drawn!

Requirements: This short mental routine for two people is as simple as it is effective. In both cases, the information is relayed to the medium via a thumb tip writer worn by the performer, but the ruse employed is slightly different in each case.

These thumb writers are on sale at all magical dealers and are of two general types. One is a short thumb tip with lead attached to the ball of the thumb. The other is a small clip which attaches to the thumb nail itself. Only a few trials are necessary to ascertain which is the most practical for each individual. Besides a thumb tip, two slates are required, as well as a pack of cards and a fairly long piece of chalk. On one side the chalk has been shaved a bit so as to make a nice flat surface on which a few pencilled notations may be made.

Presentation: In introducing this effect, the performer holds a slate and a piece of chalk and outlines briefly the details of the test and just what the medium, who may be blindfolded, will attempt to do. He requests the full cooperation of everyone in the audience; and suggests that if they will but concentrate at the proper time the tests should be a success. From this point on not another word is spoken by the performer until the first test is completed.

The performer seats the medium in a chair next to a table with her back to the audience. He lays the slate on the table, picks up a deck of cards and hands it to someone to make a selection. The performer stands facing the audience during the removal of the card with his right hand dropped to his side. On his right thumb he has his thumb writer, and this hand also has retained the piece of chalk.

It is but the work of a second to slip the chalk into position between the fingers and to thumb write the initials of the selected card on the flat surface of the chalk. The moment the performer writes down the initials of the card, he picks up the slate from the table and hands it, along with the chalk, to the medium. She quickly works up to her first climax by writing on the slate the name of the card she finds noted on the chalk, and then holds the slate above her head for all to see what she has written.

The performer again takes the slate and, while quickly erasing it, asks a spectator if he would like to assist in another test but a much more difficult one. He will, of course, agree, so the performer hands him another slate with the suggestion that he draw some simple design or geometrical figure; and then show it to the rest of the audience so that all may concentrate upon the figure. The performer still holds the medium's slate, and is again wearing the thumb writer. His arm hangs naturally at his side. Once the performer catches sight of the figure being drawn he reproduces it on the edge of the slate, via the thumb nail writer, as well as he is able under the circumstances. Since these figures are seldom more than a triangle, circle or parallelogram, the medium should be able to make it out.

During this time she has been listening to the spectator writing on his slate, and as soon as the sound of the scratching chalk ceases, she cries, "I have an impression." The performer immediately hands her the slate he is holding. With appropriate pauses and flashes of inspiration, the medium quickly reproduces the drawing and stands up, slate in hand, to reveal it and take her bow.

SLATE IMMORTALITY

Robert Parrish

The effect of this startling variation in Living and Dead Tests first appeared in Annemann's publication "Sh-h-h!! It's a secret."

On an unprepared slate the performer writes a row of six figures from

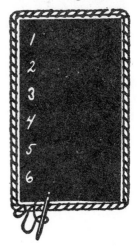

1 to 6 in a column down the left side. The slate is handed to a spectator to write the name of some dead person, known only to himself, after any one of the six figures. This is done while the performer's back is turned.

The slate is handed to another person who writes the name of a living person after any of the remaining figures. This is repeated until six names are written on the slate, one of which is a dead person's name among five "living" names.

The performer is given the slate and, concentrating upon it, he asks the spectator who wrote the "dead name" to think of the person as he last saw him. The performer starts rubbing the slate with a cloth. Then he asks the spectator to speak the name aloud. Turning the slate over, the audience is shown that all the living names have been erased and *only the dead name is left untouched!*

This is truly a nice effect and is accomplished by the simplest of methods. It is only necessary for the performer to know which name has been written first. After the first person has written the dead name, the performer approaches him and takes the slate by the top with his left hand. Calling attention to the fact that he does not make any attempt to see what has been written, the performer transfers the slate to his right hand, taking it with the thumb behind and the second finger on audience side, the finger being near the top edge on the right side. The finger is far enough in on the slate so that it rubs across the name as the right hand slides downward to grasp the slate firmly near the bottom. This action is perfectly natural and the finger merely slips over the slate surface without any pressure. Thus, the dead name, wherever it may be, is crossed and a resultant blur of its chalk is made with a very slight streak visible below.

This is done as the slate is handed to another person within two or three seats of the first. After this name (living) the performer handles the slate again, but from then on merely directs each spectator to pass the slate to someone near him.

It is only necessary now for the performer to take the slate and erase all names except the streaked one.

This effect is one of perfect mental misdirection for the onlookers always seem to believe that it is necessary for the performer to *know* the name, they do not realize that it is only necessary for him to know *where* the name is. There is no conceivable way in which he can know *what* the name is, so they are completely thrown off the right scent.

A Variation: Mr. Parrish has worked out a completely novel effect using this principle, basing his patter on the identification of individuals through their handwriting. Have a column of three figures on the slate. Three different people each write a word before one of the numbers. The performer now looks at the slate and tells which person wrote each word, though his back was turned during the writing.

Proceed with the first person just as described in the first effect. Ditto with the second person, only your finger is extended a bit more than before. No trickery is employed with the last writer. Now by looking at the slate, the performer will find two slight chalk traces below the word written by person No. 1, and only one streak under the word written by person No. 2.

HALF AND HALF
STEWART JAMES

Do not pass up this effect because of the layout of the tables. The effect is stunning and is truly a miracle from the audience's viewpoint.

Effect: The visible apparatus consists of three dice, an apparently meaningless list of letters, two slates and a piece of chalk.

The list first used is that shown in Figure 1. You write something on one slate and place it to one side. No one sees what you have written.

An interested spectator rolls the dice until satisfied that they are fair. Then comes the important throw of the cubes. The total is noted. Let us say that it is ten. The spectator locates the pair of letters tenth from the top of the column and proceeds to write them on the second slate. The letters will be found to be NK.

The performer hands the spectator a second list which, when placed beside the first, reveals a completed list of eighteen words. They read as per the list shown in figure No. 2.

The word at the tenth position is PLANK, the last two letters of which the volunteer has just written on his slate. Your slate now is turned so that its writing side faces the audience as it is placed beside the spectator's slate. The word is completed. The performer's slate bears PLA, the first three letters.

#1	#2
WD	CROWD
IC	MAGIC
HT	TIGHT
TE	WROTE
PE	GROPE
NT	BRUNT
TY	PARTY
NE	SHONE
RA	ZEBRA
NK	PLANK
IL	DEVIL
YS	FRAYS
HE	LATHE
IN	SATIN
SH	FRESH
CE	TWICE
ST	YEAST
ID	SOLID

Preparation: With three dice, the smallest number that can be thrown is 3 and the largest will be 18. If an odd number is tossed, you have volunteer count off that many rows of letters and note what comes up next. When an even number is thrown he is directed to count to that number and note the letters at that number. In either case, only letters at an even-numbered position may be selected.

As two cannot be thrown this narrows the possible selections to 4, 6, 8, 10, 12, 14, 16, or 18.

You also have eight separate lists for the groups of three letters, as illustrated. The numbers shown over the lists are for your personal use and knowledge, and, of course, do not appear on the lists proper.

In my own case I carry each list in a separate envelope with the numbers lightly penciled on the inside of the flap.

In preparing for the trick, arrange the envelopes in your pocket in a known order. Four, six and eight are in your left coat pocket; ten and twelve are in your inside coat pocket; and fourteen, sixteen and eighteen are in your right coat pocket.

Routine: Introduce the list (Figure 1) of two-letter combinations, the dice and the slates. Secretly print PLA on one slate and place aside as volunteer tests the dice. The dice now are rolled and the total taken. In most cases you can total the dice quickly and remove the proper list from your pocket before the volunteer has announced the result.

Suppose the total to be eleven. You have removed the envelope, secretly marked twelve, from your inside coat pocket and are holding it. Tell him to count down eleven two-letter combinations, note the next and write it on his slate. It will be YS.

4	6	8	10	12	14	16	18
CRO	CRO	CRO	CRO	CRO	CRO	CRO	CRO
MAG	MAG	MAG	MAG	MAG	MAG	MAG	MAG
TIG	TIG	TIG	TIG	TIG	TIG	TIG	TIG
PLA	WRO	WRO	WRO	WRO	WRO	WRO	WRO
GRO	GRO	GRO	GRO	GRO	GRO	GRO	GRO
BRU	PLA	BRU	BRU	BRU	BRU	BRU	BRU
PAR	PAR	PAR	PAR	PAR	PAR	PAR	PAR
SHO	SHO	PLA	SHO	SHO	SHO	SHO	SHO
ZEB	ZEB	ZEB	ZEB	ZEB	ZEB	ZEB	ZEB
THI	THI	THI	PLA	THI	THI	THI	THI
DEV	DEV	DEV	DEV	DEV	DEV	DEV	DEV
FRA	FRA	FRA	FRA	PLA	FRA	FRA	FRA
LAT	LAT	LAT	LAT	LAT	LAT	LAT	LAT
SAT	SAT	SAT	SAT	SAT	PLA	SAT	SAT
FRE	FRE	FRE	FRE	FRE	FRE	FRE	FRE
TWI	TWI	TWI	TWI	TWI	TWI	PLA	TWI
YEA	YEA	YEA	YEA	YEA	YEA	YEA	YEA
SOL	SOL	SOL	SOL	SOL	SOL	SOL	PLA

On handing him your list to place beside his, he finds that the word at that position is PLAYS. Holding the two slates together, with the writing on both showing, the word PLAYS is revealed.

Although the word was selected so fairly, to all appearances you must have known what word it would be. As a matter of fact, you don't as no particular word is forced. Reasoning further, the list is not exchanged for half of it is already in the volunteer's hands. The prediction is not switched for your written-on slate is never again touched by you. The prediction is direct with no double meaning.

NUMERO!
AL BAKER

Here is one of those rare effects that has an anticlimax but becomes greater because of it. The basis of the trick, the addition part, is not new but Mr. Baker has woven around it a bit of chicanery which dresses up the problem in a not easily forgotten guise.

Effect: A spectator is chosen for the problem, and is handed a folded paper upon which the performer has scribbled something. Showing a large size slate, the performer hands him chalk with the request that he write down a line of figures as they come to mind. Immediately under this row the performer jots a row and the spectator follows with a third. Then the performer finishes quickly by writing a fourth and fifth line. Drawing a line underneath, the spectator is handed slate for adding. The total is read aloud and shown. Opening the folded paper, the spectator finds prophecied the correct total! So far nothing original has happened, but wait! The performer shows the back of the slate on which has been inscribed the letters of the alphabet, each letter followed by a numeral from 1 to 0, see illustration. The spectator is asked his first or last name. *Substituting letters for the figures of the problem's total, this spectator's name is found to be revealed by that row of figures!*

It will be realized immediately by many that this also makes a valuable effect as a publicity trick with a pad of paper. Although it will puzzle a mathematician, and it will confound magicians who know only the addition effect, the mechanics are so simple that it practically becomes an impromptu stunt.

Preparation: First you must know the name of the person with whom you are going to work the effect. It may be either his first or last name, so long as it isn't more than six letters long, in which case another name is secured. On the back of the slate or pad have the alphabet and numerals written as per the chart.

A	1	K	1	U	1
B	2	L	2	V	2
C	3	M	3	W	3
D	4	N	4	X	4
E	5	O	5	Y	5
F	6	P	6	Z	6
G	7	Q	7		
H	8	R	8		
I	9	S	9		
J	0	T	0		

Before the test, write down the name of the person, and with the chart, substitute the letters for figures. If the name were Harry, the letters would equal 81885. This is all you need know before starting. On a piece of paper write the five figures and place a 2 in front of them, making a number prophecy of 281885 for the spectator to hold. Now add 2 to the last figure of the number representing the name of the person, in this case changing the number to 81887. This number is your key number to be remembered. If the last figure of the original name number is an 8 or 9, this rule holds good although adding the 2 affects the last two figures of the number instead of only the last one. If the number were 71288 it would change to 71290 by adding the 2.

Routine: Present the problem by handing the correct person the folded slip and ask him to place it in his pocket or otherwise hide it. Without showing the chart side of the slate or pad, ask him to write a row of five figures. Have him put down the same number of figures in the row as there are letters in his name, although you don't tell him this. Thus, in this case, you have him write a row of five figures. If the name were John he would be told to write four. You quickly put down the second row under his, and write the key number you have memorized. He writes the third row and you write the last two. The rule that governs the writing of the last two rows is the "nine" rule relating to the top and the third lines. Thus, in writing the fourth line, you watch the first line and put down figures which, added to the figures directly above each one, total nine. If the top row is 63052, the fourth line will be 36947. The fifth row is written while watching the third row and the same rule applies. Then the line is drawn and the spectator adds the problem.

The resulting sum will be exactly what you have prophecied on the folded slip he has pocketed. That's the first climax. Now explain that you will go further and that there is an unknown force or power at work when the spectator jots down his numbers at random. Ask him for his first or last name, as the case may be. Then turn over the slate or pad. On it is the list of letters and figures as listed here. You may remark that you have numbered the letters over and over somewhat as is done by numerologists. Don't say "as done *exactly* by them" because numerologists leave out the zero in their computations. There will be, in each case, one more figure in the total than there are letters in the name. Say, therefore, that you will use only the correct number of figures as they were written down in the total. Counting from right to left you cross out the first figure. He names the first letter, H. The figure after the letter H is 8, so you write H under the 8 in the total. He names the second letter, A. The figure after A is 1, so A is written under the second figure in total. This continues until finished *and the name of the spectator assisting is seen to coincide exactly with the total of the problem he helped assemble!*

The presentation of this effective idea may be varied by using two slates. One contains the chart, while the other is used for the problem. Start by having the spectator who assists put the chart slate (without it being shown) under his chair, or in a safe place. Now you write something on one side of the slate and announce that it is a prophecy. Don't show it but continue by having the problem written on the other side. When the total is read aloud, turn the slate over to show your prognostication correct. Now have the spectator take his slate and show the chart. Ask him the first letter of his name. He says H. Ask him what figure is after the letter on the slate. He say 8. Then you openly write H under the first 8 on your slate. Continue to this manner, which is very effective, as the audience doesn't realize you know the name beforehand and it is fascinating to watch the name build up under the total.

Although, at the start, this stunt may appear a bit complicated, I doubt if anyone will have trouble understanding and making it work if he will just try it out on a piece of paper to get the idea clearly in mind. Many who know the nine principles of the addition are still thrown off, because even that part is not done in the same order as the old trick. The smart ones generally look for adjoining lines to total nine, disregarding separated lines.

There are but two operations before presenting it; changing the name to figures, followed by memorizing the key number. Try to use last names whenever possible.

THE SUPER SLATES

ANNEMANN

For many years dealer's catalogues have listed the "Spirit Slates" where two slates and one flap make a spirit message possible. A moot question is, "why does a message appear only on one side?" In this version, after the two slates have been shown and numbered openly on four sides, they are opened to show a genuine chalk message on the inside of each slate, and they may be left with the audience for thorough examination. It would be best to follow these directions with a pair of slates and a flap in hand.

Put a message on one side of one slate and in the upper left corner of the slate write the figure 1. Cover this with the flap. On one side of the second slate write another message, or continue the first message. Mark this side with the figure 4. Lay this slate, with the message side down, on the first slate with the flap and keep all numbers to the front end towards the audience.

Pick up the slates, and holding them together and tipped forward a little, so that the top surface can be seen, the first or top slate is slid off and put under the second slate. State that you will number each side, and chalk in the figure 1 on the upper left corner of the top slate (flap). With the same move as before, slide this slate off and put it underneath. Mark the new surface with the figure 2. Now turn the two slates completely over (never end for end—numbers always stay at the front end) and mark the new surface with the figure 3. Lift this slate off and put it underneath (the flap has dropped off onto the top of the bottom slate) marking the new surface (back of flap) with the figure 4. Now—with a remark about the slates having been marked, slide the top slate off about an inch to the right and, grasping it near the upper right corner with the right thumb underneath and fingers on top, turn it outward—end for end—and at the same time bring it underneath the top slate and square them. The flap is on this slate, held in place by the fingers, and the two slates are placed on the table for a moment. You pick up a ribbon, or preferably a large and heavy rubber band. Now pick up the two slates, leaving the flap behind. Remarking that they will be securely tied together, make the same move as just described, turning over the top slate and bringing it back under the other. The messages are now both inside and the slates are fastened together. When revealed, everything can be examined and the numbering all checks perfectly.

Be careful when handling that the undersides of the slates cannot be seen as the messages are there several times. These moves are all simple and, although it may take several readings with the slates in hand to master the moves, you will be more than satisfied and pleased with the result. You can vary the effect by having the names of cards appear, one on each slate. Or again, have on each slate the answer to separate questions. Finding writing on both slates after openly numbering them will fool everyone, even well posted conjurers.

GABBATHA
J. G. THOMPSON, JR.

Dabblers in things of a spiritualistic nature should be interested in the following effect which has been routined for small gatherings of the intimate type. It can be carried in the vest pocket and performed practically impromptu at any time. Its running time is about seven minutes.

The performer asks a spectator to write the initials of a dead person on one of seven small white cards, explaining that from this point on the card will represent the deceased person and that his burial will be re-enacted. On the six remaining pasteboards, the spectator is told to write the initials of six living persons who will act as pall-bearers for the "dead" man.

This done, the "dead name card" is to be placed somewhere in the stack of pall-bearers, while the performer stands at a distance. Picking up the stack of seven cards at finger tips, the performer drops them in a borrowed hat, calling this the "cemetery."

He then explains that the dead man was a sincere believer in spiritualism and that he had left a pair of sealed slates with a friend sometime before his death, stating that he would attempt to "come back" and manifest his return. At this point the performer exhibits two small slates, numbers the four sides, binds them together with a rubber band, and hands them to a member of the audience.

Suddenly remembering the "pall-bearers" are still in the "cemetery," he remarks that it might be a good plan to see that they got home safely. Holding the hat high above his head, he has a spectator reach in and mix up the cards after which six of them are removed, one by one, and laid face down on the table, leaving one in the hat.

The performer now asks the spectator to examine the cards to see if the correct one was "buried." The cards are turned face up and prove to be the six "pall-bearers." The slates are opened by the person holding them, and on one side are the two initials which match those on the "dead name card" remaining in the hat! Gabbatha!

Requirements: You will need two miniature vest pocket slates, 2" x 2¼", with flap; seven plain white cards, 1¼" x 2"; and a rubber band. To prepare the cards for use in this effect, one of them is coated on one side with Simonize (auto polish), allowed to soak for a few minutes, then polished briskly with a piece of cotton and set aside to dry over night. With a card thus prepared in a pile of ordinary cards, the packet will cut at the "slick" card with a slight pressure and pushing movement to either side.

Take the flap of the slate and write the figure "2" on one side of it. Now stack the slates with the flap, written side down, on the upper surface of the lower slate. Place the rubber band in your right trouser pocket and you are set to start.

Routine: The spectator writes the first and last initials of the "dead name" on the smooth side of the "slick" card; the living names on the ordinary cards. He then mixes up the cards and returns them to you, and you very carefully take them by your finger tips with the right thumb underneath and the first and middle fingers on top of the stack. You now place the stack of cards in the hat, but as your hand momentarily goes out of sight, tilt it a bit and with your thumb push lightly on the cards towards the right. The packet will cut at the "slick" card and the "dead" initials can be read. Slide the "dead card" to one side where it can be reached easily when the hat is next picked up. Set the hat aside for a moment.

Show the slates freely, then stack them and place them lengthwise on your left palm with one end pressed against the base of the thumb, and with your left fingers curled around the other end.

Write "1" on the upper surface, then turn the slate over by grasping the edge farthest from you and turning it towards your body. Apparently write "2" on the new upper surface of the slate, but instead write the "dead name" initials you just glimpsed. Turn the slate as before and then turn both slates completely over together. This action will cause the flap to drop onto the lower slate and cover the initials you just wrote and, at the same time, will bring the "2" previously written on the flap into its correct position. Write "3" on the new top surface, and finally turn the single slate over writing "4" on the last side.

Make a final turn and place this slate below the other which brings the flap surface uppermost. With your left thumb slide the top slate to the finger tips, holding the flap in place with your thumb. Exhibit it on both sides, showing figures "1" and "2," and pass it to the right hand, which is held with the back to the floor. The slate is held with its side edge towards the floor and laying along the forefinger, the right thumb being on the upper edge. As the left hand exhibits the other slate to show the sides marked "3" and "4," the right hand tilts slightly towards the body and the flap falls into a perfect finger palm on the second and third joints of the middle and third fingers.

Slide the left hand slate behind the one in your right hand, and then the left hand goes into the left pocket searching for a rubber band. Not finding it, you transfer the slates to your left hand and carry the palmed flap to your right pocket, where you deposit it and bring out the band. This is snapped around the slates before handing them to the spectator to hold.

As the hat is picked up by the right hand to have the cards mixed, your right thumb goes outside of the brim with the fingers inside, where they pull the "dead name card" against the side of the hat. Hold it here during the subsequent mixing and withdrawal of the six pall-bearer cards.

While it has taken some time and space to describe the actual movements throughout, the actual working is smooth and the patter scheme fits all of the action. Although slightly long, it makes an excellent press stunt where the occasion permits.

GHOST WRITER

CLAYTON RAWSON

Effect: A freely selected card, inserted face up into the face down deck while all is held behind a spectator's back, is further protected by his wrapping the cards in a handkerchief. The performer shows two slates, puts them together, and the deck in its covering placed on top. After an incantation the pack of cards is unwrapped and spread. The card below the faced one is shown. The performer slides the slates apart to show its name written on one surface. Then the card above the reversed one is revealed. And the performer shows, written across the surface of the other slate, its name, too!

Preparation: This is a favorite of mine because of the simplicity plus the effect gained. The slates have the usual flap. On the flap write the name of the top (face down) card of the deck. On one slate write the name of the second card from the bottom of the deck. Put the two chalked sides of flap and slate together, and you are set.

Routine: Dovetail shuffle the deck, keeping the two important cards in place. Fan the deck for a selection. Square the deck, and have the selected card placed face up on the face down deck. Instruct the spectator to insert his card somewhere in the deck while he holds it behind his back. As you put the deck behind his back, merely turn it over. He inserts what he thinks to be the top card into the deck. Then he is told to cut the pack several times. And lastly you take out your breast pocket handkerchief and have him wrap up the deck, still behind his back. No one living could know the result of his action. Yet the face up card he chose now rests between the two pasteboards you have wanted to force, and the wrapping keeps everyone from discovering that the deck was turned.

The slates are shown, put together, and the flap dropped. From here on it is simply a case of revelation as described.

NONPAREIL
STANLEY COLLINS

In the almost innumerable versions of the slate effect, the conjurer has to force the choice of the particular figure, word, phrase, etc., he desires to magically produce. The trick I am about to describe enables the performer after having offered a perfectly *free selection* of any card from a pack, to produce an enlargement of it on a previously marked slate.

Preparation: Of the two slates in use, one is previously provided with a large figure 1 drawn from one corner to the other through a chart sketch of a pip card, say, the 8 of Spades, as large as the slate itself.

To mask this preparation, the familiar flap is again requisitioned, one side of which is marked with a large figure 3. Before placing the flap on the slate, the 8 of Spades is removed from the pack and laid face downward on the sketch of itself. The figure 3 on the flap must face the prepared side of the slate so that when in position both sides will appear blank.

Routine: Advancing with the ordinary and the unprepared slate in left hand, the flap is marked openly with a large figure 1, and the opposite side of slate with a large figure 2.

The second slate is numbered with a 3 on one side and a 4 on the other, these numbers, as the performer explains, being written for identification purposes. Presenting a well shuffled pack of cards to a spectator, he or she is asked to draw one and place it face downward on slate 1 without looking at it. The patter must be arranged so as to misdirect the real motive for this action, emphasis being laid on the fact that no one must know the card selected. The slates are now placed together, care being taken that the figure 3 on one side faces the 1 on the flap of the other.

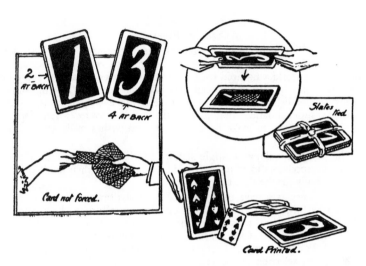

While they are being tied with a ribbon, the positions are reversed so that the flap slate is on top of the other. By this arrangement the flap will fall onto the 3 side of the unprepared slate, carrying with it and hiding the selected card. (If the slates were to be separated at this point, the writing and the duplicate force card would appear.) And this is exactly what happens when the slates are untied! The 8 of Spades, supposedly the selected card, is revealed laying face up on the No. 3 (flap) side, while the top slate's inside surface is seen to have its picture in chalk. The entire action of this slate maneuver is shown in Figures 1 and 2.

The right hand tips the card from the flap slate over onto the surface of the left hand slate with sketch and the flap slate is tossed with flap side down upon your table as you come forward and pass the left hand slate out

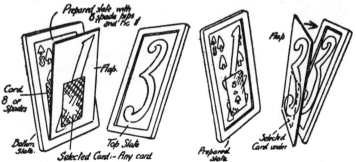

to the selector of the card. Saying, "And here is your material proof of something beyond the veil working in our interests," you then take back the slate, continuing, "You may keep the card as a constant reminder of occurrences strange. I need the slate for future attempts to pass an hitherto unsurmountable barrier."

MY CASE

CLARENCE HUBBARD

Effect: "There are people," begins the performer, "who just don't believe in anything, even when they see it before their very eyes. They are the skeptics of the world who hold back and retard progress in almost every line of creative endeavor. My experiment now is to duplicate the accomplishment of many spiritualistic mediums—that of receiving a written message from "the happy summer land," that part of the veiled universe where departed souls live, and strive to make their thoughts and wishes made known to us still among the living."

The performer shows a single slate to be clean on both sides. He asks two close-by spectators to initial each side, one of whom then holds the slate close to his body for the time being.

"While messages have been received countless times under as stringent conditions as this," he continues, "the unbelievers talk of trickery, and that is why I want to try and prove otherwise. I don't want to know what is going to be the result, that is, if we are successful in establishing a contact with the far beyond. For test purposes I cannot ask any certain one of you to help. We must leave that selection to chance."

The performer-medium passes out ten envelopes, each containing a blank card. He calls attention to the fact that each envelope is numbered from 1 to 10. Each spectator receiving one is to write a simple query upon his card and then seal it inside the accompanying envelope. The performer follows this up by collecting the envelopes on a tray, and dumping them into another person's lap.

"It's best that I don't touch your envelopes," he says. Next he takes from his side coat pocket a handful of counters. "There are ten of these," the performer blandly remarks, as he drops them into the hands of still another person. "You see?" He takes them back. "One counter and only one will be picked." He drops them back into his side coat pocket and, shaking the pocket, holds it open for a selection by the spectator. "The number?" asks the wizard. Perhaps it is 8. He turns toward the man with the envelopes. "Find the envelope numbered 8, open it, and read aloud so everyone can hear the question inside."

The spectator does so. It might be something such as, "Will a state of war exist between the United States of America and Germany?"

The performer nods to an acknowledgment of the question, and tells the man with the envelopes to pass the rest of them around, as they are of no further use.

"And thus we've found and determined upon a question which no one of us could have foretold would be asked or selected." The performer says this as he approaches the man who has been guarding the slate. "Honestly, now," he asks that person, "Do you think that anyone has had access to the slate you hold, or that any entity of an invisible nature might have been close by?" It's a tricky question and the person will have to hesitate. The audience takes this for indecision and you take advantage of the stall by reaching for the slate and asking, "Those are your initials, aren't they?"

Then you call the other "initial man" forward. He sees the other side of the slate and agrees when you ask if his initials aren't there also.

Then you turn the slate around towards the audience. It bears a chalked on message! and the writing could read something like, "WAR IS HELL!" which is a perfect answer to the question asked. We would like to finish by saying, "And that, my friends, is proof enough that from another level of being has come an answer as well as a warning."

Preparation: A single slate bearing a flap with a semi-circular piece cut out of one corner, and a metal or wooden tray, built on the lines of the "money tray" so as to deliver an extra envelope at the right time. See illustrations.

To get back to the flap slate. The answer to your forced question is chalked onto the slate, a semi-circle is drawn in one corner and this side is covered with the flap. This is laid on the table, together with the envelopes and the tray. In the false bottom of the tray is your extra envelope, marked No. 8, in which is sealed your force question.

MESSAGE ON
SLATE COVERED
BY FLAP

FLAP

TRAY WHICH ADDS
EXTRA ENVELOPE

Routine: Pick up the slate and show it on both sides as you talk, and at that time you chalk on a semi-circle in one corner on each side. When marking your semi-circle on the flap side, your chalk follows the cut edge of the flap. The chalked line effectively hides the line of demarcation between the flap and the slate proper. It is in this corner that the first spectator marks his initials, which go onto the slate itself. At this time you go back and drop the slate onto your table. Then, as an afterthought, pick it up again, minus the flap, and have a second person step forward. He initials the unprepared side in its designated corner, and you push the slate under his coat, asking him to hold it.

The envelopes are stacked on your tray, so you pick it up and pass among the spectators, asking several people to take one until they are gone. You hold the tray at the opening side for the distribution, and also for the collection of them. Thus you do not handle the envelopes at any time, which is a strong point in your favor. There are only 9 envelopes in your stack instead of ten, but no one will notice this. After collecting the envelopes, change the tray to your other hand, thus freeing the opening in the false bottom, and dump the trayful of envelopes into someone's lap. The extra No. 8 envelope falls with them.

Next comes the force of that added envelope with the question, the answer to which is on the slate being held. All suit coats are made with a small change pocket at the top of one or both of the side pockets. In the pocket proper put ten counters bearing the same number, in this instance 8. In the little pocket put ten counters numbered consecutively beginning at 1. It is from this little pocket that you take the counters which you hand someone and take back. You put them back into that little pocket, and shake the entire pocket as you hold it open for a selection. If the coat pockets have flaps, so much the better. Keep the flap open for the first showing and return. Then turn the flap inside and let the spectator reach freely. The little pocket is covered. Otherwise merely hold your hand there in an effort to keep the pocket open and make the spectator's task of reaching in easier.

The rest you know. Just remember that no matter what question you may use, keep it topical, be certain that the answer definitely fits the question so that no checkup with its writer is necessary, and keep the answer short so as to show up on the slate. When you apparently get an acknowledgment after the question first is read aloud, it's a lie—for you look around and then nod with a gesture at—the Lord only knows whom. No one else will know either, but you've made a subtle point.

THE 20th CENTURY SLATE TEST
Jean Hugard

Jean Hugard has a clever and subtle method of handling a flap in this effect and I know it will find favor with not a few club and close-up workers. All in all, the general effect has not been changed much insofar as a message or name still appears on the slate. Mr. Hugard's subtlety consists of making the conditions appear stricter by the application of a piece of newspaper cut to slate surface size. After showing the slates as usual and cleaning them, a piece of newsprint is stuck to one side of one slate by its corners with bits of wax.

Unbeknown to the audience there is a message already written on one slate, which has been covered by a duplicate piece of newspaper stuck to the slate, and this newspaper in turn has been covered with the usual flap. The paper the audience first sees is dutifully stuck to the flap and the two slates are placed together. Mr. Hugard gave me no definite excuse for the paper, but I suggest that patter be formed regarding the necessity of absolute darkness and suggesting further that failure has resulted at times when even the slate frames were not exactly true and even.

Concluding this bit of patter, the performer separates the slates again and has a spectator, who is later to open the slate, initial the paper with a crayon. Of course, he initials the piece of paper covering the message, the flap bearing the piece of paper which the audience has seen having been dropped to the other slate. The slates are placed together again with the message slate on top and they are held by the spectator until it is time for the climax. The performer again takes them and separates them, and discards the lower slate bearing the flap. The spectator identifies his markings on the top slate, removes the paper and finds the message. This leaves the slate and paper in the audience, and all evidence of trickery has been done away with very neatly.

THE SCHOOLBAG
Peter Warlock

Now for a slate effect in which two messages are obtained on one slate. The operator picks up a schoolbag, and opening it withdraws a number of books, a slate, a piece of chalk and a duster. The patter theme runs along the lines that the schoolbag belonged to one little Willie, since departed, and how now, strange things happen inside the bag. Cleaning the slate the operator marks it on one side with a name or an initial. Whilst this is going on the schoolbag can be examined by a member of the audience. Receiving the schoolbag again, the performer places the slate and piece of chalk inside it. The bag is then hung by its strap on the back of a chair. Advancing with the books, four or five in number, one is selected by a member of the audience. The selector of the book is then asked to open it to a page which is decided upon and to read aloud the first line on the page. However, in arriving at a page number, the performer has noted down several freely suggested numbers on a pad and totaled the column, arriving at 91. When this is handed to another spectator to check, he reminds the performer that a mistake has been made and that the total should be 94. It is page 94 then to which the book is opened and the line read.

The performer now calls upon little Willie to manifest himself by writing on the slate, in chalk, the line selected. The slate is withdrawn from the schoolbag and it is shown to contain the written line. However, the man with the book says it's not the correct line. "What a pity," says the performer, "he never could count. It's probably the line from some entirely different page; let's give him another chance." The slate is cleaned and replaced in the schoolbag. After the necessary interval it is withdrawn and the correct line found written on the slate.

A subtle point in this routine is that the first message to appear is really the first line of page 91. Acting on the suggestion proposed in your patter given above, the man with the book is sure to check page 91 after the effect is successfully concluded. He'll tell the others for certain thus adding a decided punch to the whole effect.

Although only an ordinary flap slate is used in the making of this effect, it will be noted that two messages are produced instead of the usual one; also that there is no doubt in the minds of the spectators that both the slate and the schoolbag are free from preparation, as both are passed into the hands of the audience at some time during the presentation.

Requirements: One schoolbag, scribbling pad, pencil, tray, dust cloth, a flap slate, a piece of chalk and a number of books, one of which you will force. In making the necessary preparation, write the first line of page 91 on one side of the slate. On the flap write the first line of page 94, and place the written side of the flap against the written side of the slate so that the slate now appears blank on both sides. The dust cloth is rolled into a ball and put in a corner of the bag. The slate and other articles are dumped into the bag and you're ready to present the effect.

Presentation: Introduce the bag and remove all the articles except the dusting cloth. Hand the bag to someone to examine and he'll bring out the cloth—thus subtly proving that there's nothing left in the bag. The books and the cloth are placed on the table or a chair while the slate and chalk are held. Asking for a name or someone's initials, you write this on the non-flap side of the slate. Take back the bag and replace the slate. Directly that it is inside, tilt the bag, causing the flap to fall out of the slate and against the side of the bag. Now force the correct book from among five on the tray, using the usual equivoque. Pick up the scribbling pad and pass from one member of the audience to another, asking them to suggest numbers which you write down in a column. However, you mentally keep track of the total.

When it has reached the total of not less than eighty-five and not more than ninety, you thank them and start to total the column. In the course of doing so, you deliberately add the figure necessary to make the column total 94, but actually you put down 91. Hand the pad to the person with the book, or his neighbor, who will of course correct your addition. The assistant now look up the first line on page 94.

Remove the slate from the bag, leaving the flap behind. It is handed to the spectator ostensibly for him to read what is written, and also to allow him to handle the slate and convince himself that it is unprepared. The sentence proves to be the wrong one, so you pick up the duster and erase the writing and then replace the slate in the bag. This time you place it behind the flap, *i.e.*, so the blank side of the flap comes against the clean side of the slate. When removing the slate the second time, the flap is removed with it, it being an easy matter to slip it into the slate frame and hold it in place as the fingers withdraw the slate. The correct line now appears to be written on the slate. Simultaneously with the withdrawal of the slate, the schoolbag is turned over with the other hand, allowing the chalk to drop to the floor, thus mutely calling attention to the fact that the bag is otherwise empty.

KNOCKOUT!

HENRY FETSCH

Effect: The performer chooses a prominent member of the audience and hands him a piece of chalk and a slate and stands him at one side of the stage, or across the room. The performer stands at the opposite side of the stage and also holds a slate and a piece of chalk. Four more volunteers are asked to stand at their seats in the audience.

The first volunteer is asked to concentrate upon his year of birth. The second thinks of the year in which his wife was born. The third person mentally selects any important year, in the last 20, during which an event of consequence has happened for him. To further vary the numbers selected, the fourth assistant thinks of the first four figures of his telephone number, license number, Social Security Card, etc. After a bit of concentration, the performer writes upon his slate the total of these four mentally chosen numbers.

The four audience standees are now asked to call out their selected numbers, and the assistant on the stage writes them down in a colum on the slate he holds. He is requested to add them and call aloud the total, and then show it to the audience. (You can invite members of the audience to take down the numbers and add them for a double check—and this is a very strong point.) The climax arrives when the performer shows his slate to contain the correct total of the four numbers!

Routine: There are points in this presentation that afford exceptional clearness and directness of action. Magicians, especially, expect trickery either in the adding operation or in the performer's handling of his slate and chalk. However, there is no evident trickery at any time, and all material is unprepared. After such a buildup, I can see some readers quitting when a plant is mentioned. I only hope they'll follow through and try it out. The plant is the fourth person to stand.

The selection of volunteers is made according to the following table:

1st—Between 25 to 30 years of age.

2nd—Between 25 to 30 years of age.

3rd—Any age.

4th—Is a stooge who knows the total to be reached; we shall say 7595.

INSTRUCTION TABLE

1st—Think of the year he or she was born.

2nd—Think of the year his wife or her husband was born.

3rd—Think of any year within the last 20, of importance to him or her.

4th—Think of the first four figures of license, telephone, etc. (???)

By following the above tables, the selected number will always fall within a certain range of years. See the first table in conjunction with the following.

1st—1906 to 1921

2nd—1906 to 1921—due to the fact that husband and wife ages are nearly alike, or within ten years' difference.

3rd—1924 to 1944

4th—The first two digits of your stooge's number to be called is 18. He acquires the other two digits as follows. As each of the first three calls his number to be written down on stage, the stooge makes a mental addition of the last two digits only. He then subtracts this total from the last two digits in the prearranged number (95) and gets the last two digits of the number he is to call. He puts 18 in front of them, and calls out the four figure number. The addition of the four sets of selected numbers now totals the prearranged total of 7595.

EXAMPLE

1st—1910	The stooge's thoughts— 1st—10	
2nd—1913	2nd—13	95
3rd—1924	3rd—24	47
4th—1848	—	—
————	47	48
7595—the prearranged total	18 before the 48 remainder—1848	

This is one effect where a stooge is never suspected. The explanation to a prospective plant is simple and easily understood. Give it just one try.

A SLATE AND A NUMBER
ORVILLE MEYER

The subtlety used in this number divination feat is quite ingenious, and a perfect example of misdirection. The routine is simple, direct and convincing.

Effect: Three people write mentally selected numbers on a pad of paper. The performer has correctly prophesied the total on a slate, and although this effect is not new, the method is certainly a psychological improvement over others of the same nature.

Preparation: Use a small scratch pad about 2 by 3 inches. Take the backing off so either side may be used for writing. On one side, using two styles of writing, put any two two-figure numbers, for instance 34 and 86. I suggest using two numbers whose total ends in zero, as the total of these two figures must be kept in mind. For the above figures, you would remember 120.

Routine: Select a spectator on your left and have him think of a number from ten to one hundred. With pad and pencil in hand, as though you were about to jot it down, ask him to whisper his number to you. When he does so, start to write it down, then pause a moment, and state that before you start the test, you will write a prediction which will not be revealed until the test is finished. Write something on the slate, and put it writing side down in full view. Ask the first person to keep his number in mind for a minute while you go to a person on your right. Hand the pencil and pad to him (don't worry about the numbers on the bottom of the pad, as they never turn it over) and ask him to write a number of two digits. Another person near the center is asked to do the same.

Now return to the first person on your left, and as you approach him, the left hand at side turns the pad over, bringing the previously written numbers to the top. Ask the spectator if he is still thinking of his number . . . then have him write it below the two previously written numbers on the pad. For further identification have him initial the paper, tear it off and keep it. You pocket the pad.

As you walk away, stress what has been done. Three numbers were thought of, and you wrote on the slate before anything at all was written down. The spectator with sheet adds the numbers, and then stands and reads the total aloud. The slate is shown and the predicted sum is correct.

HOW? Because after the first spectator gave you his number, you remembered (?) to make the prediction on the slate, and this predicted total was his whispered number plus the total of the two already written by you on the underside of pad. Thus, with 34 and 86 you would have kept in mind 120. If the first spectator had whispered 24, the prophecy would have been 144.

I suggest taking the paper from the spectator after he has read the total, and show it to one or two people nearby. Then pocket it and reveal what is on the slate. This principle gets entirely away from the old 9 principle which many know, and the fact that the last writer keeps the paper and adds does away with any thought of exchange.

GHOST WRITER
R. M. JAMISON

With the routine employed in the following trick, the slates may be shown high up in front rather than to one side, and two successive messages can be obtained.

Effect: We say "effect" when in truth this is merely a description of that part of an effect in which you produce one or two spirit messages on two slates. However, the handling has some nice points as you will see. The performer shows two slates, the sides of which are numbers from 1 to 4. These are exhibited quite freely and are put together. When taken apart a few minutes later, the numbering is still intact, but each slate bears a message on its inner side.

For those who want to produce two messages, or one long message with half of it on each slate, or as Ted Annemann suggested—a message on one slate with an important detail missing, which is later found on the second slate, then we can recommend this routine.

Preparation: The numbers and messages are written with No. 98 Sanford White Ink, using a small camel's hair brush. The contrast and reading is better than with chalk. The writing may be washed off later if you want to change the messages for another trick.

To arrange the slate set up, place Nos. 1 and 3 on one slate, and on the "1" side, one of the messages. With this message face up, and the numbered end of the slate AWAY from you, place it on the table to your right.

The other slate is numbered 2 and 4 with the message on the "4" side. Pick up this second slate with the "2" side up and with the numbered end TOWARDS you and place it on the table at your left.

Now number your flap 1 and 4, but on OPPOSITE ends. Take the flap with the "1" side up and towards you, and place it on the slate to your right covering the message on the first slate. Now pick up the slate to your left and place it on the right slate. No. 2 side will now be on top.

Routine: Pick up the squared slates and hold them in front of your chest, with your hands at the sides, so that the No. 2 side will be facing audience, with the number at top. Slide the rear slate (the one nearest you) off to the right, holding the flap on its front with the right forefinger. Thus the audience sees one side of each slate numbered respectively, 1 and 2.

Put them back together and turn them over end for end. Separate them exactly as before, the flap having dropped to the new rear slate during the turn over, and show the audience the sides numbered 3 and 4. Nothing could be fairer! The audience has now seen all sides of the slates!

Lay the slates on the table, remembering which message you want first, so that you can have either the No. 2 or the No. 3 side uppermost. To reveal the message, pick up the slates together, slide off the top slate and show the message it contains. Let the under slate with the flap be seen carelessly as devoid of writing, and drop it on the table—flap side down—as you rub off the message on the slate you are holding. Do not, however, rub off the number. A damp cloth will clean the slate very nicely.

Pick up the second slate, leaving its flap on the table. Remember that this second slate contains a message on its lower face, so do not let the audience get a flash of it. Place it on the slate you have just cleaned. Give them to someone to hold, and when they are separated a second message appears! Everything may now be examined, as the numbering is correct as at first.

If you use Annemann's suggestion, do not erase the first slate whose message is minus some important detail. After showing the message, pick up the second slate (containing the missing detail), place it on top of the first slate and give them to someone to hold. When separated, the spirits are found to have added the missing details on the second slate!!! The effect is thus brought to a surprise finish, and leaves the slates perfectly numbered and with writing on both.

THOUGHT RAYS
Dr. L. E. Duncanson

Effect: In this very effective mystery simplicity reigns supreme. A slate and a piece of chalk are given to a spectator who faces the audience. The performer is isolated in any fair manner, preferably by turning his back and standing in a far corner. The spectator is requested to think of a word or name and write it on the slate. Secondly he is asked to think of a number and to write that also. Finally he thinks of some geometrical design and draws that, as well.

Everything he has put on the slate he now shows to the audience. The performer directs everything from where he is located, and makes it very obvious that it is impossible for him to receive any clue as to what had been written. Once everyone has seen what the assistant has written and drawn, he is asked to erase it, lay it on the table and resume his seat.

The performer picks up the slate and the chalk and, standing facing the audience, asks everyone to concentrate on the word that was written. Then he writes something on the slate. Anyone now calls the word on which they have all been concentrating, and the performer turns his slate around and shows that he has actually written that very same word.

Erasing this, they are all asked to concentrate on the number while the performer again writes. Someone else names the number, the performer turns his slate and he is right a second time. The number is erased and, while all think of the picture, the performer succeeds in duplicating it! The effect is presented simply as a case of "thought rays" emanating from a large group all thinking of the same subject.

Preparation: You use nothing but the slate, chalk and a piece of dry, soft cotton cloth for the erasing. But beforehand, there is a slight preparation. Clean the slate well with ammonia water and let it dry. This is to remove all traces of oil from the surface.

Take a piece of white chalk and let it soak in Three-And-One Oil, then dry the chalk so that it is not oily to the touch. Anything now written on the ammonia cleaned slate with this prepared chalk, and afterwards erased, will leave a very light oily line tracing on the slate. This can be read by you if the slate is tilted slightly at an angle under a light, yet the surface itself appears void of writing.

Routine: The working now becomes clear when the effect is reread. I advise having the spectator stand where there isn't an overabundance of light but there need be little fear on this score. The effect may be presented under the most trying conditions and will not be found wanting.*

FATAL NUMBER

HENRY CHRIST

Here's a slate effect that is considerably off the beaten path, so far as its impression on the audience is concerned.

Effect: The performer shows a large display board (it can be made to fit the suitcase, or fold to fit a briefcase) upon which can be seen a long list of Kings who, throughout history, have either been murdered or deposed (see illustration). It is shown that the fatal number 2 has been in evidence constantly and that around these rulers there existed something unknown, something far greater than mere coincidence can explain away.

Two slates and a packet of cards containing the names and countries of the 18 rulers are at hand. The slates are shown blank on all sides, secured together with two elastic bands, and two spectators each hold an end of them.

Two more spectators step forward and one mixes the packet of cards thoroughly. The other spectator stands beside the large display board (containing the list of 18 deposed rulers as illustrated here) and is told to start at the top and tap each name deliberately and slowly down the column, stopping wherever he may please (this is NOT a force). At the same time, the man with the shuffled packet of cards holds them

THE FATAL NUMBER

The FOLLOWING LIST OF KINGS HAVE EITHER BEEN MURDERED OR DEPOSED

NICHOLAS	II	—	of RUSSIA
WILLIAM	II	—	of GERMANY
JAMES	II	—	of ENGLAND
FRANCESCO	II	—	of SICILY
CHARLES	II	—	of FRANCE
CHARLES	II	—	of ENGLAND
CHARLES	II	—	of ANJOU
FREDERICK	II	—	of GERMANY
WILLIAM	II	—	of ENGLAND
ALEXANDER	II	—	of RUSSIA
MANUEL	II	—	of PORTUGAL
JEAN	II	—	of FRANCE
RICHARD	II	—	of ENGLAND
PETER	II	—	of RUSSIA
HAROLD	II	—	of ENGLAND
FRANZ	II	—	of GERMANY
EDWARD	II	—	of ENGLAND
ETHELRED	II	—	of ENGLAND

face down and deals off a card each time the first man touches a name. He stops dealing when the man stops pointing. The name and country is read aloud. The second man turns over the last card he dealt and shows it. *It bears the same name and country!*

The first coincidence having been proven, the performer has the card dealer turn over the next card and call it aloud. The performer takes back the

---

* **Note by Annemann:** Zancig sold an effect like this for $10 shortly before his death, but it was for two people. The medium was guarded while the items were being written on a blackboard. The performer secretly copied them on a piece of chalk with flat sides, and substituted this for the piece in use. The medium on return used this written-on piece of chalk and thus secured the necessary information. I'm not violating any confidence by revealing this because it has long been off the market, and besides it can be found on page 295 of Carrington's "Physical Phenomena of Spiritualism," which was published first in 1907. I think that Mr. Duncanson's method for one person is an ingenious improvement that really modernizes the entire effect.

two slates and shows the inside surface of one. On it is a large and heavy chalked signature of that ruler. Stating that he will go a bit further, the performer announces that he has not only secured the signature from a ghostly land, but has also managed to get a picture of the ruler as he is today. Turning the other slate, he shows a large chalked picture of a skull!

Requirements: Practically everything used is familiar. The two slates have a common and not too tight flap. The signature of, say the tenth king, Alexander, is written on one side of the flap. The skull is drawn on the inside of one slate. Cover with flap and mark the frame on other side so you know later which is which. Get blank playing cards from your dealer and make two sets of 18 cards each, according to the list of rulers and countries. Now make an extra card for the tenth name, Alexander II of Russia.

On the back of the display board is fastened a simple chair back servante used for cards and found in every magical catalogue. The small bag has just above it a clip in which is resting one of the 18 card packets, arranged from back to face EXACTLY the same as the list of names on the board from top to bottom. The board is placed in front of a chair, resting on the floor. The extra card is put in the performer's right trouser pocket. The other 18 card packet is setting on the table together with slates. Two elastic bands are at hand.

Routine: Attention is called to the list and the story told of the apparently gruesome curse. The two slates are shown casually, placed together and fastened with the two bands. Two people assist in holding them.

Two more spectators help. One is given the packet of cards to read a few aloud and shuffle well. The performer takes them back in his left hand as he asks the other person to stand near the board and touch the names. In explaining this part, the performer picks up the board with his left hand at top, thumb in front, and the packet of cards he holds goes out of sight for a second. It drops into the bag and the fingers grasp the substitute deck as the board is picked up and placed on the chair seat against the back. This switch to arranged deck is perfect and most natural.

The first man having been told how to point, the other is given back his deck. No matter where the first man stops in his pointing, the second man must be at the same name with his cards. As this is being done, secure the extra card from your pocket. When the man stops pointing, take the remaining cards from the second man while he turns over his last card dealt. Add the force card to the top of this packet and, after this part of the effect, hand the packet back to him and ask that he turn over the next card and call it out.

Take back the two slates. Remove the bands and hold them flat with the marked side upward. Remove the lower slate (with flap) and show the correct signature. Lay aside, and talk for a moment about getting a picture of the ruler as he is today. Then you can freely turn the other slate up and show the skull!

FAMILIAR SPIRIT
KENT ARTHUR

This test is a prize example of audience befuddlement. There are performers who will take hold of an experiment of this sort and build it into a feature number.

Effect: The performer shows about 20 blank pieces of cardboard. Or he may use his own business cards for the purpose, as they are always left behind with the audience. The people present now call out two figure numbers and these are written upon the cards, a single two figured number to each card. As each card is so inscribed it is dropped into a bowl or hat and at the conclusion of the procedure any spectator gives the cards a violent mixing.

Now passing to two others of the company, the performer asks each to reach in and draw out a handful of the numbers. Those remaining are kept by the man who mixed the cards and passed the container. During this time the performer has not touched the container or had any part in the procedure after writing the cards when the numbers were called.

Standing for a moment before each spectator, the performer gazes into his eyes and then inscribes something on a small slate he carries. Each of the three spectators is now asked to add together all of the numbers he has in his possession. During this interval the performer is seen to be adding numbers on his slate. He finally puts down a total and erases the other inconsequential numbers on the slate. The slate is placed writing side down to one side and another picked up.

Each of the three persons now gives his total and these are openly written on the second slate for all to see. A line is drawn under them and these, in turn, are added and a total reached. The performer recalls that the numbers used have been selected by the spectators at the start, and that in all selections and adding, the procedures have been entirely under their own control.

Picking up his first slate the performer shows what he wrote at the beginning. *It is the same total arrived at by the spectators!*

Method: Little has to be said about the solution for it is really simple. The entire swindle, for it is but little more than that, lies in the cards written upon at the outset. Although the performer asks for two figure numbers called at random from 10 to 99, and then apparently writes each upon a card, he actually writes only HALF the numbers called. For example: The first number called is, say, 28. The performer writes this upon a card and drops it into the hat or bowl. When the second number is called *he completely disregards it,* and really writes that number which, when added to the number called before, will total 100, in this case 72. And so he proceeds through the cards, writing what the audience calls on the odd cards and then what will bring it to 100 on the evens.

Now it will be seen that although the cards be mixed eternally and added in any combination, the grand total of 20 cards will always be 1000. More than 20 or less than 20 cards will give proportionate grand totals, figuring 100 for each pair of two cards.

1000 would be a suspicious total, so to offset this defect the performer on the last card deliberately adds a number which would be more than 100, or less than 100. For instance the number called on the next to the last card might be 73. On the last card, instead of writing 27 as should be done (to make 100 total for the two cards), the performer could write 51, or 24 more than necessary. Now the grand total will be 1024 instead of an even 1000. By writing a number less than 27, the grand total would be correspondingly less than 1000.

An alternate and very easy way to accomplish this "different total" at each performance is to have an extra, or 21st, card. The performer follows the rules through the first 20, each pair totaling 100. On the last card he writes exactly what is called and that number itself, added to 1000, will be the grand total. This eliminates any figuring upon the performer's part. The audience automatically makes the grand total different each time merely by naming the last, or 21st, number.

Be sure to make a great show of mixing and the selection of the numbered cards. Keep away from the operations after the start so that it all appears more than fair. The audience gets tangled up in the simple solution, always looking for a complicated maze of formulae.

For the performer who is really a showman, this is a very worthwhile effect.

THE PSYCHIC SLATE
HERBERT HOOD

Effect: The performer puts a single slate and a pack of cards on the table. Before leaving the room he asks a spectator to shuffle the deck (all of this after he is out of sight, of course), cut it several times, and then put the top card face down under the slate. The mystic returns when this has been done. He peers at the blank upper surface of the slate. He may state that he is going to prove that man can, with proper training, use his eyes and brain to surmount normally impassible barriers. He draws a picture of a card on the upper side of the slate. He steps away. His picture is seen and named. The slate is lifted and the card beneath turned over. It's the same one drawn by the performer!

Preparation: Use a marked deck and stack it in the Si Stebbins order or the "Eight-Kings" arrangement. Use a marked deck that will not take too much squinting to decipher the top card.

Routine: Step away and let someone give the deck a shuffle. As you get almost out of talking distance tell him to cut the pack a couple of times. Then he takes the top card and puts it under the slate. You return, pick up the piece of chalk on the table and concentrate. It is easy enough for you to see the top card of the deck laying close by, catch its identity, and count one back in the stack system. That gives you the name of the card under the slate. Why? And after the shuffle? Simply because a stacked deck can be hastily shuffled by anyone and still remain stacked in sections too many to mention. After this shuffle it is cut once or twice. The percentage is terrific in favor of the top two cards being mates. Therefore, when one is taken from the top and put under the slate, the next can tattle if you know how to read its marks.

It but remains for you to draw its picture on the slate—the card beneath, and, in the remote case of failure, just admit of a "fog" and try again, turning the slate over and having the deck cut again for another selection. It will be an event in your life when you must try the second time.

A THOUGHT OUT THOUGHT
HERBERT HOOD

Effect: The performer shuffles a deck before a volunteer and gives it to him for further mixing. He cuts, looks at the top card, and buries it in the center of the deck, or thereabouts. Next he is asked to fan the deck out and hold it with faces toward himself. All of this time has seen the performer at a far side of the room.

The performer now holds a slate and chalk. He attempts to get an impression, but is dissatisfied. He moves toward the spectator, asking him to hold the fan of cards up and directly before himself. The spectator is told to try and see his card among all of the others. The performer comes close and raises or lowers the spectator's arms to an eye level. Then he steps away and does another picture. The spectator names his card—and the slate is shown. It is pictured there.

Method: Again we have used a marked and stacked deck—and again we have presented the effect in such a manner as to deceive the most erudite. The first shuffle by the performer was false, a mere matter of cuts. The spectator's shuffle was slight—the performer didn't let much time elapse before telling the person to cut the deck, pick off the top card, look at it, and bury it. The first bit of writing on the slate was fakery. Then the performer approached the spectator with his fan of cards. His maneuvers here amounted to nothing, except, he was able to see and read the identity of the top card of the deck—at his (performer's) right end of the fan. Counting one back he knew which card to draw actually on the second attempt.

PSYCHIC TYPE
STANLEY COLLINS

Effect: This very effective experiment, built around the trick of a slate with a loose flap, offers sundry points of novelty. Two slates, after being marked on both sides with identifying numbers, are tied together with a piece of tape and entrusted to someone in the audience to hold. The titles of well-known magazines are called out by various spectators and written down in succession by the performer on plain postcards, each name being verified as it is written by a gentleman who stands at the performer's side. About half a dozen having been suggested, the cards are openly handed to the man on the stage to be shuffled, after which he is requested to retain any one of them and return the others to the performer. The selected card, the name upon which is only known to the helper, is placed by him in an envelope chosen from a packet and having been carefully sealed and marked is handed to the person holding the slates. Upon separating the slates a few seconds later, the selected name is discovered written in chalk upon one of them, while the envelope, bearing the initials of the second person, on being torn open reveals the title page of the selected magazine instead of the card.

Preparation: Despite precautions to eliminate forcing, one of the slates contains a previously chalked name of a popular periodical, certain to be called, on one side covered with a flap. The title sheet of this magazine is folded and put into an envelope after subjecting it to a little preparation. A triangular piece cut from the top of a postcard is pasted to the sheet's back, so that when it is inserted in the envelope the top edge of a postcard alone is visible, and the presence of the title is never suspected. The envelope containing this faked sheet is deposited on the top of the packet to be utilized for the experiment.

Now the postcards. Of these, a dozen will be required, five of which are prepared beforehand by writing on the blank side the name to be reproduced between the slates. Place them on the table with printed sides up, and the seven unprepared cards on top of them.

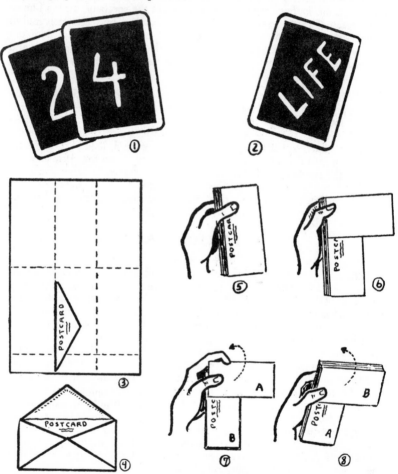

Routine: Having numbered the slates, they are placed for a moment on the table while the tape is shown and when again picked up to be tied, the flap is allowed to remain behind. The next step is to write the called out names of the various journals, and it is at this part of the effect that a very subtle deception is employed.

Taking the dozen postcards from the table, the performer nonchalantly takes about half of them and hands them to the assistant for scrutiny. He hands them back and the performer puts them on top of the others which he holds in his left hand, as per Fig. 5. While asking for the first name, the top card is apparently taken in the right hand, turned over and placed on the stack as in Fig. 6, the bulk of the cards forming a pad to facilitate ease in writing. In reality, however, the TWO top cards are taken as one, turned over as described, and the first name is written as called out. Five other cards are added, one by one, each receiving a name given by members of the audience.

Now, while asking for the next name, a peculiar turn over is given to the two packets which should be readily understood by studying sketches 7 and 8. The two packets are caused to make a revolution by altering the positions of thumb and first finger, the former being passed below the packets and the latter above. A slight upward pressure of the thumb causes the revolution and leaves the packets to all intents and purposes the same as they were a second previously. The card A in Fig. 8 will now be the one that was behind the first one drawn, consequently a blank card, and it is quickly placed on B to hide from the assistant's view the name already written on it, and the remainder very deliberately placed on the table. It is advisable to have a friend call out the required name at this stage, i.e., seventh, so that the last name may be verified as were the previous ones. Should, however, the name be called out earlier, it must be written down again instead of the last name called, care being taken that the gentleman does not see this. Having written on the last blank card, the packet is handed to the spectator to be shuffled, which, of course, does not affect the trick in the least, as all the six cards will have the same name written on them.

Having made his selection of a card, the gentleman takes one of the envelopes spread before him, and into this he places the postcard he has chosen. It is handed back to the performer and is promptly changed for the top envelope of the pack in the act of turning to put them on the table. Then, openly, the card seen in the envelope is sealed and the flap marked. When opening the envelope at the conclusion, care must be taken that the fake piece of card is not exposed as stuck to the rear of the title page.

MIXED MYSTERY
H. C. MOLE

Effect: Saying that he wishes to demonstrate an example of the ultimate in coincidence, the performer shows a glass bowl full of one-inch square cardboards, each bearing a letter of the alphabet. These may be shown freely as there is nothing wrong with them in any way. A spectator is asked to reach into the bowl and take therefrom a small handful (say, 7 or 8) of the letters. These he drops into a letter envelope which is sealed and given to him to hold for the time being.

Next, on a pad, three spectators write rows of three figures each, one under the other. A fourth person adds up the columns while the performer returns to the front and picks up a newspaper which he gives someone close by. Then he takes a school slate, piece of chalk, and speaks to the man who has added the figures.

As this total of 4 figures is announced, the performer writes upon the slate (suppose 4382 to be the total) PAGE—4, COLUMN—3, LINE—8, WORD—2. Then, turning to the one holding the newspaper, the performer asks that he open the sheet to the fourth page. Next he is to pick out the third column. When this has been done he is requested to count down to the eighth line, and lastly count across that line to the second word. Then he is to draw a circle around that word which has been so fairly picked.

The magician now shows his strange knowledge of coincidence by having the chosen letters called off by their selector. As they are named he writes them across the other side of the slate. But, instead of making a word as written, the letters could look like A H E T E R W. The performer blandly asks the man with the newspaper if that is the word at which he has been looking. It could be a typographical error, of course. The answer is "No."

The slate is turned over and a quick check through of the position numbers made. Everything is in order. The spectator names the word. The performer says that coincidence supplied the correct letters but they were read out in the wrong order. The man with the letters calls them through correctly. *Finally calling upon his powers as a magician, the performer turns the slate around to show that the letters have rearranged themselves and now correctly spell "Weather," the selected word!!*

Preparation: With such an effect at hand, probably most of the readers would find no difficulty in constructing a method. There really are three separate parts—the selection of the letters, the reaching of a desired total, and the transposition of letters written on the slate. Apparatus necessities are small.

Secure or make three sets of the alphabet on one-inch square cardboards. A pad of paper with no backing, a pencil, a slate with a loose flap and chalk, a newspaper, and a faked envelope complete the requisites.

Open the paper and locate a page numbered with a single digit, preferably 2, 3 or 4. This page must contain a column of reading matter which starts at the top with no headlines or other confusing data. Look for an expressive word (not "the," "and," "there," etc.) somewhere among the first nine lines. Then jot down your four figures which find this particular word as described in the effect. That's your total.

Next originate a three row three figured addition problem, that, when added up, will result in the desired total. Take the backless pad. Being careful not to tear off the sheets, copy this problem on the under side of both the top and bottom pages. Each line should appear in different handwriting. Do not draw any line underneath.

On one surface of the slate, write the word you have picked in large chalk letters. Cover this with the flap.

Pick out, from your bowl of letters, the ones which spell out the chosen word. Get two letter envelopes. Trim the ends and bottom of one which leaves only the front and flap together. Insert this inside the other envelope. Between the flaps drop the letters you have selected, separating and spreading them so as not to make the envelope noticeably bulky. Lastly seal the flaps together. A secret compartment has thus been made.

Routine: The first spectator makes his small grab from the bowl. From your inside pocket you remove the envelope. The letters are dropped in, you seal it and the spectator keeps the envelope for the time being. Taking the pad from the same pocket it is handed to someone for the writing of three figures. He passes it to another, and he does likewise. Taking the pad you start towards the front, tear off the back (unused) page and give it to someone for the adding. No matter which side the first person has started writing upon, the other side, when torn off and given a spectator, bears the desired problem. This subterfuge which gives freedom in handling is credited to Dave Allison.

During the addition process, the paper is given out and the slate, with flap, picked up. On its unprepared side is written the figures of the total together with the page, column, line, word designations. The man with the paper looks up the word and scores it.

The rest of this action must be followed closely, for soon an impression must be created that the performer is slightly bewildered. The magician lays down the slate, flap side UP, and steps to the man with the envelope. "Have you been guarding those letters you picked?" he asks. He takes the envelope, tears off the end, and dumps the contents into the spectator's hands. Of course, the envelope is pinched open to allow of only those letters in the rear compartment leaving. "Call them out to us," says the performer as he goes back to the front and picks up the slate. He has crumpled up and taken the envelope with him, dropping it on the table as the slate is retrieved.

The letters as called out are written on the flap in their jumbled order. Almost always a few of the spectators, upon hearing the word called, will see that the letters are there though mixed. At this point you turn the slate over and ask the spectator if he has the right spot in the paper according to the figures. He says "Yes" and you lay down the slate again, but this time with flap side down, and approach him to get a quick glance at the word.

Light now seems to dawn and you explain that you had the letters but in the wrong sequence. Ask the man with the letters to stand and pick them out correctly, calling each one aloud. While he does this you reapproach the front, pick up the slate carelessly and appear to be checking the letters as named. The flap has been left behind. Next, and last, call upon the powers of darkness and evil to make good what they have made wrong. Then turn the slate to show the word in correct lettering.

More often than not the audience figures that the spectator with the letters has done his part wrong by his reading them off in an incorrect order. Then you apparently step into the breach and save the day by a bit of magical prowess in the rearrangement.

CHALK ON METAL SLATES TIP

Here's a worthwhile tip for those who have painted metal slates which are smooth and don't take chalk very well. Don't try sandpaper. Just put a spoonful of Dutch Cleanser or Babbo, etc., on the surface and then scour with a damp cloth. Paint will come off but it gives a new roughened side which takes chalk as it should be taken.

CONTROLLED CURRENCY
ANNEMANN

The following effect, which is a combination mental routine and conjuring, was one of Ted Annemann's favorites. You will find it clean cut and direct and injected throughout the routine are a number of clever subtleties that are baffling to the layman and confounding to magicians.

Effect: The performer borrows two dollar bills and has them folded and inserted in two pay envelopes. One of the audience is selected as the subject and takes the envelopes, mixes them and selects one. The performer asks him to open the envelope and look at the number on the bill. As soon as he begins to concentrate on the number, the performer reads his mind and calls out the number.

The subject now opens the second envelope and reads aloud the number on the other bill. This bill is sealed in another envelope which is burned. While it is still burning, the performer reaches into his pocket and brings forth a small metal box which is locked with a combination lock. This box is handed to the person who had loaned the bill. By now the bill and the envelope have been reduced to ashes, and the performer announces that he intends to restore the bill and have it pass into the box which is being held up in view of everyone. He removes a card and reads off the combination of the lock, and the person with the box opens the lock, lifts the lid of the box and finds the bill intact.

Preparation: Obtain five new dollar bills, with numbers running consecutively, from one bank. Also another set of five bills from a second bank. Now select two bills from each set of five, and erase the last figure of the number on each bill. This leaves you with two pairs of bills, each pair of which are duplicates.

Next soak these four bills in wine for an hour or so. While they are still wet, crumple them a bit and then dry them between sheets of newspaper under pressure. When dry, these bills will be just about half way between new and old ones in texture.

You will also need two metal boxes with hinged lids. These boxes should be about the size of a pack of cards, and the lids are secured in each case with a combination lock for which a key is not necessary. Two cards, bearing the combination for the locks will also be needed, as well as a packet of drug size envelopes, one of which has a slit in its face.

Take the first pair of duplicate bills, insert one in a drug envelope, and fold the other, once the long way and twice the short way, with the green side out. Place this folded bill in your left trouser pocket. The envelope with the duplicate bill sealed therein is placed in one of the metal boxes, the lid closed, locked and the box placed in your left hip pocket. Follow the same procedure with the second pair of bills, but fold one of these bills with the black side out. Place this bill in your right coat pocket, and its duplicate in an envelope goes into the second metal box which is locked and placed in your right hip pocket. With each box goes the card bearing the lock's combination, and in each pocket with the folded bills is placed a drug envelope. Place the slit envelope in your left coat pocket.

Lastly, but most important, memorize the numbers on the two bills, or write the numbers in ink on your two thumb nails.

Routine: Ask for a bill, "Perhaps $100, maybe $50, how about $20 please, $10 or $5," and compromise on $1 with the remark, "You can't blame the lender as he undoubtedly has seen magicians before." The spectator folds his bill according to instructions, and at the same time you place your left hand in your left trouser pocket and palm the green bill, if that's the way the spectator is folding his; otherwise you palm the other bill from your right pocket with your right hand. Just watch the spectator carefully, you'll have plenty of time to get the bill matching his.

The folded bill is taken from the lender and switched for your palmed bill, as explained in "Dollar Bill Switch" page 216. As the switch is made, gesture towards your left and ask another person to stand. Without mentioning the word "bill", remark that it is important this second party keep everything in view for the rest of the audience to see. It's this psychology that tends to make the audience feel that you are doing the same. Your right hand, or left, as the case may be, goes to the pocket from which you palmed the dummy, leaves the spectator's bill and comes out with the drug envelope. Present the dummy bill with one hand and the envelope with the other to the person standing, requesting him to seal the bill in the envelope. While he does so, you immediately turn to the audience and request a second bill, saying, "After all, two can grieve better than one—when they have something in common."

While obtaining this second bill, you palm the other dummy. Receiving the second bill, you fold it yourself with the proper side out, switch it and hold the dummy up in view. Reach into your pocket, deposit the spectator's bill and bring out the other drug envelope. Have the person who is standing, seal this second dummy in the second envelope and mix the envelopes. He is then told to step to a far corner of the room, or the auditorium, and put one of the envelopes in his pocket.

As he does so, explain to the audience, "Two of you have loaned me dollar bills with which I shall conjure, both mentally and physically. The first test will be mental". Turn and point to the man in the far corner, saying, "Do you want to exchange the envelope now—or do you wish to keep the one you have selected by yourself?"

Whatever this spectator does, it matters not. You tell him to open the envelope of his choice, remove the bill and look at the number on it. Remark to the audience, "Maybe it's a ransom note. The fact that every government bill has a different number running into the millions makes possible a lot of arrests and convictions"—turning to both the lenders—"I am sure you aren't giving ME that kind of currency?"

Addressing the man in the corner, say, "Think of the first figure on that bill you have selected." Put your fingers to your forehead, pretend to concentrate and say, "It's a . . . " Here you name the first figure of either bill, both of which you know—either from memory or from a glimpse of your thumb nails. If the spectator says, "Yes", you know you are on the right bill and continue throughout correctly. If the spectator says, "No", you say, "Try the last figure. (pause) It's a . . . ". The answer to this must be "Yes" for you have named the last figure of the number on the other bill. At hearing "Yes" to this maneuver, shrug your shoulders and say, "I'm going backwards, that's all. At times when you look into a stranger's mind, you get a reversed impression. It's like looking into a mirror." Then continue revealing the number backwards to a climax."

At this point, Annemann usually stopped all applause for he believed this move on his part was very effective (editor's note). Call the person with the bill back to the stage, relieve him of the bill and pass it back to the lender, saying, "It may be yours or his"—pointing to the other lender—"but a dollar is a dollar, and what do you think I am, a psychic? Reading minds is difficult enough."

"There's one bill left," you continue addressing the man with the envelope. "Open the envelope, take it out please, and read the number on it out loud." Then turn and address the owner of this second bill, saying, "Listen carefully to the number, for this is your bill, the one you're going to get back." The number is read and you repeat each number as it is called. Don't tell anyone else to listen, they will. While they won't remember each and every figure, the audience as a whole will get the swing of it and realize that it is the same number when they hear it read later. Each individual gets a portion of the number. Together they make an error improbable of being accepted, and combined they give you acclaim.

During this, take out of your pocket another drug envelope with the well-known slit in its back. The second bill (dummy) is inserted in this envelope and out through the slit into your palm. Deposit this palmed bill in your pocket as you reach for a box of matches. Ignite the envelope and hand it to the assisting spectator who will struggle with it for a minute or two and then will let go of it. "You shouldn't be so careful," you say, "it never was your bill. Why burn yourself for someone else's money?"

During this burning, pull from the correct pocket the box containing the duplicate of the bill you have apparently just burned. Hold the box on your outstretched palm as the audience enjoys the comedy of the burning envelope. "Look", you say, "Here's a sort of tin box. There have been politicians who kept money in such places. Now, politicians are said to have all the money that's loose. Therefore, all money burned up in the public interest, and I'm here in your interest—as an entertainer—should gravitate to the tin box." "You have spent the cash," you say to the assistant who has

just burned his fingers, "and that's about all you can do. Thank you for playing a villain's part." You thus dismiss your assistant, and then turn to the
lender of the second bill, saying, "And you, sir, take the box and stand so
all can see a taxpayer coming into his own."

Reach into your pocket, the same one from which you took the box,
bring forth the combination card and say, "That's a combination lock. I'll
read you the turns, and you'll have the satisfaction of getting back what you
gave out for no good reason." The spectator opens the lock, lifts the lid and
finds the envelope. He removes it, tears it open and finds his bill inside. You
then ask him to read aloud the number on the bill.

Conclude the effect by saying, "I didn't mean to inject any political talk
with this test. Please excuse me for wandering from my theme. In my en-
thusiasm, I unconsciously saw what I talked about. Actually, I wanted only to
show you the difference between a mindreader and a magician. I'll leave it
up to you to decide whether I'm a better mindreader than a magician, or
vice versa."

A MENTALIST WITH MONEY
ANNEMANN

If ever there was an impromptu mental novelty, this should be it.

Borrow a derby or soft hat. Say that you'll show a test of clairvoyance
and telepathy combined. Ask for the loan of seven or eight one dollar bills.
However, before starting to collect them, step up to one volunteer and ask
him to write his name in pencil on his bill so as to identify it later. Ask him
to fold it over and over until it is in a small flat square. At the same time
have the rest of the donors do the same. While the key subject is writing and
folding, you can pick up one or two of the other bills that are ready. Collect
them with your right hand and drop them into the hat which you are holding
in your left hand. When you take the marked bill, pretend to put it with the
rest, but slip it under the fingers of your left hand inside the hat, and then
collect the rest.

Hand the hat to a spectator who stands at the other side of the room.
The left fingers keep hold of the stolen bill. Don't try to palm anything.
Just keep it in the fingers and let the left hand be natural and out of direct
use. Don't stall around but keep moving at this point. Walk away to a far
corner. Tell the man with the hat to pick out a bill while your back is turned,
hold it up, and say, "All right". You turn your back. When the spectator
speaks, say, "Put it on the table, and take another." Next time you say, "No,
still not right, put it aside and try again." In the meantime you have been
standing with your back turned and have gestured with your right hand. The
left, however, has opened the stolen bill and you note the number and refold
it. You'll find when you try this that you have more time than you think.
Also you may think it hard to remember the number but if you'll try this first
before saying you can't, you'll be surprised. If you are familiar with
mnemonics use it here. On the third or fourth pick, stop the selector and say,
"That's it." Walk over to him and take the bill he holds with your right
hand. Without a pause, walk to the one who signed the bill. When almost to
him, pretend to pass the bill to your left hand, actually palming it in your
right hand and bringing the marked bill into view at the tips of the left
fingers. Hand the marked bill to its owner, and return to your position
beside the hat. Ask him to open the bill and see if it is his. It is!

Now take the hat from the person who has been assisting you, and set it on the table. As you lay it down, drop the palmed bill into it from your right hand.

Return to the person holding the marked bill and ask him to open it and look at the number. For your climax, announce the number slowly and deliberately. Then ask the owners of the other bills to raise their hands so that you may return the borrowed bills.

You will find that it will help a bit in handling the marked bill if you borrow one that is rather well used.

DOLLAR BILL SWITCH
L. VOSBURGH LYONS

Dollar bills are always of interest to an audience. This original exchange, which is the last word in constant visibility, can be used for any number of tricks which require substitution either for another bill, or for a dummy duplicate bill.

First we shall describe the switch, and then attempt to "hint" and per-

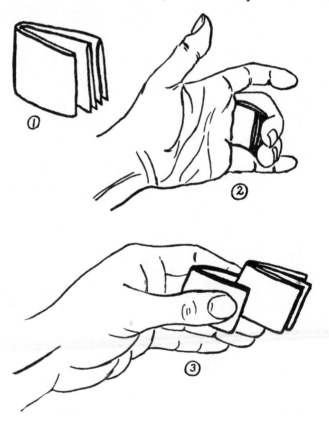

haps "build" upon the reader's imagination as to its possibilities. Sketch No. 1 shows how the dummy bill is to be folded, i.e.: first the long way, then twice to make a packet 1½" x 1¼" in size. The No. 1 sketch is shown in the position, as to its folding, by which it is finger palmed in sketch No. 2. This is important.

We shall suppose, right off, that you have the bill finger palmed as described. The borrowed bill is folded once the long way and twice the opposite way. You take it in the right fingers. The left thumb helps in letting the palmed bill spring open, and the finger tips of both hands come together as if to further crease the bill just received. The right hand bill, the borrowed one, is deliberately pushed into the open folds of the left hand dummy bill; the right thumb and fingers grasp both bills at their near edge and the left hand moves away with the palm obviously empty.

It is now absolutely impossible, from any angle, to recognize more than a single bill in the right hand. The right thumb now moves back just enough to let the outside fold snap open a bit through its own resiliency, and then rests the ball of the thumb on the inside borrowed bill. At this position the inside bill, still folded, is ready to be drawn back into a finger palm and to leave the dummy alone in view. Note also that the two bills, the outside one open and the inside one folded, may be transferred to the left fingers, and the borrowed bill palmed by that hand. It all depends which of your hands is more naturally proficient, the switch being a "7-11" either way.

As will be seen, this switch is ideal for any number of tricks, and may be used with paper billets just as readily. So far as the bill is concerned, let us mention right here that a safety factor which is imperative when the spectator folds the bill (and that should be allowed and encouraged as often as possible) is to have two dummy bills ready, one folded green side out and the other black side out.

In a great many instances, the switch will be used merely to leave a bill in sight for a few minutes while the borrowed bill is inserted in a prepared envelope, wallet, etc. The receptacle being left with the owner of the original bill while the duplicate is vanished by whatever means you like. The bill, when first borrowed, is initialed by the lender and subsequently exchanged for a duplicate which is retained for a while by another spectator, or in his closed hand, in order that any slight difference in wear and tear may not be noticed.

MYSTIC PERCEPTION
HENRY HARDIN

Effect: The performer asks a spectator to take a dollar bill from his pocket, note whether the number on the bill is odd or even, and then to cover the numbers with his thumbs. The performer, places his finger tips on the spectator's forehead and correctly divines whether the number was odd or even.

Secret: The secret on which this is based is very old, but still is little known today. Examine a dollar bill and you will find on its face a minute letter in the upper left and lower right sections. These letters run from A upwards through the alphabet and they are the key to the whole stunt. They designate whether the bill is odd or even in the following manner. A is odd,

B is even, C is odd, D is even, etc. To do the trick as baldly as this is but to present a puzzle. But see what happens when you apply the original Hardin technique.

Presentation: Anyone takes a dollar bill from his pocket. He is asked to note whether the number is odd or even. Then he places his right and left thumbs over the two numbers on each side of the face of the bill. The performer approaches him, deliberately places his left hand down over the spectator's thumbs and bill, puts his right fingers against the spectator's forehead and says, "Odd, even, odd, even, etc." After a few more studied and thoughtful repetitions, he declares, "It's even", or "It's odd", as the case may be. All he has to do, of course, is to note the key letter.

In short, Hardin's presentation is a case of mind reading rather than a trick with a bill. The dollar just ceases to exist after serving its purpose to provide one of two thoughts. The placing of the performer's left hand gave him just that split second's time to glimpse the letter, and the repeating of the two words, while his right fingers played against the spectator's forehead, let him count in the alphabet to the proper designation.

PAY DAY
JACK VOSBURGH

Effect: This is a mental coin effect based on a mathematical system. On the table are three small coin envelopes labeled respectively: Office Boy, Janitor, President. Also there are five different coins: a penny, nickel, dime, quarter, and half dollar.

Three spectators are asked to participate and each is given a small typewritten sheet or card called a "Salary Schedule". While the performer's back is turned, one of the three men picks up the three employee envelopes, mixes them well, selects any one for himself, and passes the other two on to a second man. This person mixes the two remaining envelopes, selects either one, and hands the third envelope to the third spectator.

Each man reads the label on his envelope and sees what employee he is to be. Then he reads his salary schedule and sees which coin that employee is to receive. Each of the three men puts into his envelope the coin designated in the schedule. The envelopes are pocketed or held out of sight, and the performer turns around and faces the spectators.

He takes from his pocket a fourth envelope labeled "Income Tax," and into it he puts the two remaining coins. Pocketing this envelope he looks at each of the three men and tells what job he holds and how much money is in his pay envelope.

Routine: As I have said, the method is mathematical. The three salary schedules are all different, as will be noted from the table here:

#1		#2		#3	
President	10c	President	25c	President	50c
Office Boy	10c	Office Boy	5c	Office Boy	5c
Janitor	1c	Janitor	1c	Janitor	50c

These are passed out writing sides down, so no man knows what the cards of his neighbors say. The performer must remember to which man each of the schedules goes. Because of the system involved, the two coins left on the table, after the three coins have been put into the envelopes, tell the story.

And the rest of the trick is a table written upon the back of the "Income Tax" envelope. This table is secretly referred to while placing the two remaining coins into the tax envelope. Here is the table:

	#1	#2	#3
6.....	Boy	Pres.	Jan.
	10c	25c	50c
26.....	Pres.	Boy	Jan.
	10c	5c	50c
30.....	Boy	Jan.	Pres.
	10c	1c	50c
35.....	Jan.	Boy	Pres.
	1c	5c	50c
60.....	Jan.	Pres.	Boy
	1c	25c	5c
75.....	Pres.	Jan.	Boy
	10c	1c	5c

To read the table add the value of the two coins left and read from this total in the first column. Reading across from this total you find the offices and the salaries held by the holders of schedules #1, #2, and #3.

NUMISMATIGIC
STEWART JAMES

This is one of those mysteries, in which the astute performer will see at once the possibilities for a veritable miracle. It almost can be made into a challenge effect and has practically no explanation.

Five coins are shown and examined. Four of them are United States nickels and the fifth is a Canadian nickel or five cent piece. They are sealed in borrowed envelopes which the performer never has seen or touched. After mixing, they are handed to the performer, one at a time, behind his back. He correctly divines the location of the Canadian nickel among the rest while the sharpest eyes can be watching the precedure.

The secret is quite astonishing. It just so happens that Canadian five cent pieces are magnetic, while those of United States coinage are not. In that fact lies the secret. Under your coat, and hanging from the back of your shirt or vest, is as strong a magnet as can be obtained and carried. The envelopes containing the nickels are applied to the magnet behind your back as they are received, and there is no difficulty in ascertaining the location of the Canadian coin as that envelope will sway towards the magnet. The envelopes should be held by one corner so the coin drops to the bottom.

Mr. James obtained a real heavy magnet bar from a flour mill, one of those used in the chutes to catch any metallic substances before they pass through the rollers. A very good magnet for this effect may be obtained from a slot machine repair man. The magnet used in the "one armed bandit" type is only about two inches long and can be concealed easily in your hand. They are used in the machines to stop iron and steel slugs.

The readers who can see in this principle good possibilities for a master pocket and publicity trick will no doubt devise their own method of handling and concealing the magnet.

The fact that both the envelopes and coins are totally unprepared and are handled freely by the spectators is what makes this a challenge trick that can't be duplicated.

THE KNICKEL OF KANADAH

L. VOSBURGH LYONS

This effect may well follow Stewart James' "Numismatigic", thus you may immediately repeat the trick but by an entirely different method of handling.

Effect: Five nickels, 4 American and 1 Canadian, are placed secretly in a small cardboard slide which in turn is hidden in two envelopes. Despite these precautions, the performer can always name the slot occupied by the Canadian coin. Everything may be examined and furthermore, the two envelopes employed positively preclude any possibility of the performer catching a glimpse of the coins.

Preparation: In a piece of rather heavy cardboard, about 2 x 7 inches, cut out five holes just large enough to hold five nickels. Paste a piece of heavy paper over the bottom of the cardboard and label the holes 1, 2, 3, 4, 5.

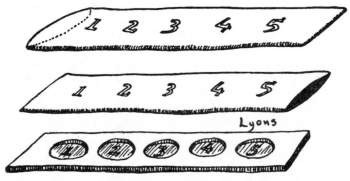

Next make a paper envelope to fit over the card with its opening on the right end. Place this envelope over the cardboard slide and number the envelope with large numerals, 1 to 5, corresponding with the numbered holes in the slide. Remove this envelope. Also make another envelope, large enough to slide easily over the first envelope, but with the opening at the left end. Number this envelope in the same way as the first envelope, but starting with the numeral 1 nearest the open end.

Secure a small piece of Alnico magnet. The base of one of the novelty magnetic Pups is just the thing from which to saw off a piece about a quarter inch long. Have this piece in one of your pockets where it may be secured easily, or keep it in the pocket with the nickels where it will adhere to the Canadian nickel.

Routine: Bring out the handful of coins with your left hand. Pick out the nickels and drop them, one by one, into a spectators hand for his inspection. As you do this you retain the magnet in your left hand, ready for use. Explain that for the purpose of the test one coin must be different from the rest, and so you are substituting a Canadian nickel for one of the American coins.

Next hand out the cardboard slide together with the envelopes. Turn your back and ask the person with the coins to put one in each of the holes in the card. When he says he has done so, remind him to make note of which hole the Canadian coin occupies. Another person now takes the coin slide and, holding it so that the coins cannot fall out, pushes it into the first envelope. He is asked to be careful that the numbering on the outside of the envelope corresponds with the numbered holes in which the coins are arranged.

A third person now encloses the package with the second envelope, which goes on in the opposite direction, but making certain that the numbers correspond with the numbers on the first envelope.

You explain that this use of two envelopes, opening at opposite ends, prevents any possibility of the coins being seen. Now turn around and take the envelope package with your right hand. The magnet, you remember, is finger palmed in your left hand. Transfer the package to your left hand with a sort of sliding motion which immediately attracts the magnet to the bottom of the envelope directly under the spot occupied by the Canadian nickel. You needn't have any fear of the magnet falling off, it will stay there. Grasp the left end of the package with your left thumb and first finger, and hold it flatwise towards the audience with the numbers being right side up. The fingers of the right hand, kept open to let the hands be seen empty, are passed back and forth in front (audience side) of the envelope. Keep the fingers at least two inches away. Don't let an impression be given that there is any "feel" necessary. Then grasp the right end of the package with the right thumb and forefinger, while the left hand goes back and forth, also obviously empty.

It is this freedom of movement and obvious absence of gimmicks that impresses the audience. Through all these movements, the magnet clings to the back (your side) of the package. Now announce the number under which the Canadian nickel is secreted.

As the first person acknowledges that you are correct, you hand the package to one of the spectators to verify your assertion. In doing so, drop the package backwards into your left curled fingers and, as it is pulled away from your hand, the magnet is disengaged and finger palmed in your left hand. While the package is being opened and examined you can pocket the magnet.

D A T E S
CHARLES T. JORDAN

A number of coins are collected in a borrowed hat which is set, crown down, on the table. Announcing the date of a coin, the performer reaches into the hat and brings forth a coin which he immediately passes for inspection. It bears the date he named! He repeats with the others. One advantage of this method is that no extra coin is used, and another is the fact that the spectators may note the dates on their own coins before dropping them into the hat. Thus each may claim his coin immediately its date is read.

It is necessary that the wizard perform some feat requiring the loan of a half-dollar at some time earlier in his program. Pretending to give it back, he must substitute a half-dollar of his own, prepared by rubbing it previously (on either side or in the milling) with a piece of soap. By not allowing too much soap to collect on the coin, its presence never will be suspected. In borrowing a number of coins for the experiment to be explained, the performer must make certain that this prepared coin is included among those collected in the hat. The first date he names is that on the prepared coin!

Reaching into the hat standing on the table behind his back, the performer will find it very easy to distinguish the soaped coin from the others. It has a soft or greasy touch that cannot be mistaken when one is feeling for it. Securing it, the performer at the same time picks up another one of the coins between the first and second finger tips and, by bending the fingers inward, lodges it in the crotch of the thumb. It is easy to tell by sense of touch where the date is on the half-dollar. On the older coins, the stars on the "tails" side have a feel possessed by no other portion of the coin's surface. On the newer ones, the waist of the figure on the "tails" side is a good distinguishing sign.

In bringing the hand forward with the soaped coin held plainly in view at the finger tips, it is a fairly simple matter to read the date of the second coin which you have thumb palmed. The prepared coin is given to the owner (?) and the performer reaches into the hat for another. This time the one just glimpsed is named and a third coin concealed in the thumb crotch to be read as the hand is held forward. In a similar manner each date is read up to and including the last.

DUPLEX DATE READING
CHARLES T. JORDAN

In this day and age, when publicity is freely given to those who apparently can see through all sorts of blindfolds, etc., this old trick should be an excellent impromptu test. Argamasilla, the Spanish nobleman who confounded New York critics for a short time with his reputed ability to see through metals, could have used this stunt to good advantage for press interviews.

Effect: Two people note the dates on their own half dollars and then place the date sides of the two coins face to face. The performer holds them in that condition at the tips of his left fingers, rubs them with his right palm, and then takes them with his right finger tips and rubs them with his left palm. Again taking them with his left finger tips, they are passed back to the owners, still with the date sides face to face. Everything seems absolutely fair, yet the performer is now able to name correctly the date on each of the borrowed coins.

Routine: Though simple, the effect is exceedingly impressive. It all lies in a subtle exchange and re-exchange of one coin. Have an extra half dollar in the right palm with its date side away from the palm. Take the two borrowed coins by their edges between the left thumb and finger tips which are bunched in a circle about the coins. The right hand, in stroking the upper coin, silently leaves the extra palmed coin on top of it. At the same instant the left fingers allow the borrowed coin on the bottom to fall into the left palm, date side up, where it can easily be read. Nothing seems changed, as two coins are still visible at the finger tips, upper one date side down. The right hand rubs them, and then takes them from above by the finger tips, exactly as the left hand held them. Turning the right hand over, the date of the former upper borrowed coin is exposed. Now the left hand in rubbing them leaves the borrowed coin on top, date side down, and the performer's coin falls into his right palm. The left hand again takes the coins and returns them to the company in the very same position as when received. The right hand pockets the extra coin as the performer reveals the two hidden dates in as impressive a manner and with as much dramatization as possible.

Blindfold Reading

PAR-OPTIC VISION
ANNEMANN

Here is a most unusual test that requires no preparation and may be introduced into your program at any time. It is one of those mental tests that can be done before any sized audience, yet is just as effective when presented for a single person. Professional performers know how rare such an effect is and how hard it is to find one.

Effect: The performer borrows a deck of cards and states that he is about to do a test that should not be confused with card tricks or sleight-of-hand. It will be left to the audience as to what senses are employed by the performer in gaining his subsequent knowledge. The working of the effect is so clean, and obviously free of trickery, that this point being stressed at the start will emphasize it and will be remembered afterwards.

One person is chosen, always a man, and shuffling the deck of cards, the performer has three taken and placed by the assistant in his pocket. The assistant is cautioned against peeking at the cards at this time in order to guard against the possibility of the performer reading his mind. (After all, this is a test of par-optic vision, not of mindreading.)

The performer now allows the assistant to blindfold him and to lead him to a distance of 30 or 40 feet, turning him so that when the action starts he will have his back turned towards the assistant. When set, the performer says, "Reach into your pocket and draw out a card." The spectator does so. The performer names the card. "Drop it," says the performer, "and take out another." This is done, and again the performer names it! "There is only one of them left, isn't there?" remarks the performer. The spectator acknowledges this display of astuteness. "Don't take it out," cautions the man with the many eyes. Then slowly, but accurately, this master mind calls the color, suit and value of the card still in the spectator's pocket!

Routine: This is an effect that's all effect. The three cards taken by the assistant and placed in his pocket are forced. It is important, however, that the first and third force card should be of the same color but of different suits; while the middle card is of opposite color.

Once the assistant has them in his pocket with the backs of the cards outwards, and in the known order, it is up to you to then direct him to produce them in the same order. Nine times out of ten, he will withdraw the cards by grasping the outside one first, the middle one next (it never misses being second) and that's exactly what you want him to do. By keying your patter and hurrying the man up when he is producing the cards, he will usually follow the line of least resistance and withdraw the cards just as you wish.

We have now reached the point where you are blindfolded and are standing at a distance from the assistant. When set, you ask him to put his hand in his pocket quickly and withdraw but one card. If he has reacted as you expect, he will now be holding the first or outermost card and you are ready to tell him what card it is. You do so, as follows, which allows you considerable leeway and guarantees that you will name it correctly.

Name the color first, followed by the suit, to double-check. If it isn't the color you name, then, of course, you know it's the middle card and so call it. If it isn't the suit, then you know it's the other card of the same color, and so name it. Thanks to your set up of the force cards, you can't miss by following this method of elimination, although the audience do not realize you are "pumping" information.

As I mentioned before, the middle card never misses being the second one withdrawn. The third card, which is left in the pocket, you know without any trouble, so it's up to you to make the most of it and build up the effect for all it's worth!

Note: Sometimes you will run up against one man who will withdraw the cards in reverse order. This rare specimen will invariably keep on the way he has started.

A simple and direct force with a borrowed pack is to reverse the three force cards on the bottom of the deck. Now give the deck a dovetail shuffle without disturbing or flashing these three cards. Next explain to the assistant, as you lay the deck backs up on your left hand, that three cards are to be selected without either of you seeing what they are. Put your left hand behind your back and ask him to reach behind you and, with his left hand, cut off a bunch of cards. He does so, although he can't see what he's doing, as you are both facing front. As he brings them out in front, you say, "You know how impossible it is for me to know how many you have cut off. Now reach back again and take the next three cards for yourself and place them in your pocket without looking at them." During this interim, you have turned the deck over and he gets the three force cards. As soon as he has them, you right the deck, bring it forward and drop it on the table. The whole maneuver is executed with one hand and there isn't a bit of lost motion.

So much for the impromptu method. On the other hand, if you are using your own deck then any number of subterfuges are open to you. You can use a stacked deck, either the "Eight Kings" or "Si Stebbins." With such a set up, after the three cards are taken in a bunch, all you have to do is glimpse the bottom card of the pack, as you lay it down, and you're all set—for the three selected cards all follow this "key card" in the stacked sequence.

For a possible repeat performance at a later date, and for those who don't want to touch the deck after the selections, one can use a three kind alternating force deck with every third card wide and long. This is made by cutting all other cards short and narrow. False shuffle and cut. Put the deck on the table and have the assistant cut off a bunch and then take the next three cards and place them in his pocket.

NEW SHEET READING
ANNEMANN-HULL

Burling Hull brought out the original of this effect, and subsequently I revamped some of the details to make it even more effective.

Effect: As it stands now, this is the effect. Not more than twenty drug envelopes and cards are distributed together with pencils of the bridge scoring type. In the corner of each envelope is a large and heavy figure (1 through 20) of the gummed type sold by stationery stores. These numerals can be seen easily at quite some distance. Now questions, names, sentences, numbers, etc., are written on the cards which are then sealed in the envelopes.

A spectator collects them and comes forward to assist with the test. The medium is introduced, seated in a chair, blindfolded and covered with a sheet.

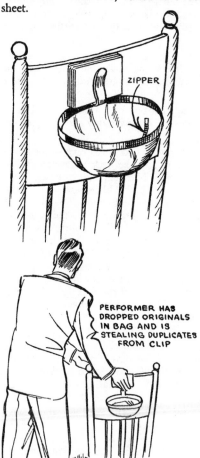

The assisting spectator mixes the envelopes and hands one to the performer, calling its number as he does so. The performer holds it against the medium's forehead and she immediately reveals its contents. This is continued until all the envelopes have been read. The medium is uncovered, and the assistant takes the unopened envelopes into the audience and returns them.

Preparation: Probably the most important factor in this presentation is never seen, which is as it should be. The modern dealer's catalogs seem to have lost sight of one of the most valuable accessories in magic. It's the old deck changing servante to be attached to the back of a chair. A five-inch bag hangs from a metal band and above this, against the chair back is a clip which holds a pack of cards laying on its side. Let us say that the clip holds an arranged pack. The performer has a shuffled deck in his right hand. He needs a chair for the trick, or wishes to move one out of the way. He moves it by grasping the top of the chair's back with his right hand (the one containing the shuffled deck), while the left hand takes hold of the chair's seat. Or if it is a light chair, he may move it with his right hand alone. Regardless, the deck in his right hand has been dropped into the servante bag, and the clipped deck is brought forward as the right hand leaves the chair.

Having obtained or built one of these silent servantes, cut a slit across the bottom of the bag and sew a zipper along the slit. These zippers can be obtained in department stores, etc.

In our case we're going to put something of value INTO the servante instead of taking it away, and we're going to use a packet of No. 2 size drug envelopes instead of a deck of cards.

The envelopes should be white. The numbers should be placed in one corner for an important reason. A dummy set of envelopes are made up and blank cards sealed inside. This set can be used a number of times until they become soiled. Another set of envelopes is prepared and ready with cards and pencils. The cards are of good quality bristol board and the pencils are of the No. 2 (or softer) lead type.

The sheet used is opaque insofar as seeing movements through it, but it is white and of the bed sheet type which lets light through it. The medium has a good pocket flashlight on her person, and should test it before each performance.

Routine: The medium is not in view when the effect begins. The performer passes out the writing material himself and returns to the front. A spectator is chosen to collect the sealed envelopes. As he comes forward the performer takes them and stands the assistant to one side.

Introducing the medium the performer steps to the chair, upon the seat of which is the sheet, and upon the back of which is the servante with the dummy set in the clip. He moves the chair forward a foot or so and the medium is seated. The package of envelopes has been exchanged.

While the medium sits holding the sheet, the performer explains that she will assume a clairvoyant condition and attempt to attune herself with members of the audience. As he talks he hands the (dummies) envelopes to the spectator for mixing. While this is being done the performer stands before the medium, opens the sheet out and drops it over her. As the sheet is opened out the medium sits back and upright in the chair, reaches both hands around behind it and secures the original envelopes from beneath the bag. This action is completed while the performer adjusts the sheet by stepping around behind and pulling it well over into place and, at the same time, closes the zipper in the bag himself.

By this time the medium has the flashlight in her lap and has started sorting the envelopes into three or four piles. She has also slumped in the chair, which gives her more lap space and, as the sheet covers her from knees to head, she can work quite unhampered.

The performer has innocently stalled for a few seconds while the spectator completes his mixing of the envelopes and finally picks one, calling out the number on it. The performer takes it and asks for that person's acknowledgment. Then he approaches the medium and holds it against her forehead with the number towards the audience. This has given her ample opportunity to pick out the correct envelope, lay it on top of her flashlight lens and turn on the light. She reveals the information as she reads it through the envelope! There is no need to worry about the flashlight being seen, if the medium is careful not to turn it on when there is no envelope on top of it. If she is seated as near bright lights as possible, they will help cover any accidental flash.

The action continues until the next to the last envelope is reached. The medium gets this as soon as she hears the number, and also the next one as soon as possible, for it is the last. She starts on the last and says it is none too clear as her power is weakening. Under the cloth she has concealed the light and squared up the packet of envelopes. She moves restlessly as she talks and, as she turns a little in the chair to arise—still under the sheet, deposits the packet of envelopes in the servante clip.

The performer has kept all the answered envelopes (dummies) in his left hand during the procedure, and now transfers them to his right hand. The medium stands and the performer moves the chair back, again making the exchange. The sheet is removed. The performer thanks the assistant from the audience, and hands him the bunch of original envelopes for redistribution to their owners, who may want to inspect them.

THE MYSTERY OF THE BLACKBOARD
ANNEMANN

This is one of those effects that can be built into feature proportions due to its many possibilities for spectacular presentation.

It is strictly a one man stunt and needs practically no apparatus or preparation. I say again, and make it emphatic, that the secret is subtle and never suspected by the audience, because it all takes place right before their eyes and in a very natural manner.

Effect: On platform, stage, or at the front of room is a blackboard facing the audience. Chalk and eraser are at hand. The performer states that he will attempt a most difficult test of telepathy and will need the assistance of three people from his audience. They come forward and stand near the blackboard. Follow this in your mind and you will realize the effect of the set up on the audience.

The performer takes a heavy piece of silk or a handkerchief and says that he will be blindfolded and led to a corner of the stage. Each one of the committee is then to write on the blackboard. One is to write a number of three figures, another is to write a word of not less than seven letters, and the last is to draw the first geometrical diagram that comes to his mind. The performer states that in this way, he will have covered all means of expressing oneself in writing, figures, letters and lines.

The performer is now blindfolded and led to a corner of the stage. The committee is then asked to draw the picture, and write the figures and the word. When they announce that they have finished, the performer asks the audience to remember what the committee is thinking of. Never tell them to remember what is on the blackboard.

The performer now tells them to erase the blackboard, and to lead him to it and give him a piece of chalk. Taking it, the performer, still blindfolded, makes a few marks and finally writes the number as best he can. This is followed by the correct word and finally the picture. This is the point where the performer can make or break the effect.

Preparation: I know that this must sound difficult but it is far from being so! In the first place, although you stand as per diagram with back turned towards the committee, the blindfold is faked in your favorite way as long as you can see straight ahead. I sincerely advise the old folded handkerchief as the best.

It is simple and looks like just what it is—a handkerchief. I never did like the tricky looking blindfolds that are obviously made up for that purpose. Use a large size man's handkerchief. Have it folded over and over from opposite corners until the rolls meet at the center. Now fold and put it in your pocket. When it is on, you can see through the one thickness and that is the point.

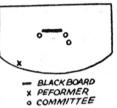

— BLACKBOARD
x PERFORMER
o COMMITTEE

Routine: Stand in your corner and direct the proceedings up to the point where you ask the audience to remember what the committee is thinking of. Then waving your hand back towards blackboard, say, "Now gentlemen, erase the blackboard and leave it clean so that there is no trace of what you have placed there." *As this gesture is made, you swing half around and in a flash you have the information you need!* You swing right back into position, but for a split second you have gestured as you talked and did what any natural person would have done. Therefore, I'll guarantee that no one will ever notice your actions. Besides, they are used to you being turned away from blackboard and they know you are blindfolded. Besides that, they don't know yet exactly what you are going to do.

Now the committee comes over to you and leads you to blackboard. I advise that you close your eyes the moment you have seen what you want, and don't open them again for any reason. You won't need them anymore, and you will act more like a blindfolded person as you are lead back and when you do your writing. Just write as best you can. You will be legible enough. Remember, keep your eyes closed, you can't help but do it right.

I suggest that you write two of the items, the number and the word, and then stop. Take off the blindfold, remark that for the picture test you would like to have the committee at a distance, and send them back to their seats. Now make the drawing, have one of the committee say "Right" or "Wrong," (the audience knows anyway) and you are through to a climax with an empty stage.

I know this effect is good. If I have convinced you, you'll have one of the best and most practical tricks in a long time. If I haven't convinced you, it will only be a matter of time until you see someone do it and then realize the effect upon the audience.

IN THE MIND

HENRY FETSCH

If this routine is given the proper practice and presentation it will prove to be a reputation builder. After steady use for four years I know it is good. It can be done at any time and anywhere with borrowed material.

Effect No. 1: First of all the magician is securely blindfolded. I always borrow two coins, half dollars or quarters, and place one over each eye. Then a pad of gauze is placed over each coin, followed with a cloth blindfold over all. This is a genuine blindfold and the method has a decided appeal to the layman.

The magician then requests the loan of a deck of cards which are thoroughly shuffled before they are handed to him. Any card is now freely selected, revealed to everyone except the magician, and returned to the deck. The performer then runs the card with faces towards the audience, from one hand to the other, telling everyone to mentally think the word "stop" when the selected card comes into view. And under such conditions as these he succeeds in stopping on the chosen pasteboard.

Effect No. 2: Saying that due to the favorable conditions which resulted in his being able to discover the chosen card, he will attempt to go a step further. He proceeds to have three cards selected, revealed to all, and returned to the deck which again is shuffled and cut several times. Once more the performer runs the cards face outward from hand to hand and stops at all three of the chosen cards.

Effect No. 3: The audience is now cautioned to pay strict attention to the final effect. Any card is once more taken, shown to all, returned for shuffle and cuts, and the magician builds up the climax. He refers to the blindfold, the free selection of cards, etc., and finally says that he will attempt to reveal the chosen card by name. The spectator is asked to visualize a picture of the card and the performer succeeds in his revelation!

I have described exactly the effect as seen by the layman. Never have I been questioned on any part of the routine, which gradually builds to a climax that they remember. It is presented strictly as a test of mental vibrations, which is why everybody is asked to help send their mental commands to the performer. The blindfold is to exclude all light and normal perceptions that might tend to confuse the demonstrator.

Preparation: It is best to work this routine standing up behind a table with the audience all around you. The only preparation necessary is to have a card, say the Four of Spades from a regulation size deck, in your left coat pocket. A duplicate of this card, from a bridge size deck, is in your right coat pocket. Have a regulation blindfold handy, or a large handkerchief, several small gauze pads and, in case you aren't able to borrow any, a couple of half dollars in one of your pockets.

Routine No. 1: Pass the cards from one hand to the other, cards facing your audience, and have one selected. While the card is being revealed to everyone, crimp the lower left hand corner of the top card. Cut the deck retaining the top half in the right hand, in position from the regular overhand shuffle. Have the selected card returned to the top of the left hand portion, then shuffle the right hand portion on top in the regular overhand fashion, with the crimped card going on top of the selected card at the beginning of the shuffle. Have anyone shuffle and cut the cards, but hurry him along in this action—in other words, time your patter so that you have him cutting the cards before he really gets a chance to shuffle them properly.

Now, with the deck in the left hand, remove the cards one at a time with the right hand so that the lower left hand corner of the card passes under the thumb of the left hand which is resting on top of the deck. Because of this position, when you come to the crimped card, you will feel the crimp as it goes under the left thumb. All that remains to do is to stop on the next card which will be the one selected.

Routine No. 2: At the finish of the first effect you cut the crimped card to the top of the deck. Then have any three cards selected freely and shown to all. Explaining that you will use just part of the deck to shorten the effect, start dealing the cards into three face down piles, one at a time, with the bottom card of the first pile being the crimped one. After you have dealt about four cards onto each pile stop and ask someone to stop you at any time. Then continue dealing.

No matter when the signal comes for you to stop, you continue dealing that row across. In other words, each pile must finally contain the same number of cards. And as you deal you count. You must know how many cards there are to a pile. Thus, if you finish the row with the 21st card dealt you know that there are 7 in each pile.

Using that number as an example you tell the people with chosen cards to replace them, one on the top of each pile. While this is going on, you casually place the remaining cards in the side coat pocket which contains the Four of Spades to match the deck being used. These cards are so placed that the Four of Spades becomes the new bottom or face card of the deck. It's a natural move to put the cards in your pocket, for the hands must be free for handling the cards on the table. Being blindfolded, it's about the only place one could put cards without fumbling.

The three piles are assembled in any order, and cut several times by you and the audience. Do not try any fancy cuts or shuffles. Remember, you are blindfolded, so it is best to appear clumsy in handling the cards throughout the routine. It is this clumsiness plus the blindfold that impresses the audience the most.

From this point remove the cards as you did in Effect No. 1, except that as each card is removed it is placed back on the bottom of the packet held in your left hand. Keep passing the cards in this manner until you come to the crimped card. Following it is one of the selected cards upon which you stop, and then lay it on the table. Now you pass seven more cards to the bottom of the packet, and the next card will be another of the selected cards. Stop on this card and lay it on the table also.

Pass seven more cards to the bottom. The next card is the last selected pasteboards. This you stop on and put with the first two laid out. To "halt" a wise person who may count, or get the impression of sameness in the length of passing, go a couple of cards beyond the last one—say you aren't positive because impressions aren't as clear as at first—ask the selector to concentrate upon each card showing—and, one by one, deal backwards until you reach the proper card upon which you stop and that is the one you lay down.

Just remember that the number of cards in each pile before the selected cards are returned, is the number of cards you pass each time after the revealing of the first selected card which follows the crimp.

Routine No. 3: Replace the selected cards from effect number two on top of the cards in your left hand—and then give them to anyone to shuffle and cut. While this is going on you take the rest of the deck from your coat pocket and riffle shuffle it thoroughly, keeping Four of Spades on the bottom. The spectator places the other cards on top of your packet. Then you give the entire deck another riffle shuffle, still keeping the Four of Spades on the bottom. This action has served to convince all that the deck has been well shuffled by both you and the audience. The riffle shuffle is advocated for it is best suited to conceal the difference in back design of the Four of Spades.

Now comes the force of the Four of Spades. Hold the pack normally in the left hand and, with the right thumb and forefinger at the sides, pull out a portion from the center of the deck. Run off these cards, a few at a time, onto the top of the left hand pile in the Hindu Shuffle manner. You ask, during this, for someone to stop you as he wishes. However, you have timed your talk and shuffling off so that you've run out of cards before a command can come. Without hesitating, you pull out a new section, not from the middle this time but from the bottom portion—run as many off the top as you can until the "stop" comes, and immediately turn over the right hand packet to show the face card (the Four of Spades) to those watching.

At this point, you remark that everything has been done openly, and they must realize the impossibility of you knowing at what card they are looking. You recall that you have so far successfully located the cards upon which they were concentrating—and add that you wish to go a step further.

During this talk, and after they have had a chance to see the Four of Spades, you put the right hand packet underneath the left hand packet which keeps the Four of Spades on the bottom. Then you riffle shuffle the deck a time or two, all the while, of course, keeping the force card on the bottom.

The selector of the forced Four of Spades approached you and you place your fingers upon his forehead. This always entails a bit of difficulty, so you drop the deck into your side coat pocket for the time being and proceed to use both of your hands. While he thinks of his card you give as dramatic a presentation of mindreading as you can, and reveal the identity of the chosen card.

You ask immediately for the removal of the blindfold. While it is being untied, you remove the deck from your pocket minus the odd Four of Spades. Then the coins, borrowed for the blindfolding, and the cards are returned to your host and all is over.

This is a thorough description of the trick as I present it. I've done it long enough to realize the salient points and their effect on the audience. I would suggest that the feat is best presented as a test of extra-sensory perception—with a perfect-plus (Professor Rhine) conclusion as a finale. You, as the performer, receive impressions from the audience, and act upon them. Then, as a final test, you succeed in revealing a chosen card. It all should be very scientific, and not presented as a trick.

(Editor's Note: It would seem that this stunt would lend itself to a most effective presentation with ESP cards. The fact that there are duplicate symbol cards in an ESP pack shouldn't detract from the effect. Passing over one or two duplicates before finally settling on a symbol card would make the effect that much stronger, for it should be obvious that someone in the audience was not concentrating hard enough! Furthermore, if you knew the name of the crimped card—and that should present no difficulty—you could dispense with the pocket subterfuge by cutting the crimped card to the bottom of the deck in readiness for the Hindu force.)

WITH SIGHT UNSEEN
L. E. DUNCANSON

Here is an effect that is a veritable stunner when properly presented. From the audience's standpoint it appears to be genuine clairvoyance.

Effect: The performer is blindfolded, has his hands tied behind his back and is stood by an accommodating committeeman so that his side (performer's) is towards the audience. In this position everything the performer handles behind his back is visible to the audience. He asks the committee to pick up a deck that is on the table, shuffle it and withdraw a half dozen cards. These are handed to the performer behind his back and he correctly names and identifies each card. He then asks the committee to supply a watch and to set it at any time they choose. When this is handed to the performer he announces at what time it has been set. Then the committee picks up a slate and jots down a series of numbers, letters and some simple geometrical figure. No matter what they have written the performer is able to identify everything, and thus finishes his test.

Preparation: First take a small mirror of any nature, but preferably not over an inch and a half in diameter. Now, if you will stand with your feet about three and a half inches apart, and lay the mirror on the floor between them at the insteps, you will quickly grasp the principle employed. Stand straight and look down into the mirror. Lean slightly forward, if necessary, and hold your hands behind your back so that you can see them reflected in the mirror. Now if you take a playing card and hold it in your hands, you will be able to catch its reflection in the mirror. Furthermore, if you stand sidewise to the audience, the mirror cannot be seen yet you can see reflected everything you hold in your hands. So much for that. The next thing is the detailed explanation of the mirror's use and operation in this effect.

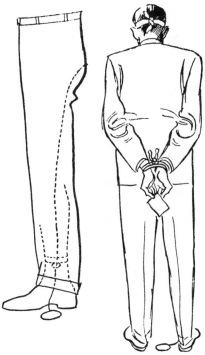

A sort of anklet wristlet is prepared on the order of a wrist watch strap. This is placed on the ankle about three or four inches above your trouser edge, and on the inside of the ankle. On the strap is a small eyelet of metal or cord. Now two small mirrors are secured, and these are cemented back to back. Fasten a length of black fishline to the double mirror. Run this line up through the ankle eyelet, up the trouser leg to just above the seat, where it is then threaded through to the back with a needle. Take up the slack till by pulling the thread you raise the mirror, and then cut off the line about six inches from where it comes out of the trouser's seat. Fasten a hook to the end of the thread, the hook end of which is sharpened.

When this line is pulled down in back, the mirror is drawn taut against the eyelet on your ankle, and thus it's out of sight and out of the way. Bring the hook down and pin it on your trouser leg, and it will be just hidden by the edge of your coat where you can get at it quickly. Now you are ready to work the effect.

Routine: You will find that having your hands tied behind you will make the best impression. Let one of the committee supply the handkerchief for the tying. Of course the tying isn't necessary, but afterwards it will serve as a reminder that your hands couldn't have been brought to the front at any time. Now pick out the location where you will stand, with either side to the audience. Always face according to whichever ankle the mirror is attached. This should be on the inside of the leg nearest the audience. Have your feet about three inches apart and side by side. Turn your body slightly towards the audience and have one of the committee bind your hands behind you. As you make this slight turn, your fingers in back release the hook, and the mirror slides down between your feet into position on the floor. As the mirror is double sided it can't go wrong. At once the left foot pivots a little on its toe, the heel touches the right foot and the mirror is completely hidden under your insteps. Thus the committeeman, who is tieing your wrists, is prevented from seeing the mirror. After your hands are bound, the committee then blindfolds you with another handkerchief which, of course, does not prevent you from seeing down along your nose.

Ease and simplicity are paramount from here on. The cards are handed and you proceed to read them as desired. The mirror remains hidden until wanted, and by slightly moving the heel you get a picture of what you have behind you. The blindfold prevents anyone from seeing you look downwards. The test with a watch is very effective but in all cases remember that your hands can be seen and therefore act accordingly. Keep turning the watch or article over and over as if trying to feel out the information that you give. It will easily be seen that with this principle the tests are unlimited. At the finish your actions are practically the reverse of the beginning. Ask to have your hands freed for the last test as you will need more freedom in handling the slate. Then, after revealing the majority of items, turn your body a little towards the audience when revealing the last few; and the right hand holding slate masks the left as it pulls down cord and at once you can turn around freely and pull off the blindfold.

MEPHISTO THOT

J. G. THOMPSON, JR.

Effect: An assistant from the audience distributes nine numbered slips of paper and the performer asks each person receiving one to write a question or bit of personal data. The written slips are then collected and sealed in an envelope. This is left in full view of everyone on a table and another assistant is recruited to watch it.

The medium is now introduced and is seated with her back to the audience. While the performer blindfolds her, the person who has the envelope in his care burns it in a nearby ashtray.

Next a large slate is shown to contain a square divided into nine smaller ones, three across and three down. The assistant, as soon as he has finished burning the envelope and slips, is handed the slate together with a piece of chalk and is asked to number the squares from 1 to 9 in any order he pleases. He is then given a pointer and is asked to point to any number that he pleases. As soon as he has indicated a number, the person who wrote on the slip bearing that particular number stands. Immediately the medium answers his question or correctly reveals what had been written on that person's slip. This is continued haphazardly until all the squares have been indicated and all the nine questions answered.

As a climax, the medium calls out several numbers which the performer puts under the numbered squares on the slate. These form a total across the bottom of the slate. When the three vertical columns are added, this total is found to be correct!

Preparation: The general effect of this routine is excellent. It has a set number of items to be revealed, so it does not go on indefinitely. You will need several pay envelopes, a few small slips of fairly thin paper, pencils, a large slate and chalk, a blindfold or a large handkerchief, and one of the Thornton card reels.

Bind five of six fairly large size pay envelopes together with a wide rubber band. Take another envelope, seal 9 paper slips in it and then fold its length in half with the flap outside. The creased edge of this folded envelope is stuck under the rubber band on the flap side of the stack. Square up the stack and, referring to the illustration, the folded envelope occupies position ABCD, the band concealing the fact that this envelope is folded. Hold the packet securely in your left hand like a deck of cards.

The reel is concealed in the folds of the blindfold and both are in the medium's possession. Now you're all set.

Routine: Step into the audience with the envelope packet in your left hand and with the 9 slips and the pencils in your right hand. Have the paper slips passed out and the questions written. When completed, pull one of the ordinary envelopes off the back of the envelope packet and hand it to a spectator. Ask him to gather the slips, seal them in the envelope, and then fold the envelope in half. Take it back and lay it on top of the packet of envelopes so that it occupies the position EFGH. Hold the packet above your head with the genuine envelope facing the audience and return to the stage. Step to the table and pull the previously prepared envelope out of the packet and stand it tentwise on the table. As you do so place the packet of envelopes in your pocket. This is a perfect switch and is quite indetectable.

At the moment of pocketing the envelopes, the medium is introduced and makes her entrance from the right side of the stage. A spectator is asked to come up on the stage and watch the envelope on the table. You seat the medium, blindfold her and have the spectator burn the envelope at the same time. The process of blindfolding is more important than it would seem. The bandage is placed a bit high so that the medium can see downwards along her nose. Stand facing the audience at the medium's left as you fasten the blindfold at the back. While in this position, the medium reaches into your pocket with her right hand and removes the envelope with the genuine questions enclosed. She also has time to fasten the reel to her dress or holds it tightly between her knees. Now, as you move to her right side to adjust the blindfold, she slips the button at the end of the reel thread into your left hand.

By this time the envelope is burned. Pick up the slate with your left hand (button is inside your hand and the thread passes through your fingers, at the roots, to the medium) and hold it with fingers behind and thumb in front while your right hand chalks in the squares. Hand the slate to the spectator and have him number the squares. He now points to one of the numbered squares and the person in the audience, who originally had the correspondingly numbered slip, stands and concentrates on his question. As he

stands, you fold your arms and step back a bit, keeping the slate in view. With your arms folded so that your right hand is hidden under your left arm, you have an opportunity of catching the thread with your right fingers. (You are standing with the medium to your left and your assistant to your right.) You are all set now to signal the numbers as they are selected. During this time, the medium has opened the envelope and has arranged the slips, being careful to keep her arms tightly against her side throughout. Once arranged, she grips the thread and is ready.

The signal code itself is simple. One short tug means one, and one long tug means add five to the shorter number. Thus 4 would be four short tugs. 5 would be one long tug. 6 would be one long tug followed by a short tug. Zero, when it comes up in the final total of the three columns, is signalled by two long tugs.

Actual practice will smooth out the action and show you that the figures for the final addition can be transmitted while the medium is giving the answer to the last question. There is no rush for this. The moment the last slip has been described you send the first number of the answer. Tell the assisting spectator to add the columns, and in this interval you send the medium the remaining figures in the total which you have already added mentally. Then without a word being spoken, the medium announces the correct total of the three columns. Just as she calls out the last digit, let go of the thread and it will snap back into the medium's reel. She pockets it with the papers and envelope, stands, removes the blindfold and takes her applause.

MAGIC VS. MENTALISM

ANNEMANN

This effect is unusual in theme and makes a neat opening number for a mental routine or act.

Effect: The performer states that many have asked him the difference between a mindreader and a magician, and that he will attempt to make the difference clear.

He produces two packs of playing cards in their cases and asks the help of a spectator. The spectator selects one of the decks and places it in his pocket for the time being. Taking the other deck from its case, the performer says that a magician would always fan the cards and have one selected, looked at, replaced, and then after a shuffle would locate the correct card in some mysterious fashion. On the other hand, a mindreader would only fan the cards with the faces towards the spectator and ask him to merely think of one that he liked.

Suiting the action of his words, the performer fans the cards and the spectator thinks of one that he sees. Closing the deck, it is given a shuffle and the performer hands it directly to the spectator. Now the performer states that he has no further control over the cards and that the spectator is to name, for the first time, the card he merely thought of. This is done and then the spectator is asked to deal the cards, one at a time, on to the performer's hand, face down. As the cards are dealt the performer spells the named card aloud, letter by letter, and when the last letter is reached the spectator is stopped. Once more the performer calls attention to the fact that the card was merely thought of and not selected by removing it or touching it. The spectator holds up the last card, and it is the one thought of!

After this denouement, the performer explains that the effect could only have been accomplished by his reading the spectator's mind, and then putting the correct card in the proper position. But then the performer asks the spectator if he thinks that the performer knew what card he was going to select before the performance started. The answer is, of course, no!

The spectator is now asked to remove from his pocket the deck which he had selected and placed there at the start of the test. He is told to take it from its case and to repeat what he did before—deal the cards, one at a time, as he again spells out the name of his originally selected card. On the last card he is stopped, before he has a chance to look at its face, and is asked, "If that is your thought of card, will you be a true believer in the powers of mindreading and prophecy?" This invariably gets a laugh regardless of the answer, and then the last card is shown. Again it is the correct card!

The performer then turns to some other person in the audience, and says, "Perhaps, Sir, you may have some doubts about the genuineness of this experiment."

Whatever the reply, the performer says, "To prove that I definitely foretold what card this gentleman would mentally select, I wrote its name down, sealed it, and put it here in my pocket. Would you kindly take it out and read aloud what card I thought would be chosen."

He does so, and, of course, the prediction is correct!

Preparation: The method is simply the old automatic spelling principle with six cards, each spelling with a different number of letters. Take, for instance, the following set up: AC—6H—JS—8H—9D—QD. Place these on top of your deck with the Ace of Clubs the top card; then on top of these place any nine other cards. Now any one of these will spell out automatically as follows: "Ace of Clubs" with the Ace turning up on the letter "s"; "Six of Hearts," with the 6 turning up on the "s"; and so on throughout the set up. When your deck is set, place a short card below the Queen of Diamonds, or alternately pencil dot the back of the Queen on its upper left and lower right corners. This is so that you can quickly locate the Queen as you riffle the deck or fan it.

Make exactly the same preparation with the second deck, and place each deck in its own case. Now write six predictions on slips of paper, naming a different force card in each prediction. Seal each of these slips in a separate envelope, and then place the envelopes in six different pockets of your suit according to a memorized order.

Routine: Ask any spectator to assist you, hand him the two decks and ask him to choose one and place it in his pocket till later. As you come to the part where you explain what a mindreader would do, cut the deck you are holding right below the Queen. Lift the cut off portion with your right hand and fan the bottom six cards, face down, with the Queen at the face of the fan. Hold this group up facing the spectator as you ask him to think of one card that he sees and likes. Remember to have the spectator at your left so that the audience cannot see exactly how many cards are visible. From the patter they assume that you are giving him a choice of a goodly number of cards.

Drop the packet back on top of the cards in your left hand, square up the deck and give it a good riffle shuffle *below* the top fifteen cards. Hand the deck to the spectator and ask him to deal the cards onto your palm after he has named his card aloud. You spell out the card, letter for letter for each card that he deals. On the last letter, the mentally chosen card turns up. Then the second deck is brought forth, the card spelled, and again it turns up correctly.

The finale with the envelopes was suggested by Leslie May and forms an extraordinarily striking climax to this fine effect. The working of the envelope prediction is, of course, obvious to the reader. All you have to do is have some other spectator reach into the correct pocket of your suit, remove the envelope he finds there, open it and read your prediction.

A CARD TO BE THOUGHT ABOUT
ANNEMANN

Impromptu thought card tricks have always been welcome, and the following is one I have found to be very effective. I'll explain it exactly as I have been using it.

Effect: The deck is spread out face down and a spectator is asked to remove three cards and hold them. He is to study them carefully and make a mental choice of one which he is to keep firmly in mind. Squaring up the deck, you have the three cards replaced and give them a shuffle. Now putting the deck behind your back, you try to locate the thought-of card by drawing one card out and throwing it face up on the table. You are wrong, of course, and explaining that the spectator is not concentrating enough, you fan the deck facing him and ask him to spot his card once more. This time you locate his mentally chosen card without fail.

Routine: The procedure you follow is simply this. When the original three cards are returned to the deck in a group, bring them to the top. Now when you place the deck behind your back, transfer the top one to the bottom, and the second one you slip into your hip pocket. Run the third one silently into tenth place, by counting off ten cards, slipping the top card to the top of the deck and then replacing the nine remaining cards on top of the deck. Turn the deck face up and repeat this same move so that the bottom card is transferred from the bottom to tenth from bottom.

Placing these three selected cards takes but twenty seconds. When set, draw any card out of the center of the deck and throw it face up on the table. It is, of course, the wrong card and they tell you so. Now bring the deck to the front, fan it facing the spectator and ask him if he sees his card as you slowly thumb through the upper half of the deck. Nine times out of ten if he sees it he'll say so. If he has seen it then it must be the card tenth from the top, so you can spread the deck across the table and pick it out with an appropriate line of patter about impulses, etc.

If the card hasn't been seen, hand the deck to the spectator and let him finish running through the cards himself. If he then sees it, it is the tenth card from the bottom of the deck. If he can't find it at all, he is asked to name it and you then remove it from your pocket. Always pocket the middle card of the three as it improves the percentage quite a little in favor of this latter finish.

MIND OR MUSCLE?
ANNEMANN

You will find this trick will create considerable discussion, because it appears to be a genuine test of mindreading as well as a novel interpreting of involuntary muscular reactions. The routine is carefully worked out, and the problem is presented directly, simply, and without sleights or manipulations.

Effect: Three people each select cards and return them to the pack in a manner which allays suspicion. The deck is returned to the performer who ribbon spreads it face up across the table. The first card is found by holding the person's wrist and passing his hand over the pasteboards. The second card is found in the same way. And the third card is named by the performer who touches his fingertips to the forehead of the person selecting the last card.

Preparation: Two decks are used. One is a regular deck of cards and the other is a single force deck with all cards alike. Arrange the regular deck in the familiar Si Stebbin's system. Put the force deck in your right coat pocket. Have the regular deck handy when you are ready to begin.

Routine: Commence by having the first two cards selected in this manner: Fan the deck freely and allow any card to be removed. Cut the deck at this point which will bring the "key" card to the bottom, but don't look at it. Pass to a second person and have another card removed. As it is taken, carelessly drop the card above it to the floor. Close up the deck, stoop down and pick up the fallen card, your second "key" card, and drop it on top of the deck regardless of whether you have seen it or not.

Now hand the deck to the first person and ask him to push his card anywhere into the deck. He then passes the deck to the second person, who also pushes his card into the deck at any place he pleases. The deck is then returned to you. To the spectators this method of handling the cards appears more than fair. And it is, because up to now you do not know the names of the two selected cards, or where they are in the deck. And furthermore you did not force either card. However, you do know where the two necessary "key" cards are—the "key" for the first selected card is on the bottom of the deck, and the "key" for the second selected card is on the top of the deck.

You now spread the deck face up across the table. The first spectator comes forward and his card is found by apparent muscle reading. There is ample time for you to note the bottom card, which is your first "key" card. Just count one ahead in the Si Stebbin system and then look for that card. The same thing is done with the second person by noting the top "key" card and determining the identity of his chosen card.

Now state that you have developed your powers to the nth degree and ask for a third person to volunteer for your last test. Pick up the deck and shuffle it. Explain that the volunteer is to put the deck in his pocket. Then he is to take out any card from the deck that he wishes, note it, and then put it in his opposite side coat pocket without letting anyone else see it. As you explain this, do it by dropping the deck into your side coat pocket alongside of the single force deck. (This is an Al Baker subtlety.) Take out one card from the force deck, keeping it with its back towards the audience, glance at it, and then put it into your opposite coat pocket. Having thusly illustrated the procedure, take out the force deck (with its back to the audience), add to it the card you passed across without showing it, and deliberately put the deck into the spectator's side coat pocket. Turn your back and walk away while he transfers one card. Step back, ask if he is concentrating upon the color, suit and value of the card he chose. Point out that under the strict conditions imposed, the only possible way to learn the card's identity is by thought vibration, and that he alone can help by thinking intently of the card he chose.

As you explain this you put your right fingertips against his forehead, and at the same time take the remainder of the deck from his pocket with your left hand and drop it into your pocket next to the other, regular deck. Proceed now to name the card correctly, giving first the color, then the suit, and finally the value. Have the spectator show it, and then suggest that he keep it as a souvenir of the occasion.

Seldom, if ever, will anyone want to look at the cards.* They were seen and handled freely at the start, and the last test makes a deep impression and a great finale.

YGGDRASIL
ANNEMANN

The following effect takes advantage of the publicity garnered by Professor Rhine and the Duke University experiments, and makes use of a deck of Extra Sensory Perception cards. With these cards but one or two tests will suffice the usual audience, because many people look upon these tests as genuine telepathy; know that laboratory tests have not gone far; and too much from the performer causes them to suspect chicanery.

Effect: The performer introduces the test with an opening address somewhat along these lines:

"It has become public knowledge that, in recent years, universities all over the world have been experimenting and testing the little known powers of the mind. Professor J. B. Rhine of Duke has gone further than the rest, however, by systematically recording several million tests, using as a base a set of 25 symbol cards; cards bearing only 5 different designs and repeated 5 times. These designs were selected for their difference from each other, and the experiments involving their use have been termed extra sensory perception. This term is rather all embracing and does not mean telepathy or mind-reading in itself. Those are but the more commonly given explanations. Extra sensory perception merely indicates and searches for a sense outside of those which all of us normally have. I want to try several short tests with these cards, in an attempt to prove that there is something beyond all that we know. What it is, and why it is, can only be left to your own judgment."

With these few words, the performer picks up a deck of ESP cards and, opening the case and removing the cards, explains that the deck consists of but 5 different symbol cards repeated several times. He hands the deck to someone willing to assist, and asks that five of the different cards be removed. These are fanned before the spectator and he is asked to mentally choose one. The performer then places the fan of cards behind his back and, while the spectator concentrates on his card, withdraws one and places it back out, in his trouser pocket. He then slowly counts the remaining four cards, one by one, onto the deck, and asks the spectator to name his selected card. The performer removes the card from his pocket and it is the correct one! The first test has succeeded!

The performer offers to repeat the test. This time the five different symbol cards are picked out of the deck and laid face down on the table. The performer turns his back as a second spectator picks up one card, looks at it

---

*(**Editor's Note:** For those who like subtleties, here is a fine point. In anticipation of someone wanting to see the deck after the trick has been completed, follow this procedure: When picking up the regular deck which has been spread on the table, divide it at the duplicate of the force card bringing this card to the top of the pack. Later if someone wants to see the deck, reach into your pocket and bring out the regular deck—minus the top card—and give it to him. Thus, when the third spectator adds his card to the deck, he will be holding a complete deck.

and then lays it on the table again. The cards are then moved about a bit, so that the performer cannot tell which one might have been selected. He turns around, gathers up the cards, still face down, and places them in his inside coat pocket. While the spectator "thinks" of his card the performer finds it successfully a second time.

A third test is suggested and the performer has the deck shuffled and then places it in his trousers pocket. A third person comes forward and is told to stand behind the performer, and when the performer gives the word he is to plunge his hand into the performer's pocket and pull out one card. The performer explains that some people have a hidden sense, and that this final experiment will show whether this third gentleman is endowed with it. The spectator follows instruction, grasps a card and just as he withdraws it, the performer announces the card's name. Climax!

Requirements: You will need two decks of ESP cards, although but one is used openly. A deck of these cards consists of twenty-five cards, being made up of five separate and distinct symbols, repeated five times each. The symbols represented are a Square, a Star, a Circle, a Cross and a set of Wavy Lines. See the illustration.

These cards should be in a regular fan, one behind the other, from left to right, so that when squared up they will retain their memorized order.

To prepare for the effect, take 5 Stars from one deck and discard the rest. Put 4 of these Stars face outward under your belt in the back, allowing the lower half of the cards to protrude below the belt; or suspend them from a paper clip, sewn to the inside of your coat, so that they hang within an inch of the bottom edge of your coat. Then from the deck you will use, take one each of the five designs, place the Star at the face of the packet and place them in your inside coat pocket. The extra Star card is left in the deck, and the deck is replaced in its case.

Routine: Open with the patter outlined under "presentation," then pick up the card case, show it openly and name the 5 designs which make up the deck. Say that you will use the 5 different symbols, and hand the case to someone, asking him to remove the cards. Take the cards from him, run through them, select the five different cards, and fan them, making a mental note of the sequence. Hold the fan face towards the assisting spectator, as illustrated.

Ask the spectator to look them over and to finally settle his mind on but one design. He is to think of the design as a mental picture, rather than as a name.

Square the cards face down in your left hand. Place both hands with the cards behind your back. Transfer the packet of cards to a position between your right fingers and thumb, while the left hand secures the four Star cards from the clip under the back of your coat. Hold these face down in your left palm. While you are doing this, say, "You are thinking of a symbol. I shall remove one card," bring your right hand around in front of you, holding the packet squared as though it were but one card, and put it in your right trouser pocket. As you do so, say, "One from five leaves four," and bring your left hand in front of you and deal the four (Star) cards face down on top of the deck, which should be on the table.

Now ask the spectator to reveal the design he chose, at the same time inserting your right hand into the right trouser pocket, where your fingers separate the five cards (one finger going in between each card) whose sequence you already know.

As the spectator names the design he selected, you ask, "Why did you choose the . . .? Is such a design connected with your everyday life? Did it remind you of something?" This slight stall gives you an opportunity to secure the correct card, and you should have it half out of your pocket and in view as he answers. You finish with, "Well, you concentrated upon it very thoroughly and steadily. Some force directed me to that very symbol." Show the card to be correct and toss it onto the deck.

The deck now contains the 5 added duplicates of the Star (one was already there and you just added the four from the clip under your coat.)

Look at someone else and say, "We shall try it a bit differently. The five designs shall be left on the table." As you patter, run through the deck with the faces towards you and apparently remove five different cards. Instead, however, you pick out the five Stars and drop them, face down, in a row on the table. Say, "This time I'll turn my back and leave the selection up to chance alone. There won't be any opportunity for me to take advantage of a possible liking on your part for any particular card. Please step to the table, pick up and look at any one design. Put it back in its place, and then slightly move each card a bit so as to prevent leaving any clue as to which card may have been picked up."

The second spectator does as instructed, and then you turn around, pick up the five cards and place them, face down, on your left palm. Transfer them to your right hand, as your left hand opens your coat and removes (without a word) a couple of letters or papers from your inside coat pocket. Lay whatever you've removed on the table, and then transfer the packet of cards back to your left hand. Your right now takes hold of your coat lapel on the right side, and pulls the coat open a few inches. Your left hand pretends to place the packet of cards in the inside coat pocket, but actually deposits them in your upper vest pocket with thumb and forefinger, while the other fingers go on into the coat pocket for effect. Now open the coat out wide so that all may see the inside pocket.

Ask the spectator to think hard of the card he selected. You reach into the inside pocket with your left hand and remove a card with its back to the audience and the spectator. Look at it, shake your head and toss it face up on the table. This card is any card but the Star, which as you remember faces the inside of your pocket. Repeat this with the next three odd cards, tossing each one face up on the table. This will leave the Star card for last. As you toss the fourth card down, say, "You aren't thinking of any of those. It must be the last. Will you name your symbol and then reach into my pocket and remove it yourself?" He does so, and, of course, finds but one card and that one is the Star card which he selected!

The added duplicates are now safely out of the way (in your vest pocket), and only four different cards remain in your right trouser pocket. These are, as you will remember, the four cards left over from the first test, and you also know the order in which they are arranged.

Continue with the effect by saying, "We have tried this by mental selection and by chance selection. Now we shall turn about and see whether or not someone here in the audience is endowed with a hidden sense." Select a third person, or accept a volunteer, and have him shuffle the deck until he's satisfied that the cards are well mixed. Take the pack face down and put it into your right trouser pocket *under the four cards that are there*. You know the top card of this packet of four, and this card now becomes the top card of the deck. What is just as important is that this known card is also the nearest card to the outside of your pocket. Placing the cards in your pocket takes but a minute, so you continue to address your new assistant, "You, sir, shall stand behind me. When I snap my fingers, please reach into my pocket with your right hand, pull out a card and look at it behind my back. No one will see it but yourself." There won't be one time in fifty that this person will miss getting the top card. It's the only one he can get quickly and without effort. To be sure that he will grasp the right one, you hurry him along, and just as he dives into your pocket, you snap your fingers and say, "You are going to select a . . . !" (You name, of course, the top card.) As he withdraws the card you swing around and ask, "What is it?" He shows it, and everyone sees that it is the card you named! Climax!

Remarks are superfluous. The deck is now a complete one, and it is at this time when all who are interested in such tests will ask to examine it. Tricks no end can be done, but this routine has stood me well for several years and it has been ironed out through actual performance. Both the patter and the effects are logical, nothing is claimed, and the spectators are left to mull it over in their own minds and arrive at any conclusions they like. Don't, however, becloud the tests by using these ESP cards like an ordinary bridge deck, and then complicate things with fancy sleights and intricate effects for which the symbol cards were never intended.

THE SECRET ORDER OF THE ACES
Annemann

The following mental routine is a novel, two person telepathic effect using four Aces from any deck. It is my simplified version of an effect published by Hugh Mackay in 1925. You will find it quite different in theme from other similar problems of the same nature.

Effect: The lady assistant retires to another room with a spectator as guard. Any pack of cards is used and handed to someone who removes the four Aces. He mixes the Aces, and lays them, or stands them, in a face out row in any order. Lastly, he turns over (so that the backs are outward), either the two red Aces, or the two black Aces. The audience having noted down the position of each Ace in the row, and the color reversed, a spectator mixes them up and leaves them on the table. The lady now returns and her blindfold is removed at the table, after the performer has been put under guard. The lady immediately carries out the exact movements which took place while she was absent.

Secret and Routine: The whole thing is pure presentation plus the finger nail bump. If you hold a card between the tips of the forefinger and thumb, and press sharply with the nail of the forefinger against the card over the ball of thumb, a slight bump is raised which can be detected instantly by passing a thumb or finger over the surface of the pasteboard.

I suggest that the cards be stood against something rather than laid on the table. All can see the row better, and it makes it easier for you. After the row has been placed in the desired position by a spectator and the color reversed, you ask someone to jot down the order of the Aces as they stand. You pick up the first, saying, "Clubs" (or whatever it is), and toss it to the table. Repeat with the rest, and finally mention, for notation, the color which was reversed. You only have to nick three cards. And it does not matter whether the card is facing one way or another as the three marks can't get mixed. The first card's bump is anywhere along the end; on the second it is somewhere around the center; and on the third it is anywhere along the side. The fourth need not be marked. After all notes have been made and the cards have been well mixed, you ask someone to go out and call in the lady assistant. If you send out a lady, the reversed color has been black; if a gentleman, red. If you are working before only one sex, arrange with your partner beforehand which of the two people you'll send.

The lady returns, picks up the Aces, looks them over. She puts up the second or third Ace, then another, another, and finally moves one and puts the other between, all of which builds up the effect of concentration and uncertainty. Lastly, she turns over the correct pair of colors.

PARALLEL THOUGHTS
ANNEMANN

This effect is a perfect follow up to the preceding one, "The Secret Order of the Aces." It bears a similarity, but its general appearance is different, and the conditions are strict, which will counteract any thoughts your audience may have about the first trick.

Effect: The performer requests his assistant, or medium, to step into an adjoining room for a few minutes. He now borrows a deck of cards and has it shuffled or well mixed. Remarking that he will not touch the cards even once, the performer has someone spread the deck out and has four cards removed. These are placed in a face up row on the table. Now, the selector is asked to take his time, change his mind as often as he desires, but finally to settle upon one of the four. When he has decided, he touches the card with his finger. Someone else gathers up the four cards, and shuffles them as much as he likes. While he does so, the performer steps into a closet or into another room, where he will not be able to contact the medium.

When the medium returns, she correctly reveals the card upon which every-one is concentrating.

The fact that any four cards are removed for this test, and the fact that the performer never touches them, make this quite foolproof.

Secret: The secret lies in the possibility of any four cards being men-tally known as 1, 2, 3 and 4. The lowest in value is recognized as 1. The next is 2, the next is 3, and the highest is 4. Where duplicate values are among the four, the suits have preference in a pre-arranged order. Use the suit values common in Bridge, *i.e.*: Clubs, Diamonds, Hearts and Spades, which Spades the top value. Thus there can never be any confusion between you and your medium as to the secretly recognized order, no matter what cards are being used.

Routine: After the final selection of one card, and the subsequent shuffling of the four, you either have a lady or gentleman, as the case may warrant, take the cards to the medium; or go and bring her back to the room, where she stands next to the table gazing at the cards.

If the cards are taken to the medium by a lady, she knows the selected card is No. 1; by a gentleman, No. 2. If a lady fetches her, but has left the cards on the table, then the selected card is No. 3. If a gentelman goes to fetch her without the cards, then it's No. 4.

In the first two instances, she looks over the cards and arranges them in order. She then selects the correct card, and returns to the room with it in her hand, but held face down. The selector names it, and she turns it face up. It's correct!

On the other hand, if she is lead to the table, she spreads the cards face up, looks at them, picks them up and removes a card without showing it. The selector names his card and the medium turns it over, showing it to be the one she's holding.

This presentation, together with the subtlety of using any four cards, will be found to fool the most erudite.

VOLITION

ANNEMANN

Effect: The audience sees four envelopes passed out, and four cards taken from the pack by the people receiving the envelopes. The cards are sealed in the envelopes and a fifth person collects them, mixes them, and lays them in a row on the table which stands between the performer and the audience.

Now the performer speaks out. He explains that he intends to show that a sympathy exists between people and the objects they have touched. To emphasize that sympathy he will let each of the four people pass through a sieve of chance.

Each of the four persons is given his chance. Each, in turn, selects an envelope and places it in his pocket. The performer then says, "Ladies and gentlemen. Four of you have selected cards, sealed them tightly in separate envelopes, so that no one but them know what cards were chosen. The envelopes were then mixed and, finally, each of the four assistants reclaimed one envelope by chance selection. This you have all witnessed. When I started this experiment, I mentioned coincidence. I ask you now to check, carefully on an occurrance that you will rarely ever see duplicated again. Mr. —————, the name of your card? Open your envelope. It's the same one you selected. Good. Show it to the audience, please. Mr. —————, you picked what card? The —————. Open your envelope, please, etc."

Each person shows the card in his envelope and it is seen to be the very one he originally selected. Is it coincidence that all found their own cards? It's either factual evidence or accurate fancy!

Routine: The envelopes, handed out in a careless manner, are marked. It doesn't matter how, but the containers are capable of being identified from each side as 1, 2, 3, 4. When the fifth person lays them down in a row, the performer's first mental effort is to note how they lie.

First he patters about leaving all to chance. He knows the people as 1, 2, 3, 4. Therefore he knows to whom each envelope belongs. First, he looks at the envelope second from his left. He motions, offhandedly, towards the person to whom he knows it belongs. "Give me a number between one and four—quickly." If "three" is given, he asks that person to step forward, count to it, take it, and step back. If "two" is mentioned, he looks down, counts deliberately to two and offers it. From each side of the row the same card has been "sold" to its owner.

You now push the three remaining envelopes together to close up the empty space. This action permits you to see the mark on the middle envelope. Looking upward, after the arrangement, you ask another of the "four" to step forward. Naturally, it is he to whom the middle envelope belongs.

Pick up your right hand envelope and give it to him. Say, "Just touch one of the others." Should he touch his own (original center) you continue, "Keep it for yourself." Should he touch the right end envelope you say, "That puts both out of the way. Pick up that envelope on the table and put it in your pocket."

No matter what happens, he gets his own. You put the two remaining envelopes side by side, and call either one of the two remaining people. And you know which envelope belongs to the person who comes up.

Ask him outright to pick up one. As you request him to do so, look at and motion for the last person to come forward, too. Pretend to ignore the person who is selecting the envelope, but note which envelope he has selected.

As the fourth person steps up, you have two "outs." Should the third man pick up the envelope belonging to the fourth man, and that man is coming forward, tell the selector to give it to the fourth man. Then indicate that the selector is to take the remaining envelope. On the other hand, if he should select his own envelope, let him keep it and, of course, the fourth man takes the last envelope, which is his own.

Now ask all the people with envelopes to come forward and stand around you facing the audience. Explain what you hope will happen and have them all open their envelopes and show their cards to the audience.

One thing that you must remember is to make your presentation very deliberate, without a show of hesitation. The patter must be timed with the action, and should be very matter of fact. Since you do not care, apparently, how the envelopes are returned and selected, then the only answer the audience can arrive at is that it was all a matter of pure chance. Pass blithely, but accurately, through this part of the trick. Save your showmanship for the opening announcement and the closing one just prior to the climax.

You will find the effect on the audience to be terrific, provided, of course, that you present the stunt as an experiment to test an unknown but suspected quality in everyone to veer towards that which is his own. Your attitude throughout should be that your assistants do the trick—not you!

WAITING PLACE FOR UNKNOWN THOUGHTS

JAMES-ANNEMANN

"Somewhere, every thought that you will ever possess is waiting to be brought into the world. I ask you to think of something—a word will do—in a manner that requires some conscious effort on your part. That gives me time to project my astral body to the waiting place for your unborn thoughts. Your conscious effort removes a thought and brings it into being on our earth. As I am on the spot, by psychic vision, I see that thought removed, and can tell, upon coming out of my trance, what is on your mind." Thus, the performer prepares his audience for the following miracle of modern day mindreading.

Effect: Your subject is given a packet of 52 alphabet cards—just enough so that the alphabet may be repeated twice with one letter to each card. He steps to a distant spot, cuts the packet where he may please, and removes three cards. No one else sees them.

If it is possible for him to form a word from the three letters he holds, he does so. Should he not be able to do so, he discards them and takes three more.

You do not handle the cards again, ask any leading questions, or even have him write the word, but you know it.

Method No. 1: (by Mr. James): Although the packet of cards is referred to as two complete sets of the alphabet, they bear only three letters repeated throughout, as: C-I-E-C-I-E-C, etc. An indifferently lettered card or two may be put at the face of the packet. The volunteer cuts and removes three cards. It does not require much thought on his part to form the word ICE—the only word possible with these letters. Telling him that if he cannot form a word from the letters chosen he may take three more is merely misdirection. Other letters may be substituted as long as the formation of a word is readily apparent and only one word can be made.

Method No. 2: (by Annemann): This honey of an effect reminded me of a much popularized book test method I introduced called, "Between the Lines." It requires a Dunninger to nerve one's self into letting a 3-banked force deck, whether cards or letters, be handled by a spectator. Besides, wanting to use the effect, and not wishing to buy enough decks of alphabet cards to build the force pack, we sought to accomplish a near miracle with only one deck of two complete alphabets. It has necessitated eliminating Mr. James' condition that no leading questions be asked, but experience has taught us that a person can ask lead questions when trying what is evidently a most impossible feat, and build up the opinion that he is working hard mentally against a subject not quite perfect at concentrating. At any rate, accept this variation at face value, please.

Set your alphabet deck as follows: Q-H-J-C-S-V-X-N-U-T-K-F-O-G-M-R-E-D-Z-L-I-P-W-B-A-Y. Now repeat this formation of letters with the second half of the pack.

Show the case, explain about it containing alphabet cards, along with your theme patter. Remove the deck and pick a spectator to be the subject, at the same time false shuffle the cards and fan them to let the faces be seen. Just before giving the deck to the spectator cut about 13 cards from the top to the bottom.

The spectator cuts the deck and deals three cards face up on the table. You have your back turned. Ask if he can make a word from them. "No? Push them aside and deal three more. No? Push them away and try three more. Yes?" Have him hold the three cards and discard all the others.

He is to think of the first letter. "R? No. Try the last letter. P? No. Let's take the middle letter. U? No. Concentrate. It's the name of a place? No. We'll try by having you feel the word as though you were with it. Ah! It is a clammy feeling. The word is 'Fog.' Right."

It seldom will be that long. We've given you the longest possible ritual. With the set-up given, but 5 three letter words can be formed and they are: Red, Lip, Nut, Fog, and Bay. No other possible combinations can be formed. To remember these words easily, memorize the following sentence:

"With *red lips* she ate *nuts* while sailing on a *foggy bay.*"

Your system of "pumping" is always the same. The moment you get a "Yes," you know the word. On the last two the "name of a place" separates "Fog" and "Bay."

Those who try this stunt will soon realize that errors on your part really enhances the effect, so long as the positions of the thought of letters are changed each time (first, last, middle). These errors, plus the fact that the spectator may have to make several deals before he gets a word, convinces the audience that you are attempting an impossible feat. When you succeed, as you do, the effect is a phenomenon so far as they are concerned.

THE BRAIN WAVE DECK
DAI VERNON

This card effect of causing a mentally chosen card to automatically and instantly reverse itself in a deck, is probably the finest mental effect known today. It is not only the most subtle but also the most incomprehensible feat imaginable from an audience's viewpoint. It has tremendous possibilities when properly presented as a problem of mental coercion. One well known mentalist has garnered reams of newspaper publicity by using it as a long distance telephone test.

Effect: The performer tosses a card case containing a deck of cards onto the table, or hands it to someone to place in his pocket. The performer explains that he is going to make the spectator think of one of the 52 cards in the deck. To prove that the spectator will think of and name a certain card, the performer explains that he has already taken a particular card with a different colored back and has inserted it in the deck, but in a reversed position. The spectator thinks for a moment and then names the first card that comes into his mind. Picking up the deck, the performer removes it from its case and fans the cards. In the fan but one card is reversed, and that one card is the very card just named by the spectator. It is removed from the fan and turned back up, when it is seen that its back is red whereas the backs of all the other cards in the deck are blue!

Preparation: A special deck of cards will have to be prepared for this trick, or you can buy the deck all ready made up from any magic dealer. The deck is arranged as follows: All the Hearts and Diamonds are Blue backed cards, while all the Spades and Clubs are Red backed cards. Lay out the cards face up from RIGHT to LEFT, starting with Ace to King of Diamonds followed by the Ace to King of Hearts, in a horizontal row across your table. Now directly under these cards lay out, face up, the Ace to King of Spades followed by the Ace to King of Clubs—but starting from the LEFT end of the row and continuing on towards the RIGHT, as follows:

KH QH JH 10H 9H 8H 7H 6H 5H 4H 3H 2H AH KD QD JD 10D 9D 8D 7D 6D 5D 4D 3D 2D AD

AS 2S 3S 4S 5S 6S 7S 8S 9S 10S JS QS KS AC 2C 3C 4C 5C 6C 7C 8C 9C 10C JC QC KC

Now prepare the face of each card with roughing fluid, obtainable at any dealers. To assemble the deck, turn each card in the top row face down on the card under it in the bottom row. Assemble these pairs by putting the left end pair on to the next pair to the right. These are put onto the next pair to the right, etc. You now have a pack of double back cards, one side of which is blue, the other red. When the blue backs are up the first face up card, the lower one of the top pair, is the Ace of Spades; and when the deck is reversed with the red backs up the first face up card, also the bottom one of the top pair, is the Ace of Diamonds.

The deck so assembled may be fanned and each of the pairs of cards will adhere, so that you may fan it from either side and the audience will see nothing but the backs of the cards. Now to cause one of the face up cards to appear, all one has to do is to apply a little pressure with the fingers when you reach the proper pair and they will separate, revealing the bottom card face up. As the Diamonds and Hearts run from Ace to King in two complete cycles, all you have to do is to hold the deck with the Red side up and push the cards off into the right hand with the left thumb, counting mentally one, two, three, etc., until you reach the Diamond you want. To get a particular Heart just continue counting in the same fashion. To help in counting the second cycle of Hearts, the 14th pair from the top, which has the Ace of Hearts face up as the lower card, is pencil marked on the back with a small dot in its upper left and lower right corners. Thus to find a Heart quickly just fan the cards to the pencil marked one and start your count from there.

Now turn the deck over so that the Blue backs are on top, and you will be able to locate the Spades and the Clubs in the same way as you did the Diamonds and Hearts, by running and counting the cards from your left hand into your right. Mark the 14th card with pencil dots, as already explained, and this will be your key to the run of Clubs.

The only other preparation necessary to make the trick complete is to be sure to use a card case of a neutral color, such as a white Fox Lake case. In this way, the deck may be removed with either the red or the blue backs of the cards showing, which will be less obvious than if you removed a red backed deck from a blue case, and vice versa. When placing your assembled deck in its case, mark the outside of the case on one side to indicate which color backs will be facing that side of the case. Thus you can pick up the case and, knowing which side of the cards are red and which are blue, you will be guided accordingly.

Routine: The presentation should now be obvious. Toss your deck on the table, tell your audience about the insertion of a different colored card in the deck and how you are going to attempt to make one of them name that very card. If the card named is a red one, the deck is removed with the red side up; if a black card, the deck is removed with the blue side up. You now deliberately fan the cards and count to the spot where you know the named card is located, pushing the cards into the right hand, one at a time, as you do so. Be sure to maintain your fan formation as you push the cards into the right hand. When you reach the spot where the named card lies, apply a little pressure and split that pair, bring the selected card into view and face up in the fan. Draw the face up card out of the fan and drop it on the table, saying, "I didn't want anyone to think I was a sleight-of-hand artist, so I used a card with a different colored back." Then turn the card over and show its back.

If you intend to do some further mental stunts with cards, then drop this deck into your pocket, while they examine the back of the selected card, and switch it for an ordinary deck with backs to match. You will, of course, need to have two ordinary decks, one red back and one blue, and have them in readiness, one in each side coat pocket.*

I'LL READ YOUR MIND

JOHN CRIMMINS, JR.

Effect: Here is a variation of the "You Do as I Do" card trick that borders on the miraculous. A spectator thoroughly shuffles a deck of cards and steps into a corner of the room. There he turns his back on the performer and the audience, while he fans out the deck. He is invited to select any two cards he likes and to reverse them in the deck.

While the spectator is making up his mind—and incidentally trying his darndest to select the two cards most unlikely to be known to the magician— the performer picks up a second deck and announces that he will likewise turn his back and reverse the same two cards in his deck, that the spectator is now

---

* (Editor's Note: This remarkable card feat has a most interesting history. Research indicates that this feat of causing a mentally chosen card to reverse itself automatically in the deck was first marketed by Bagshawe of London, England, when he introduced his "Reverso" deck. This English deck relied for its working on pairs of cards, set up as described above, but an ingenious and mechanical arrangement was depended upon to hold them together. One card had a small projection on its back that caught into a declivity in the card above it thus causing each pair to slide off the deck as one card. Max Holden, then in England, purchased one of these decks and a short time later introduced the trick to America's magic circles. For quite some time he had such card manipulators as Nate Leipzig and T. Nelson Downs running around in circles, until he finally presented the deck to T. Nelson Downs. About this time Mr. Holden opened the first of his now well known magic stores and featured this deck as one of his most exclusive tricks. Finding that the English make was too difficult to have manufactured, he hit on the idea of holding the pairs together with wax. This was most satisfactory and for years he advertised the trick in his catalog as the "Sympathetic Reversed Cards." In both the Bagshawe and Holden version the deck was held with backs up throughout the trick. Subsequently Dai Vernon was working with the same principle and really popularized the deck. In his version, he used beeswax to hold the pairs together, and treated each card on its back so that he worked with a face up deck. Needless to say, the finesse with which he handled the deck, soon elevated the trick to a place unsurpassed in its field. Paul Fox suggested the variation of using a red and blue backed pack, and then with the advent of roughing fluid Dai Vernon finally perfected the trick as we have it today.)

selecting. When the spectator announces that he is ready, both he and the magician face the audience and fan their decks. Impossible as it seems, both the spectator and the magician have reversed the same two cards. The effect may be repeated immediately with another spectator.

When you consider the startling effect, the absolute fairness of the procedure and the futile effort of the spectator to outsmart the performer, the effect comes pretty near being a perfect mental masterpiece.

Routine: The secret depends entirely upon the use of a "Brain-Wave Deck." However, the cards must all be of one color—not red and blue backed. The first spectator uses his own or any unprepared deck. Ask him which color suit he prefers, red or black. This is important as the Brain Wave Deck only allows showing two reversed red, or two reversed black cards, at the same time. You must, therefore, know the color before you pick it up, so as to fan it correctly. As the spectator turns to face the audience, ask him to announce the names of the two cards. Have him fan his deck to prove it, as you fan your deck to expose the same two cards which you have supposedly reversed.

The effect can be repeated immediately with a second spectator, who selects two cards of the opposite color to those chosen by the first person. All you have to do is to turn over your deck while your back is to the audience.

A PECULIAR HAPPENSTANCE
G. W. LORD AND M. D. OVERHOLSER

Effect: The performer writes a prediction upon a slip of paper which is folded and placed aside. He shuffles a deck and gives it to a person for cutting. The spectator looks at the top card of the deck and puts it face down on the table. Onto it he deals seven cards, and then deals eight cards in a pile for the performer.

The performer picks up his eight cards, remarking that the spectator knows the name of the card at the bottom of his (spectator's) pile, so therefore he will look at the bottom card of his pile—he does.

The spectator shuffles his own pile of eight cards and then also the performer's pile of eight. Each picks up his packet. Both simultaneously deal card after card face down in two parallel rows. The performer then announces the name of the card he looked at in his pile, and asks someone to read his prediction.

It reads as follows: "Your card will be opposite mine."

The spectator then turns face up, one at a time, the cards in the performer's row until he comes to the card looked at previously by the performer. He then is asked to name his card and turn over the pasteboard in his row and directly opposite the performer's card. It is the one he chose.

Method: The deck is both marked and stacked. The performer's shuffle is false, but a spectator may cut. When the performer picks up his pile of eight cards and notes the face card he can compute eight cards back and know the identity of the spectator's noted card. With either of the two rotating suit stacks the spectator's card will be of the same suit as the performer's card. This will aid in the figuring. With the Nikola system the suits will be different, but one who has learned this arrangement should know each card by its number value of from 1 to 52. In such a case, the card the performer notes has its numerical value from which is deducted 8, and the resultant figure translated gives the name of the spectator's card.

After the shuffled packets of eight are dealt in rows opposite each other, the performer can locate the spectator's card, the name of which he now knows, wherever it may be in his row. Then he determines the name of the card in his own row directly opposite the spectator's card and calls that as his noted card. The rest of the effect is automatically successful.

A neat addition to the effect is to have the spectator first cut the deck and pocket the top card without looking at it. Then the trick proceeds exactly as described.

Well marked cards can be secured from most magical marts, or from the many "houses" which advertise gambling ware in the theatrical trade papers and cheap "sensational" magazines. Most of these places have catalogues showing various backs and the systems of marking so you can take your pick.

YOU AND YOURS—ME AND MINE
HERBERT HOOD

You will like this version of "You Do as I Do" effect, if you have the required properties, because the routine requires no exchange of decks.

Effect: Both the performer and spectator shuffle their own decks of cards, secretly remove one card each and reverse it in their own decks. When the decks are ribbon spread across the table, both are seen to have selected the same card.

Requirements: Two decks of cards, one of which must be a marked deck so that the cards may be read from the backs.

Routine: The spectator gets the marked deck and you keep the one that is ordinary. Both of you shuffle well and then put your decks on the table opposite each other—both decks are face down.

Ask him to think of any number, not too large. He announces it aloud. Each of you count off cards together from your own decks until the number is reached. The last card (at number), of each pile, is put aside from the pile onto which the other cards were dealt. Then each of you peek at that card you have selected—something like looking at the "hole card" in a stud poker game.

The performer says, "Put your card back now, anywhere among the others, and shuffle. I do the same." And then, quickly, as an afterthought, say, "I'm sorry, but the cards should be face up in the decks instead of face down. I'll turn around and reverse mine that way—and you do the same, just turn your card over among the others."

You again face each other. You call for a coincidence. Have him spread his pack across the table with the backs up. In the middle there turns up his selected card facing everybody. You spread your deck in the same manner. And the card face up in your deck is the same as his!

Coincidence? No. This time it was simply a case of one marked deck. The spectator gets it and can shuffle as much as he likes. The counting is purely "business." The selected cards are laid aside, and then much ado made of the peeking at them. It doesn't matter what you have. Your ability is used for getting the name of his card from its back. The aftermath allows you to find the duplicate of the spectator's card and turn it over in your own deck.

PARADE OF THE LAMAS

BRUCE ELLIOTT

Out of the hidden and forbidden fastness of Tibet comes the background for this little excursion into improbability. A Lama, to a Tibetan, is a superman capable of little parlor stunts like levitation for an indefinite period, or a stark naked marathon run of hundreds of miles over 20,000 foot high ant hills that make up the Himalaya's. Mental projection of astral images, telepathy, all the things that we in our devious ways attempt to imitate under the guise of magic, are reported to be actualities to these fantastic sorcerors.

Shrouded in Sanskrit are directions for performing these miracles. Since, however, most of the formulae call for a twenty year residence in an isolated cave plus a meager subsistence ration, perhaps it would be easier to call on Sakya-t 'Ubpa and see what we can do with a playing card representation of the "Green Lama."

Effect: Three playing cards, printed as Green Lamas are shown. See the illustration for the type of picture to use. They are placed in a face down row, end to end. On to each are dealt two cards at right angles. Then, to one side, are dealt three indifferent cards in a pile.

The first of the original three stacks is picked up and the Lama card openly pushed between the two other cards. The master, you, mutters "Ommani-padme-hum," (a Tibetan prayer saying, "Hail the shining jewel in the lotus blossoms," and, allegorically, "Greater glory to Buddha.") The three cards are shown to be indifferent to the prayer. But the Lama card has vanished. The off-side indifferent heap is fanned face up and the Lama card is among them.

The second original stack is picked up and its Lama card inserted. In the same manner it is shown to have disappeared, and then revealed to have travelled to the off-side pile. In the last instance, some spectator holds the pack while the Lama again vanishes from its packet. The performer shows the off-side stack now containing all three Lama cards, and all is open for inspection by the unbelievers.

Requisites: Aside from the ability to mumble "Ommani-padme-hum" reverently, one needs only three Lama cards, a simple false count, a double lift, and a bit of faith.

Routine: Put the three Lama cards under the top, indifferent, card of the deck. Double lift and show a Lama card, holding it up. Then pick up the next two cards and show three Lama cards in a fan. Replace them upon deck and deal three cards face down, end to end, from right to left. Off to one side deal, singly and face down, the next three cards from deck. Actually, the first card (right end) of the row is an indifferent card, the next two beside it are Lamas, and the off-side pile consists of two indifferent cards and one Lama card.

Hold the deck in your left hand as for dealing and push a few cards to the right with your thumb. Under cover of this move get the left little finger under the third card. Bring the right hand over, square the bunch of three with the fingers at outer end and the thumb at inner, saying, "We'll put two cards from the deck with each Lama," and the squared bunch is dropped overlapping the left end card in the row on the table.

This action is repeated with the next three (apparently two) cards from off the deck, and they are dropped upon the middle card. On the last card (right end, indifferent) the move is made in the same manner but in this case it is true. Only two cards are squared and dropped upon the card.

Pick up the left end packet with the left hand. Hold it face down with your fingers on one side and thumb on the other. Really there are three, but apparently there are two. The right hand picks up the Lama card, shows, and apparently pushes it in between the left hand cards. It really goes second from the top of the three.

The mumble-jumble now takes place. You may even patter about the Lama's ability to project himself. Display the bottom card, remove it, and put it face up on the table. Show the face of the next card, and, as you reach for it with the right fingers underneath and against its face, the thumb of the same hand pushes back the top card. Thus the face card, with the Lama card behind it, is put face up upon the card already on the table. The last card is turned over to show that the Lama has gone. It is dropped face up onto the others.

The off-side pile is turned up and one Lama card is found there. It alone is dropped face down in the same spot on the table, while the first face up pile just shown is picked up with the right hand, and put face down on top of the two cards, from the off-side pile, which remain in your left hand. This packet of cards is now dropped onto the deck. Then, from the deck, are dealt two cards onto the off-side Lama card.

The next, or middle, packet is handled in the same manner as was the first. But, this time, when you put the shown cards (with Lama concealed) on the deck, either slip the top card to bottom deliberately or make an idle shuffle to accomplish the same result. There is a Lama on top of the deck now, so you double lift and show an indifferent card apparently in that position. Replace the card (pair) and deal off the Lama card onto the off-side pile, face down.

Have a spectator hold the pack tightly. This time you do not show the Lama card as it is put into its group (the last pile, all of which are indifferent cards, and only three) but by this time you have convinced all, at least subconsciously, of your fairness. Build up this finish, bellowing "Om-mani-padme-hum" in a rotund basso, and show the third Lama gone, using, of course, the same manner of moves as used previously, except that this time they are honest. Then fan the off-side group to show all three Lama cards together.*

THE TWIN PRINCESS
WALTER B. GIBSON

All magicians are familiar with the "Princess Card Trick," wherein a card is mentally chosen from a group, and discovered by the magician, after he has placed the group in his pocket. In its simplest form, the trick is done with five cards; in his pocket the performer has four extras. Arranging the shown group in numerical order, he has simply to put it in his pocket, bring out the four extras, one by one, faces down; then pluck the mentally selected card from his pocketed group, as soon as it's named aloud.

The trick always had two recognized draw-backs. First, that the chosen card had to be named aloud, which was not particularly serious. The other was that the extra cards could never be shown after removal from the pocket, which was a serious objection to the trick. It was overcome by DeLand's mechanical version of the trick, with "two way" cards involved, but that didn't satisfy the host of magicians who prefer tricks with a borrowed pack.

Seeking a solution to the problem, I found one, and included it in my "New Magician's Manual." The system was to use five cards that were quite similar, and to have four extras, also similar. That is, all the cards were blacks, and spots, of five, six, seven, eight, and nine denominations. This enabled the magician to finish the trick by casually showing the faces of the extra cards that he removed from his pocket, people taking them to be the originals.

Still, the trick lacked something. Analyzing it, I uncovered an unnoticed objection. It was the use of the pocket. The process wasn't natural. Since the pocket couldn't be eliminated, the answer was to find a *reason* for using it. Obviously, it would be natural to put cards in the pocket, if there was nowhere else to place them. So, the idea struck, to "double up" the trick, using two sets of cards. Needing each hand for a separate action, the magician would logically have to work from his pockets.

This was more than a solution to an old trick. It doubled the effect, as well as baffling people with the use of a greater number of cards. Thus the "Twin Princess," as I shall describe it, is really a worthwhile mystery. Since the reader is already familiar with the principle, I shall concentrate upon method and presentation.

To begin with, I have reduced the trick to a choice of "one in four" instead of "one in five," which speeds the process, and is quite satisfactory, considering that it is a "repeat" proposition. In your right trouser's pocket stow three black cards: a seven, an eight, a nine; two being of one suit, the third of the opposite suit. In the left trouser's pocket, put three reds, a six, a

---

* (**Editor's Note:** This startling stunt can be done with blank playing cards on which you have had printed your picture. Such cards to match your deck may be obtained from any magic dealer. At the finish of the effect, these cards can be left with the spectators as souvenirs and advertisements.)

seven, and an eight, varying the suits on a two to one ratio, as with the blacks.

Now, running through the pack faces up, pick out spot cards of both colors, but make sure that you take four blacks, values six, seven, eight, nine; and four reds, of those same values. Discarding the pack, show the cluster you removed, reds and blacks together; then, casually, sort the reds from the rest.

That done, hand the four blacks to a spectator, faces down, telling him to mix them, then look at one card and remember it, mixing it back with the rest. Or, you can have him deal the cards in a row, glance at one, by picking it up, and then mixing it with the other face down cards.

You make this very fair, by turning your back during the process. You also turn away, to give the four red cards to another spectator, so that he can make a similar "one card" choice. By the time he is ready, the man with the blacks has finished. So, you take the four blacks, solemnly glance at their faces, and nod, as though reading his mind. In going through the blacks, you arrange them in order; six, seven, eight, and nine.

Since the reds are now ready, you turn to get them, and, needing both hands, you show the black packet, and put it in your right trouser's pocket, above the extras there. Go through the glancing process with the reds, fixing them in numerical order, and then, having put the blacks in one pocket, you quite logically stow the reds in the other.

Concentrating, you say "Black," and draw an extra card from the right pocket. Then, remarking "Red," take an extra from the left. Dropping the cards faces down on the table, you continue this alternating process, until you have three black cards in sight, and three red ones. To the man on your right, you say: "There are three of the blacks—and will you tell this other gentleman the name of the fourth—which might be your card?" Note, that he is naming it for the benefit of the other chooser, a fine point of psychology. Your hand is going into your right pocket, and having the four originals there, you easily get the one he names, by simply counting to the right card numerically. But, even here, you have good misdirection, for you are turning to the left, to ask the other man, the name of his card. By then, you have the black card, and are waving it, back toward its chooser, while reaching for the named card in the left pocket, as the man on your left gives it.

Again, the misdirection is perfect, and so is the climax. In drawing the left card, hold it back outward, too. Look from one card to the other; then hand them to their owners, faces in view, showing that you scored a double hit! Then, turning up the three black cards on the table, you say to the first man: "And remember—you chose the card mentally from these four!" Immediately after, you turn up the red extras, and make the same statement to the second man.

Note how easily this all fits. Sevens and eights are always confusing as to suits; sixes and nines, being reversible, are even more so. You have no fives, tens, or other "strangers" to worry about. All that remains is to merely get the cards that you left in your pockets.

Here is an excellent way of doing it. Have a card selected from half of the pack. Bring it to the top, and put that half in one pocket. Do the same with a card from the other half, and put it in the other pocket. Have the cards called by name, or just concentrated upon, and bring them out, simultaneously, a very nice effect. Then, bring out the halves of the pack, including, with them, the extra cards previously left behind.

Note: This is a good committee trick, with two spectators from the audience. You can flash cards faces front, before and after, and in drawing extras from pockets, they can be placed in the hands of your assistants, faces down. But even if they see the faces, they won't be any wiser.

CHERCHEZ LA LADY
JACK VOSBURGH

Here's a little stunt that can be built up through presentation to an effective bit for a mental routine. A similar effect was a favorite with both Sid Lorraine and Ted Annemann.

Effect: Three playing cards, a black Jack, a black King and a red Queen are handed to a spectator. He mixes them and holds them in front of him, fan-wise, with the backs facing you. You or the medium, if she is to do the trick, have stood some ten or fifteen feet in front of the spectator while he shuffled the three cards. Walk towards him, look into his eyes and say, "I am going to guess which is the Queen." When you are directly in front of him, reach up, hesitate, and then grab a card out of the fan, as though doing it impulsively. You get the Queen!

The spectator takes the three cards and mixes them again. He hands them to you behind your back, and again you find the Queen. As a final test, he places each card in a separate envelope, mixes them and hands them to you one at a time. You take each one and hold it above your head. Suddenly, on one envelope, you feel an impulse and announce it to contain the Queen. When the envelope is opened, you've hit it again!

Preparation: Use cards with one-way back patterns. Put a drop of rubber cement on the back of the Queen, and smear it around by rubbing the cement with a paper napkin in a circular movement. When dry the card will have a thin, transparent rubber coating that will not be noticeable and will not hinder the shuffling of the cards. The envelopes are unprepared.

Routine: The first effect is obtained by having the back design of the Queen reversed in comparison with the other two cards. Thus it will be easy to spot in the fan. The second effect takes advantage of the rubber cement spot on the back of the Queen. Just feel for it, and rub off the cement before bringing the card to the front. In the third effect, you hand the spectator one envelope at a time in which to seal the cards. As you hand him the second envelope, take back the first. Do the same with the third envelope. As soon as you get the one containing the Queen, turn it so that its flap faces opposite to the flaps on the other two envelopes. If you hold the envelopes flap side down at the start, this will not be noticed. Let him mix the envelopes, and you take them back, one at a time, hold them over your head and feel for the flap on the Queen envelope. That's all!

OPEN MINDS
AUDLEY WALSH

For a clean cut mental stunt with a borrowed deck of cards, this one will be found hard to beat. It is simple to follow, direct in its action and astonishing to the nth degree.

Effect: The performer hands a deck of cards to a spectator for shuffling, and that person is to think of a three figure number as he mixes the cards. The deck is given a second person who shuffles and also thinks of three figures. The same thing happens with a third person. The performer retrieves the pack, fans through them and removes four cards which he places in a face down row on the table.

Next, in order that the remainder of the pack be kept intact, he puts a heavy rubber band around its width. A fourth spectator is now asked to sign his name across one end of the face card of the deck, in this case we'll say it's the Two of Clubs. Each of the original three thinkers now jots down his mentally chosen figures on the other end of the card, which results in three rows of three figures each. And the fourth person acknowledges his signed card and adds up the vertical columns to reach a total. This he does with the single card in his own hands.

The sum is read aloud. The magician turns face up the row of four cards that he previously took from the deck. They represent the total reached by adding the three numbers thought of by the spectators!

Preparation: The entire problem is one that uses only the cards, a pencil, and a rubber band, that is, as far as the audience is concerned. No pads, slates, or other "outside" devices make their appearance to confuse the issue.

In his left trouser pocket the performer has a half card, half of the Two of Clubs. In his right pocket is a heavy rubber band. Previously he has written at one end of the Two of Clubs in the deck, a dummy problem of three rows of three figures each, scribbling so that each row might be judged as by a different person. This set of figures he has summed up and the answer of 4 figures is remembered. It is suggested that the problem be formed to total 4 figures representing a date of historical importance, such as 1492, etc., so that it cannot be forgotten.

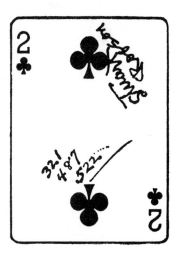

Before going further it can be suggested that, if the performer wishes to present the feat impromptu when using a borrowed deck, he carry half cards from both regular and bridge size decks. The back of the half card is never seen. Just before this effect he does one which requires his absence from the room for a minute or so. During this time, he scribbles the problem upon one end of the proper card in the borrowed deck. Upon his return and at the conclusion of his other trick, he is ready to go directly into this one.

Routine: In the beginning, the deck is mixed by three people who think of numbers at the same time. Upon taking back the cards the performer fans through the deck, removes the four cards to represent the total, one at a time, places them face down in order for revelation later. During this time he locates, and gets to the face of the deck, the written on Two of Clubs. The deck is closed and held in the right hand while the left looks for the rubber band, "to keep the deck intact." It is not in the left pocket so the cards are transferred to the left hand and the right hand dives into the right pocket and brings out the band. However, the actions have been but a ruse, for the left hand has palmed out the half card and has added it to the face card of the pack, covering the end of the card containing the writing. The band is placed around the pack and its width conceals the fact that a half card is on the face. The top and bottom halves of the Two of Clubs match, and who is there to think anything out of the way, or wrong?

A fourth spectator now signs one end of the face card, and of course he is presented the end which represents the genuine card. The writing of the first three people is done on the opposite or fake half.

Now the rubber band is removed with the right hand and given to the left to hold, as the right hand withdraws the genuine card and presents it to the fourth spectator for verification and adding. The rubber band is put back into your pocket by the left hand and the half card goes along with it.

The total is called out, and one by one, in correct order, the face down cards are turned over. The performer has read correctly the minds of the three spectators. And not only that, he has added together their respective numbers to arrive at the inevitable total.

FORCED PROGNOSTICO

SELLERS-EVANS

Effect: The performer shows four cards to be blank on both sides. A spectator selects one, and places it in his pocket. The performer then riffles the ends of a deck of cards, and the spectator inserts his finger into the end of the deck and makes a note of one card. The name of this card is then found written by a spirit hand on the card in the spectator's pocket.

Preparation: The card to be revealed is, of course, forced. For this we use one of Tom Seller's brilliant innovations. Take an ordinary playing card such as shown in Figure 1, and cut a half card as in Figure 2. This second card is more than a half card, as its length is as wide as the width of the whole card. This half card is fixed to one end of the face of the whole card as shown in Figure 3, and glued along its bottom edge to the side of the whole card as per the shaded section in Figure 3.

This prepared card may be on top of the deck, or added after someone has shuffled the deck. A spectator puts his finger into the end of the pack when you riffle it. When this is done you take the top card and insert it into the break, as shown in Figure 4. Now the card below the crosswise card is noted, and this noted card will be the half card—the one you want to force.

So much for the force. The four blank cards used in the effect need no preparation, being but ordinary white cards, blank on both sides. Do not use blank playing cards as they tend to cause the spectators to become suspicious. On one of the blank cards write in ink the name of the force card, and place it, writing side down, second from the top in the stack of blank cards. If you prefer, just sketch the outline of the card instead of writing its name. Both are effective.

Routine: Introduce the four blank cards and proceed to show them blank on both sides as follows: Fan the four cards, writing side down, and then close the fan and hold the cards in your left hand, from above, with the fingers on one long side and the thumb on the other. The fingers curl underneath the packet and thus the little finger is in a position for a simple glide sleight, as illustrated.

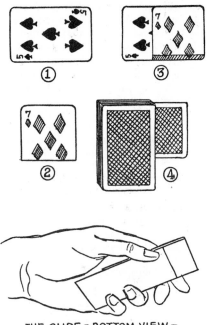

The bottom card of the packet is shown blank by turning the left hand, and then the hand turns back to its original position with the fingers facing the floor. This bottom card is now withdrawn by the right hand and dealt upon the table. In withdrawing this card, its top surface is seen to be blank, thus you have shown both sides of the card. The left hand again turns, showing the new bottom card blank, and then resumes its original position. This time the left little finger, aided as much as is necessary by the other fingers, pulls back the bottom card about an inch and the right hand takes the next card (prediction card) and deals it beside the first card on the table. Thus the prediction card, which you will later force, has been shown on both sides apparently. Now the remaining two cards in the left hand are shown and dealt in exactly the same manner onto the table beside the others. This handling

THE GLIDE – BOTTOM VIEW –
SHOWING HOW BOTTOM CARD
IS DRAWN BACK BY THE
LITTLE FINGER.

of the blank cards is a Val Evans idea adapted from an ancient card maneuver, and fits into this routine in a very natural and offhand manner.

"Point to two cards," says the performer. If the prediction card is one of them he tosses the others aside. If not among them he tells the spectator to throw aside the ones he has indicated. In either case two cards are left and the prediction is one of them. "Give me one card," next says the performer. If he is handed the prediction he continues without pause, "and into which of your pockets do you want to keep it for the time being?" And upon being told, it is put there. If the performer is given the blank card of the two he tosses it aside and tells the spectator to put the card into one of his pockets.

Then follows the noting of a card. The spectator is asked to state whether or not he thinks the performer could have known what he was going to pick. He'll say "no." "In that case," replies the magician, "do you think that there might be the possibility of an invisible spirit knowing at which card you would look?" Such a question will, of course, elicit a negative answer, and it is then that the "spirit" does "prove" his presence by writing or drawing upon the "blank" card in the spectators pocket.

THE DREAM OF A HERMIT

Dr. Jaks

Effect: The performer gives out two decks of cards, still in their original wrappers. One deck has red backs and the other has blue backs. While these cards are being removed from their cases and shuffled, the performer gives a third encased deck to another member of the audience to hold.

The first spectator is asked to select either one of the two shuffled decks for himself and to put it in his pocket. The performer places the remaining deck in his own pocket. Now both the assistant and the performer reach into their pockets, select a card and bring it forth. Without showing what card they have each drawn, they lay them on the table face down. The performer picks up the assistant's card and slides it into the deck in his own pocket. The assistant does likewise with the performer's card. Both now remove their decks and spread them, backs up, across the table. An odd red card is seen in the blue deck, and an odd blue card is seen in the red deck. These are both withdrawn and are found to match! Thus both have selected the same card. This is the first climax.

The performer now turns to the second man who is guarding the odd deck of cards. He opens the case and sets the deck face down on the table. The second spectator then spells out his name, letter by letter, dealing off one card at a time. On the last letter, the card at that position is turned face up and shown. This proves also to be the duplicate of the two cards found the first time!

Preparation: There are several subtle details contained in this method, which make the effect very simple to operate.

First, remove the Four of Diamonds from both the red and blue decks. Put them in your side coat pocket, facing the same way and towards your body. Remember which color is which. An alternate and probably better method would be to use the right trouser pocket. In the latter case, keep the cards at the top of the pocket so that you can pull the pocket out and show it is empty before placing the deck therein. After setting the cards as above, reseal the remaining 51 card decks in their original cellophane wrappers and cases. So far as the third deck is concerned, you can easily set this for the spelling finale just prior to the presentation. As you are using the Four of Diamonds, it's but the matter of a second or two to set this card in position from the top of the deck so that it will spell out to someone's name you know in the audience.

Routine: Bring forth the red and blue decks, have them opened and shuffled separately. While this is being done, pass the third "spelling" deck to the person whose name will spell out the correct card later. Ask him to put it in his pocket for the time being.

The spectator who is going to assist in the trick now selects either the red or blue deck and hands you the remaining one. Instruct him to place his deck in his pocket as you do the same with the deck he gave you. Instruct him to reach into his pocket, withdraw any one card and lay it, without looking at it, face down on the table. You apparently do the very same thing, but actually you bring forth one of the Four of Diamonds, being careful to withdraw the one that matches the deck you have in your pocket. Now, pick up the spectator's tabled card and place it in your pocket, where you immediately switch it for the remaining Four of Diamonds and insert this card into your deck. Do not remove your hand from your pocket yet, for you have to keep the spectator's card separated from the deck. Your assistant picks up your tabled card and follows your example by placing your Four of Diamonds into his deck.

Ask the spectator to remove his deck and spread it face down across the table. You do likewise with your deck, having left the spectator's card behind in your pocket. The two opposite colored cards are removed from each spread and, of course, prove to be the same card.

The second man holding the "spelling" deck, now spells out his name and brings the effect to its climax by turning up the Four of Diamonds on the last letter of his name.

MYSTIC MATCHING
Dan Bellman

I think this version of the "Do As I Do" effect is the only one that allows you to repeat the general effect immediately with the same person, and at the same time "top" the first presentation. It is ideally suited for a mental routine.

Effect: Two packs of cards are shown, a red backed one and a blue backed one. The assistant shuffles one deck, while the performer mixes the other. They now exchange packs, each takes a card from the center, remembers it, places it on top and then cuts it to the center burying it. The decks are again exchanged and each looks for the card he selected in his deck. When they are shown, they are both found to be the same card!

Now the performer offers to repeat the effect. He takes the pack he is holding and places it behind his back. The volunteer now selects any card from the pack behind the performer's back and puts it into his own pocket. The rest of the pack is placed on the table.

The volunteer then holds his pack behind his back, while the performer selects one, and places it face down on the table, or just holds it. The volunteer now squares up his pack, brings it around and places it on the table. When the two selected cards are matched they are found to be the same card! Thus, a climax is built up in a natural fashion and with telling effect.

Preparation: Needed are three decks, plus a set of indexes for the "Cards from the Pocket" trick which are available at all dealers. Set up one of your red decks in the pocket indexes, leave the other red deck in its case, and set up the blue deck in the familiar Si Stebbins order or any other arrangement familiar to you. Pocket the indexes and you're set.

Routine: The cards are removed from their cases and the red backed deck is handed to a spectator. While he shuffles, the performer false shuffles the blue deck. He notes the bottom card and then exchanges decks with the spectator. Each takes out a card, looks at it, puts it on top, cuts the deck and then the decks are exchanged again. Now while the performer is supposedly looking through the pack he now holds (the Si Stebbins set-up deck) for his card, he actually looks for his key card (the one he noted on the bottom of the deck) and starts to remove the card that is in front of the key card. This will be the other person's card, so he pulls it up in the fan a bit. Just before he remove it, he looks through the set-up to find where the spectator's card really belongs and cuts the deck at this point. He then removes the card that is projecting from the fan, which is the spectator's card and, saying that it is his card, he lays it face down on the table. After the cards have been shown alike, the performer replaces his card on top of the pack, and thus the arrangement is preserved and he is ready for the second part.

The performer holds his cards in his hands behind his back, but stands facing the audience. He tells the assisting spectator that he is going to pass the cards from hand to hand and he would like to have the spectator select one. As he runs them from hand to hand, the performer mentally notes each card. As he had glimpsed the bottom card of the deck when placing it behind him he has no trouble starting his count at the top of the deck. Thus, when the assistant takes a card, the performer knows immediately what card it is. (The easiest method of accomplishing this is to use the subterfuge taken from the original Hugh Johnston manuscript on the use of a stacked deck. Mentally designate each of your right four fingers as a suit, in the order the suits are arranged in the deck. As you fan the cards from left to right, merely repeat to yourself the values or numerals as they go by, letting the fingers take their turns in rotation as they pull over the cards from left to right, aided by the left thumb above. Each finger thus comes into contact with a card. When the spectator removes one, the performer knows the value, and whichever finger is on the card at that point automatically designates the suit.)

Tell the spectator to put the card he just drew in his pocket and then take the deck and set it on the table. As he does so, and while you are still facing the audience, you also place one of your hands in your trouser pocket and secure the duplicate card from the proper index. The assistant is now instructed to stand facing the audience with the red pack behind his back. Thus the assistant provides perfect cover for you to bring out the duplicate card palmed in your hand, and then pretend to remove it from the pack the assitant is spreading for you to make a selection.

The rest is showmanship. The performer holds his card with its back to the audience and asks the assistant to lay his deck on the table. The assistant now removes the card he has in his pocket, shows it to the audience, and then the performer turns his card around and shows he has selected the very same card. Nothing could be more direct and to the point!

MENTAL RESCUE

L. VOSBURGH LYONS

Effect: Two spectators, A and B, are seated opposite each other at a table. The performer hands a pack of cards to A, who shuffles and returns the cards face down on the performer's outstretched left hand. The second spectator B then cuts off any number of cards for himself, and the remaining lower half of the deck is placed in front of A. The performer stands at a little distance and directs each to deal five cards, face down, in a row before himself.

Both A and B now select one card from among those in front of him. Each notes his card and is told to remember it. Then each puts his card, face down, in among those spread out in front of his partner. (A's card goes in B's pile, and vice versa.) Each picks up the pile in front of him and shuffles them well.

Both A and B are told to deal their five cards face up on the table. Each in turn is asked if he can positively, and without chance of failure, pick out his partner's selected card. The answer must be "No." It is quite obvious to all that the performer has had no part in the proceedings to date, but he comes to their assistance at this point, and says:

"I have been standing at quite some distance from the table and consequently I do not have any idea as to what your two cards may be. However, I'll try to find them. I must depend upon mental vibrations, your reactions, and what recently has come to be known as extra-sensory perception. Look directly at me, please (to A). In your mind think of the color of your card, now the suit, and now the value. Lastly, repeat the name of your card to yourself silently. Thank you. Was this . . . . your brain picture?"

With this sentence, the performer reaches into B's pile opposite, and picks up the correct card!

Without a pause, the performer turns to B, and says, "Don't bother with the separate features of your card. I must start like that to become en rapport with the conditions surrounding us here. Just look directly at me while I count ten, and imagine your card as a large picture surrounding me." The performer counts quickly and evenly. "Thank you, too. It developed into a very clear image of the . . . . This one right here." The second card is picked from A's group and handed to B.

Preparation: Before the test, select five cards from the deck you will use, any five cards arranged in the Si Stebbins order. I suggest that you always use the same five for speed. Deposit these five cards, in order, in your right trouser pocket, or hang them, faces to body, under the lower edge of your coat on the right side. A paper clip sewn or pinned there will hold the cards very nicely till you need them.

Routine: Spectator A shuffles the deck and places it on your left palm. You turn to your right, swinging the left hand over for B to cut off a bunch. As he does so, your right hand drops to your side and steals the five cards from under the edge of your coat. Now swing back towards the left, pick the remaining half off of your left hand and drop the palmed cards on top of them as you do so. Lay these in front of A. Step away and proceed with the test, as described. When you come to the point where you have to step in, all you have to do is pick the strange card from among A's known set, and the "stacked" card from among B's.

COPY CAT

CHESBRO-THOMPSON

This effect is an easy version of the "You Do As I Do" effect, but avoids the exchanging of the two decks used.

The deck handed to the spectator is arranged in "Si Stebbins" order, or any other favorite stacked manner. The one retained is a "Brain Wave" Deck of all blue backed cards with a short Joker on its face. The face-up card of the tenth pair from the top, or back, is turned face down. The spectator's deck contains no Joker.

Instruct the spectator to duplicate all of your moves, only, however, after you have completed them. Cut your deck several times finally cutting it at the short locator card so it is once more on the face. Have the spectator do likewise. Fan through the cards until you come to the card previously turned face down. Separate the pack at the outer end at this point so that it forms a "V" retaining a grip on both portions, on the top of the lower portions of which is the reversed card. Remove it with right hand, and hold it still face down. Turn the deck over by revolving left wrist (the pack will appear O.K. since there are face up cards on both portions) push the card in between the two packets, square the deck and turn it face down again.

Now, as the spectator repeats your moves with his deck, note the bottom card of top portion as he turns the pack over (he has to turn it toward you!). Figure one ahead in the stacking system and you know the identity of the card he is holding face down.

There is a fifty-fifty possibility that you will have your deck facing the wrong way to show the duplicate of his card reversed. To make the effect 100% workable, just as the spectator begins to fan through his cards, draw off your short face card back up and use it as a pointer to demonstrate where and how his card is to be replaced, etc. This provides plenty of mis-direction if a turn-over of the pack is necessary. In either case, the Joker is then replaced so that becomes the face card of the deck.

Cut your cards several times, finally cutting once more at the short card. Have the spectator cut as many times as you did. Fan through your deck face down until you come to the correct pair, i. e., the one containing the face up duplicate of the spectator's card, separate the cards and throw the reversed one upon the table. When the spectator locates his card, the two cards are seen to be the same.

The trick can be repeated immediately if you replace your card in the deck *face down* at the same spot from which you withdrew it, remembering later where to find it and use it as your reversed card at the beginning of the effect.

Since all of your actions take place first, a presentation can be employed in which you "teach" or "allow" the spectator to do a trick by himself.

GHOSTATIC TOUCH

HENRY FETSCH

Effect: (1) The performer has any person freely select a card from a shuffled red deck, and another person select any card from a freely shuffled blue deck. When the chosen cards are named, it is found that both persons have selected the same cards. Both Jack of Diamonds!

(2) The red deck is shuffled by one spectator and then placed in the performer's inside coat pocket. The other spectator shuffles his blue deck and places it in his own inside coat pocket. This person then reaches into the performer's pocket and removes any card. Now the performer reaches into the spectator's pocket and also removes one card. Once again the selected cards are alike! Both Eight of Spades!

(3) The decks are again shuffled by the spectators, and a deck is placed in each of the performer's side coat pockets. He reaches into both pockets at the same time and removes a card from each deck. These two cards also are alike! Both Four of Diamonds!

(4) The decks are again shuffled and each spectator places a deck in his own side coat pocket. The performer reaches into their two pockets, removes a card from each, and still the two cards are alike! Both Ace of Diamonds!

(5) For the climax, the spectators reach into each other's coat pockets and remove a card. And to the amazement of all, the two freely selected cards are the same! Both Ace of Spades!

Preparation: The following cards and decks are arranged. Once made up they may be used over and over, for the effect will be an outstanding one on any program:

1. A red deck consisting of all Eight of Spades, with a Jack of Spades on top .

2. A blue deck consisting of all Aces of Spades, with a Jack of Spades on top, plus the following three prepared cards at any position in the deck where you may care to place them: The Four of Diamonds, a short card; the Eight of Spades, a long card, and an Ace of Diamonds, a wide card.

3. A second red deck consisting of all Aces of Spades, plus the following two prepared cards at any position in the deck: The Four of Diamonds, a short card, and the Ace of Diamonds, a wide card. Before the routine, this deck is placed in your top right vest pocket.

Routine: Here are the actual mechanics of the effects as described at the beginning.

1. False shuffle and force the top card of each pack. Use any force you can do well.

2. The only card the spectator can possibly select is one of the Eight of Spades. You can find the Eight of Spades in his blue deck easily because it's a long card. At the finish, bring out the deck in your vest pocket instead of the deck they saw you put in your inside coat pocket.

3. Locate both of the Four of Diamonds (short cards), and remove them from your pockets.

4. Locate both the Aces of Diamonds (wide cards), and remove them from the spectator's pockets.

5. This works itself due to all cards in each deck being Aces of Spades.

In conclusion, you will find the routine truly mystifying. The repetition only serves to heighten the effect, and the last coincidence really floors them. Even magicians fail to figure a force deck due to the number of times the coincidence appears. Work this one smoothly and with a bit of speed, and you'll never do a show without it, for it's one of the few card routines that can be presented under any and all conditions.

THE GUIDANCE OF FATE

Orville Meyer

Effect: The performer introduces two decks of cards, one of which he hands to a spectator. Both shuffle their own decks. The performer now covers his deck with a handkerchief, and the spectator cuts off a portion by lifting the portion through the cloth. The card below this cut, i. e., the one on top of the lower half being held by the performer, is laid aside. The spectator now is asked to cover his deck with the handkerchief. The performer cuts off a portion, and the spectator removes the card on top of the portion he retains and lays it on the table with the first card. The two freely chosen cards are now shown and are found to be alike!

This effect is clean cut, and very practical for club audiences. Both shuffles are genuine, the decks are not confusingly exchanged, and the spectator's shuffled deck is never touched by the performer, excepting when he cuts it through the handkerchief.

Requirements: One long card in a shortened deck is all that is needed.

Routine: The pack given to the subject is the short deck with the long card. In your deck, on top or bottom, is a duplicate of this long card. Both decks are shuffled, and you finish your shuffle by bringing your duplicate card to the top, or retaining it there, as the case may be. Cover your pack with an opaque handkerchief, and under cover of this turn your deck face up.

Ask the spectator to lift off a few cards but stop him before he removes this cut completely. This gives you a chance to reverse the lower half (actually the original upper half of the deck) as you ask him if he is satisfied with where he has cut. Then bring out the lower half, have him remove the top (force) card and lay it on the table. You take the handkerchief from him, reach under it, remove the cards he cut off, and toss them on the table turned over.

Now have the spectator square his deck, and, as you give him the handkerchief, note the position of the long card. Have him cover his deck with the handkerchief and hold it out so that you may cut off a few cards, exactly as he did previously. As you cut, you can feel the long card through the handkerchief. Press down on the ends of the long card with your thumb, making a break, and cut off all the cards above it in one packet. This will leave the long card on top of the portion being held by the spectator. He draws this card off and lays it on the table, next to the first card. Naturally, when they are turned face up, they match!

HYPNOSTHESIA

NEWTON HALL

Removing from his finger an odd appearing ring the performer states that it has a peculiar occult power and originally was a valued possession of Merlin of legendary fame. It seems that after looking at the ring, a person sees the last object with which the ring came in contact, regardless of what other object actually is held before him. The performer offers to demonstrate this uncanny situation.

Effect: A spectator is asked forward to act as a custodian of the truth. A pack of cards is mixed, spread across the table, faces down, and the spectator freely pushes out any one. The performer then touches the back of this card with the ring for a second, whereupon the card, without its face being seen, is dropped into a silver box and held by the assistant.

The performer now has a person gaze at the ring for a moment. This person then selects a card from the fanned pack, notes it, and replaces it in the pack.

A second spectator is approached and allowed to look at the ring. The deck is then riffled, he says, "Stop," and notes the card at that place.

The third person looks at the ring, and then cuts the deck at any place. He looks at the card and the performer puts it into his own pocket.

The performer now returns and gives the deck to the assistant holding the box. Each of the three assisting spectators is asked to stand and name the card he selected and looked at. *All three say the Three of Spades.*

Calling attention to the fact that it could hardly be a coincidence that all three should look at the Three of Spades, and that they actually didn't, the performer explains that the ring has caused them to think they did. The performer asks the third man to reach into his (performer's) pocket and remove the card which proves to be a totally different one. Then he tells them that if all three men thought they saw the Three of Spades, that must have been the last thing that was touched by the ring. And the last object touched by the ring was the card that was put in the silver box and has been guarded by the custodian of the truth. This assistant looks over the deck and states that there is no Three of Spades in it. He opens the box and takes out the card for all to see. It's the Three of Spades!

Requirements: A Petrie-Lewis card box and one duplicate of any card in the deck, for instance, the Three of Spades. Empty the right side trousers pocket and place any indifferent card therein with its face to body. Put one Three of Spades face down in the regular compartment of the card box, and leave the false compartment open in the lid. (Annemann suggests that it would be a good idea to carry the ring in this false compartment which will keep the lid from closing and be a good excuse for using the box.) The duplicate Three of Spades is placed on top of the deck, which is left on the table or handy in your side coat pocket.

Presentation: Remove the card box from your pocket, take out the ring and patter along as described. Set the box and ring on the table; pick up the deck of cards and give them a riffle shuffle keeping the Three of Spades on top. Now ribbon spread the deck, face down, on the table and have someone push out any card. Without looking at this freely selected card, it is touched with the ring and then placed into the false top compartment of the card box which is closed and given to the assistant to hold. Drop the ring into your right coat pocket, and pick up the deck of cards.

You now have to force the Three of Spades on three different spectators. For the first person, make the pass and use a straight fan force. If, by chance, you miss, have him pick three or four other cards and lay them all down on the table for the old elimination force. Bring the Three of Spades to the top of the deck again.

For the second person, use the riffle force and slip the top card, the Three of Spades, to the center of the deck as you separate the halves at the point where he inserted his finger. After he replaces the forced card, bring it again to the top and go on to the third spectator.

For this last force, hold the cards face down on the palm of your left hand. The third spectator cuts anywhere he pleases, reverses his cut off portion and replaces it on top of the lower portion. Your left hand, which has been holding the deck, now spreads the cards across the table and the spectator makes a note of the top card of the lower portion, i. e., the first face down card below the string of face up cards. He gets the force card on this, because as you spread the cards you turn your left hand face down to start the spread, which automatically brings the original top card of the deck, the Three of Spades, into the force position, although the spectator doesn't realize it. He naturally thinks the card he looks at is the top card of the lower half of the deck, marked by his own free cut. (This is a perfect force and beautifully deceptive. Ed.)

This third forced card is handed to you and you deliberately put it in your right trousers pocket. As your hand comes out, however, you palm it and return it to the top of the deck.

Now returning to the assistant who has the box, you hand him the deck of cards, minus the top card, the Three of Spades, which you retain in your palm. As you walk away from him, insert your right hand into your side coat pocket, and deposit the palmed card as you bring the ring forth.

Continue with your patter story and have the three spectators stand in turn and announce the name of their individually chosen cards. They all name the same card, the Three of Spades, as already described. Now have the third man reach into your right trousers pocket and remove the card that is there. He brings out an entirely different card than the Three of Spades which he thought he had given to you to put there.

For your climax, have the assistant holding the box lay it down for a second while he looks through the deck for the Three of Spades. After he announces that he cannot find it, he opens the card box and removes the card in question. Obviously it's been there all the time, thus proving your assertion about the influence of the ring!

MENTAL NUMBERS

VINCENT DALBAN

This item forms an effective opening for a mental act and requires but very little preliminary preparation. The effect is based on an idea suggested in Blackstone's "Secrets of Magic." However, it will be seen that a

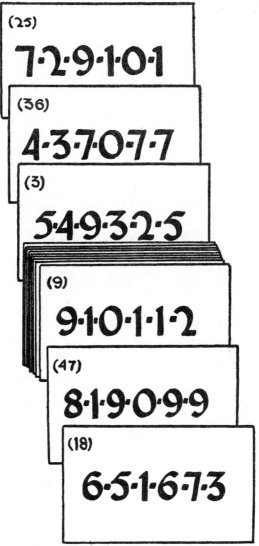

new principle and method of handling is brought into play which will confuse those who may know the older secret.

Effect: The performer shows a packet of cards, say from 50 to 100. Each card is blank on one side; the reverse side carries a six-figure number. The packet of cards is shuffled and several members of the audience each select and retain a card. The performer eventually names the numbers on the selected cards.

Preparation: It is not necessary to memorize any numbers. Each card bears, in addition to the six-figure number, a serial number 1, 2, 3, 4 and so on, in small type on the same side of the card, and it is on these serial numbers that the six-figure numbers are based.

In making up the six-figure numbers, as will be detailed further on, it must be carefully noted that the six-figure number and the serial number from which it is made do not appear on the same card. The six-figure number is always on the card next below (when packet is held number sides downwards). The six-figure number made up from the serial number on the bottom card of packet appears of course on the top card of the packet. From this it will be seen that on a card being withdrawn from the packet, a glance at the serial number of the card next above it will enable the six-figure number of the selected card to be built up and announced. Thus very little memory work is required.

Make the cards as follows: Add 9 to the serial number and reverse the total for the first two figures of the six-figure number. (For example, serial number 36—add 9 making 45 reverse and give 5-4 as the first two figures.) For third figure, add the first two together and give total (if more than 10 drop the figure 1). For serial number 36, 5 plus 4 (first two figures) total 9.

The fourth figure is obtained by adding the second and third. 4 plus 9 equals 13. Drop the 1 and give 3.

The fifth figure is obtained by adding the third and fourth figures. 9 plus 3 equals 12. Drop the 1 and give 2.

The sixth figure is obtained by adding the fourth and fifth figures. 3 plus 2 equals 5.

Therefore the six-figure number made up from serial number 36 is 5-4-9-3-2-5.

In making the cards, number each blank card first with a serial number, 1, 2, 3, 4 and so on, and then thoroughly shuffle them so that the numbers are not in consecutive order. The cards must henceforth always remain in this order and although the packet may be fairly cut, it must not be shuffled, unless falsely so.

Now make up and letter the cards with their respective six-figure numbers as described, being certain that you make up a number from the serial number of one card and put it on the next card below. The accompanying illustration makes this all apparent.

Routine: To present, the cards are falsely shuffled, a quite perfect method being that described in "Extra-Sensory Perception," page 157. A card is withdrawn by a spectator, whereupon the performer cuts the cards immediately above where the card has been withdrawn and, in passing to another person, the index or serial number of the bottom or face card is noted. A second selection is made and the cards are again cut and the key card noted. A third card may be selected if desired, but care must be exercised to ensure that it is not taken from a position immediately following either of the previous two selections.

Remembering the index numbers noted, the performer then puts the packet aside, and returning to the first, then second, and lastly the third person, impressively reveals the number for each. The first can be revealed slowly by holding the spectator's pulse. The second is given in two parts, the first three and last three, the spectator holding his card to back of the performer's head. The last number is given completely at one time, as "Six hundred and fifty-one thousand, six hundred and seventy-three," the spectator having pocketed the card and then concentrates on the number as the performer looks directly at him.

I originally used blank cards (1¾ x 3 inches) for this, but by using your own business cards with name and address on one side, a good thing can be made of it as the cards chosen can then be left with the three spectators. It is no job to make up the two or three missing ones after each performance. As you now know, the serial number gives no clue whatever to the six-figure number on the same card.

Keep your packet of cards in some sort of a case, on the outside of which you have a list of the serial numbers in the order originally set. The missing cards can be replaced without any trouble or searching.

AS IN A MIRROR DARKLY

ROBERT BRETHEN

Here is one of those infrequent ideas well worth the evening's labor to make up.

Effect: The performer writes a prediction on a slip of paper and drops it into a hat. He next introduces a deck of cards, shuffles them and asks a spectator to think of any card. Fanning the deck before the spectator, he is asked to point to his mentally chosen card. This card is deliberately withdrawn and dropped, face down, into the hat with the prediction slip. When the name of the card is announced, a second spectator removes the card and the prediction slip from the hat and finds that they both correspond. The performer has, therefore, succeeded in predicting a card that was merely thought of!

Preparation: Secure a new deck of regular (not bridge) size cards, several packages of cigarette papers, and paste-pot and pen and ink. Seat yourself at a well lighted table, and on 53 papers write in ink the names of the 52 cards and the Joker, such as, "The thought of card will be the ...." These papers are folded, writing inside, once each way.

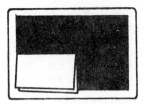

As each paper is so prepared it is secured by a daub of paste, no larger than what can be applied with the head of a pin, to the lower right corner of the back of the card to which it refers. The illustration will make this part clear. The extra Joker or Score card is used to back up the deck and conceal the last paper. The use of cigarette papers keeps such a prepared deck from being too bulky, and, of course, the faces of the cards are well mixed. Now follow the presentation from start to finish and see for yourself how clean cut and direct this mental effect is.

Routine: Writing a prediction upon a slip of paper, drop it, after folding, into a deep dish or hat. However, the paper is retained in the hand and is left in the pocket as you immediately reach for the deck in its case.

A spectator is asked to step forward. Stand at his left. Tell him that you are thinking of a card in the deck and that he is to look you directly in the eye and remember well the first card that enters his mind. Impress upon him that he is not to change his mind once that he has an impression.

You remove the deck from the case which is tossed aside. Step forward a bit and turn towards the spectator which action turns your back somewhat to the audience. Fan the deck from left to right with the faces towards the spectator. He looks for the card of which he is thinking, and at the same time the audience sees quite a little of the backs of the cards.

It is possible to further heighten the assumption that all is fair by using the subtle Hindu Shuffle described of late in several books on cards and explained fully with effects in Jinx No. 56. The deck is first shuffled with faces showing and front of deck held downwards with the attached papers at that end. The audience sees cards genuinely mixed, and several times the performer can show the backs (?) of the cards, saying, "The 52 backs are mixed also but as they all look alike I have my subject think of a face so that there can be no mistake."

When the deck is fanned towards the subject he touches his card when he sees it. The performer immediately pulls it upwards in the fan about half an inch, saying, "This is the card you thought of while I was concentrating?" As he acknowledges the statement, or query to be true, you step towards the hat which is behind and to the right of the spectator. As you do this, say, "Then tell everybody what card flashed into your mind. I'll put it here with the prediction I originally wrote for you."

You have cut the deck to bring the selected card to the back and you now are turned so that the face of the deck is towards the audience. At this point it is not necessary to be finicky or too particular about the audience seeing the cards. Remember that they have seen the deck fanned, and seen the spectator find his card. It is therefore impossible for you to do anything underhanded with the cards now. The card is withdrawn, keeping the paper attached covered with the fingers of the right hand and dropped into the hat, and at the same time the paper slip is dislodged by a squeeze between fingers and thumb.

Pick up the hat with the same hand and give it to another spectator nearby. Ask him to name and show the card which the spectator thought of. Then have him remove the paper and read aloud what you predicted.

Each performer will work out his particular method of presentation, I know, but it is suggested that you first try it as given here.

For those who use only this one effect in their program which requires cards, the deck may be recased and put out of the way. For those who wish to continue with some other effect, there is ample opportunity for an exchange of the deck during the interval when the spectator takes the card and paper from hat to read.*

NEW $1000 TEST CARD LOCATION
Annemann

Effect: For the first part of this effect do Brethen's "As In a Mirror Darkly," described above. Then announce that what you have just done was a test of prophecy, and that now you would like to show a test of mindreadinging. Hand the deck of cards to someone, ask him to shuffle them, cut them and then select one card. All this time you have had your back to him. Ask him to hold the selected card to his forehead and to concentrate on it. You turn around and, walking up to him and placing your finger tips on his forehead, you name the card!

Preparation: Have another deck of cards, with backs to match the "Brethen Deck" on your table with the rest of your apparatus. This deck is stacked according to your favorite system, Si Stebbins, etc.

Routine: Remove the Brethen deck from its case and toss the case onto the table, close to the stacked deck. During the finale of the Brethen trick, step back to the table, lay your faked deck down behind a crumpled handkerchief and, at the same time with your left hand, pick up the stacked deck and the case. You now are facing the audience at the very conclusion and excuse your assistant.

Explain that you have shown a test of prophecy, although the critical people before you might not believe in that solution, and say that it was merely a matter of your will forcing the thought upon the spectator's mind. Put the deck into the case as you say this, and then decide to show how it is possible to read the mind of some willing subject.

Toss the encased deck into the audience and ask whoever gets it to come forward. He removes the cards and gives them a shuffle, but you hurry up the procedure to prevent the mixing of more than a few cards by saying, "Put the deck face down on your left hand." Then, as an afterthought, say, "You've shuffled the deck—now give it one complete cut."

Continue, "Look at the top card, whatever it may happen to be. Your selection has been made by chance with no conscious liking for any card, or my will-power influencing you. (Your back is turned during the cutting and picking off of the card). Hold the card against your forehead with your right hand covering it completely." Now you turn around and approach him.

* (Note by Annemann: The self contained feature of Mr. Brethen's deck carries this mental effect quite a distance beyond any of its predecessors. When body work can be eliminated, it always helps both in presentation and serviceability.)

Take the remainder of the deck from him and toss it on to the table. In doing so you glimpse the bottom or face card, count one ahead in the system, and you know what he is holding. Touch his forehead with your finger tips, and slowly reveal the color, suit and value of the pasteboard. Have him acknowledge that you are correct with each step.

If wrong on any one of them, say that you won't guess, and that he isn't thinking hard enough. Hand him back the deck for a cut and a second selection. This never will fail twice, once you have become acute at letting a person shuffle and then stopping him by giving additional directions. I first published the idea in slightly different form back around 1932 and it has been featured by many performers since, especially the late Nate Leipsiz. However, you take it for what it is worth to you, and I suggest it as a finish to the Brethen mystery so that the deck is handled and shown to be quite unprepared.

UTILITY ROUTINE
J. G. THOMPSON, JR.

Effect: The performer writes a prediction on a slip of paper and lays it aside temporarily. One spectator selects a card from a well-shuffled pack and remembers it. A second spectator withdraws a card and remembers the number of spots on it. The deck is now divided equally and the first spectator takes one half, the performer the other. The performer places his half in his pocket and the spectator looks through his half for his card, but can't find it. A third spectator puts his hand in the performer's pocket and finally selects a card as performer counts up to the selected number. This card is withdrawn and proves to be the selected card. The performer's prophecy is also correct, as is the number to which he counted.

Requirements: A "single ender" deck of cards with 26 duplicates of one card cut short and with matching backs. For the sake of clearness let us suppose that the duplicate cards are Aces of Diamonds.

Preparation: Stack the deck in your favorite order such as "Si Stebbins" or "Eight Kings," being sure that the back designs of the deck all point in the one direction. Cut the cards so that the Ace of Diamonds is on top, and remove it. Now cut off 25 cards and place them in your upper right vest pocket.

Reverse the order of the remaining 26 cards, so that what was the bottom card now becomes the top one. Place a duplicate short Ace of Diamonds between each card, with the result that you have assembled a typical "Svengali" deck in which the 26 ordinary cards are prearranged in your favorite order.

Presentation: On a slip of paper write, "The Ace of Diamonds will be selected." Fold it and lay it on the table in full view. Remove the deck from its case, false shuffle it several times and have a card chosen by riffling the end of the pack for a spectator to insert his finger and withdraw a card. He will, of course, get a force card, the Ace of Diamonds.

As the card is taken out, the portion of the deck above it is cut off and a second person asked to look at the card just below the first one that was removed. The spectator is to remember it as a number only, rather than as a card, i.e., the Nine of Hearts will represent the number 9, the Queen of Clubs, the number 12, etc., paying no attention to the suit. While this is being done, and both cards are being returned, secretly note the value of the card on the face of the cut-off portion in your right hand. Counting one value backwards in the stacking system, the performer immediately knows the value of the card chosen by the second person. The cards are returned to their original positions and the top portion is dropped on top and the deck is squared.

The deck is handed to the first person who is asked to deal the cards into two face-down piles, one card at a time to each pile. This action separates all the Aces of Diamonds into one pile, and the ordinary cards into the other pile, at the same time reversing the stacked arrangement. The first spectator is now asked to indicate a pile, and the ordinary pile is forced on him.

He is told that with 26 cards out of 52 he must stand a pretty good chance of holding his card. He is to fan through and see if it is there. It is not, so the packet is taken from him and placed aside for the time being.

A third spectator is now requested to lend a hand. The pile of 26 Aces is picked up, still face down, and placed by the performer into his own inside coat pocket. The second spectator is asked to concentrate upon the number he has in mind. The third assistant is told to put his hand into the performer's pocket, and to grasp a different card for each number the performer calls out. He is to drop that card as the performer calls another number, then grasp another card, and to continue doing this as long as the counting continues so that when the performer stops counting he will be holding but one card. When the selected number is reached the performer stops counting, and tells the assistant to withdraw the card he is then holding and place it on the table, face down.

As the performer turns to the second spectator to ask if that is the number he has in mind, his left hand apparently removes the remainder of the cards from the inside coat pocket. Actually, however, the performer removes the packet of 25 ordinary cards from his upper vest pocket where they have been from the start. These are laid on top of the pile lying on the table.

Having received a confirmation from the second spectator that it was the correct number, the first spectator is asked to name his card. He answer, "The Ace of Diamonds." The third man turns over the card he withdrew from performer's pocket and finds that it is the Ace of Diamonds.

Congratulating the third man upon his success, the performer remarks that he will have to be pretty good to top this feat, but that he thinks he has done so. Now have the prediction slip opened and there is the correct prophecy of the Ace of Diamonds.

Add the Ace withdrawn by the third spectator to the top of the deck, and you have a full pack of cards which may be casually shown all different, yet which are now arranged in your favorite stacked order.

Need we mention that some tricks with a set-up deck may now be performed; then a few with the "one way backs"; and as a final control there's still the "short" Ace for a key card effect!

ONLY AN IMAGE

Eddie Clever

This effect will be found to leave a striking impression and, at the same time, will create unusual interest. In effect you ask everyone present to think of a card while you pass around a small pad upon which several people write the names of cards of which they are thinking. Someone else takes the pad, secretly crosses out any one of the cards listed, tears off the page and puts it in his pocket. You now state that you will attempt to take a thought photograph or thought image of the card which has been crossed out. Showing a blank playing card, you place it face down on a spectator's palm and ask him to place his other hand over it so that it will be completely isolated. The person who crossed out the card is asked to concentrate on it and to try to visualize it as clearly as possible.

After a moment, the blank card is looked at and a faint impression of the Ace of Spades is found on the card's face. The person who has been concentrating says that is incorrect, whereupon you ask who was thinking of the Ace of Spades. Someone acknowledges this card and you request him not to think of it so intently, as he is shutting out the influence of the right card and is confusing the experiment.

The ghostly Ace of Spades is now placed in a small envelope so as to further isolate it, and given back to be held by the assisting spectator. This time when it is looked at, a clearer impression of another card has taken the place of the Ace of Spades, and this new card impression is found to be the correct one.

Requirements: A small pad without cardboard back; six playing cards including the Ace of Spades; five double pay envelopes; a pencil with a good hard rubber eraser. Your preparation consists in writing the names of five of the cards, in different style handwriting, on the top page of the pad, then reversing the pad so that the bottom, blank page becomes the top sheet of the pad in working. Now take five of the cards, excepting the Ace of Spades, and rub them over lightly with the eraser till the spots become somewhat faint and ghostly. This clever idea was originated by Larsen and Wright in their book, "Take A Card." Mark an X with your pencil on the upper right hand back corner of each card. Place these cards in the back section of your five double envelopes and put them in your right coat pocket in a known order. Bridge size cards fit the usual drug envelopes which should be used, although in some cases you may have to trim the sides of the cards a bit so that they will slide in and out of the envelopes with ease.

Take the sixth card, the Ace of Spades, and erase it until it is even more faint than the others but still capable of being seen for some distance. Lightly daub two opposite corners of the face of the Ace with diachylon and stick it to the back of a blank face card. Place this double card in a card case which has a cover design matching the backs of the cards used. If you can't find such a case, just take the Joker from your deck and paste it on one side of the case, back out, and you are set. In the corners and center of the design on the card case smear a goodly quantity of diachylon. Place the case in your left coat pocket, or set it on the note pad on your table.

Routine: Ask everybody present to think of a card. This will make certain that one or more in the audience will think of the Ace of Spades! With pad in hand, blank side up, pass among the spectators and have five people write the names of their thought of cards on the blank, top page. Many times the Ace of Spades will be one of these cards, but it doesn't matter as it is just as startling when someone else is found to be thinking of it.

In going to the sixth person, the pad is turned over and, of course, one of the five forced cards is crossed out. You have turned your back as this is done. Now ask the person to tear off the sheet and keep it. There is no danger of his turning the pad over. However, if you are a little skittish, just tear off the force sheet yourself and hand it to the person to cross out a card and keep.

After the card is crossed out, you remove the blank card from the card case and show it. You are holding the card case in your left hand, so you lay the blank card on top of it (over the design side) as you mark and X on the card's back in the upper right hand corner. To steady the card case while you are marking the card, you have inserted your left fingers into the case. Now press down on the back of the blank double card which will cause the blank card to adhere to the back of the card case. The top card (the faint Ace of Spades) can now be pushed off with the thumb, and the card case is tossed aside and out of the way. This is a perfect get-away. Place the card on someone's hand and have him cover it with his other hand.

The person who crossed out a card concentrates. When the apparently blank card is turned over and shown, a faint impression of the Ace of Spades is seen. Ask if it is the right card, and allow it to be passed around. The person concentrating will disclaim this card. Say, "I seem to feel conflicting thoughts. Who has been thinking of the Ace of Spades?" When someone acknowledges this card, ask him to banish the thought of it from his mind for the time being. If, by chance, no one does acknowledge it, just remark that someone must have been thinking of it and has now changed his mind. Rarely, however, will this be necessary. Now say, "To make sure we don't go wrong again, what was the card you crossed out. The . . . . ? Thank you, Now will everybody please think of that one card. This time we'll isolate the card a little better."

Remove the correct envelope from the pocket and seal up the Ace. After a moment, tear off the end, pull out the other card half way and let a spectator remove it. This time a better impression is seen of the correct card, while the faint impression of the first card has vanished.

This is almost a card trick without cards and makes a stunning spirit test. One might ask why not have 52 cards in envelopes, but such a thing has been tried and the packets are too bulky to be practical.

Editor's note: Ted Annemann used this trick with tremendous effect. It is one of the most intriguing and provocative tests of modern mentalism. With proper presentation it can be made one of your most talked about effects. Unlike its bigger brother, the Spirit Paintings, this trick can be done close up for intimate audiences—and is all the greater for it. It is an illusion in miniature, and is definitely different. We urge you to try it!

CRYSTAL-VISO

DR. JAKS

Effect: The performer hands a spectator a deck of cards, asks him to shuffle them and then select any card he likes while he still has the deck in his own hands. The performer now turns his back and requests the spectator to hand him the selected card behind his back. Turning sideways to the audience, so that they may see the card is still in his hands, the performer reaches for a crystal ball on his table. He holds this in front of him with his free hand and by looking into it divines the name of the selected card.

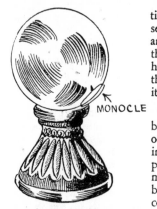

MONOCLE

The crystal ball is handed for examination and, when it is returned, the performer sets it in its base on the table. He now has another card selected, after which he picks up the ball and stand and going to a likely subject has him gaze into the ball. Shortly the image of the card becomes visible and this person names it correctly!

Preparation: A deck of cards, a crystal ball and stand, and an ordinary celluloid monocle upon the center of which is written, in index form, the name of a card. For our purpose we'll use the Two of Clubs, so on the monocle inscribe the figure 2 with a Club spot below it, just as it would appear on the index corner of a playing card. Now file notches around the edge of the monocle, so that it will be easy to palm, and place it in your right coat pocket.

Routine: Let the spectator take the deck in his own hands and select a card. Turn your back and ask him to hand you the card. Turn to face the spectator and tear off and finger palm the index of the card in your right hand. Pick up the crystal with your right hand, turn sideways to the audience so they may see the card you are holding, with the torn corner covered by your left fingers, glance into the crystal and reveal the card from the palmed index. Bring the card around to the front, show it and pass out the crystal for examination.

Reach into your right coat pocket, deposit the torn corner and palm the monocle. Pick up the deck of cards, bury the torn one you are holding and set the deck down. Then take back the crystal ball and set it in the stand, leaving the monocle under it as in the illustration.

Now force the Two of Clubs and have the person put it in his pocket. Pick up the ball and stand and go over to one of the guests. Ask him to gaze into the ball and tell everyone what he sees. He names the Two of Clubs! You can now pass the ball out with your right hand as your left palms the monocle.

What makes this such a nice effect is that the monocle cannot be seen through the ball, and the writing on it looks as if it were really inside the crystal. The slight curvature of the monocle aids also in keeping it close to the ball.

"BEFORE YOUR EYES" BUSINESS CARD

CHARLES NYQUIST

For those who liked "Before Your Eyes," page 168, then here's an impromptu method that makes a pocket trick of this effect. Use your own business cards instead of a slate. Write the words, "Ten of Hearts," on the back of the card in black crayon, spacing them as in the slate effect. Switch this card for one prepared according to the original trick with Frick & Fleming's "It's A Pip" liquid. Stick this card in your upper, outside coat pocket leaving a good two-thirds of it in view (the switch could be made at this point). Now force the Ten of Hearts on someone, and then take card out of breast pocket to show your prediction. The spirits evidently have not answered as yet, so just rub your thumb over the card and your message disappears leaving the correct name on the card! The spectator, of course, keeps the card as a souvenir and as an ad for you.

CONTROLLED LUCK

NEWTON HALL

Effect: Two spectators are chosen from the audience, and to one is handed a hat full of numbered cardboard squares. The performer offers these for examination and explains that they are numbered from 1 to 52. The assistant is told to mix them thoroughly, and from this point on the performer never touches them again.

Now a pack of cards is given to a second spectator to be shuffled, and he is asked to stand to one side of a table. The first spectator holding the numbered squares stands at the opposite side of the table. The performer now moves away about ten feet, stands facing both assistants, and announces that he will write a prediction about events to happen. This prediction he writes, either on a pad or on a business card which he has just borrowed.

The spectator with the cards we will designate as "A," and the spectator with the numbered squares as "B." "A" is now directed to draw the cards off the deck, one at a time, to hold them up before his eyes and to look intently at the face of each card. Then he is to drop it face down on the table without mentioning what card it is. Simultaneously, as "A" holds each card up, "B" reaches into the hat and draws out a number which he calls aloud.

This procedure goes on until the performer calls, "Stop." "A" is now holding a card and "B" a number. The performer steps forward and hands his prediction to a third spectator who reads it. The prediction says:

"When 'B' calls the number twenty-six, 'A' will be looking at the six of Spades."

Spectator "B" has, of course, just called the number 26 and holds it in his hand, and spectator "A" holds up his card for all to see. This is the climax—it is the Six of Spades! This makes a new and different effect, and the best part of it is that all the numbered squares and the cards may be examined and will be found to be unprepared in any way.

Requirements: The cardboard numbers are without preparation, and the spectator who has charge of them draws them freely from the hat. Some performers may prefer to use wooden counters numbered from 1 to 52, something like those used in the game of Lotto. The deck used is a Bicycle League Back deck, at the center of which is a three-wing design that makes a perfect reverse mark readable from a distance of ten to twenty feet. However, there are decks on the market now with picture backs that make excellent reverse designs without being too obvious.

Beforehand, the deck is set with all backs pointed one way except for one card which the performer knows. This is the predicted card. The only necessary gimmick is one of the now popular thumb writers sold by all dealers.

Routine: Follow it as already described with the performer giving the cardboard squares into the keeping of one spectator, and the deck of cards to another. As performer hands out the cards, he gives them a little overhand shuffle which will serve to "force" the spectator to mix them the same way without disarranging the backs. While the first spectator is looking over the numbered squares and the second fellow is shuffling the cards, the performer picks up or borrows a calling card, affixes the thumb nail writer in place and steps away a bit ready to write his prediction. (It might be mentioned here that Haden's "Swami Holdout," which delivers and does away with your thumbnail writer, can be used here with telling effect. This pencil holdout may be obtained from any dealer.)

To continue, the performer explains what's to be done; then writes his prediction, but leaves out the number. He puts the pencil in his pocket, holds the card in his hand with the prediction towards him, and stands watching the procedure with as much interest as the rest of the audience. Spectator "B" is calling a number for each card spectator "A" holds up and looks at, and the performer is watching for the reversed card to show up. The moment it pops up, he calls out, "Stop," and at the same time fills in the number just called with his thumbnail writer in the space he had left vacant in his prediction. Stepping up to a third spectator, the performer hands him the prediction card and asks him to verify what he has written. This person reads aloud what performer has written and the person with the deck turns over the card he is holding. Both the card and the number called coincide with performer's prediction!

A MENTAL TEST REVAMPED
HERBERT HOOD

Effect: The performer hands a pack of cards to the spectator with the request that he fan it and choose one card mentally. He is then given a slip on which to write the name of the card. This slip is burned and the mentalist picks up the deck, fans it, draws out a card and lays it on the table. The mentally selected card is named, and the one on the table is turned face up and found to be it!

Routine: In your left coat pocket have a deck of cards and a match or two. Give the pack to a person with the request that he look them over and merely think of one. Take back the deck and put it in your pocket again.

Hand him a slip of paper with the request that he write down the name of his thought-of card. Then he is to fold the paper once each way. You take it from him, holding the closed corner of the doubly folded paper to the upper left and tear the paper through center the long way. Put the outside or right-hand section in front of the other piece and tear these in half. Put the right hand pieces in front and the left thumb draws back with the folded middle of the slip still untorn. The right fingertips take the loose pieces in view, and deposit them on an ashtray, as the left goes to coat pocket, leaves the torn-out center and brings out a match. The match is given to the writer to burn the pieces.

Now, as the paper burns, your left hand drops to your pocket and opens out the torn center portion of the slip against the face of the pack. Bring out the pack slightly spread, and fan it towards you. Pretend to look over the card, as you read the writing on the torn center piece. Now draw out the correct card and place it face down on the table. Return the rest of the deck to your pocket together with the paper. The thought-of card is named as you turn over the one you placed on the table, which proves to be the correct card!

This will be found as fine a way as any of doing a "thought card" trick without impressions, switches, guesswork, pumping, or preparation of any sort.

DIABOLICAL INFLUENCE
Harris Solomon

Of all the bare-face swindles to cross my path, I consider this original effect of Mr. Solomon's worthy of the highest award. I only fear the reader will think it all too simple, and not give due consideration to the effect upon the witnesses. I believe it to be the acme of drawing room conceptions.

Effect: The performer has a deck of cards, a gummed sticker, a pencil and a piece of paper. He starts by taking a card from the deck, for instance, the Two of Diamonds, on the face of which he makes a notation and covers the writing with the sticker. Asking someone for his initials, they are written on the sticker, and the card is placed face down on the table. Fanning the deck, a spectator selects and pockets a card. Placing the deck on the table, the performer leaves the room from where he directs the proceedings.

Someone is asked to call out a number from 5 to 50. Whatever the number may be, he is asked to count down in the deck to that position and remember the card. The performer then tells him to shuffle the deck again, and to write the name of the card looked at on the piece of paper.

Another person is now asked to name any card that comes to his mind, and this is also written on the paper under the name of the first card.

Lastly, a fourth person is requested to name any three numbers from 1 to 100 and, after doing so, he is asked to write them on the paper directly below the names of the two cards.

The performer now suggests that the deck be squared following a good shuffle, and be placed face down on the table. On top of the deck is to be placed the sticker card, also face down. The tabulated paper is to be turned over with the writing side down.

Reentering the room, the performer picks up the deck and, after asking if his requests have been followed, turns the top sticker card face up on the table and, on either side of it are dealt the next two cards face down. The first spectator, who counted down to a number, names his card, and the performer turns up the first of the two face down cards and it's the correct card! The second person, who mentally selected a card now names it, and the performer turns up the other face down card, and that, too, is correct! Next the performer looks at the person who has a card in his pocket and names it correctly! Lastly, the person who wrote the three numbers is asked to add them and announce the total. The initialed sticker is torn off of the Two of Diamonds, and the performer is found to have correctly predicted the sum!

Preparation: The only things needed are two duplicate decks of cards, two stickers, a pencil and a sheet of paper. The two decks must be stacked alike. Use your favorite system, or shuffle one deck and then arrange the other deck in the same order. On the top of each deck have the Two of Diamonds, followed by a card you know. Keep one deck and one sticker in your pocket. The audience is not to know of this deck.

Routine: Come forward with the other deck, remove the Two of Diamonds and pretend to write a prediction on its face. Cover your prediction with the sticker by moistening only the edges of the sticker, so that it may be removed easily later. Lay this Two of Diamonds to one side, face down, on the table. Write someone's initials on the sticker. Force the next card, the one you know, and have it placed in someone's pocket. Put the deck on the table and leave the room.

The moment you are out of sight, remove the other deck from your pocket together with the sticker. Write on the sticker the same initials you noted on the sticker which you stuck to the card in the other room. Next a number is named aloud and while it is being counted to, you do the same with your duplicate deck and remove the card. When a card is named, remove that also from your deck. When the three numbers are called out, add them quickly and write the total on your Two of Diamonds. Now stick your duplicate sticker over this number. All of this will take but little time and you will have ample opportunity while the folks in the other room are noting the same information on the sheet of paper.

Before you reenter the other room, remove the top card of your deck (the duplicate of the card forced) and place it in your right pocket. Place the deck of cards in an upright position in your left pocket. Now palm the two duplicates of the selected cards, in the order in which they were chosen, with the sticker card as the top card of the three.

When the folks in the other room announce that everything is in order and the deck has been squared up, you enter, move directly to the table and pick up the deck, adding the three palmed cards as you do so. Ask if everything has been followed. As you ask, turn over the top card with sticker and lay it face up on the table. This is a subtle point for they have all seen the sticker card on top a minute before! The initials also are another misleading factor. Then deal the next two cards, face down, one to the right and one to the left of the face up card. As you ask for the name of the first card counted to, your left hand drops the deck into your left pocket so that it lays on its side. At the same moment your right hand turns up the first face down card. Ask for the name of the second card and turn this one up also. Then turn to man with the card in his pocket and name the card. Next ask to have the numbers added. While this is being done, you take the duplicate deck (the upright one) from your pocket, shuffle it carelessly and lay it on the table. When the sum is announced, have someone pick up the Two of Diamonds, remove the sticker and your prediction is found to be correct. Everything may now be examined, and when the first selected card is returned, the deck will be a complete one.

WEIRD WIRE

ANNEMANN

This is one of those ingenious effects of the type that Ted Annemann revelled in. It's the perfect phone test and is completely inexplicable to laymen and magicians alike. However, the simplicity of the code used makes it an ideal two person mental test for nothing need be memorized—the medium relying solely on a short printed list for her information.

Effect: The performer offers to try a thought projection test over the telephone, and before he commences he gives the medium's telephone number to the person who is to act as the subject. The performer then draws a series of five extra sensory perception symbols (see "Yggdrasil" on page 241) on a piece of paper, and asks the subject to make a mental note of but one design. As soon as the subject decides upon one, he picks up the phone himself and calls the medium. She correctly names the symbol selected!

The subject is then invited to try another test. He selects several playing cards from a deck, looks up and encircles any word in a magazine, and then calls the medium again. She asks him to concentrate on the word, then she names it! When he admits that she is right, she follows right along and discloses the names of the cards which he selected, as well!

So much for the effect, which is a stunner in that it may be done impromptu at any time. Of course, I have already tipped my hand by mentioning a code in the opening paragraph, but frankly it is very simple and easy to work. It's the combination of drawings, word and cards that serves to make it look complicated to the audience, and it is these very factors that creates the mystery by keeping the subjecs mind busy.

The E.S.P. Symbol Projection

The five designs you use are those made famous by Prof. J. B. Rhine of Duke University in his extra-sensory perception experiments. In order they are: A Circle, a Cross, a set of Wavy Lines, a Square and a Star.

To start, you draw these designs on a sheet of paper. Ask the subject to look them over as long as he cares to, and finally choose any one. If he takes one of the first three, you ask him to call your wife, or the person who is acting the part of the medium, and ask her what is on his mind. If he takes one of the last two, you tell him to call and ask her which one of the drawings he is thinking about. Thus he either gives away the fact that he has something on his mind (symbols 1, 2 or 3), or that he is thinking of a drawing (symbols 4 or 5). This detail takes care of segregating the symbol cards into two groups, and is the first thing the medium must know.

If the subject mentions drawings, the medium starts by telling him it is some kind of a simple diagram. She knows its either 4 or 5, but needs a little more information to determine which one. If he asks "which," or mentions "drawing," she continues.

She asks him to think of it and then tells him he'd better draw it quite large on a piece of paper and look at it intently. He can either reply that he has already done so, or take a few seconds out to do it. His reply or action gives a further clue. She knows it is one of the symbols in the second set (4, 5), and if he has already drawn it, the answer is 4. If he hasn't drawn it, the answer is 5. In such a case she lets him do it, tells him to concentrate, and then reveals the identity of the drawing he has made.

If, on the other hand, the medium determines from the opening conversation that she must work in the first set (1, 2, 3), she immediately suggests drawing it. If it is not already on paper she knows it to be 3. But if he replies that he has drawn it, she knows it to be 1 or 2. And then, to get the final result she asks him to burn it. And he either has done that very thing, or hasn't. If he says he has, the answer must be 2. If he takes time out to do so, it must be 1. We have used figures in explaining this, but, naturally, the medium's talk is always about the drawings themselves. Here is the set-up which the performer knows and which the partner has beside the phone.

(1) Circle—what? On paper—not burned.

(2) Cross—what? On paper—burned.

(3) Wavy lines—what? Not on paper.

(4) Square—which? On paper.

(5) Star—which? Not on paper.

The performer, on the scene, has operated a bit backwards according to the chart. Thus if the "cross" were to be chosen he would ask the person to draw it on a sheet of paper, look at it for a full minute intently, and then burn it and imagine he can see the diagram in the smoke. Then he would be told to call up the psychic and ask her what's on his mind.

On the other hand, should the Square be selected, he would be told to draw it, concentrate upon it, and then be told to call and ask which of the drawings he is thinking about.

The beauty of using the five Rhine symbols for the test lies in the fact that they are a logical group as a whole. A query as to which is being thought about does not seem to be strange, as it might if any other small group of unrelated objects were used.

If once out of a hundred times, something goes amiss and the subject's initial request is wrong or not clear, the medium has an even chance of things working out as she continues. If it hits, all well and good—but if she misses, she immediately says she's sorry and "will you please ask the performer to try something else with you and call me back? I've had a lot of things on my mind today. I'll wait for the call, if you will."

The subject, not knowing you would have done another test immediately anyway, is carried along into the next test which can't very well fail!

The Word Projection

So much for that part. The subject is given a copy of a current magazine. I suggest Reader's Digest because it's coat pocket size, but most any magazine or book will do. As he looks it over you take out a deck of cards, shuffle, and place them face down before him. The subject is asked to cut them once or twice, and then deal three cards in a face-up row from left to right. If a picture card shows up among them, the performer pushes them aside, saying, "Try three more. Picture cards are too confusing to use." This action is repeated until three cards are dealt with no picture cards showing up. Then the subject is told to consider the first two cards as indicating a page in the magazine. Thus if an 8 and a 3 showed up, the page would be 83. When the page has been found, the last, or third, card indicates the word, counting from the beginning of the reading matter on the page.

This principle was devised by me several years ago for a book test. Here it serves as a book test again, but has been extended for use over a phone and the naming of the cards. Use a deck stacked in the Si Stebbins order. Each card is three above its preceding card in value, and the four suits rotate in the order of Spades, Hearts, Clubs and Diamonds.

If the instructions have been followed there are only four possible words that can be selected in the magazine used. This is probably the most subtle psychological part of the stunt! By discarding all combinations containing a court card, but four combinations of three cards remain. The four combinations, and the word each designates are as follows:

A, 4, 7 . . . . Locates the seventh word on page 14

2, 5, 8 . . . . Locates the eighth word on page 25

3, 6, 9 . . . . Locates the ninth word on page 36

4, 7, 10 . . . . Locates the tenth word on page 47

With the one man version as explained in "Between the Lines," page 53, the performer turned his back during the selection of cards and word. In this instance he watches the proceedings which eliminates any chance of error by the spectator. It is needless to say that the medium has the four words listed, together with the values of the three cards which locate them.

With only four possible words from which to choose, the performer resorts to the dodge of having the subject call and ask either "what" he has on his mind this time, or that he is "thinking of a word." That is as far as the revelation goes, however. In the first case, "what" signifies to the medium that the word is on a left hand page, or, 7 on page 14 or 9 on page 36. In the second case she is made aware that the word is on a right-hand page, in short, either 8 on page 25 or 10 on page 47.

With this much to go on, she asks the person to concentrate (in the first case revealing that he is thinking of a word) and then names the first letter of one of the two words. If she hits it, all well and good. If she doesn't she merely asks him to try the last letter and then she names the last letter of the other word and works backwards. Thus she reveals what almost seems to be impossible except for telepathy.

The Card Projections

The performer put over a very cute bit of business just before the gentleman phoned. He picked up the three cards used to find the word, keeping them in order with the smallest valued card at the back, and put them into the subject's right hand coat pocket with their faces nearest his body. After naming the chosen word, the medium turns her attention to the cards. She says, "How did you pick the word? By mixing up numbers or with a deck of cards?" Then she says, "Where are the cards now?" And then she says, "Take just one out of your pocket and look at it very intently."

The old dodge of having cards thus removed from a pocket holds good here. The subject never fails to reach in and bring out the cards in order, starting with the outside one first. It is very difficult for him to do anything else. The medium now makes a stab in the dark at the color of it. She knows the value because of the word giving her the "value" identity of all three cards. If right, she then names a suit. If wrong on color she makes a stab at one of the other color suits. And if wrong all the way, she says, "I'm not getting a good impression at all. You must be getting tired. All I can see are . . . . . . hazy spots." And she names the correct number.

Then she says, "Take another card out and try to picture yourself either wearing a big diamond, shaking a big club, digging with a spade, or receiving a valentine in the shape of a big heart." And immediately she names the suit correctly. This is no trouble, for after getting the suit of the first of the three cards she knows what the other two are because of the stacked order. And the naming of the last card is no more difficult except that she asks him to keep it in his pocket and she will try to project her mind to that very spot and attempt to name it!

The performer can even add to things by saying that he doesn't care to know the word himself. And so the mystery is unfolded. Drawings, a word, and cards have been revealed from a distance!

THOUGHTS IN THE AIR
ANNEMANN

I consider this a very practical and mystifying little conception with a big effect. It is impromptu and can be done anywhere at any time, something pretty rare for worthwhile effects of this nature. It can be learned with an assistant, in five minutes, which is another point in its favor.

Effect: No apparatus is needed. Any pack of cards is borrowed from the host or hostess. Mixing the cards, the performer requests that the assistant, or medium, be sent to a distant room for the time being. He now states that one person must be chosen and, so that it may be left entirely to chance, he will deal the cards around to each until the first Ace shows up which will automatically elect him. This is done. This selected person is asked to look through his pockets (or her pocketbook) and take out some small personal article which he is to hide somewhere in the room, but not on the person of anybody. This person then selects someone else who is asked to select a card from the deck. The deck is placed face down on the table and the second spectator inserts his card at any spot, squares the cards and leaves them there. Now the performer leaves the room before the return of the medium who spreads the deck face up, moves her hand across the cards and picks out the selected one. Following this she moves around the room and locates the article. Once more in circling the room, the medium gives the article to its owner!

Preparation: Nothing but the cards is used at any time. Previously the performer and the medium have agreed on a force card, and also who is to be the first subject. Starting at some spot, the people present are numbered from left to right around the room. The performer, who is doing another trick or so, has ample opportunity to set an Ace to fall on this person. If there are five people present, and the subject is number three, the Ace can be placed eighth from the top to hit him on the second round.

Routine: The subject is asked to select some small personal object from his pockets and to hide it anywhere within the room. While he does this, the performer gathers up the cards, and runs through them, remarking

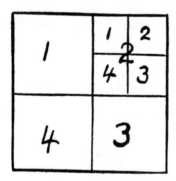

offhandedly that the Joker is the only card with a bad influence and should be out of the deck. Really though, he looks for three cards, cards which will tell where the article is hidden! Impossible? Not at all. Imagine the room as being divided into four squares by lines running through the center each way. The sketch will make this point clear. Then imagine each of those squares being divided the same way, and then each of these smaller squares divided again. Supposing the article were hidden behind something in the far right corner of the room. The numbers 2—2—2 would signal the medium into this very corner!

It will thus be seen that three figures can direct your medium to any small portion of the room. She also knows the article to be small, knows it to be of a personal nature, and knows that invariably it will be an object that is obviously out of place wherever it may be. Knowing these things, and the spot where it lies, it is no trick at all to locate it successfully.

The performer therefore runs through the cards and brings to the top in correct order three cards that signal the correct imaginary squares from the largest to the smallest. And at the same time he locates the card to be forced on the second subject! This person is now picked by the first person and, in his best liked way, the performer forces a card. Putting the deck face down on the table, he asks that the card be returned to any spot, the deck edges squared, and cards held by the selector. Then he leaves the room.

The medium returns, spreads the deck face up on the table and after "the business" picks out the card. A glance at the top three cards of the deck and the medium solves the three number combination that gives her almost the exact spot where the article is hidden. She walks aimlessly around the room and gradually works into position and locates the object. Then, knowing who the owner of the article is, it is returned after another walk around the room. Whereupon the performer is called back to rejoice, and highballs are in order.

The effect is excellent subterfuge. The only thing that is ever remembered is the location of the object and the return of it to the owner. The use of the cards is incidental, and the card selection accepted as a fill in, and a use for them after the first part. You will find that they are forgotten immediately afterwards and the article business discussed all by itself.

THE EYES HAVE IT

J. G. THOMPSON, JR.

Here's an idea for communicating silently with your partner or medium by signalling with your eyes. The code is not complicated and it may be learned in a few minute's time.

Sit or stand opposite your assistant. Catch her eye. That's dead center. Now shift your glance to the right of her head, say about a foot. Shift your glance to the left or her head about a foot without stopping on dead center or catching her eye. Then check with her that she has seen your glances. It's amazing how just a bit of a side glance registers on another person who is looking at your eyes.

Next glance directly above her head about a foot, and, staying on this new level, glance to the right and then to the left. Lastly look to a spot a foot below her eyes, and then cover the right and left positions.

This gives a square of nine positions with the assistant's eyes always determining dead center, or the center square. And before going any farther determine once and for all time whether your assistant wants the squares numbered:

1	2	3		3	2	1
4	5	6	or	6	5	4
7	8	9		9	8	7

depending upon whether she wants to count them from left to right or right to left. Five is the only square not affected by the change.

The figure 0 is signalled simply by letting the glance go away out of the phantom square of nine. The stop is when the performer's gaze drops to his hand or hands.

Now take a deck of cards, but for the moment pay no attention to the faces of the cards. Fan them before you and an imaginary spectator. You both are facing your assistant who is at a little distance facing you. Look at the spread of cards and think of a number of two figures. Glance up carelessly and let your gaze hit the proper square for the first figure and then shift (without moving your head) to the second position. Then it drops to the fan of cards again, and your assistant should now have that number, i. e., any number from 1 to a hundred. For repeats of the same figure the gaze merely does a repeat—first to the number, to the hand, and immediately back to the number, and back to the hand.

Practice this for the next half hour and let the assistant call out the numbers as sent each time. Then consider the cards. The first thing to do is give the suits a value. For example: Clubs—0; Diamonds—13; Hearts—26; Spades—39. That's all!

When a card in the fan is indicated to the performer by a spectator he notes the suit, remembers the value for that suit, adds to it the pip value of the card, and sends that total to the assistant. She merely subtracts from the number received the nearest suit value which is less than the number transmitted. That leaves her with the pip value, and the number subtracted indicates the suit. Thus if the Queen of Hearts were chosen, Hearts would mean 26 to which would be added the pip value of 12. The total is 38 and that is sent. The next value less than 38 is 26 whereupon the medium subtracts 26, indicating Hearts, and gets a remainder of 12 which tells her all she has to know.

A variation of having a spectator indicate a card facing both him and the performer would be to have one chosen from the deck, noted and returned. Just before this the performer would make it clear that he would like the spectator to ask the medium himself, and in his own words, the identity of his pasteboard after the performer had concentrated for a moment. The card returned would be shuffled to the top or bottom and glimpsed while the pack was being squared on the hand. A glance at the spectator would get him started and a follow up glance at the medium, as the spectator puts his question, would do the trick.

On the other hand, the performer might be up against another condition where the spectator might like to keep his card. Mentioning that he may pocket the card he takes, the performer, having noted the top or bottom card of the mixed deck, glances her way and transmit the card. She, of course, being ready after such a remark. Then the card is deliberately forced and she names the card without hesitation.

Once learned by two people, this system will never be forgotten. Even if not used for months it cannot help but work.

A PRACTICAL CARD CODE

Orville Meyer

Many times I've been asked for a good practical method for coding cards. I've always been a believer in verbal codes for real practical work. Of course, there are times when a silent code can be used to good advantage, but for general use I advise the verbal type. Mr. Meyer developed the following code. I like it and believe many will make use of it. Certainly, the wife or sweetheart who is invariably cajoled into assisting won't be able to use the common excuse that there is too much to remember!

LAYOUT OF CODE

"Tell us"—Diamonds.
"Now tell us"—Clubs.
"Tell me"—Hearts.
"Now tell me"—Spades.

"What"		"the name"
1 2 3	4 5 6	7 8 9	10 J Q
"Yes"	(Silence)	"Yes"	(Silence)

1	2	3
"Yes"	"That's right"	(Silence)
"Right"	"You're right"	

K

"The card"

Now for an explanation with examples. The selected card is known to the performer by whatever method he wishes. He may have it drawn from a face up deck or he may use a stacked pack and after a free selection a glimpse at the next card will give him the same information. This is no doubt best, because the performer apparently never sees the card. The assistant may be standing or seated with back to audience. The use of a blindfold is optional.

Asking the assistant to name the card being thought of gives her some definite information, but this offhand query always sounds the same to the audience if they are acute enough to notice. After this first question by the performer the assistant replies but always withholds part of her knowledge, and thus gains the name of the card by the performer's answers or his silence as the case may be.

Example: Suppose someone selects the Five of Hearts. The performer says, *"Tell me what* card this gentleman is thinking of." "Tell me" indicates that the card is a Heart. The key word "what" indicates that the card is *among the lower six* in value. Had the performer said, "Tell me the *name* of the card," the assistant would then know that it was one of the higher six, or from the Seven to the Queen.

Knowing definitely the suit of the card, the assistant now reveals only the *color*. She says, "It is a red card," and waits for the performer's immediate reply. As will be seen, the group one to six is divided into two groups of three each. The performer's reply or silence to this first statement by assistant informs her which group of three contains the card. In this case there is no reply and after a few seconds, she knows that the card is in the second group of the lower six, either the four, five or six. However, she remarks, "The person is thinking of a Heart." Once mores she listens for the reply which will indicate the actual card. One of the three is to be transmitted as per the lower table under 1, 2, and 3. Any reply consisting of *one word* shows that the chosen card is the first in the final group; any reply of two words will make it the second; and no reply at all makes it the last of the group of three. In this case the performer says, "That's right," giving her final knowledge. She finishes with, "and the name of the card is the Five of Hearts."

One more example will clarify the procedure. This time we shall take the Seven of Clubs. The dialogue is as it is given.

Performer: *"Now tell us the name* of this card."

Assistant: "It is a black card." (Knowing it to be a Club and one of the two higher groups).

Performer: "Yes."

Assistant: "In fact it is a Club." (Now knowing it to be the 7, 8 or 9.)

Performer: "Yes." (Which indicates the 7.)

Assistant: "And I'm sure it is the Seven of Clubs."

Kings are always sent in the initial sentence by saying "the card" instead of "what" or "the name." Thus a King can be rattled off in the *same manner* but without the performer ever saying a word more.

Practice on this for half an hour will make it easy. Try to make it natural and don't ask the questions stiffly with emphasis or make the replies as though a life depended upon them. Try to answer back immediately so that there is no break in the continuity of the assistant's speech. Make it look as though she reveals the card practically all at once with no delay. Watch these points and you have as nice a code as you could want. Do it four or five times, then vary or finish by forcing a card you have both agreed upon beforehand and without a single word being spoken she names it. It is a little twist at the last moment that will always befuddle the wise guy who may think of a code.

A COMPLETE "SILENT THOUGHT TRANSMISSION" ACT

CHARLES T. JORDAN

No originality is claimed for the separate components of this startling performance, but the arrangement is original and all that could be desired. We will describe it as a complete performance, but it might better be presented in parts that appeal to the individual reader and arranged in a smooth running performance.

When having several cards drawn have each spectator keep a written note, for the cards are apt to be forgotten. One, or two at the most, card tests are enough for any performance. There is no verbal code, and every test is simple to learn although a certain amount of rehearsal is necessary. I have used every test explained with fine results, and the information is conveyed to the medium in so many different ways as to make detection impossible.

Effect: The performer announces a few tests of telepathy and steps into audience with a pack of cards on a napkin-covered tray. Anyone cuts and deals 25 onto the tray and the performer pockets the rest. The tray is carried along and five spectators each select a card. The last selector takes the pack and shuffles back his card, handing it to one of the others who does likewise until all cards have been shuffled by the spectators themselves. The tray is handed off to assistant (later the medium) who gives the performer a pack of envelopes and pencils. Each envelope contains a slip of paper and these are distributed with the pencils. The shuffled cards are handed to a spectator, who is requested to take them up to the platform and spread them out in five rows of five cards each along five cleats which are attached to a sort of drawing board standing on a chair seat to right of the audience.

The persons having envelopes are all asked to write the name of some living person except one, who is to write the name of someone deceased. A volunteer collects the sealed slips in a borrowed hat and holds it till later. The medium is now introduced and blindfolded. At the center of the platform, well forward, is a blackboard, and to its right, but a foot farther back, stands a small plain table on which various articles lay, as will be described later.

A committee of two leads the medium from the room to prevent communication. When she has left, the performer brings forward a slate and chalk. Three spectators each write a three digit number, and a fourth initials the slate. Without exchange, it is placed number side down on the table, and a glass with several pieces of colored chalk is brought forward. A color is chosen, the glass put back and a deck of cards is then produced. It is cut in half and the halves fanned before the spectators. A card is selected mentally from each half and their names are whispered to the performer.

A spectator advances to the table and throws two dice. They are covered with a cup where they fall. Six half-dollars are borrowed, carried to the table by a spectator and placed in a stack with dates down. The performer's watch is then set at any hour and minute and placed face down with the rest of the articles. A matchbox, or cigarette case, is borrowed and the number of its contents is noted. It is placed on the table.

The performer now gives a resume of what has happened, and states that to start, he will have to perform a test or two with the medium in order that she will become 'attuned.' A trusted person goes after the medium and the committee. She is led to the blackboard and given a piece of chalk. The committee surrounds her. The performer shows a deck to be well mixed and has one selected, well back in the audience. The selector, himself, asks the medium to name it, whereupon she instantly draws its likeness on the blackboard. Borrowing a half-dollar, the performer passes it to another who asks the medium for the date and what he has. The medium draws a half dollar and dates it correctly.

From now on the performer says nothing. The medium divines everything that has taken place during her absence. When adding numbers on slate, the medium asks a committeeman to hold the glass of colored chalks near her. She picks out the chosen color and writes the total of the numbers on the back of the slate. She then locates and names the five cards chosen at the start, which are displayed with backs out on the board. Finally the person with the envelopes in the hat is asked to step forward and stand at the medium's left. With chalk in right hand she reaches into the hat, withdraws an envelope and throws it aside. This is repeated several times until finally she grows tense and instantly writes a name on the blackboard. The committee opens the envelope and the writer acknowledges it as the dead name. This makes a perfect climax to the act.

Explanation: The pack you bring down to the audience is really composed of but 50 cards. The last 25 are arranged in the same order as the first 25 and are duplicates. Wherever the pack is cut, the same 25 cards will be dealt off. You place the balance of the cards in your pocket to get them out of the way. On the tray is spread a napkin. It is folded so that its center forms a flap that will just reach either side of the tray (Fig. 1). Under this flap lies a packet of 20 (different from any of the first 25) cards. You walk up the aisle and have five cards chosen from the "25 packet" which lies face down on the side of the tray not covered with the flap.

When the five cards have been drawn, you turn to go back to the front. As you do so, you turn over, or reverse the napkin flap, covering the exposed cards and revealing the other twenty. The spectators then return their cards to this heap. While they do so, you return to the platform and hand the tray to your assistant who, at the same time, hands you envelopes and pencils. The pencils you immediately place in your outer breast pocket. Unsuspected by the audience, UNDER the stack of envelopes, face up, is a packet of cards, duplicates of the "25 packet" from which spectators' cards were drawn, and arranged in some simple order known to your assistant. Hold the envelopes low so as to conceal the cards and distribute about three envelopes, together with pencils. At this point in the distribution you arrive at the person who has shuffled the 25 cards. Hand him an envelope, take the cards from him and carelessly place them upon the heap of envelopes which you turn over as you cross the aisle. Nonchalantly hand the arranged packet of cards, now on top of the envelopes, to a person and tell him to take them to the stage and spread them out in five rows on the board.

Meanwhile the left hand holding the envelopes goes to side pocket and leaves the cards. You have now distributed four envelopes without intimating your purpose. Hand out another making five. The next envelope, the sixth, you open and extract from it a slip of paper. Placing this on the plain side of envelope (so spectator will unconsciously use envelope for a "pad") you hand it to an obliging person together with a hard pencil. "Will each of you who have an envelope please open it and use the slip of paper inside on which to write the name of some living person, with the exception of you, sir (this to person to whom you handed sixth envelope), you will please write the name of a deceased person. Let no one see what you write."

The sixth envelope is prepared by cutting out the address side of another envelope together with the flap. It is pasted by the corners to a good piece of carbon paper (carbon side down). The flap of another envelope is moistened and this prepared front slipped inside, the flaps laying coincident and stuck together. It seems entirely unprepared, but anything written on the slip of paper held against its address side will be transferred to the inside envelope front by the carbon.

When all have written the names, you address them, "I want the slips folded like this. Let me see—Oh yes, let me have your envelope a minute please, no, keep the paper. I don't want to see the paper or the name you have written on it." You take the envelope from the party who has written the dead name, and remove a second slip of paper previously placed there purposely. "I want you to fold the paper like this," you direct. You naturally lay the prepared envelope on top of the stack and place the entire stack under the arm. You now show how to fold the paper, and then take the stack from under your arm, but reverse side up! The prepared envelope is now on the bottom of the stack, and the former bottom envelope on top is unprepared except that beforehand you have pressed a needle point into each of its corners. No matter what corner is grasped by the medium, she'll know the dead envelope. This envelope you hand the person in which to seal the dead name.

Everyone is now directed to seal their envelopes and someone asked to collect them in a hat, which he is to hold until later. You gather up the pencils and return to the front, handing them, together with the unused envelopes to your assistant who carries them off and returns a moment later with a handkerchief. The medium is then blindfolded (but still can see under the handkerchief) and a committee leads her to another room.

The assistant has employed her time well. When she first carried off the tray, she lifted the napkin flap and learned what cards were missing from the 25 by comparing these with the 20 left, using a list. As she knows the order of the 25 cards now on the cleats of the board, she either memorizes the names or the positions of each card chosen. When you handed her the stack of envelopes and pencils, she seized the chance to open the faked envelope and learn the name of the dead person whose name was written on the sixth slip.

You now bring down into the audience the slate and chalk. On the slate someone writes a number of three figures. You read the figures as you hand the slate to a second person a few seats removed. When you pass the slate from the second person to the third, you add the first person's number to that of the second and keep the total in your head. As you hand the slate to a fourth person for his initials, you add in the last person's number. This adding of three digit numbers is extremely easy, or if you prefer do it with two figure numbers. Return to the platform with the slate and confirm your total as you do so. Place the slate and chalk on the table and immediately bring forward the tumbler containing the six pieces of colored chalk.

"But," you ask, "how are you going to get the slate total to the medium." YOU HAVE ALREADY DONE SO. Before going further, it may be well to explain the principle employed, and in detail.

The information for the next few tests as well as this one depends upon HOW and WHERE you place the various articles on the table. But don't be disgusted and say that would be "raw". It will, if you stand with the article in your hand and figure around as to where and how you should place it. But, if you do your figuring on your way back to the table and nonchalantly place the article down, *at the same time picking up another article for the next test or asking for the loan of an article for the next test, and keeping your eyes anywhere but on your hands*, it will never be suspected. And I know from practical experience. The tests following are the finest I know for impromptu demonstrations. Any square or oblong table may be used, about two by three feet being a most practical size. Fig. 2 represents the table top. It is well, at first, to practice with a diagrammed piece of paper just covering the table. Fig. 2 shows the scheme.

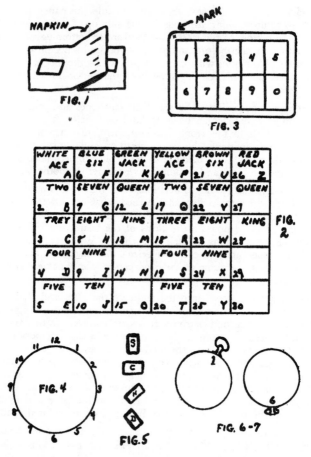

FIG. 1

FIG. 3

FIG. 2

FIG. 4

FIG. 5

FIG. 6-7

There are 30 squares, each row of 5 numbered vertically, and if you wish to convey initials, etc., they are lettered in the same manner. Also 1-13 and 16-28 represent the 13 denominations of playing cards. The top row horizontally represents colors, numbers, etc., and when this is all laid out practice setting things naturally on the proper numbers and colors. Then remove the diagram and practice the same thing with the bare table top. The medium's reading of the signals set is simplicity itself, as she stands at the blackboard and can look down sidewise at the table from under her blindfold. What takes practice in this act is naturalness (without stalling or straining) in placing the various articles in position.

However, many of the signals do not depend upon placing, and the mixing up of these tests is what makes the method so misdirecting. The slate is ordinary but one corner on the side that will be up is marked so as to be readily recognized. The slate is mentally divided into ten parts, each signifying a digit as shown in Fig. 3. X is the marked corner. The total of the three 3-digit numbers cannot possibly be over 3,000 so the first two figures of the answer can be indicated by some one square on the table top. The first two figures of the sum are therefore communicated to the medium by placing the marked corner of the slate on the proper imaginary square. The chalk should be tapering but short. The third digit of the answer should be indicated by placing the chalk on the slate, so it lays in the proper imaginary square number. The last figure of the number is shown by considering the chalk (small) end as a clock hand (Fig. 4), and having it point to the proper number. This imaginary clock dial is square with the table, and the position of the slate on the table has nothing to do with it. The procedure is to figure the thing out on your way to the table and, with your left hand, place the slate on the proper spot. The right hand, a second later, lays the chalk on the slate in the proper square and pointing in the right direction. It would be best to have one side of the chalk flat so that it cannot roll accidentally.

At the same time the right hand does this, the left hand should be picking up the tumbler of colored chalk. The color is selected and indicated by placing the tumbler, as carelessly as possible, on the correct color square, and picking up the pack of cards with free hand at the same time. The pack is cut in half and one card in each half pointed out to you. Advance to the table and place the halves, one in each hand, face down in their proper squares. Suits are indicated by their positions as per Fig. 5.

A spectator advances to the table and throws a pair of dice. You cover them with a cup where they fall. The handle on the cup is placed clock fashion to tell the total thrown. If using a dice cup, a mark has been placed on the edge of the bottom which is used as an indicator the same way. The medium should note if the number thrown is 2-3-11-12. In these cases she can apparently read the dice singly, saying, "Two Aces, An Ace and a Deuce, Two Sixes, or a Six and a Five."

In the left hand trouser pocket you have a stack of six half-dollars, dates facing one way and their order memorized by the medium. They will remain stacked well. Don't announce that dates are to be read. Borrow six half-dollars from as many spectators, with the right hand. The left hand, which carelessly has been in left pocket comes forth with the coins. Apparently transfer the coins from the right hand to the left, immediately handing the stacked coins in your left hand to someone to place on the table. The right hand disposes of its coins in your left vest pocket as it removes the watch, which should not be running. The spectator sets it at any hour and minute, showing it to you. You put it on the table with the stem indicating the hour (Fig. 6) and the square in which watch goes tells the minute. If under 30 minutes, bow is turned UNDER as in Fig. 7. If watch is set 48 minutes after the hour, turn bow up and place on square 18. Medium knows by bow that she must add 30 min. to 18.

The number of matches or cigarettes in a box or case can be indicated by the square on which you place the container. With a little practice, a match box can be tossed to the proper square. At the very start, when the medium returns and you present the card and coin tests to "attune" yourselves, a single card is forced, and the borrowed coin is switched for one of known date and value in passing it to a person across the aisle.

A NEW METHOD OF TABULATION
RALPH W. READ

The following original idea by Ralph Read will be of inestimable value to many performers.

Having stolen, or otherwise secured original written questions, or duplicates thereof, this new method of tabulating them for secret reference later is one of the cleverest means yet devised for the mentalist. It is so innocent looking and so easy to handle that no suspicion can possibly be aroused.

You have backstage a writing tablet about 8" by 10", the ordinary kind with a gray cardboard back and a flexible cover which is hinged at the top. The stolen questions are copied in abbreviated form on the outside of the cardboard back two or three questions on each line. The questions to be answered first are on the bottom line, and others on the lines above.

Write the bottom line about one-half inch above the bottom edge of the cardboard. The exact distance is determined by opening the front cover and folding it clear over so it rests flat against the cardboard back. In this position, the cover won't reach clear to the bottom, so you write the bottom line of questions so as to be concealed underneath the bottom edge of cover. Thus all the writing is concealed when the cover is folded over against the back.

When questions are copied, cover is closed on front of pad and, together with a thick black marking pencil, is placed on a stand to be seen on the stage when act is opened. After opening talk you dump collected questions on stage, pick up crayon and tablet, open and turn back cover as you sit down in a chair. Explain that concentration is necessary and you use tablet to inscribe impressions. Having memorized one question (not on pad) you hold tablet on left arm and in full view scribble with crayon while talking something like this —

"I get a jumble of letters . . . a 'B' (make a small B) . . . no, it's not a B, it's an R (make a bold R) . . . and now an L . . . yes, it's an L (make a large L below the R) . . . and now I see an A (make an A below the L) . . . but the A seems to be in the wrong place . . . it should come first. Now I see something crooked, snake-like (make a large S) . . . and there is something supporting it (make S into a $) . . . is A. L. R. here? . . . yes, I see you . . . do you recognize this mark here?" You hold up tablet in left hand, fingers on front and thumb on back near bottom edge of cover (the cover now being towards you, of course).

A slight upward pressure of left thumb, and the cover slides up enough so you can see bottom line of tabulated questions. Secretly read and remember one or more of them. A second is all you need. A. L. R. acknowledges the $ sign and you continue . . . "it looks like a good sign for it means money for you . . . you want the better things in life you haven't had before, in fact you'd like to be rich, etc., etc."

You tear off the A. L. R. "impression sheet" and throw it aside, proceeding with the next question—the one you have just noted on the back. With each question you will find some article, or dramatic element, that you can illustrate on the sheet with crayon. Even if your drawing ability is poor and the picture crude, the spectator will readily see the connection, if not the exact likeness, and that is sufficient excuse for your going ahead with the answer. For questions about marriage draw a heart or hearts; about trips draw a train, boat or auto; about babies, draw a nursing bottle.

Using a tablet in this manner offers many advantages apart from its simplicity and ease in handling. All of your written "impressions" may be freely shown or examined; they are bold enough so all can see them, and this maintains a dramatic interest on the part of the entire audience. When putting your "impressions" on pad, the top hinged end is downwards, the "impressions" are written in full view right side up to you, but upside down to the audience, until you later turn tablet around and hold it up for identification—a perfect excuse for thus turning it around for them to see and read.

With three questions per line, and eight or ten lines, you will have 24 to 30 questions, enough for most acts. In other words, you use only about 3 or 4 inches at the bottom of cardboard for copying. With a tablet in hand you will quickly discover how easy it is to slide cover upwards enough to bring uppermost lines into view. The cover then slides back the instant you have glimpsed line, and everything is again hidden from view. Use a new tablet for each performance.

MOONLIGHT MADNESS
J. G. THOMPSON, JR.

This is an explanation of a principle which, for several years, has served me well. Mrs. Thompson and I have used it to fool large audiences as well as small groups of friends. Everyone has been taken in by it. Close acquaintances have seen us perform on more than one occasion and still are not near a solution. The principle has been tested time and again, for it has been the first method of transmission to stand up under practically every condition to which a pair of mindreaders is subject. It's to the credit of a device that it is simple, and in that lies a baffling quality. There are few purely magical effects using as little apparatus and needing so little practice as the device offered here.

A two person mental act seems always to find favor with audiences, especially those of the intimate home and club type. It is difficult for people to solve such work for the reason that most people think along magical lines of manual trickery, aided by numerous exposures, and because there are very few double mental acts in comparison to magic acts.

While magic has continually made strides by making use of principles unknown but a decade before, mental acts have stagnated and the mentalists themselves have kept to outworn and laboriously learned systems. One look at a system, by a neophyte with sincere intentions, is enough to discourage him.

I was dissatisfied. Dissatisfaction bred revolution. And that, plus a minor rebellion on the part of my wife, caused me to delve for an almost non-study, natural, and practical (even if time has elapsed since the last show) method of transmission.

The Principle: Briefly stated, the means of signalling is a flashlight bulb attached to the rear of the vest, under the coat, and connecetd with a combination battery holder and switch in the trouser pocket.

Construction: At a 5 and 10 cent store purchase a single battery metal pencil type flashlight with a spring bottom switch at one end. Also purchase twenty inches of flexible (tinsel cord, preferably), and an old flashlight bulb, a radio panel light socket stripped to the bare necessities, and a safety pin. See your nearest electrical supply store for these.

One end of the tinsel cord is split and the two wires are soldered to the panel light socket—one to the side, the other to the bottom. The safety pin also is soldered to the side of the socket and a bit of tire tape wrapped around to hold all connections secure. The bulb is removed from the flashlight and screwed into the panel socket. The glass top is broken from the old bulb and everything removed from inside. The other end of the tinsel cord is split. The insulation is stripped back just enough to make a connection—one wire being soldered to the inside of the base and the other to the terminal connection at the bottom of the base. Keeping the two wires apart the bulb case is filled with hot sealing wax and allowed to harden. Then the base is screwed into the flashlight case from which the good bulb was removed to be placed into the panel socket. With a 1½-volt battery in the case, pressure upon the spring switch will cause panel bulb to light. Release of pressure extinguishes the light at the end of the tinsel cord.

By means of the safety pin, the socket is fastened, bulb up, near the lower edge of your vest about six inches above the rear trouser pocket opening. The case is passed through the belt strap into either side trouser pocket. I use the left for no particular reason except that it leaves my right hand free.

To eliminate absolutely any visible movement in the pocket while operating the switch, close your entire hand around the case and press your fist, thus formed, firmly against your leg. Your thumb operates the button by alternately pressing and releasing. The apparatus can be worn from morning until night without difficulty. The accompanying sketch shows the entire outfit.

With coat on, and with back towards the medium, you silently signal, by short and long flashes which are clearly visible through the cloth. No one, however, but the medium is directly behind you to see the code flashes. This holds true even should both of you, and the audience, be in total darkness.

The Code: Almost everything can be broken down to numbers, and in this case a short flash equals 1 and a long flash 5. Using these two signals any digit can be transmitted to take care of license numbers, telephone, bill, street, social security numerals, birth dates, coin and paper money denominations, addition totals, etc. The reader must remember that we are not attempting to duplicate the intricate acts of article defining with their speed of accomplishment despite the outmoded methods invariably used. We offer a neat, clean-cut, and practical method of doing impossible seeming stunts at a moment's notice without a lifetime of labor to learn.

The Setting: The medium is best at one end of the room while you station yourself at a distance with the spectators before your table. At home parties you can seat the lady at an advantageous spot according to conditions, and approach the seated people about the room, stepping back a little for the denouement. As the device gives off no reflection or glow other than a

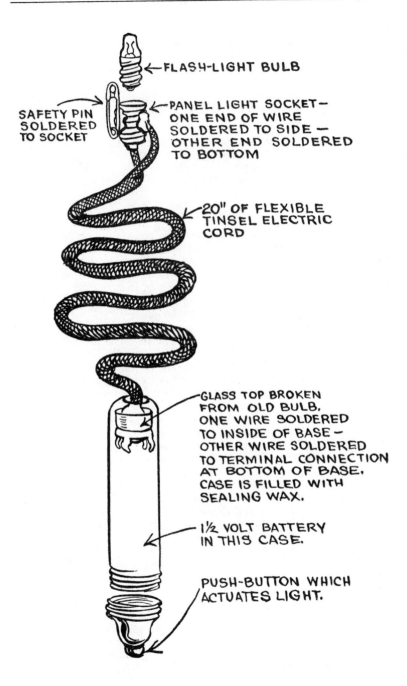

← FLASH-LIGHT BULB

SAFETY PIN
SOLDERED
TO SOCKET

←PANEL LIGHT SOCKET—
ONE END OF WIRE
SOLDERED TO SIDE —
OTHER END SOLDERED
TO BOTTOM

20" OF FLEXIBLE
TINSEL ELECTRIC
CORD

GLASS TOP BROKEN
FROM OLD BULB,
ONE WIRE SOLDERED
TO INSIDE OF BASE —
OTHER WIRE SOLDERED
TO TERMINAL CONNECTION
AT BOTTOM OF BASE.
CASE IS FILLED WITH
SEALING WAX.

1½ VOLT BATTERY
IN THIS CASE.

PUSH-BUTTON WHICH
ACTUATES LIGHT.

single spot of light at a place where the medium is looking for it, you have more freedom of movement than you would suppose. It isn't good policy for the medium to look continuously at your back. She can rest her head upon her hand and peer quite easily between her fingers. We'll discuss the blindfold angles later.

The size of the audience has not, so far, altered the effectiveness of the routine for us. It was evolved for home gatherings, but we have had excellent results before a group of 400 persons.

What Can Be Accomplished: A volunteer assistant sits at a table with his back to the medium. The performer stands to the left and slightly to the rear, cutting off the medium's view of the table. Emphasis should be placed on the fact that the assistant always asks all the questions and that you, for once, propose to remain silent.

GENERAL TEST

If the assistant is requested to empty his pockets and wallet onto the table, much material will be found suitable for transmission. Have a memorized list of ten or twenty common pocket articles. Immediately you can pick up one article and another, sending the list number of the first while the subject still is getting out the stuff. If you prefer, another good general test is to have the spectator write down, at your direction, miscellaneous personal data, such as mentioned under The Code paragraph.

A very convincing book test can be presented by having a spectator read silently a passage from one of several books available. The assistant closes the book and takes ALL of them to the medium who picks out the right one, finds the page, and reads back the passage. The performer stands at ease and in silence while this is carried out, but he has signalled the number of the book, the page number, and the paragraph or line number, having had ample time to do it.

Professor J. B. Rhine's (Duke University) prize psychology and "extra-sensory perception" students can be outdone by handing a deck of ESP cards out for mixing, while you relate what has been done and the results obtained. Your subject lays the cards before him, turns one up at a time and concentrates, and then taps upon the table as a signal. (See illustration.) The medium names the design correctly! At the same time he turns the card so the audience can see it. As Rhine star apostles of ESP don't get as many as 9 out of 25 on an average, it's quite effective when your medium gets 25 out of 25, although we would suggest you jiggle the switch enough to keep her down to about 19. You merely know the five cards by number. The circle (1) is made with one line; the cross (2) uses two lines; the wavy lines (3) are three in number; the square (4) has four lines; and the star (5) has five points.

As for playing cards, both of you remember the four suits in a certain order, knowing them as 1, 2, 3 and 4. A short signal is given over and over to signify each suit until the correct one is reached. Then, following a short pause, the value is transmitted; a Queen, for instance, being sent with two "longs" and two "shorts." If performing where it is possible for the spectators either to sit or congregate around the table, you should have the medium do more than just name a card or two. Try this effective routine:

Ask a spectator to shuffle the deck, remove any number of cards, say 10, and lay them in a face up row. Then ask for questions from various people in regards to the layout. By using two "shorts" for "No" and three "shorts" for "Yes" in addition to the regular system, all information can be sent in regards to positions of cards, their relationships with others in the row, and names. As a clincher test spread the deck face up and station someone at the light switch with instructions to plunge the room into darkness as soon as he hears another

spectator select a card by thumping it heavily with his forefinger. There is no opportunity to signal between time of selection and the time room is darkened. Yet a moment or two after the lights are out the medium names the chosen card.

A more elaborate, but very convincing test of either telepathy or clairvoyance, is to have a bunch of cards laid out as before, whereupon the medium begins to speak immediately, something like this:—

"Before you ask me questions I have a few things to tell you. Looking in a general way at the mental picture of cards that you have formed, I see that there are nine cards on the table. Of these, there are six with spots and three face cards. Insofar as suits are concerned, that is, Clubs, Diamonds,

Hearts and Spades, I perceive that all of them are represented. I see also that there are three Clubs, two Diamonds, three Hearts and one Spade. To be specific the Clubs are the two, seven and Jack; the Diamonds are the ten and Queen; the Hearts are the Ace, nine and King, and the Spade is the eight. That is all I can immediately visualise, no, wait a minute. There is another card I have missed—its very faint, but I am sure it is the Seven of Diamonds." An examination of the face card of the pack shows it to be that card.

Analysis: As quickly as possible count the number of cards laid out and code it at once. The medium has memorized the order in which the various items will be "sent," so she knows automatically what each signal represents. Having received the first item she starts talking as outlined. Meanwhile count the face cards and code this number. Simple subtraction in her mind allows her to continue with more information. Now note which suits are represented and wait until medium says—"Insofar as the suits are concerned, that is Clubs, Diamonds, Hearts and Spades"—As each is mentioned, if there are any, flash a short signal so that medium is almost immediately able to name all of the suits represented. Mrs. Thompson assigns the name of a suit to each of her four right fingers and bends the "suits" into her palm as signalled. Next is sent how many of each suit there are, using a set order of suit rotation. It is simple to remember the information received as 4012, or, as in the example given here 3231. In sending the values always keep to the same suit order and start with the lowest value. For the second card, signal a number which, if added to the first value already sent, equals the value of the second, etc., for all of the cards. As the medium knows from her bent fingers the suits, and from the total remembered exactly how many there are of each suit, she knows which is the last of each suit and, therefore, when to start on the next suit.

When cards are first withdrawn from the pack and laid on the table, contrive to see the face card of the deck before same is put aside. Its suit and value are signalled last after the medium has taken care of the cards on the table.

Thus the outline to be followed by both performer and medium is (1) No. of cards; (2) No. of face cards; (3) No. of suits represented; (4) No. of cards in each suit; (5) Value of cards in each suit; (6) Final card on face of deck. In this routine it must be remembered that the medium is trying to create the impression of genuine mindreading and not show how fast she can reveal the facts.

Letters and Words: Recently I have been attempting to perfect a system for sending alphabet letters. Those familiar with the Morse cords are set. Those who are not probably will not want to devote the necessary time to it. At least I didn't and therefore developed the following:

Since there are but two signals available, allow a short flash, or dot, to equal a straight line, and a long flash, or dash, to equal a curve. An examination of the capital letters of the alphabet will show that each is made up of a combination of straight lines and curves. In coding, send just what you see, starting either at the left or at the top of the letter depending upon its construction. It is not necessary to learn any code. For instance, if the letter is B, you will see at the left a straight line, hence signal a dot. Next, two curves (a curve is always considered a semi-circle) are transmitted. An O would be two dashes, a G a dash and dot, et cetera. The complete code looks like this:

I	.
T, L, V, X	. .
A, F, N, H, Y, K, Z	. . .
E, M, W	. . . .
D, P	. —
R, U	. — .
B	. — —
C	—
O, S	— —
G, J	— .
Q	— — .

The flashing is comparatively simple. A glance at the complete code, however, shows that the chief difficulty arises in the receiving. The medium need not necessarily memorize the code for it may be on a card in her hand. How is she to know which letter is being sent when more than one is in the group coded? In each case where there are more than one, the letter most likely to appear is given first and the others follow in order of probability of appearance. Where there are only two the medium names the first in a hesitant manner. If she is correct, signal a dot, whereupon she becomes positive. If not correct, there is no signal and the medium switches to the other letter in a positive manner. In the EMW group she starts with an E. If wrong she says, "No, it seems to be turned the wrong way. Perhaps it is an M——," or "Yes, I see now, it is a W." You, of course, signal a dot at the right point. That leaves two groups in which difficulty might be experienced, namely TLVX and AFNHYKZ. Here the medium can state that she sees many letters, none of which are very clear, and then proceeds to name all in the group one by one until she receives your signal. Or, during her talk of cloudiness, you may send a few dots to denote which of the letters in the series is the one. Then her vision clears. It must be realized that a lot depends upon common sense when coding a word. There are many letters which couldn't possibly follow others, and experience plus acuteness will make things much easier than they read.

Questions: By employing a principle outlined by Larsen and Wright in their mss. "Mental and Spirit Mysteries," it is possible to transmit the gist of a question which some spectator either writes upon a blackboard for all to see, or whispers to the performer. Messrs. Larsen and Wright nicely classified all possible subjects upon which questions can be asked, as follows:—

(1) Business; (2) Love; (3) Health; (4) Journies; (5) Lost and Found Articles; (6) News (Will I hear from my brother? Will the parcel-post arrive? etc.); (7) Conflict (Can I trust my partner? Will the quarrel be patched up? etc); (8) Success (Will I succeed? etc.); (9) Politics (Who

(Note by Annemann: I think the principle of dot-dashing as applied to the groups and requiring no practice or memory for the sender is very clever and worthy of being studied. As it stands it is excellent for initials, and, while some may consider it just as well in the long pull to send figures from 1 to 26 to designate letters, we think an advantage to many will be that the assistant-medium-wife-sweetheart won't have to study long and hard. The ingenious grouping of letters with simple signals offers untold possibilities.)

will be elected? etc.); (10) Crime; (11) Children (Will it be a girl or boy? etc.) (12) Miscellaneous.

To be brief, the performer quickly classifies the spectator's question and sends the number. This mechanical end of the test is simple enough, but it is the medium, here, who carries the burden. She must be quick witted, possess a vivid imagination, and be fluent of speech. She must be able to say a great deal about nothing and convince the spectator that she is actually answering his individual query.

For instance: Having received signal No. 1, she might speak as follows: "I see a matter concerning you which is about to come up in the near future. In some manner it seems to be concerned with papers and signatures. You may rest assured that the outcome will be for the best, though it will not be exactly what you may expect at the present moment, for I see the future as very bright." One can give a surprisingly detailed reading by hazarding a few guesses and following up any correct surmises. As soon as she makes a mistake, signal a short flash, whereupon she corrects her statement. Frequently you can signal two groups, the combination of which will paint a clear picture.

Questions written that do no classify with your list are signalled No. 12 and it means "Go slow." Such questions can be skirted if the medium says, "I'm sorry, sir, but it seems to me inadvisable to answer that question in public at this time."

An easy query can be forced if you handle it by addressing a spectator: "What are you most interested in at the moment—some matter of business, or affairs of the heart, or a matter of health?" You'll be surprised how a person will pick up one of these suggested lines.

Additional Suggestions: In many of the tests suggested, if performed before a sizeable group seated some distance from the table, a great deal of the effectiveness may be lost by people not seeing what is going on. In the case of cards I use a plain, unvarnished, folding (fits into a brief-case), wooden stand with two ledges on which the spectator places Giant cards as shown in the illustration. The two black lines are made by cloth tape and form two pockets thus enabling use of smaller cards numbered from 1 through 9. (See illustration.) A spectator thus can arrange the cards in horizontal rows and the medium names any one pointed to, finally giving the total of the vertical columns for type of blindfold to use, see par. 1, page 229.

HIT PARADE

ORVILLE W. MEYER

A very cute musical thought transmission effect was contained in the book "Sh-h-h. It's a Secret!" I've played with it off and on since its appearance, and it has been satisfactory because one man can use a strange pianist practically impromptu.

During this time I have added a few details which, to my way of thinking, simplify things a bit and possibly add to the effect. I save time on the presentation by using lists of songs prepared in advance, and this is made possible due to the fact that The Billboard (theatrical trade weekly), Variety (same), and other similar publications publish a list of the ten top-ranking songs of the week. A dozen or so small typed lists are made. Early in the evening give the pianist one of these lists, and also the following "key" list, see illustration, explaining to the pianist that the first word of whatever you say immediately after you ask somebody to think of a song will be the cue to the proper song on the list.

In presenting, explain that you have the ten top-ranking songs of the week, in the order of their popularity, as judged by national polls, listed upon a number of cards. Then pass out all but two or three of the cards to convenient spectators.

1	Name
2	Tell
3	Please
4	Think
5	Keep
6	Ask
7	Say
8	Don't
9	Try
10	Make

And here is the second time you've simplified things, for you retain two or three cards and the uppermost of these contains not the list of songs, but the list of code words. A glance at this, if and when necessary, will arouse no suspicion.

Someone holding a list is approached and asked to point to one of the titles and think of that melody. Immediately it is coded to the pianist who hears the first word of the sentence and knows what to play. If, for instance, the fifth title were touched, the performer woud say, "Keep concentrating on that tune, and perhaps Miss ———— will catch your thought vibrations." The pianist notes that "keep" is the fifth word on the key list, and therefore plays the fifth hit tune.

The use of the tunes of the Hit Parade gives a LOGICAL reason for a list prepared in advance. The next detail is one that might be used to climax this routine, or it can be used as a separate item by itself. Often I use it for groups where, previously, I have already used the regular telepathy act as described.

A totally unknown pianist is asked to sit at the piano and is given a list of the songs beforehand, but no cue list is necessary. She is told to play any one of the ten she pleases when the time comes.

Again you have a dozen or so tune lists, plus three additional cards which bear the wording as shown in the following illustration. You are careful to remember to whom these three cards are given. Try to pick people where others nearby won't have an opportunity to read the cards also. If crowded, give the cards out in three's, that is, to three persons sitting together. The first person gets a song list, the second gets the special card, and the third gets another song list. Thus, the two on the outside will be looking over their lists while the center man can read his card unobserved.

BE A SPORT.

When asked, pretend to think of a tune, but whatever is played, say "That's it." Thanks for cooperating. Please don't tell anybody how we did it!

The rest of the procedure is obvious. Go to one of the three persons, apparently at random, and taking the card from him ask if he has chosen one of the listed songs. Ask him to concentrate upon the tune. The pianist starts playing and the spectator admits "That's it." This is repeated with the persons holding the other two fake lists.

Many of my readers will shed bitter tears over the thought of such barefaced "cheating," but I'm certainly far from the first to use this impromptu confederate gag. (See Annemann's Impromptu Frame-Ups, page 97.) When 297 people, including the pianist, out of 300 are completely baffled, why worry? You'll be lucky if your other effects score as well!

A CATALOG OF SELECTED
DOVER BOOKS
IN ALL FIELDS OF INTEREST

A CATALOG OF SELECTED DOVER

BOOKS IN ALL FIELDS OF INTEREST

CONCERNING THE SPIRITUAL IN ART, Wassily Kandinsky. Pioneering work by father of abstract art. Thoughts on color theory, nature of art. Analysis of earlier masters. 12 illustrations. 80pp. of text. 5⅜ x 8½. 23411-8 Pa. $4.95

ANIMALS: 1,419 Copyright-Free Illustrations of Mammals, Birds, Fish, Insects, etc., Jim Harter (ed.). Clear wood engravings present, in extremely lifelike poses, over 1,000 species of animals. One of the most extensive pictorial sourcebooks of its kind. Captions. Index. 284pp. 9 x 12. 23766-4 Pa. $14.95

CELTIC ART: The Methods of Construction, George Bain. Simple geometric techniques for making Celtic interlacements, spirals, Kells-type initials, animals, humans, etc. Over 500 illustrations. 160pp. 9 x 12. (Available in U.S. only.) 22923-8 Pa. $9.95

AN ATLAS OF ANATOMY FOR ARTISTS, Fritz Schider. Most thorough reference work on art anatomy in the world. Hundreds of illustrations, including selections from works by Vesalius, Leonardo, Goya, Ingres, Michelangelo, others. 593 illustrations. 192pp. 7⅛ x 10¼. 20241-0 Pa. $9.95

CELTIC HAND STROKE-BY-STROKE (Irish Half-Uncial from "The Book of Kells"): An Arthur Baker Calligraphy Manual, Arthur Baker. Complete guide to creating each letter of the alphabet in distinctive Celtic manner. Covers hand position, strokes, pens, inks, paper, more. Illustrated. 48pp. 8¼ x 11. 24336-2 Pa. $3.95

EASY ORIGAMI, John Montroll. Charming collection of 32 projects (hat, cup, pelican, piano, swan, many more) specially designed for the novice origami hobbyist. Clearly illustrated easy-to-follow instructions insure that even beginning papercrafters will achieve successful results. 48pp. 8¼ x 11. 27298-2 Pa. $3.50

THE COMPLETE BOOK OF BIRDHOUSE CONSTRUCTION FOR WOODWORKERS, Scott D. Campbell. Detailed instructions, illustrations, tables. Also data on bird habitat and instinct patterns. Bibliography. 3 tables. 63 illustrations in 15 figures. 48pp. 5¼ x 8½. 24407-5 Pa. $2.50

BLOOMINGDALE'S ILLUSTRATED 1886 CATALOG: Fashions, Dry Goods and Housewares, Bloomingdale Brothers. Famed merchants' extremely rare catalog depicting about 1,700 products: clothing, housewares, firearms, dry goods, jewelry, more. Invaluable for dating, identifying vintage items. Also, copyright-free graphics for artists, designers. Co-published with Henry Ford Museum & Greenfield Village. 160pp. 8¼ x 11. 25780-0 Pa. $10.95

HISTORIC COSTUME IN PICTURES, Braun & Schneider. Over 1,450 costumed figures in clearly detailed engravings–from dawn of civilization to end of 19th century. Captions. Many folk costumes. 256pp. 8⅜ x 11¾. 23150-X Pa. $12.95

STICKLEY CRAFTSMAN FURNITURE CATALOGS, Gustav Stickley and L. & J. G. Stickley. Beautiful, functional furniture in two authentic catalogs from 1910. 594 illustrations, including 277 photos, show settles, rockers, armchairs, reclining chairs, bookcases, desks, tables. 183pp. 6½ x 9¼. 23838-5 Pa. $11.95

AMERICAN LOCOMOTIVES IN HISTORIC PHOTOGRAPHS: 1858 to 1949, Ron Ziel (ed.). A rare collection of 126 meticulously detailed official photographs, called "builder portraits," of American locomotives that majestically chronicle the rise of steam locomotive power in America. Introduction. Detailed captions. xi+ 129pp. 9 x 12. 27393-8 Pa. $13.95

AMERICA'S LIGHTHOUSES: An Illustrated History, Francis Ross Holland, Jr. Delightfully written, profusely illustrated fact-filled survey of over 200 American lighthouses since 1716. History, anecdotes, technological advances, more. 240pp. 8 x 10¾. 25576-X Pa. $12.95

TOWARDS A NEW ARCHITECTURE, Le Corbusier. Pioneering manifesto by founder of "International School." Technical and aesthetic theories, views of industry, economics, relation of form to function, "mass-production split" and much more. Profusely illustrated. 320pp. 6⅛ x 9¼. (Available in U.S. only.) 25023-7 Pa. $9.95

HOW THE OTHER HALF LIVES, Jacob Riis. Famous journalistic record, exposing poverty and degradation of New York slums around 1900, by major social reformer. 100 striking and influential photographs. 233pp. 10 x 7⅞. 22012-5 Pa. $11.95

FRUIT KEY AND TWIG KEY TO TREES AND SHRUBS, William M. Harlow. One of the handiest and most widely used identification aids. Fruit key covers 120 deciduous and evergreen species; twig key 160 deciduous species. Easily used. Over 300 photographs. 126pp. 5⅜ x 8½. 20511-8 Pa. $3.95

COMMON BIRD SONGS, Dr. Donald J. Borror. Songs of 60 most common U.S. birds: robins, sparrows, cardinals, bluejays, finches, more—arranged in order of increasing complexity. Up to 9 variations of songs of each species. Cassette and manual 99911-4 $8.95

ORCHIDS AS HOUSE PLANTS, Rebecca Tyson Northen. Grow cattleyas and many other kinds of orchids—in a window, in a case, or under artificial light. 63 illustrations. 148pp. 5⅜ x 8½. 23261-1 Pa. $5.95

MONSTER MAZES, Dave Phillips. Masterful mazes at four levels of difficulty. Avoid deadly perils and evil creatures to find magical treasures. Solutions for all 32 exciting illustrated puzzles. 48pp. 8¼ x 11. 26005-4 Pa. $2.95

MOZART'S DON GIOVANNI (DOVER OPERA LIBRETTO SERIES), Wolfgang Amadeus Mozart. Introduced and translated by Ellen H. Bleiler. Standard Italian libretto, with complete English translation. Convenient and thoroughly portable—an ideal companion for reading along with a recording or the performance itself. Introduction. List of characters. Plot summary. 121pp. 5¼ x 8½. 24944-1 Pa. $3.95

TECHNICAL MANUAL AND DICTIONARY OF CLASSICAL BALLET, Gail Grant. Defines, explains, comments on steps, movements, poses and concepts. 15-page pictorial section. Basic book for student, viewer. 127pp. 5⅜ x 8½. 21843-0 Pa. $4.95

THE CLARINET AND CLARINET PLAYING, David Pino. Lively, comprehensive work features suggestions about technique, musicianship, and musical interpretation, as well as guidelines for teaching, making your own reeds, and preparing for public performance. Includes an intriguing look at clarinet history. "A godsend," *The Clarinet,* Journal of the International Clarinet Society. Appendixes. 7 illus. 320pp. 5⅜ x 8½. 40270-3 Pa. $9.95

HOLLYWOOD GLAMOR PORTRAITS, John Kobal (ed.). 145 photos from 1926-49. Harlow, Gable, Bogart, Bacall; 94 stars in all. Full background on photographers, technical aspects. 160pp. 8⅜ x 11¼. 23352-9 Pa. $12.95

THE ANNOTATED CASEY AT THE BAT: A Collection of Ballads about the Mighty Casey/Third, Revised Edition, Martin Gardner (ed.). Amusing sequels and parodies of one of America's best-loved poems: Casey's Revenge, Why Casey Whiffed, Casey's Sister at the Bat, others. 256pp. 5⅜ x 8½. 28598-7 Pa. $8.95

THE RAVEN AND OTHER FAVORITE POEMS, Edgar Allan Poe. Over 40 of the author's most memorable poems: "The Bells," "Ulalume," "Israfel," "To Helen," "The Conqueror Worm," "Eldorado," "Annabel Lee," many more. Alphabetic lists of titles and first lines. 64pp. 5$\frac{3}{16}$ x 8¼. 26685-0 Pa. $1.00

PERSONAL MEMOIRS OF U. S. GRANT, Ulysses Simpson Grant. Intelligent, deeply moving firsthand account of Civil War campaigns, considered by many the finest military memoirs ever written. Includes letters, historic photographs, maps and more. 528pp. 6⅛ x 9¼. 28587-1 Pa. $12.95

ANCIENT EGYPTIAN MATERIALS AND INDUSTRIES, A. Lucas and J. Harris. Fascinating, comprehensive, thoroughly documented text describes this ancient civilization's vast resources and the processes that incorporated them in daily life, including the use of animal products, building materials, cosmetics, perfumes and incense, fibers, glazed ware, glass and its manufacture, materials used in the mummification process, and much more. 544pp. 6⅛ x 9¼. (Available in U.S. only.) 40446-3 Pa. $16.95

RUSSIAN STORIES/PYCCKNE PACCKA3bl: A Dual-Language Book, edited by Gleb Struve. Twelve tales by such masters as Chekhov, Tolstoy, Dostoevsky, Pushkin, others. Excellent word-for-word English translations on facing pages, plus teaching and study aids, Russian/English vocabulary, biographical/critical introductions, more. 416pp. 5⅜ x 8½. 26244-8 Pa. $9.95

PHILADELPHIA THEN AND NOW: 60 Sites Photographed in the Past and Present, Kenneth Finkel and Susan Oyama. Rare photographs of City Hall, Logan Square, Independence Hall, Betsy Ross House, other landmarks juxtaposed with contemporary views. Captures changing face of historic city. Introduction. Captions. 128pp. 8¼ x 11. 25790-8 Pa. $9.95

AIA ARCHITECTURAL GUIDE TO NASSAU AND SUFFOLK COUNTIES, LONG ISLAND, The American Institute of Architects, Long Island Chapter, and the Society for the Preservation of Long Island Antiquities. Comprehensive, well-researched and generously illustrated volume brings to life over three centuries of Long Island's great architectural heritage. More than 240 photographs with authoritative, extensively detailed captions. 176pp. 8¼ x 11. 26946-9 Pa. $14.95

NORTH AMERICAN INDIAN LIFE: Customs and Traditions of 23 Tribes, Elsie Clews Parsons (ed.). 27 fictionalized essays by noted anthropologists examine religion, customs, government, additional facets of life among the Winnebago, Crow, Zuni, Eskimo, other tribes. 480pp. 6⅛ x 9¼. 27377-6 Pa. $10.95

FRANK LLOYD WRIGHT'S DANA HOUSE, Donald Hoffmann. Pictorial essay of residential masterpiece with over 160 interior and exterior photos, plans, elevations, sketches and studies. 128pp. 9¼ x 10¾. 29120-0 Pa. $12.95

THE MALE AND FEMALE FIGURE IN MOTION: 60 Classic Photographic Sequences, Eadweard Muybridge. 60 true-action photographs of men and women walking, running, climbing, bending, turning, etc., reproduced from rare 19th-century masterpiece. vi + 121pp. 9 x 12. 24745-7 Pa. $12.95

1001 QUESTIONS ANSWERED ABOUT THE SEASHORE, N. J. Berrill and Jacquelyn Berrill. Queries answered about dolphins, sea snails, sponges, starfish, fishes, shore birds, many others. Covers appearance, breeding, growth, feeding, much more. 305pp. 5¼ x 8¼. 23366-9 Pa. $9.95

ATTRACTING BIRDS TO YOUR YARD, William J. Weber. Easy-to-follow guide offers advice on how to attract the greatest diversity of birds: birdhouses, feeders, water and waterers, much more. 96pp. 5³⁄₁₆ x 8¼. 28927-3 Pa. $2.50

MEDICINAL AND OTHER USES OF NORTH AMERICAN PLANTS: A Historical Survey with Special Reference to the Eastern Indian Tribes, Charlotte Erichsen-Brown. Chronological historical citations document 500 years of usage of plants, trees, shrubs native to eastern Canada, northeastern U.S. Also complete identifying information. 343 illustrations. 544pp. 6½ x 9¼. 25951-X Pa. $12.95

STORYBOOK MAZES, Dave Phillips. 23 stories and mazes on two-page spreads: Wizard of Oz, Treasure Island, Robin Hood, etc. Solutions. 64pp. 8¼ x 11. 23628-5 Pa. $2.95

AMERICAN NEGRO SONGS: 230 Folk Songs and Spirituals, Religious and Secular, John W. Work. This authoritative study traces the African influences of songs sung and played by black Americans at work, in church, and as entertainment. The author discusses the lyric significance of such songs as "Swing Low, Sweet Chariot," "John Henry," and others and offers the words and music for 230 songs. Bibliography. Index of Song Titles. 272pp. 6½ x 9¼. 40271-1 Pa. $9.95

MOVIE-STAR PORTRAITS OF THE FORTIES, John Kobal (ed.). 163 glamor, studio photos of 106 stars of the 1940s: Rita Hayworth, Ava Gardner, Marlon Brando, Clark Gable, many more. 176pp. 8⅜ x 11¼. 23546-7 Pa. $14.95

BENCHLEY LOST AND FOUND, Robert Benchley. Finest humor from early 30s, about pet peeves, child psychologists, post office and others. Mostly unavailable elsewhere. 73 illustrations by Peter Arno and others. 183pp. 5⅜ x 8½. 22410-4 Pa. $6.95

YEKL and THE IMPORTED BRIDEGROOM AND OTHER STORIES OF YIDDISH NEW YORK, Abraham Cahan. Film Hester Street based on *Yekl* (1896). Novel, other stories among first about Jewish immigrants on N.Y.'s East Side. 240pp. 5⅜ x 8½. 22427-9 Pa. $7.95

SELECTED POEMS, Walt Whitman. Generous sampling from *Leaves of Grass*. Twenty-four poems include "I Hear America Singing," "Song of the Open Road," "I Sing the Body Electric," "When Lilacs Last in the Dooryard Bloom'd," "O Captain! My Captain!"—all reprinted from an authoritative edition. Lists of titles and first lines. 128pp. 5³⁄₁₆ x 8¼. 26878-0 Pa. $1.00

THE BEST TALES OF HOFFMANN, E. T. A. Hoffmann. 10 of Hoffmann's most important stories: "Nutcracker and the King of Mice," "The Golden Flowerpot," etc. 458pp. 5⅜ x 8½.   21793-0 Pa. $9.95

FROM FETISH TO GOD IN ANCIENT EGYPT, E. A. Wallis Budge. Rich detailed survey of Egyptian conception of "God" and gods, magic, cult of animals, Osiris, more. Also, superb English translations of hymns and legends. 240 illustrations. 545pp. 5⅜ x 8½.   25803-3 Pa. $13.95

FRENCH STORIES/CONTES FRANÇAIS: A Dual-Language Book, Wallace Fowlie. Ten stories by French masters, Voltaire to Camus: "Micromegas" by Voltaire; "The Atheist's Mass" by Balzac; "Minuet" by de Maupassant; "The Guest" by Camus, six more. Excellent English translations on facing pages. Also French-English vocabulary list, exercises, more. 352pp. 5⅜ x 8½.   26443-2 Pa. $9.95

CHICAGO AT THE TURN OF THE CENTURY IN PHOTOGRAPHS: 122 Historic Views from the Collections of the Chicago Historical Society, Larry A. Viskochil. Rare large-format prints offer detailed views of City Hall, State Street, the Loop, Hull House, Union Station, many other landmarks, circa 1904-1913. Introduction. Captions. Maps. 144pp. 9⅜ x 12¼.   24656-6 Pa. $12.95

OLD BROOKLYN IN EARLY PHOTOGRAPHS, 1865-1929, William Lee Younger. Luna Park, Gravesend race track, construction of Grand Army Plaza, moving of Hotel Brighton, etc. 157 previously unpublished photographs. 165pp. 8⅞ x 11¾.   23587-4 Pa. $13.95

THE MYTHS OF THE NORTH AMERICAN INDIANS, Lewis Spence. Rich anthology of the myths and legends of the Algonquins, Iroquois, Pawnees and Sioux, prefaced by an extensive historical and ethnological commentary. 36 illustrations. 480pp. 5⅜ x 8½.   25967-6 Pa. $10.95

AN ENCYCLOPEDIA OF BATTLES: Accounts of Over 1,560 Battles from 1479 B.C. to the Present, David Eggenberger. Essential details of every major battle in recorded history from the first battle of Megiddo in 1479 B.C. to Grenada in 1984. List of Battle Maps. New Appendix covering the years 1967-1984. Index. 99 illustrations. 544pp. 6½ x 9¼.   24913-1 Pa. $16.95

SAILING ALONE AROUND THE WORLD, Captain Joshua Slocum. First man to sail around the world, alone, in small boat. One of great feats of seamanship told in delightful manner. 67 illustrations. 294pp. 5⅜ x 8½.   20326-3 Pa. $6.95

ANARCHISM AND OTHER ESSAYS, Emma Goldman. Powerful, penetrating, prophetic essays on direct action, role of minorities, prison reform, puritan hypocrisy, violence, etc. 271pp. 5⅜ x 8½.   22484-8 Pa. $7.95

MYTHS OF THE HINDUS AND BUDDHISTS, Ananda K. Coomaraswamy and Sister Nivedita. Great stories of the epics; deeds of Krishna, Shiva, taken from puranas, Vedas, folk tales; etc. 32 illustrations. 400pp. 5⅜ x 8½.   21759-0 Pa. $12.95

THE TRAUMA OF BIRTH, Otto Rank. Rank's controversial thesis that anxiety neurosis is caused by profound psychological trauma which occurs at birth. 256pp. 5⅜ x 8½.   27974-X Pa. $7.95

A THEOLOGICO-POLITICAL TREATISE, Benedict Spinoza. Also contains unfinished Political Treatise. Great classic on religious liberty, theory of government on common consent. R. Elwes translation. Total of 421pp. 5⅜ x 8½. 20249-6 Pa. $10.95

MY BONDAGE AND MY FREEDOM, Frederick Douglass. Born a slave, Douglass became outspoken force in antislavery movement. The best of Douglass' autobiographies. Graphic description of slave life. 464pp. 5⅜ x 8½. 22457-0 Pa. $8.95

FOLLOWING THE EQUATOR: A Journey Around the World, Mark Twain. Fascinating humorous account of 1897 voyage to Hawaii, Australia, India, New Zealand, etc. Ironic, bemused reports on peoples, customs, climate, flora and fauna, politics, much more. 197 illustrations. 720pp. 5⅜ x 8½. 26113-1 Pa. $15.95

THE PEOPLE CALLED SHAKERS, Edward D. Andrews. Definitive study of Shakers: origins, beliefs, practices, dances, social organization, furniture and crafts, etc. 33 illustrations. 351pp. 5⅜ x 8½. 21081-2 Pa. $10.95

THE MYTHS OF GREECE AND ROME, H. A. Guerber. A classic of mythology, generously illustrated, long prized for its simple, graphic, accurate retelling of the principal myths of Greece and Rome, and for its commentary on their origins and significance. With 64 illustrations by Michelangelo, Raphael, Titian, Rubens, Canova, Bernini and others. 480pp. 5⅜ x 8½. 27584-1 Pa. $9.95

PSYCHOLOGY OF MUSIC, Carl E. Seashore. Classic work discusses music as a medium from psychological viewpoint. Clear treatment of physical acoustics, auditory apparatus, sound perception, development of musical skills, nature of musical feeling, host of other topics. 88 figures. 408pp. 5⅜ x 8½. 21851-1 Pa. $11.95

THE PHILOSOPHY OF HISTORY, Georg W. Hegel. Great classic of Western thought develops concept that history is not chance but rational process, the evolution of freedom. 457pp. 5⅜ x 8½. 20112-0 Pa. $9.95

THE BOOK OF TEA, Kakuzo Okakura. Minor classic of the Orient: entertaining, charming explanation, interpretation of traditional Japanese culture in terms of tea ceremony. 94pp. 5⅜ x 8½. 20070-1 Pa. $3.95

LIFE IN ANCIENT EGYPT, Adolf Erman. Fullest, most thorough, detailed older account with much not in more recent books, domestic life, religion, magic, medicine, commerce, much more. Many illustrations reproduce tomb paintings, carvings, hieroglyphs, etc. 597pp. 5⅜ x 8½. 22632-8 Pa. $12.95

SUNDIALS, Their Theory and Construction, Albert Waugh. Far and away the best, most thorough coverage of ideas, mathematics concerned, types, construction, adjusting anywhere. Simple, nontechnical treatment allows even children to build several of these dials. Over 100 illustrations. 230pp. 5⅜ x 8½. 22947-5 Pa. $8.95

THEORETICAL HYDRODYNAMICS, L. M. Milne-Thomson. Classic exposition of the mathematical theory of fluid motion, applicable to both hydrodynamics and aerodynamics. Over 600 exercises. 768pp. 6⅛ x 9¼. 68970-0 Pa. $20.95

SONGS OF EXPERIENCE: Facsimile Reproduction with 26 Plates in Full Color, William Blake. 26 full-color plates from a rare 1826 edition. Includes "TheTyger," "London," "Holy Thursday," and other poems. Printed text of poems. 48pp. 5¼ x 7. 24636-1 Pa. $4.95

OLD-TIME VIGNETTES IN FULL COLOR, Carol Belanger Grafton (ed.). Over 390 charming, often sentimental illustrations, selected from archives of Victorian graphics–pretty women posing, children playing, food, flowers, kittens and puppies, smiling cherubs, birds and butterflies, much more. All copyright-free. 48pp. 9¼ x 12¼. 27269-9 Pa. $7.95

PERSPECTIVE FOR ARTISTS, Rex Vicat Cole. Depth, perspective of sky and sea, shadows, much more, not usually covered. 391 diagrams, 81 reproductions of drawings and paintings. 279pp. 5⅜ x 8½. 22487-2 Pa. $9.95

DRAWING THE LIVING FIGURE, Joseph Sheppard. Innovative approach to artistic anatomy focuses on specifics of surface anatomy, rather than muscles and bones. Over 170 drawings of live models in front, back and side views, and in widely varying poses. Accompanying diagrams. 177 illustrations. Introduction. Index. 144pp. 8⅜ x11¼. 26723-7 Pa. $9.95

GOTHIC AND OLD ENGLISH ALPHABETS: 100 Complete Fonts, Dan X. Solo. Add power, elegance to posters, signs, other graphics with 100 stunning copyright-free alphabets: Blackstone, Dolbey, Germania, 97 more–including many lower-case, numerals, punctuation marks. 104pp. 8⅛ x 11. 24695-7 Pa. $8.95

HOW TO DO BEADWORK, Mary White. Fundamental book on craft from simple projects to five-bead chains and woven works. 106 illustrations. 142pp. 5⅜ x 8. 20697-1 Pa. $5.95

THE BOOK OF WOOD CARVING, Charles Marshall Sayers. Finest book for beginners discusses fundamentals and offers 34 designs. "Absolutely first rate . . . well thought out and well executed."–E. J. Tangerman. 118pp. 7¾ x 10⅝. 23654-4 Pa. $7.95

ILLUSTRATED CATALOG OF CIVIL WAR MILITARY GOODS: Union Army Weapons, Insignia, Uniform Accessories, and Other Equipment, Schuyler, Hartley, and Graham. Rare, profusely illustrated 1846 catalog includes Union Army uniform and dress regulations, arms and ammunition, coats, insignia, flags, swords, rifles, etc. 226 illustrations. 160pp. 9 x 12. 24939-5 Pa. $10.95

WOMEN'S FASHIONS OF THE EARLY 1900s: An Unabridged Republication of "New York Fashions, 1909," National Cloak & Suit Co. Rare catalog of mail-order fashions documents women's and children's clothing styles shortly after the turn of the century. Captions offer full descriptions, prices. Invaluable resource for fashion, costume historians. Approximately 725 illustrations. 128pp. 8⅜ x 11¼. 27276-1 Pa. $11.95

THE 1912 AND 1915 GUSTAV STICKLEY FURNITURE CATALOGS, Gustav Stickley. With over 200 detailed illustrations and descriptions, these two catalogs are essential reading and reference materials and identification guides for Stickley furniture. Captions cite materials, dimensions and prices. 112pp. 6½ x 9¼. 26676-1 Pa. $9.95

EARLY AMERICAN LOCOMOTIVES, John H. White, Jr. Finest locomotive engravings from early 19th century: historical (1804–74), main-line (after 1870), special, foreign, etc. 147 plates. 142pp. 11⅜ x 8¼. 22772-3 Pa. $12.95

THE TALL SHIPS OF TODAY IN PHOTOGRAPHS, Frank O. Braynard. Lavishly illustrated tribute to nearly 100 majestic contemporary sailing vessels: Amerigo Vespucci, Clearwater, Constitution, Eagle, Mayflower, Sea Cloud, Victory, many more. Authoritative captions provide statistics, background on each ship. 190 black-and-white photographs and illustrations. Introduction. 128pp. 8⅞ x 11¾. 27163-3 Pa. $14.95

LITTLE BOOK OF EARLY AMERICAN CRAFTS AND TRADES, Peter Stockham (ed.). 1807 children's book explains crafts and trades: baker, hatter, cooper, potter, and many others. 23 copperplate illustrations. 140pp. 4⅝ x 6.
23336-7 Pa. $4.95

VICTORIAN FASHIONS AND COSTUMES FROM HARPER'S BAZAR, 1867–1898, Stella Blum (ed.). Day costumes, evening wear, sports clothes, shoes, hats, other accessories in over 1,000 detailed engravings. 320pp. 9⅜ x 12¼.
22990-4 Pa. $16.95

GUSTAV STICKLEY, THE CRAFTSMAN, Mary Ann Smith. Superb study surveys broad scope of Stickley's achievement, especially in architecture. Design philosophy, rise and fall of the Craftsman empire, descriptions and floor plans for many Craftsman houses, more. 86 black-and-white halftones. 31 line illustrations. Introduction 208pp. 6½ x 9¼.
27210-9 Pa. $9.95

THE LONG ISLAND RAIL ROAD IN EARLY PHOTOGRAPHS, Ron Ziel. Over 220 rare photos, informative text document origin (1844) and development of rail service on Long Island. Vintage views of early trains, locomotives, stations, passengers, crews, much more. Captions. 8⅞ x 11¾.
26301-0 Pa. $14.95

VOYAGE OF THE LIBERDADE, Joshua Slocum. Great 19th-century mariner's thrilling, first-hand account of the wreck of his ship off South America, the 35-foot boat he built from the wreckage, and its remarkable voyage home. 128pp. 5⅜ x 8½.
40022-0 Pa. $5.95

TEN BOOKS ON ARCHITECTURE, Vitruvius. The most important book ever written on architecture. Early Roman aesthetics, technology, classical orders, site selection, all other aspects. Morgan translation. 331pp. 5⅜ x 8½. 20645-9 Pa. $8.95

THE HUMAN FIGURE IN MOTION, Eadweard Muybridge. More than 4,500 stopped-action photos, in action series, showing undraped men, women, children jumping, lying down, throwing, sitting, wrestling, carrying, etc. 390pp. 7⅞ x 10⅝.
20204-6 Clothbd. $27.95

TREES OF THE EASTERN AND CENTRAL UNITED STATES AND CANADA, William M. Harlow. Best one-volume guide to 140 trees. Full descriptions, woodlore, range, etc. Over 600 illustrations. Handy size. 288pp. 4½ x 6⅜.
20395-6 Pa. $6.95

SONGS OF WESTERN BIRDS, Dr. Donald J. Borror. Complete song and call repertoire of 60 western species, including flycatchers, juncoes, cactus wrens, many more—includes fully illustrated booklet. Cassette and manual 99913-0 $8.95

GROWING AND USING HERBS AND SPICES, Milo Miloradovich. Versatile handbook provides all the information needed for cultivation and use of all the herbs and spices available in North America. 4 illustrations. Index. Glossary. 236pp. 5⅜ x 8½.
25058-X Pa. $7.95

BIG BOOK OF MAZES AND LABYRINTHS, Walter Shepherd. 50 mazes and labyrinths in all—classical, solid, ripple, and more—in one great volume. Perfect inexpensive puzzler for clever youngsters. Full solutions. 112pp. 8⅛ x 11.
22951-3 Pa. $5.95

PIANO TUNING, J. Cree Fischer. Clearest, best book for beginner, amateur. Simple repairs, raising dropped notes, tuning by easy method of flattened fifths. No previous skills needed. 4 illustrations. 201pp. 5⅜ x 8½. 23267-0 Pa. $6.95

HINTS TO SINGERS, Lillian Nordica. Selecting the right teacher, developing confidence, overcoming stage fright, and many other important skills receive thoughtful discussion in this indispensible guide, written by a world-famous diva of four decades' experience. 96pp. 5³/₈ x 8¹/₂. 40094-8 Pa. $4.95

THE COMPLETE NONSENSE OF EDWARD LEAR, Edward Lear. All nonsense limericks, zany alphabets, Owl and Pussycat, songs, nonsense botany, etc., illustrated by Lear. Total of 320pp. 5⅜ x 8½. (AVAILABLE IN U.S. ONLY.) 20167-8 Pa. $7.95

VICTORIAN PARLOUR POETRY: An Annotated Anthology, Michael R. Turner. 117 gems by Longfellow, Tennyson, Browning, many lesser-known poets. "The Village Blacksmith," "Curfew Must Not Ring Tonight," "Only a Baby Small," dozens more, often difficult to find elsewhere. Index of poets, titles, first lines. xxiii + 325pp. 5⅝ x 8¼. 27044-0 Pa. $8.95

DUBLINERS, James Joyce. Fifteen stories offer vivid, tightly focused observations of the lives of Dublin's poorer classes. At least one, "The Dead," is considered a masterpiece. Reprinted complete and unabridged from standard edition. 160pp. 5³⁄₁₆ x 8¼. 26870-5 Pa. $1.00

GREAT WEIRD TALES: 14 Stories by Lovecraft, Blackwood, Machen and Others, S. T. Joshi (ed.). 14 spellbinding tales, including "The Sin Eater," by Fiona McLeod, "The Eye Above the Mantel," by Frank Belknap Long, as well as renowned works by R. H. Barlow, Lord Dunsany, Arthur Machen, W. C. Morrow and eight other masters of the genre. 256pp. 5⅜ x 8½. (Available in U.S. only.) 40436-6 Pa. $8.95

THE BOOK OF THE SACRED MAGIC OF ABRAMELIN THE MAGE, translated by S. MacGregor Mathers. Medieval manuscript of ceremonial magic. Basic document in Aleister Crowley, Golden Dawn groups. 268pp. 5⅜ x 8½. 23211-5 Pa. $9.95

NEW RUSSIAN-ENGLISH AND ENGLISH-RUSSIAN DICTIONARY, M. A. O'Brien. This is a remarkably handy Russian dictionary, containing a surprising amount of information, including over 70,000 entries. 366pp. 4½ x 6⅛. 20208-9 Pa. $10.95

HISTORIC HOMES OF THE AMERICAN PRESIDENTS, Second, Revised Edition, Irvin Haas. A traveler's guide to American Presidential homes, most open to the public, depicting and describing homes occupied by every American President from George Washington to George Bush. With visiting hours, admission charges, travel routes. 175 photographs. Index. 160pp. 8¼ x 11. 26751-2 Pa. $11.95

NEW YORK IN THE FORTIES, Andreas Feininger. 162 brilliant photographs by the well-known photographer, formerly with *Life* magazine. Commuters, shoppers, Times Square at night, much else from city at its peak. Captions by John von Hartz. 181pp. 9¼ x 10¾. 23585-8 Pa. $13.95

INDIAN SIGN LANGUAGE, William Tomkins. Over 525 signs developed by Sioux and other tribes. Written instructions and diagrams. Also 290 pictographs. 111pp. 6⅛ x 9¼. 22029-X Pa. $3.95

ANATOMY: A Complete Guide for Artists, Joseph Sheppard. A master of figure drawing shows artists how to render human anatomy convincingly. Over 460 illustrations. 224pp. 8⅜ x 11¼. 27279-6 Pa. $11.95

MEDIEVAL CALLIGRAPHY: Its History and Technique, Marc Drogin. Spirited history, comprehensive instruction manual covers 13 styles (ca. 4th century through 15th). Excellent photographs; directions for duplicating medieval techniques with modern tools. 224pp. 8⅜ x 11¼. 26142-5 Pa. $12.95

DRIED FLOWERS: How to Prepare Them, Sarah Whitlock and Martha Rankin. Complete instructions on how to use silica gel, meal and borax, perlite aggregate, sand and borax, glycerine and water to create attractive permanent flower arrangements. 12 illustrations. 32pp. 5⅜ x 8½. 21802-3 Pa. $1.00

EASY-TO-MAKE BIRD FEEDERS FOR WOODWORKERS, Scott D. Campbell. Detailed, simple-to-use guide for designing, constructing, caring for and using feeders. Text, illustrations for 12 classic and contemporary designs. 96pp. 5⅜ x 8½.
25847-5 Pa. $3.95

SCOTTISH WONDER TALES FROM MYTH AND LEGEND, Donald A. Mackenzie. 16 lively tales tell of giants rumbling down mountainsides, of a magic wand that turns stone pillars into warriors, of gods and goddesses, evil hags, powerful forces and more. 240pp. 5⅜ x 8½. 29677-6 Pa. $6.95

THE HISTORY OF UNDERCLOTHES, C. Willett Cunnington and Phyllis Cunnington. Fascinating, well-documented survey covering six centuries of English undergarments, enhanced with over 100 illustrations: 12th-century laced-up bodice, footed long drawers (1795), 19th-century bustles, 19th-century corsets for men, Victorian "bust improvers," much more. 272pp. 5⅜ x 8¼. 27124-2 Pa. $9.95

ARTS AND CRAFTS FURNITURE: The Complete Brooks Catalog of 1912, Brooks Manufacturing Co. Photos and detailed descriptions of more than 150 now very collectible furniture designs from the Arts and Crafts movement depict davenports, settees, buffets, desks, tables, chairs, bedsteads, dressers and more, all built of solid, quarter-sawed oak. Invaluable for students and enthusiasts of antiques, Americana and the decorative arts. 80pp. 6½ x 9¼. 27471-3 Pa. $8.95

WILBUR AND ORVILLE: A Biography of the Wright Brothers, Fred Howard. Definitive, crisply written study tells the full story of the brothers' lives and work. A vividly written biography, unparalleled in scope and color, that also captures the spirit of an extraordinary era. 560pp. 6⅛ x 9¼. 40297-5 Pa. $17.95

THE ARTS OF THE SAILOR: Knotting, Splicing and Ropework, Hervey Garrett Smith. Indispensable shipboard reference covers tools, basic knots and useful hitches; handsewing and canvas work, more. Over 100 illustrations. Delightful reading for sea lovers. 256pp. 5⅜ x 8½. 26440-8 Pa. $8.95

FRANK LLOYD WRIGHT'S FALLINGWATER: The House and Its History, Second, Revised Edition, Donald Hoffmann. A total revision—both in text and illustrations—of the standard document on Fallingwater, the boldest, most personal architectural statement of Wright's mature years, updated with valuable new material from the recently opened Frank Lloyd Wright Archives. "Fascinating"—*The New York Times*. 116 illustrations. 128pp. 9¼ x 10¾. 27430-6 Pa. $12.95

PHOTOGRAPHIC SKETCHBOOK OF THE CIVIL WAR, Alexander Gardner. 100 photos taken on field during the Civil War. Famous shots of Manassas Harper's Ferry, Lincoln, Richmond, slave pens, etc. 244pp. 10⅝ x 8¼.   22731-6 Pa. $10.95

FIVE ACRES AND INDEPENDENCE, Maurice G. Kains. Great back-to-the-land classic explains basics of self-sufficient farming. The one book to get. 95 illustrations. 397pp. 5⅜ x 8½.   20974-1 Pa. $7.95

SONGS OF EASTERN BIRDS, Dr. Donald J. Borror. Songs and calls of 60 species most common to eastern U.S.: warblers, woodpeckers, flycatchers, thrushes, larks, many more in high-quality recording.   Cassette and manual 99912-2 $9.95

A MODERN HERBAL, Margaret Grieve. Much the fullest, most exact, most useful compilation of herbal material. Gigantic alphabetical encyclopedia, from aconite to zedoary, gives botanical information, medical properties, folklore, economic uses, much else. Indispensable to serious reader. 161 illustrations. 888pp. 6½ x 9¼. 2-vol. set. (Available in U.S. only.)   Vol. I: 22798-7 Pa. $9.95
Vol. II: 22799-5 Pa. $9.95

HIDDEN TREASURE MAZE BOOK, Dave Phillips. Solve 34 challenging mazes accompanied by heroic tales of adventure. Evil dragons, people-eating plants, blood-thirsty giants, many more dangerous adversaries lurk at every twist and turn. 34 mazes, stories, solutions. 48pp. 8¼ x 11.   24566-7 Pa. $2.95

LETTERS OF W. A. MOZART, Wolfgang A. Mozart. Remarkable letters show bawdy wit, humor, imagination, musical insights, contemporary musical world; includes some letters from Leopold Mozart. 276pp. 5⅜ x 8½.   22859-2 Pa. $7.95

BASIC PRINCIPLES OF CLASSICAL BALLET, Agrippina Vaganova. Great Russian theoretician, teacher explains methods for teaching classical ballet. 118 illustrations. 175pp. 5⅜ x 8½.   22036-2 Pa. $6.95

THE JUMPING FROG, Mark Twain. Revenge edition. The original story of The Celebrated Jumping Frog of Calaveras County, a hapless French translation, and Twain's hilarious "retranslation" from the French. 12 illustrations. 66pp. 5⅜ x 8½.   22686-7 Pa. $3.95

BEST REMEMBERED POEMS, Martin Gardner (ed.). The 126 poems in this superb collection of 19th- and 20th-century British and American verse range from Shelley's "To a Skylark" to the impassioned "Renascence" of Edna St. Vincent Millay and to Edward Lear's whimsical "The Owl and the Pussycat." 224pp. 5⅜ x 8½.   27165-X Pa. $5.95

COMPLETE SONNETS, William Shakespeare. Over 150 exquisite poems deal with love, friendship, the tyranny of time, beauty's evanescence, death and other themes in language of remarkable power, precision and beauty. Glossary of archaic terms. 80pp. 5³⁄₁₆ x 8¼.   26686-9 Pa. $1.00

BODIES IN A BOOKSHOP, R. T. Campbell. Challenging mystery of blackmail and murder with ingenious plot and superbly drawn characters. In the best tradition of British suspense fiction. 192pp. 5⅜ x 8½.   24720-1 Pa. $6.95

THE WIT AND HUMOR OF OSCAR WILDE, Alvin Redman (ed.). More than 1,000 ripostes, paradoxes, wisecracks: Work is the curse of the drinking classes; I can resist everything except temptation; etc. 258pp. 5⅜ x 8½. 20602-5 Pa. $6.95

SHAKESPEARE LEXICON AND QUOTATION DICTIONARY, Alexander Schmidt. Full definitions, locations, shades of meaning in every word in plays and poems. More than 50,000 exact quotations. 1,485pp. 6½ x 9¼. 2-vol. set.
Vol. 1: 22726-X Pa. $17.95
Vol. 2: 22727-8 Pa. $17.95

SELECTED POEMS, Emily Dickinson. Over 100 best-known, best-loved poems by one of America's foremost poets, reprinted from authoritative early editions. No comparable edition at this price. Index of first lines. 64pp. 5³⁄₁₆ x 8¼.
26466-1 Pa. $1.00

THE INSIDIOUS DR. FU-MANCHU, Sax Rohmer. The first of the popular mystery series introduces a pair of English detectives to their archnemesis, the diabolical Dr. Fu-Manchu. Flavorful atmosphere, fast-paced action, and colorful characters enliven this classic of the genre. 208pp. 5³⁄₁₆ x 8¼. 29898-1 Pa. $2.00

THE MALLEUS MALEFICARUM OF KRAMER AND SPRENGER, translated by Montague Summers. Full text of most important witchhunter's "bible," used by both Catholics and Protestants. 278pp. 6⅝ x 10. 22802-9 Pa. $12.95

SPANISH STORIES/CUENTOS ESPAÑOLES: A Dual-Language Book, Angel Flores (ed.). Unique format offers 13 great stories in Spanish by Cervantes, Borges, others. Faithful English translations on facing pages. 352pp. 5⅜ x 8½.
25399-6 Pa. $8.95

GARDEN CITY, LONG ISLAND, IN EARLY PHOTOGRAPHS, 1869–1919, Mildred H. Smith. Handsome treasury of 118 vintage pictures, accompanied by carefully researched captions, document the Garden City Hotel fire (1899), the Vanderbilt Cup Race (1908), the first airmail flight departing from the Nassau Boulevard Aerodrome (1911), and much more. 96pp. 8⅞ x 11¾. 40669-5 Pa. $12.95

OLD QUEENS, N.Y., IN EARLY PHOTOGRAPHS, Vincent F. Seyfried and William Asadorian. Over 160 rare photographs of Maspeth, Jamaica, Jackson Heights, and other areas. Vintage views of DeWitt Clinton mansion, 1939 World's Fair and more. Captions. 192pp. 8⅞ x 11. 26358-4 Pa. $12.95

CAPTURED BY THE INDIANS: 15 Firsthand Accounts, 1750-1870, Frederick Drimmer. Astounding true historical accounts of grisly torture, bloody conflicts, relentless pursuits, miraculous escapes and more, by people who lived to tell the tale. 384pp. 5⅜ x 8½. 24901-8 Pa. $8.95

THE WORLD'S GREAT SPEECHES (Fourth Enlarged Edition), Lewis Copeland, Lawrence W. Lamm, and Stephen J. McKenna. Nearly 300 speeches provide public speakers with a wealth of updated quotes and inspiration–from Pericles' funeral oration and William Jennings Bryan's "Cross of Gold Speech" to Malcolm X's powerful words on the Black Revolution and Earl of Spenser's tribute to his sister, Diana, Princess of Wales. 944pp. 5⅜ x 8⅜. 40903-1 Pa. $15.95

THE BOOK OF THE SWORD, Sir Richard F. Burton. Great Victorian scholar/adventurer's eloquent, erudite history of the "queen of weapons"–from prehistory to early Roman Empire. Evolution and development of early swords, variations (sabre, broadsword, cutlass, scimitar, etc.), much more. 336pp. 6⅛ x 9¼.
25434-8 Pa. $9.95

AUTOBIOGRAPHY: The Story of My Experiments with Truth, Mohandas K. Gandhi. Boyhood, legal studies, purification, the growth of the Satyagraha (nonviolent protest) movement. Critical, inspiring work of the man responsible for the freedom of India. 480pp. 5⅜ x 8½. (Available in U.S. only.) 24593-4 Pa. $8.95

CELTIC MYTHS AND LEGENDS, T. W. Rolleston. Masterful retelling of Irish and Welsh stories and tales. Cuchulain, King Arthur, Deirdre, the Grail, many more. First paperback edition. 58 full-page illustrations. 512pp. 5⅜ x 8½. 26507-2 Pa. $9.95

THE PRINCIPLES OF PSYCHOLOGY, William James. Famous long course complete, unabridged. Stream of thought, time perception, memory, experimental methods; great work decades ahead of its time. 94 figures. 1,391pp. 5⅜ x 8½. 2-vol. set.
Vol. I: 20381-6 Pa. $14.95
Vol. II: 20382-4 Pa. $14.95

THE WORLD AS WILL AND REPRESENTATION, Arthur Schopenhauer. Definitive English translation of Schopenhauer's life work, correcting more than 1,000 errors, omissions in earlier translations. Translated by E. F. J. Payne. Total of 1,269pp. 5⅜ x 8½. 2-vol. set.
Vol. 1: 21761-2 Pa. $12.95
Vol. 2: 21762-0 Pa. $12.95

MAGIC AND MYSTERY IN TIBET, Madame Alexandra David-Neel. Experiences among lamas, magicians, sages, sorcerers, Bonpa wizards. A true psychic discovery. 32 illustrations. 321pp. 5⅜ x 8½. (Available in U.S. only.) 22682-4 Pa. $9.95

THE EGYPTIAN BOOK OF THE DEAD, E. A. Wallis Budge. Complete reproduction of Ani's papyrus, finest ever found. Full hieroglyphic text, interlinear transliteration, word-for-word translation, smooth translation. 533pp. 6½ x 9¼.
21866-X Pa. $12.95

MATHEMATICS FOR THE NONMATHEMATICIAN, Morris Kline. Detailed, college-level treatment of mathematics in cultural and historical context, with numerous exercises. Recommended Reading Lists. Tables. Numerous figures. 641pp. 5⅜ x 8½.
24823-2 Pa. $11.95

PROBABILISTIC METHODS IN THE THEORY OF STRUCTURES, Isaac Elishakoff. Well-written introduction covers the elements of the theory of probability from two or more random variables, the reliability of such multivariable structures, the theory of random function, Monte Carlo methods of treating problems incapable of exact solution, and more. Examples. 502pp. $5^{3}/_{8}$ x $8^{1}/_{2}$. 40691-1 Pa. $16.95

THE RIME OF THE ANCIENT MARINER, Gustave Doré, S. T. Coleridge. Doré's finest work; 34 plates capture moods, subtleties of poem. Flawless full-size reproductions printed on facing pages with authoritative text of poem. "Beautiful. Simply beautiful."–*Publisher's Weekly.* 77pp. 9¼ x 12. 22305-1 Pa. $7.95

NORTH AMERICAN INDIAN DESIGNS FOR ARTISTS AND CRAFTSPEOPLE, Eva Wilson. Over 360 authentic copyright-free designs adapted from Navajo blankets, Hopi pottery, Sioux buffalo hides, more. Geometrics, symbolic figures, plant and animal motifs, etc. 128pp. 8⅜ x 11. (Not for sale in the United Kingdom.) 25341-4 Pa. $9.95

SCULPTURE: Principles and Practice, Louis Slobodkin. Step-by-step approach to clay, plaster, metals, stone; classical and modern. 253 drawings, photos. 255pp. 8⅛ x 11.
22960-2 Pa. $11.95

THE INFLUENCE OF SEA POWER UPON HISTORY, 1660–1783, A. T. Mahan. Influential classic of naval history and tactics still used as text in war colleges. First paperback edition. 4 maps. 24 battle plans. 640pp. 5⅜ x 8½. 25509-3 Pa. $14.95

THE STORY OF THE TITANIC AS TOLD BY ITS SURVIVORS, Jack Winocour (ed.). What it was really like. Panic, despair, shocking inefficiency, and a little heroism. More thrilling than any fictional account. 26 illustrations. 320pp. 5⅜ x 8½. 20610-6 Pa. $8.95

FAIRY AND FOLK TALES OF THE IRISH PEASANTRY, William Butler Yeats (ed.). Treasury of 64 tales from the twilight world of Celtic myth and legend: "The Soul Cages," "The Kildare Pooka," "King O'Toole and his Goose," many more. Introduction and Notes by W. B. Yeats. 352pp. 5⅜ x 8½. 26941-8 Pa. $8.95

BUDDHIST MAHAYANA TEXTS, E. B. Cowell and others (eds.). Superb, accurate translations of basic documents in Mahayana Buddhism, highly important in history of religions. The Buddha-karita of Asvaghosha, Larger Sukhavativyuha, more. 448pp. 5⅜ x 8½. 25552-2 Pa. $12.95

ONE TWO THREE . . . INFINITY: Facts and Speculations of Science, George Gamow. Great physicist's fascinating, readable overview of contemporary science: number theory, relativity, fourth dimension, entropy, genes, atomic structure, much more. 128 illustrations. Index. 352pp. 5⅜ x 8½. 25664-2 Pa. $9.95

EXPERIMENTATION AND MEASUREMENT, W. J. Youden. Introductory manual explains laws of measurement in simple terms and offers tips for achieving accuracy and minimizing errors. Mathematics of measurement, use of instruments, experimenting with machines. 1994 edition. Foreword. Preface. Introduction. Epilogue. Selected Readings. Glossary. Index. Tables and figures. 128pp. 5³/₈ x 8¹/₂. 40451-X Pa. $6.95

DALÍ ON MODERN ART: The Cuckolds of Antiquated Modern Art, Salvador Dalí. Influential painter skewers modern art and its practitioners. Outrageous evaluations of Picasso, Cézanne, Turner, more. 15 renderings of paintings discussed. 44 calligraphic decorations by Dalí. 96pp. 5⅜ x 8½. (Available in U.S. only.) 29220-7 Pa. $5.95

ANTIQUE PLAYING CARDS: A Pictorial History, Henry René D'Allemagne. Over 900 elaborate, decorative images from rare playing cards (14th–20th centuries): Bacchus, death, dancing dogs, hunting scenes, royal coats of arms, players cheating, much more. 96pp. 9¼ x 12¼. 29265-7 Pa. $12.95

MAKING FURNITURE MASTERPIECES: 30 Projects with Measured Drawings, Franklin H. Gottshall. Step-by-step instructions, illustrations for constructing handsome, useful pieces, among them a Sheraton desk, Chippendale chair, Spanish desk, Queen Anne table and a William and Mary dressing mirror. 224pp. 8⅛ x 11¼. 29338-6 Pa. $13.95

THE FOSSIL BOOK: A Record of Prehistoric Life, Patricia V. Rich et al. Profusely illustrated definitive guide covers everything from single-celled organisms and dinosaurs to birds and mammals and the interplay between climate and man. Over 1,500 illustrations. 760pp. 7½ x 10⅛. 29371-8 Pa. $29.95

Prices subject to change without notice.

Available at your book dealer or write for free catalog to Dept. GI, Dover Publications, Inc., 31 East 2nd St., Mineola, N.Y. 11501. Dover publishes more than 500 books each year on science, elementary and advanced mathematics, biology, music, art, literary history, social sciences and other areas.